THE
TIME TEAM
GUIDE
TO THE
ARCHAEOLOGICAL SITES
OF BRITAIN & IRELAND

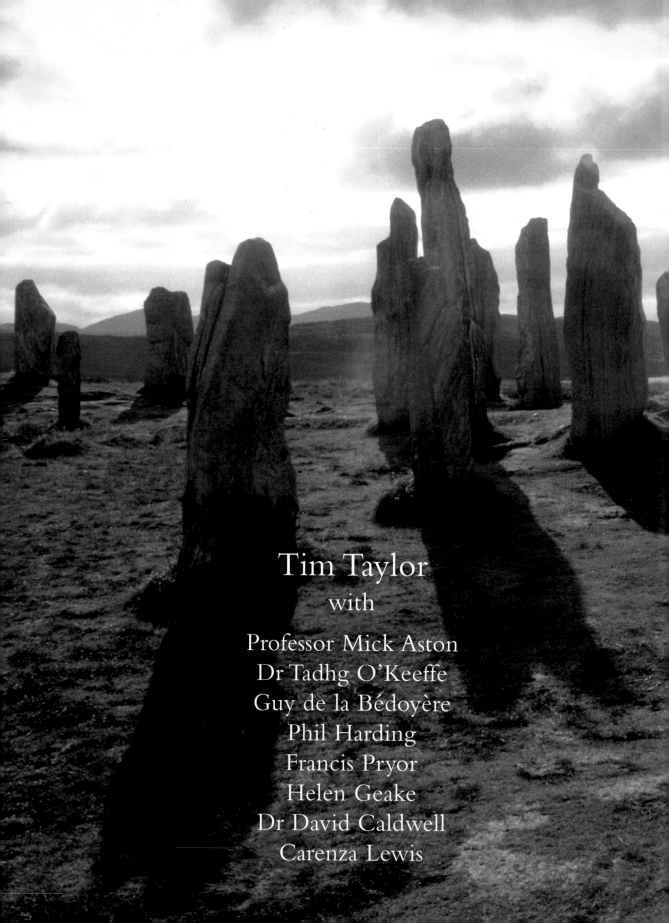

Tim Taylor

with

Professor Mick Aston
Dr Tadhg O'Keeffe
Guy de la Bédoyère
Phil Harding
Francis Pryor
Helen Geake
Dr David Caldwell
Carenza Lewis

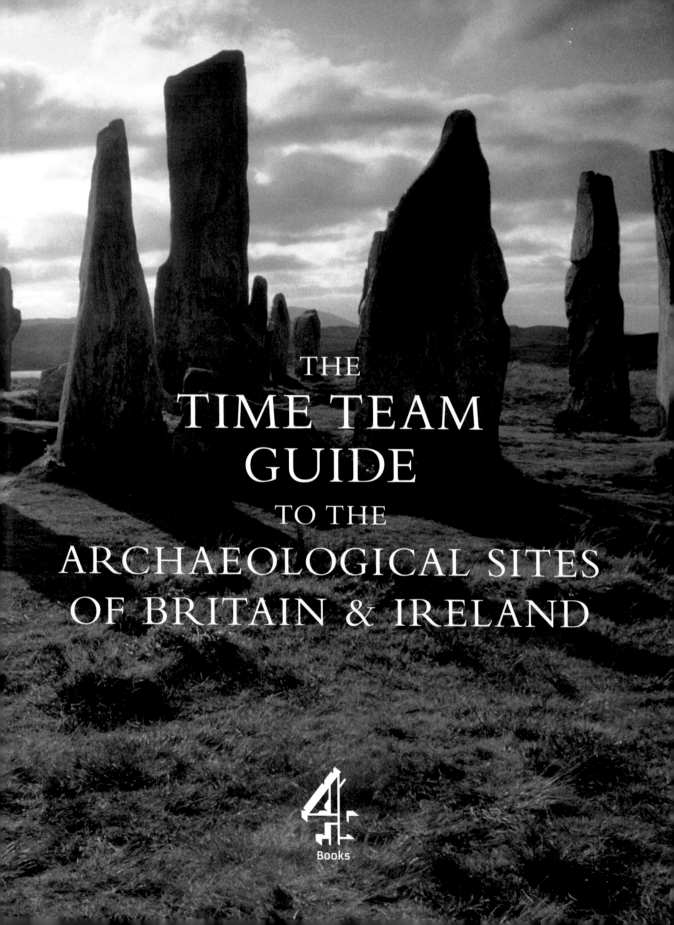

THE
TIME TEAM
GUIDE
TO THE
ARCHAEOLOGICAL SITES
OF BRITAIN & IRELAND

4
Books

TRANSWORLD PUBLISHERS
61–63 Uxbridge Road, London W5 5SA
a division of The Random House Group Ltd

RANDOM HOUSE AUSTRALIA (PTY) LTD
20 Alfred Street, Milsons Point, Sydney
New South Wales 2061, Australia

RANDOM HOUSE NEW ZEALAND LTD
18 Poland Road, Glenfield, Auckland 10, New Zealand

RANDOM HOUSE SOUTH AFRICA (PTY) LTD
Endulini, 5a Jubilee Road, Parktown 2193, South Africa

Published 2005 by Channel 4 Books
a division of Transworld Publishers

This book is published to accompany the Time Team television series
produced by Videotext Communications Ltd in association with
Picture House.

Illustrations copyright © Victor Ambrus 2005
Design by Martin Hendry
Maps by Hardlines Ltd
Picture research by Louise Thomas
Index by Christine Shuttleworth

A catalogue record for this book is available from the British Library.
ISBN 1 9050 2601 3

Printed by Appl Druck, Wemding, Germany
1 3 5 7 9 10 8 6 4 2

Papers used by Transworld Publishers are natural, recyclable products made
from wood grown in sustainable forests. The manufacturing processes
conform to the environmental regulations of the country of origin.

Contents

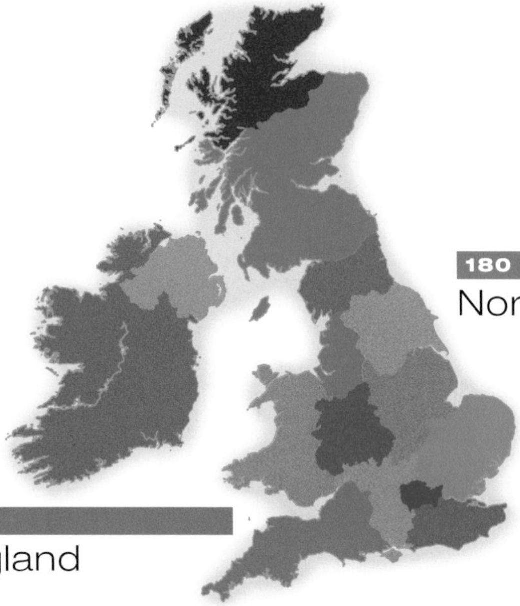

Foreword
by Tony Robinson 7

Introduction
by Tim Taylor and
the Time Team 8

10
South-west England

36
Southern England

58
Greater London

78
South-east England

96
Wales

118
Heart of England

142
East of England

164
East Midlands

180
North-west England

196
Yorkshire

214
North of England

236
Southern Scotland

252
Scottish Highland and Islands

268
Northern Ireland

280
Republic of Ireland

Top Ten sites
by the Time Team 312

What happened when? 315

Index 316

Acknowledgements 319

Foreword

AT SOME TIME IN 2005 we will be going to our 150th site. Over the last 13 years or so, Time Team has travelled all over the country. Each site we've visited, and spent our usual three days excavating, has given us the chance to get together some of the most knowledgeable archaeologists in the country. During this process we've often referred in our discussions to the nearest 'great and good' sites, and it has been fascinating to hear our experts talking about them and how they relate to the places we've been digging.

During the discussions, I've not only felt that it would be great to visit these sites with some of our experts, but also that many of these sites have new insights and new perceptions to be experienced. What you might end up reading in the booklets and on the presentation boards is not necessarily the end of the story.

Time Team has always tried to get beyond the surface story and see what was really going on, and ask the sort of questions the viewer wants answered. In this book, Tim and the rest of the team have tried to apply this approach and to give you a Time Team-style introduction to some of the sites we find the most interesting.

My own favourites relate to locations visited as part of Time Team's digs. I remember digging on Hadrian's Wall and thinking just what the Roman legionaries must have made of it, and experiencing the extraordinary richness of Orkney's archaeology and the beauty of some of Ireland's early Christian sites. Some of the sites that most surprised me were the industrial sites. People don't always associate these with archaeology, but I was particularly impressed by Ironbridge, because it seems that this really was the start, in Britain, of the world's industrial revolution.

This book reflects something else which doing 13 years of Time Team has made clear to me – the fantastic variety of Britain and Ireland's archaeology. Not only the sites themselves, but the amazing objects archaeologists have uncovered. It is also exciting and somehow encouraging to realize that on many of the sites we hope you will get to visit, secrets are still waiting to be uncovered. Many of these places were excavated generations ago, and new discoveries are still to be made. These sites and their amazing stories are alive and changing, and hopefully waiting for today's generation of archaeologists to continue the story.

I hope you enjoy having Time Team take you round Britain and Ireland, and that this guide inspires you to get out and look at some of the world's best archaeology. It is never that far from your own doorstep, and you might even bump into Time Team along the way.

Introduction

THIS BOOK IS Time Team's guide to great British and Irish archaeology. It tells the story of how archaeological sites have changed the way we think about the past and about how people used to live. And, in some cases, how we are now changing the way we think about the classic sites.

The book explores in depth more than 50 classic archaeological sites, representing those the Time Team believe are the most important and interesting in Britain and Ireland. Some of the choices are surprising, and others will make you take a second look at some of our greatest archaeological sites. In addition to these major sites, we also include more than 225 fascinating, revealing, typical and/or enigmatic places.

Our intention has been to give the reader a selection of the archaeological sites that we believe matter. For example, hillforts, henge monuments, passage graves, Roman villas, motte-and-bailey castles: these are an important part of our archaeological past, but how much do we understand them? When we wander round these sites, gazing up at the lumps of stone or magnificent fortifications that are thousands of years old, or even just looking at lumps and bumps in the ground, are we really aware of what they tell us about how people lived in the past?

We've tried to approach each site as though we were undertaking a typical Time Team piece of research. In the cases where we have dug on or near the site we will give you some of the background to the Time Team shoot. We will also be giving you an abbreviated idea of how the people lived who created the monument you are visiting, and introduce you to relevant elements of their technology. It's always been extraordinary to see Time Team's experts in ancient technology cutting the wood, melting the iron, building the wall, because it gives you a sense of the real stuff of ancient life, and it makes you appreciate the high level of skill of our ancestors. We'd like you to have in mind the skill and strength required to shape the sarsens when you go to Stonehenge, the way antler picks were used in the Neolithic period at Grimes Graves and Avebury, the magical process of creating bronze or iron, the skills of the Roman builders and surveyors as they laid out their forts in enemy territory.

We often visit sites as observers of stone and brick structures that are rather silent witnesses to the past. We are left appreciating the architectural form but have to use our imagination to recreate the effort, noise and human organization that was at work when the place was first built. Visiting a beautiful site like Rievaulx Abbey today, it might be hard to imagine the hive of activity it was in its heyday. We want to give you a sense of this.

We have also asked Mick, Phil and the rest of the team to guide you to one or two key points to watch out for – something you might miss, particularly if the site is busy. Phil, for instance, is keen for you to see a particular stone in the West Kennet long barrow – Mick will draw your attention to a specific arch at Rievaulx and Guy believes that one important piece of plasterwork is key to understanding your visit to Lullingstone.

You also get an idea about the archaeological record of excavation on the site. How up-to-date is it? Are the archaeologists' assumptions based on recent excavations and modern analysis, or are we dealing with a site last excavated in the distant past by an antiquarian enthusiast whose imagination got the better of him? A surprising

number of the great and good sites of British and Irish archaeology have had relatively little work done on them. Once a site becomes a venerable member of the canon of 'must see' visitor attractions, the archaeological authorities can become increasingly reluctant to allow unseemly intrusion. This might lead to all sorts of awful consequences – like the guidebook and interpretation signs having to be rewritten!

Another element of our sites you might miss as you hurry round are the things you can't see or that remain hidden in archaeological reports the size of telephone directories. We've tried where relevant to mention some facts that aren't obvious to the casual visitor, like the horse-shoe shaped set of stones that lies within the Avebury ring, the bodies found in and around Stonehenge, the two dead women lying under a stone bench at Skara Brae and the man with a flint arrow in his neck at West Kennet. We occasionally contemplate the effect on a party of visiting tourists of a general uprising of all sacrificed, murdered and buried dead on archaeological sites! Some of the places you will visit are not as benign as you may think.

To help you imagine what some of the sites looked like we have, as in Time Team, brought in Victor's wonderful paintings, which we hope will give you a sense of what you might have seen without removing your chance to use your own imagination to fill in the gaps.

Finally, we hope we have asked a few hard questions – Tony style – on your behalf. Why have some of Britain's premier archaeological sites remained unexcavated since the 19th century? How do the archaeologists know the accurate dates for ditches, the remains of timber buildings and other ancient buildings? We have also tried to lay to rest a few myths. Above all, we hope that this book will be the nearest we can get to giving you a member of Time Team to take you round the site.

We hope you enjoy the journey!

South-west England

Within the great moorlands of the south-west are some of the best surviving prehistoric sites in England. Mineral mining played a key role in the development of this area. Further east, the chalkland plateau of Dorset is rich in Neolithic and Bronze Age henges and settlements, and also home to the famous Iron Age hillfort Maiden Castle. In Somerset the waterlogged conditions of Glastonbury and Meare preserved a range of Iron Age archaeology that would not ordinarily survive. The Roman landscape of this region includes Aquae Sulis at Bath, probably the largest bath complex in the Roman Empire north of the Alps. At the other end of the scale, Chysauster in west Cornwall is a rare survival, a small Iron Age farming settlement.

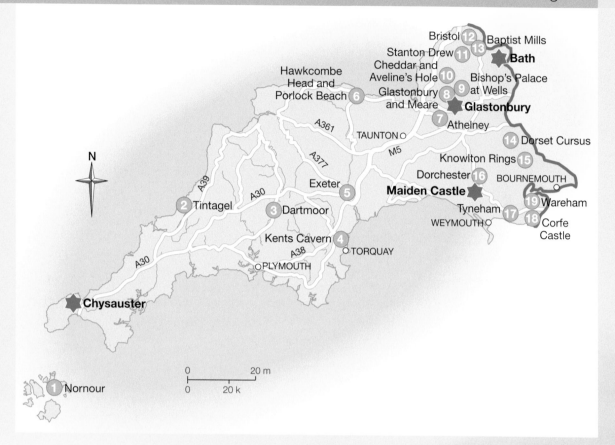

Maiden Castle
Britain's biggest Iron Age hillfort

500BC-AD300

MOST TIME TEAM members have Maiden Castle in their list of must-see attractions. Its banks enclose an area of over 19 hectares (47 acres); it's the biggest hillfort in Britain and one of the largest in north-west Europe. Mick suggests that you begin near one of the entrance points and stand in the bottom of one of the ditches. Staring up at the ridges above you, you get some idea of just how formidable this place was. And try to observe the maze-like structure of the entranceway – this forced attackers to expose their unshielded side.

Phil regards the approach from the outside as being most impressive. The idea of attacking these ramparts, all of which were within slingshot distance,

would have been daunting. When Sir Mortimer Wheeler originally excavated the site in 1934–7, he found piles of slingshot stones behind the ramparts. Early visitors to his excavation were able to purchase their own pieces of slingshot. When supplies ran low, they were added to from a nearby beach. Phil had an opportunity to use a slingshot when we excavated another site in the south-west – in the right hands it's a very effective weapon. A large pebble travelling at over 70 mph in your direction while you were attempting to scale the banks would have been a considerable deterrent.

Impressive labour

There are between 1,500 and 2,000 Iron Age hillforts in Britain and Ireland; about 20 or so fit into the Maiden Castle variety, with huge multiple ditches and banks. Maiden Castle was first occupied in the Neolithic era around 3500BC. Construction of the main ditches began

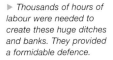

▶ Thousands of hours of labour were needed to create these huge ditches and banks. They provided a formidable defence.

around 600–500BC and this must have required thousands of hours of work and a massive amount of organization. It is the amount of labour needed to dig out these ditches that most impresses Phil. The builders had iron tools and it is likely that some form of carts were used to move material around the site. Over time the ditches and ramparts, once capped by palisades, have been rounded off, so you have to imagine something much deeper and higher with sharper edges.

Hillforts were major centres of power. Their occupiers lived in typical Iron Age roundhouses and used pits to both store food and bury waste. These pits provide important evidence for archaeologists. At Maiden Castle, most of the houses were at the edge of the enclosure and dated from the late Iron Age. Wheeler found evidence for granaries and food processing; cattle, pig and horse bones with butchery marks were also found,

as well as charred grain. Salt was imported here, and there is evidence for metalworking in bronze and iron.

Changing hands

By the end of the Iron Age this site had become the capital of the Durotiges tribe. Centres such as this one were important targets for the Romans, and it is probable that the legions of Vespasian attacked Maiden Castle. Wheeler discovered what he called a war cemetery with victims from the battle, one of whom had a ballista bolt buried in his spine. It is likely that the Romans had numbers of these kinds of giant crossbow and other mechanical devices with which to attack the occupiers, but re-excavations by Niall Sharples, in 1985 and 1986, have thrown doubt on the war graves explanation. Reassessment has led to the view that this is in fact a typical Iron Age cemetery – some of whose

▲ *Victor's reconstruction shows life within the hillfort, the family compound busy with daily chores. These are typical Iron Age round houses, and would have been surrounded by pits for storage.*

▶ *Storage pot with a typical Iron Age decorative motif.*

occupants died violently, but many of whom were buried with standard Iron Age artefacts carefully deposited as grave goods, which doesn't support the war grave theory.

Maiden Castle did come under the control of the Romans. Large amounts of Samian ware and other finds suggest a Roman fort may have been established here, and later a Roman temple was built on the site. Subsequently, the area was used for Anglo-Saxon burial. Such a prominent landmark with such excellent defences would have continued to be an attraction, but by the 600–700s Maiden Castle had begun to revert to pasture.

None the less, Maiden Castle was occupied for thousands of years, and it is this continuity that adds to its importance. Sir Mortimer Wheeler's work was of the scale needed to assess such a monument, but modern excavations have led to some reassessment of his conclusions, and provided a wealth of new evidence.

■ **GETTING THERE**
Maiden Castle is 2 miles SW of Dorchester in Dorset. See www.english-heritage.org.uk for opening times and other details.

■ **OUR VIEW** Despite Maiden Castle's importance, there is no visitor centre and the information boards have recently looked a bit tired, but one advantage of the understated presentation is that you can wander all over the site for free, enjoying what is probably the most impressive Iron Age fort in Britain. Have a good look at aerial pictures, such as that on the right, before your first visit, to appreciate the massive dimensions.

◄ *From the air you get an excellent impression of the scale of Maiden Castle, one of the biggest hillforts in north-west Europe. The impressive banks and ditches of the entrance are particularly clear from this perspective.*

Chysauster
Late Iron Age settlement

100BC–AD300

CHYSAUSTER IN CORNWALL is a rare survival: a late Iron Age 'village' occupied from the 1st century BC to the 3rd century AD, with walls that still stand up to 2m (6½ ft) high. A cluster of eight houses – each consisting of a series of rooms and byres built round a paved central courtyard – were enclosed by a wall and surrounded by walled gardens and fields for growing crops and keeping livestock.

At Chysauster you can get close to the day-to-day living conditions of the early inhabitants of south-west Britain. Archaeologists seem to have spent a large amount of time digging up palaces and castles, the homes of the great and the good, but it is often the dwelling places of the majority of ordinary people like you and me that get overlooked.

The settlement is one of a group of Iron Age sites unique to Cornwall which provide a vivid picture of life in the extreme south-west of Britain at a time when Roman towns and villas were springing up across the rest of the country. Settlements like Chysauster were centres of small tribal communities that owed their success to farming and trading in local commodities, especially tin.

Early traders
A rare recent find of a bronze spoon at the site provides a tantalizing clue to Chysauster's place in the bigger picture of Iron Age Britain, and even Europe. The spoon was probably made using local tin, and we know from Roman sources that tribes in south-west Britain were trading tin with continental merchants from the stronghold at St Michael's Mount on the Cornish coast. It's interesting to imagine the inhabitants of this tiny Cornish settlement collecting and trading nuggets of tin that ended up in bronze implements all over the Roman Empire.

The site fascinates me because it wasn't discovered until the 19th century, and then only by accident. It is remarkable that the houses and walls lay hidden in the Cornish undergrowth for hundreds of years. After their chance discovery, extensive excavations were undertaken, the first by the antiquarian W.C. Burlase in 1873, followed in the 1930s by Dr Hencken and C.K. Croft-Andrew. These excavations revealed the stone houses you see today, albeit slightly restored.

When you go there and you walk into the houses, you get a sense of the intimacy of the place and the lives of the people who lived there. You can recognize the living areas, the hearths for cooking, the sleeping spaces that were last occupied more than 1,500 years ago. I've always been surprised and a bit humbled by the fact that this kind of archaeology tells us that their concerns and ours are strangely similar – a good place to sleep away from the draughts, a handy shelf for important personal items and a lamp, and in the centre of the room a fireplace to warm your feet.

Home comforts
Mick says that for him, Chysauster has 'a unique quality of warmth and intimacy. It feels like a proper small village, and it's not hard to imagine living there yourself.' It's the structures that he feels are interesting at Chysauster. The houses are typical of the elaborate, durable native structures that can be found particularly in the west and north during the Iron Age. Just as in Scotland you have brochs (see page 260), here in Cornwall you can see the Iron Age population using the local stone to build structures in a distinctive tradition, using techniques that go back thousands of years.

Underground passages

One aspect of the village that's hardest to understand, however, is its 'fogou'. Fogous are enigmatic underground chambers that have been found at a few Iron Age sites in south-west Britain. The one at Chysauster has collapsed, but may originally have run for up to 15m (50ft). You can find it 120m (400ft) to the south-east of house seven. Archaeologists argue endlessly about the function of these underground passages – they could have been used as storage spaces, as a place of refuge in troubled times, or even for some ritual purpose – but there's little evidence to provide any clues.

Time Team excavated on a fogou site in 1996 at Boleigh in Cornwall, and after spending some time in the underground chamber it was hard to believe that they had a purely utilitarian use. As storage chambers they appeared to be rather deep and damp, and this use would not explain some of the complex structural elements, such as the small chambers that are often found to each side. As places of refuge, they had many disadvantages, too. When you visit them, you equally might have a sense that they had a spiritual purpose, but not many archaeologists would agree with this. More intact fogous can be seen at Carn Euny near Land's End, and at Halliggye at Trelowarren near the Lizard.

The interesting point about the Chysauster fogou is that antiquarian records suggest the village once extended as far as the fogou used to run – it seems likely that the settlement was much larger than just the area covered by the existing remains.

▲ *Each cluster of dwellings provided a series of rooms complete with drainage. A modern reconstructed roof can be seen in the top right-hand corner.*

■ **GETTING THERE** Chysauster is 4 miles N of Penzance, Cornwall; off the B3311 to St Ives. See www.english-heritage.org.uk or telephone 07831 757934 for opening times and other details. Admission charge. A similar Iron Age village can be visited at Carn Euny, slightly further down the peninsula (near the village of Sancreed). Finds from both sites can be seen at the Royal Cornwall Museum, Truro.

■ **OUR VIEW** In some ways house five is the best place to start. It has a range of features typical of the other houses. For example, you can see a water channel running through the house both to supply water and to allow drainage.

Bath
Ancient spa town
AD60s to the present

THE AMAZING THING about Bath is that, among all the traffic and tourists, you get the chance to see preserved Roman architecture. It's one of the few sites in Britain – Lincoln and Leicester being others – that give a sense of Roman stone and architecture, although at Bath you have to descend below the current street level to view it. To our Saxon and medieval predecessors, having an ancient Roman building in your area meant an endless supply of beautifully cut building stone and brick, and that's why so little of it survives, and why Bath is such an exceptional site.

▼ *The Victorians built their columns right on top of the ancient footings at Bath, recreating some of the atmosphere the Roman pilgrims to the spa experienced. But the original Roman bath here had a roof to keep wind and rain out.*

Come down the main road from the hills into Bath, however, and the image that most comes to mind is of a much earlier prehistoric scene. Tens of thousands of years ago, our ancestors must have stared in wonder at the sight of steam rising from the natural hot springs on the valley floor. Given the British winters, it must have felt like a gift from the gods to have a supply of mysterious warm water. The mystery of the springs is what Bath has always been about, and there's no doubt that prehistoric cultures were using the waters here long before the Romans and the elite of Georgian society arrived.

Roman soldiers
The first step in creating the Roman baths was the damming of the spring, around the 60s and 70s AD. Guy de la Bédoyère points out the likely military

origins of the Bath spa, and that tombstones and other evidence indicate that many of the visitors were soldiers – perhaps battle-weary veterans needing to recuperate. Certainly Bath became a cult centre dedicated to the Celtic deity Sulis united with Minerva, a Roman goddess of health. As well as having healing properties, cult status meant that it was a place where people could make offerings to the gods. Among the coins and votive objects, lead sheets inscribed with curses have been found by archaeologists.

Bath was an incredibly popular site in the Roman period, attracting visitors from all over the empire. The baths themselves consisted of a huge complex of buildings designed to accommodate the visitors, whether they'd come for health, religious or social reasons. When you look at the excavated remains today, they bring home how incredible Roman construction was: stone was quarried on an industrial scale, materials like mortar, lead and brick were used, and buildings were erected on a scale never seen before in Britain.

Hot water for free

The bath complex contained a series of huge heated rooms and pools, fed by pipes and lined with lead. The hot springs – rising at 46°C – at the site meant that the baths here were of exceptional size and layout. Normally, Roman baths contained only small plunge pools because of the effort and expense of heating water, but at Bath the complex could contain a series of large hot pools for swimming in and many heated rooms. The main pool – the Great Bath – was a vast vaulted room containing a pool nearly 2m (6½ft) deep, fed directly by the sacred spring.

With the springs producing a million litres of water a day, the baths also had a sophisticated engineering system to

◀ The Romans had a genius for controlling water. Taming the hot springs and draining the swamp at Bath meant installing a system of pipes, drains and sluices. Some still work today.

deliver the water through the complex and then drain it away into the nearby river Avon. However, rising water levels meant that flooding and silting became an increasing problem, and with the collapse of Roman administration in the 5th century, the baths weren't maintained and were gradually abandoned.

However, the ruined Roman buildings and streets became the basis of a growing Saxon and medieval city. The hot springs found new popularity in the 18th century, when people came to take the waters. Huge swathes of the city were rebuilt in this period and resulted in the city's world-famous Georgian architecture. It was during this building work that the remains of the Roman baths were uncovered, whose grand scale inspired the classical style of architecture of the spa buildings we still have today.

■ **GETTING THERE** The city of Bath is in North Somerset. The city centre is unsuitable for cars. For the baths, see www.romanbaths. co.uk or telephone 01225 477785 for opening times and other details. Admission charge.
■ **OUR VIEW** If you risk the modern health warnings and dip your hand in the waters, you'll experience the sensation the earliest visitors to the site had: hot running water, coming magically from the earth.

Glastonbury Abbey
Celtic and Saxon monastery
AD500-1539

WHEN WE STARE at that amazing hill, preferably at sunset or sunrise when it has fewer visitors, what do we know about life in early Glastonbury? Well, thanks to the excellent work of a good friend of Mick's, Philip Rahtz, we do have some solid evidence, and it has little to do with Arthur or the Holy Grail.

Glastonbury Abbey was one of Britain's largest, wealthiest and oldest medieval monasteries. Its origins date back to the 5th or 6th centuries AD – the time after the collapse of Roman administration in the south-west, but before the arrival of the Saxons – when Christian monasteries were a new phenomenon in Britain, inspired by communities of holy men and women in the rest of Europe.

Over one thousand years, Glastonbury Abbey grew from a small group of hermits to a major institution that wielded enormous religious and political power. It became one of the biggest landowners in the south-west, dominating the landscape of Somerset in particular, and a centre for international pilgrimage. The monastery itself became a vast collection of buildings within a walled precinct, and the town of Glastonbury developed around it. But the abbey's wealth and fame couldn't save it in the 16th century, when it became one of the last monasteries in England to be closed by Henry VIII. The elderly abbot was executed for treason, and the abbey's valuable lands and buildings sold off.

A place for visionaries

Glastonbury is a site so cluttered with modern interpretation and projected fantasy that it is difficult to see the archaeological wood for the trees. However, it's worth remembering that throughout its history, Glastonbury has attracted characters keen to impose their fantastic visions on the place. In fact, we probably owe the origins of the Glastonbury legends to its medieval monks. In the 12th century, they claimed

▼ Today, the site of the abbey is dominated by ruins that date from the 12th century AD or later, but decades of excavation have revealed an older and more complicated history.

◄ Glastonbury's complex history includes its distinctive hill. Mick says, 'Whenever I climb the Tor, I like to imagine a group of hermit-like early monks occupying the windswept top.'

to have found King Arthur's bones and those of his queen Guinevere (an early archaeological excavation). They knew exactly what such speculation was likely to do for visitor numbers and the monastery's revenue.

Glastonbury's inspiring topography seems always to have been important. Even today, to see Glastonbury Tor from a distance rising out of the mists is impressive, and in the past, when the flat, marshy Somerset Levels were partially flooded throughout the year, the high ground around the Tor would have been more of a true island than it is today. Excavations suggest that the first monks lived hermit-like on top of the Tor, and only moved below to the later abbey site in the 8th century with the coming of the Saxons.

The site of the Saxon and medieval abbey feels completely different from the Tor. The tenacity and dedication of the first monks who clung to the hilltop is impressive, whereas the scale of the later abbey ruins laid out in beautiful rolling grass makes me think how astute the later Saxon and medieval monks were, not just in choosing a more workable site, but in building on the reputation and wealth of the abbey over the centuries (and starting some of those legends!), to create the vast institution still hinted at by the ruins today.

Early monasticism

Mick points out that the nature of early monastic structures and the lifestyle of the first monks mean that archaeologists have very few artefacts to discover from this period. However, the evidence from Glastonbury Tor is good enough to suggest a number of timber buildings, while animal bones and metalworking hearths suggest they were eating good meat and manufacturing bronze objects, including a small head found on the site.

Although the 6th- and 7th-century finds from Glastonbury Tor are limited, they're important, says Mick, because only a handful of these early monastic sites in Britain have so far been investigated. 'I think sites like Glastonbury represent an early "British" form of monasteries, found in the south-west, Wales and Ireland, with hermits living in inaccessible places like hilltops and islands. These hermit communities were overtaken by a new type of Saxon monasticism in the 8th century, which needed a bigger range of buildings. That's why the monks at Glastonbury moved to the larger, flatter site at this date.' The Tor retained its importance, though, and a small Saxon hermitage was followed by a medieval church, the tower of which survives. It was here the Abbot of Glastonbury was hanged by Henry VIII, so in many ways the story of Glastonbury Abbey ended where it began, 1,500 years before.

■ **GETTING THERE** Glastonbury is in Somerset. For the abbey, see www.glastonburyabbey.com or telephone 01458 832267 for opening times and other details. Admission charge. For the Tor, see www.nationaltrust.org.uk or telephone 01934 844518 for details.

■ **OUR VIEW** The ruins of the abbey are open to the public, complete with small museum; the abbey barn at the edge of the monastic precinct contains the Somerset Rural Life Museum. A walk up the Tor is a must.

Other sites to visit

❶ Nornour, Isles of Scilly

The small island of Nornour – less than 1.6 hectares (4 acres) in size – in the Eastern Isles group of the Isles of Scilly is home to a major prehistoric settlement site, dating from the Bronze Age through to the Romano-British Iron Age. In 1962, lengths of wall above a small beach were exposed during violent storms, and archaeological work in ensuing years revealed a settlement consisting of an uneven row of 11 stone-walled circular houses, inhabited from about 2200BC onwards. In the Romano-British Iron Age, the settlement was reused as a shrine, and the site has produced a large quantity of bronze remains of this date, including coins, complete miniature pots, finger rings, goddess figurines, as well as domestic pottery and fragments of small clay figures made in moulds. Unusually, Nornour contained large quantities of Roman brooches, which were first thought to suggest a bronze-working workshop on the island but are now thought to be votive offerings deposited at a shrine. A holy beacon flame may well have been kept alongside the shrine as a guide to mariners.

When this site was inhabited the Scilly Isles were one island rather than an archipelago. The archaeological remains on Nornour are probably only part of the original settlement, much of which has been lost to rising sea levels.

■ **LOCATION** Isles of Scilly.
■ **ACCESS** Finds from Nornour are in the Isles of Scilly Museum, Church Street, St Mary's; telephone 01720 422337 for opening times and other details. Nornour is uninhabited and access is difficult. Contact Catharine Sawyer 01720 423326 for guided tours (summer only).

❷ Tintagel

Joined to the Cornish mainland by a narrow neck of land, and facing the full force of the Atlantic, Tintagel is in a dramatic setting with a romantic history to match.

It seems that after a period as a Roman settlement and military outpost, Tintagel became an important trading settlement and stronghold of the Celtic kings of Dumnonia – a kingdom made up of Cornwall, Devon and parts of Somerset. In addition to numerous 5th- and 6th-century buildings, a quantity of imported luxury goods has been unearthed. A large defensive ditch also dates to this time. It restricted access to the headland, and probably gave Tintagel its name: Din Tagell, or Fortress of the Narrow Entrance.

The secluded Tintagel soon became steeped in mythology. Since medieval times, it has been associated with King Arthur. When Richard, Earl of Cornwall, built his breathtaking castle on the headland in 1233, he probably did so to associate himself with the already popular Arthurian legends, rather than because the site offered any strategic advantage. By the 15th century the castle was in ruins.

Much later, Victorian poet Tennyson revived this connection with Arthur in his *Idylls of the King*. Then, in 1998, came the discovery of a slate with two Latin inscriptions dated to the 6th century AD. The second reads: 'Artognou, father of a descendant of Coll, has had [this] made.' Some have, probably erroneously, suggested that Artognou refers to King Arthur. Whatever the truth, Tintagel's history is complex and compelling.

■ **LOCATION** 13 miles N of Padstow, Cornwall; on coast, off B3263.
■ **ACCESS** See www.english-heritage.org.uk or telephone 01840 770328 for opening times and other details. Admission charge.

◄ *Tintagel faces west into the Atlantic and has been a natural fortress and trading post over centuries, with a history of legends to match its variety of archaeological finds.*

BRONZE AGE LANDSCAPE

❸ Dartmoor

Dartmoor is extraordinary. There can be few parts of the country that within so small an area contain such a wealth of archaeological riches. The Dartmoor National Park, covering just under 370 square miles, contains over 1,000 sites scheduled as Ancient Monuments by English Heritage, and has probably the best preserved and most extensive Bronze Age domestic and ritual landscape in Europe. Tree clearance on the moor was probably well under way by 4000BC, the beginning of the Neolithic, and largely complete by about 1500BC, the middle Bronze Age. A major system of linear field banks called reaves, running straight across country often for miles, covers large areas of the moor, and was laid out probably around 1700–1600BC. Small clusters of roundhouses, and networks of trackways, were fully

▼ *The rocky outcrops of Dartmoor tower above one of the most extensive Bronze Age domestic landscapes in Europe. They are good vantage points from which to view an area scattered with barrows and stone circles.*

incorporated into it. But Dartmoor also contains literally hundreds of Bronze Age barrows, roundhouse remains, stone rows and circles, and enclosures of various kinds, scattered across its landscape. Many of these sites are fully accessible, and visitors can hardly avoid stumbling across them.

Dartmoor's medieval landscape is much less well known but in its own way almost as important, with the remains of field systems and entire deserted hamlets surviving. The settlement at Hound Tor, in the parish of Manaton on the eastern side of the moor, is probably the best example.

■ **LOCATION** Dartmoor, Devon; W of Exeter.
■ **ACCESS** See www.dartmoor-npa. gov.uk for details.

❹ Kents Cavern

In the heart of Torquay lies Kents Cavern, which has provided the oldest evidence of human occupation in Britain, and is rightly regarded as one of the most significant prehistoric caves in the whole of northern Europe. Some of the evidence found in this limestone cave system dates back over 700,000 years, while five hand-axes discovered here are believed to have been made by the early hominid *Homo erectus* approximately 450,000 years ago.

Kents Cavern has also given up a wealth of Neanderthal flint implements, together with the jawbone and teeth of another early human species from 31,000 years ago, *Homo sapiens*, suggesting that the two species existed side by side, although the manner of their interaction is the subject of much debate. Ancient animal relics have also been found over the years, including the remains of a 500,000-year-old ancestral cave bear (an ancestor of contemporary bears), the bones of an ice-age cave lion, the 400,000-year-old canines from a sabre-toothed cat and teeth and bone belonging to a woolly mammoth.

Kents Cavern has been under the ownership of the Powe family for five generations. Francis Powe

▼ *The impressive west front of Exeter Cathedral with its 14th-century screen of saints, which would originally have been painted. The cathedral stands in the centre of the historic part of the city.*

acquired the caves when he purchased the land in 1903. The running of the caves as an attraction was passed down through successive sons until Nick Powe took over in 2000. Recognized by the *Guinness Book of Records*, Kents Cavern is the oldest scheduled monument in the British Isles.

■ **LOCATION** Ilsham Road, Torquay, Devon.
■ **ACCESS** See www.kents-cavern.co.uk or telephone 01803 215136 for opening times and other details. Admission charge.

CIVIL WAR

❺ Exeter

The city of Exeter has a long history of suffering as a result of conflict, and never more so than from 1642 to 1646 when civil war raged between Charles I and Parliament. Exeter endured terrible damage, which saw a great deal of the city destroyed. The population was divided in its loyalty between the two warring factions, which did not help in the defence of the city. Exeter was held by Parliament until its seizure by the Royalist armies in 1643, after which it was retaken by Parliamentary forces in 1646. It had been a prestigious centre of power, wealth and authority, as symbolized by the city's defensive wall. Nevertheless, damage caused by the war was extensive, with the suburbs razed to the ground.

Rebuilding commenced in earnest during the 1650s and had progressed considerably by the time of the Restoration under Charles II. Modernization lessened the necessity for the city wall but large parts remain standing today, with much of it impressively intact. The original wall circuit had been built by the Romans, then utilized by the Saxons, before being improved upon throughout the ages up to the Civil War itself.

One of Exeter's most enduring historical relics is the 12th-century

Hayes Barton manor house, birthplace of Sir Walter Raleigh. It was renovated many times over the centuries but what remains is a fine example of Tudor architecture. Oak features greatly in the construction, as was typical of the Tudor era, and the house's 'E' shape was allegedly a compliment to Queen Elizabeth I.

■ **LOCATION** Exeter, Devon.
■ **ACCESS** Historic Exeter is located around the cathedral. No public access to Hayes Barton Manor, Budleigh Salterton.

STONE AGE TO WARTIME

❻ Hawkcombe Head and Porlock Beach

Porlock Beach lies on the coast of Exmoor and, together with nearby Hawkcombe Head, has yielded evidence of the earliest human activity in the region. The discovery of flints dating from the Mesolithic period (about 8000–4000BC) suggests that groups of hunter-gatherers roamed the region; their movements have also been traced across the wider landscape beyond this area.

Excavations at Hawkcombe Head, ever since A.L. Wedlake discovered the site in 1942, have unearthed thousands of flints, including cores – lumps of flint that are left over after the more useful flakes have been knapped away – and microliths, while the predominant use of beach pebble as a raw material for making the tools is also apparent.

The nearby pebble beach at Porlock has yielded similar flint deposits also dating from the Mesolithic era, suggesting a link with the site at Hawkcombe Head. First observed in the 19th century, the most significant archaeological aspect of Porlock Beach are the stretches of submerged forest containing tree stumps and branches that date back around 5,000 to 6,000 years.

Porlock Beach was also used as part of the Invasion Stop Line during the Second World War and several buildings remain standing

today. Furthermore, the movement of the beach, caused by wave action, instigated the recent archaeological discovery of bones belonging to an Aurochs (an extinct species of ancient cattle), dating from around 1500BC.

■ **LOCATION** Porlock Bay is 5 miles W of Minehead, Somerset; on A39. Hawkcombe Head is 3 miles SW of Porlock (OS grid reference SS 844 457).
■ **ACCESS** By road and footpath. See www.exmoor-nationalpark.gov.uk and www.porlock.co.uk/visitorcentre for details.

KING ALFRED'S VICTORY

❼ Athelney

Athelney lies to the south-west of Glastonbury in a location infamous for being where Alfred the Great plotted his successful guerrilla warfare against the Vikings. Since the AD790s, the Vikings had plundered England at will. Over time they began to establish permanent settlements. During the AD800s, the Vikings seized the Anglo-Saxon kingdoms of York, East Anglia and Mercia, leaving Wessex to stand alone. Numerous battles ensued and the forces of Wessex, under the command of King Aethelred and his brother Alfred, offered staunch resistance. However, defeats soon outnumbered victories and Aethelred died, leaving 21-year-old Alfred to assume the mantle of King of Wessex.

In early 878, the Vikings seized Chippenham, which meant they now had a base from which to strike at Wessex. Alfred was forced to flee and withdrew to the Somerset marshes. Adopting Viking tactics, Alfred built a fortified base at Athelney in order to regroup and formulate new strategies. It was at this time that Alfred allegedly burnt the cakes he'd been asked to look after.

By a combination of guerrilla warfare tactics and the advantages afforded by the difficult marshland, King Alfred defeated the Vikings in

May 878, and in so doing ensured Wessex's survival. In honour of his victory, Alfred founded Athelney Abbey, though no evidence of it exists above ground today. Historians point out that, had Alfred given in, England as a country would not have come into being, since at the time he was the only remaining Anglo-Saxon monarch.

■ **LOCATION** 8 miles NE of Taunton; off A361.

■ **ACCESS** See OS Landranger map 195 for footpaths around Athelney Hill and the Saxon village at East Lyng.

IRON AGE VILLAGES

❽ Glastonbury and Meare

The lake villages at Glastonbury and Meare, in the Somerset Levels, are famous for the rare insight they give into daily life in Iron Age Britain. Neither site was actually in a lake: Glastonbury was on very wet swampy ground, and Meare lay at the edge of a large raised bog. Both settlements, occupied between roughly 300 and 50BC, were built on artificial 'islands' created from layers of brushwood and clay, tied together with thick tree branches laid crosswise. The Glastonbury settlement consisted of up to 40 houses, while the two separate settlements at Meare grew from tiny origins into a site that may have housed as many as 200 people.

Rising water levels appear to have forced the inhabitants to abandon the villages, but it was this flooding that preserved a huge number of organic artefacts that are normally lost. Excavation at both sites revealed timber houses whose layers of clay floors and hearths have been built up over generations of occupation. Preserved plant and animal remains show that the wetlands provided an enormously rich and varied natural resource for the village inhabitants, while thousands of smashed pots, along with fragments of weaving looms, metalworking equipment,

farming implements, jewellery, wooden bowls, wheels, even baskets and dice, give a rare glimpse of life in an Iron Age settlement on the eve of the Roman Conquest.

■ **LOCATION** Peat Moors Centre: Westhay, 2 miles NW of Glastonbury on B3151; Glastonbury Lake Village Museum: High Street, Glastonbury.

■ **ACCESS** See www.somerset.gov.uk /somerset/cultureheritage/heritage/pmc/ and www.somerset.gov.uk/museums /DIREC/G.html for opening times and other details. Admission charges.

13TH-CENTURY PALACE

❾ Bishop's Palace at Wells

The city of Wells in Somerset is the smallest city in England and derives its name from the three wells in the grounds of the majestic Bishop's Palace, which dates from the early 13th century. The palace was built when the first Bishop of Bath and Wells, Bishop Jocelin Trotman, was granted a licence from the Crown to build a residence on land south of the cathedral of St Andrew.

Fortified with battlements and a moat, the Bishop's Palace has a vaulted entrance hall made from local Doulting stone, which leads to the well-preserved undercroft with its 13th-century window openings and pillars made from Blue Lias stone from the wetlands of the Somerset

▲ *The south-west corner turret of the Bishop's Palace at Wells with the gatehouse in the background – home to the bishops of Bath and Wells for nearly 800 years.*

Levels. An exquisite Jacobean staircase leads to the first floor of the palace, where rooms refurbished in the later Victorian-Gothic style can be seen. These rooms include a portrait gallery of the bishops. The Coronation Cope (used for royal occasions) and Glastonbury Chair (one of the first 'folding chairs') are also exhibited here.

The tranquil gardens contain the ruins of the great hall, the remains of which still reveal medieval architecture and window tracery. The 13th-century chapel was restored in the 19th century and is still in use today. The windows of the chapel were made from glass salvaged from the ruins of French medieval churches. The palace has been the home to the Bishop of Bath and Wells for nearly 800 years. Recent archaeological investigation in the Virgin's Tower revealed a fragment of a wall painting depicting the face of a woman whose identity is unknown.

■ **LOCATION** City centre, Wells, Somerset.

■ **ACCESS** See www.bishopspalacewells. co.uk or telephone 01749 678691 for opening times and other details. Admission charge.

⑩ Cheddar Gorge and Aveline's Hole

The Mendip Hills in Somerset is an important area for the study of early human occupation in Britain because of its many limestone caves. In 1903, Gough's Cave in Cheddar Gorge produced the earliest complete human skeleton ever found in Britain – the Upper Palaeolithic 'Cheddar Man', who met a brutal death, aged about 23

years old, with a strong blow to the face. Subsequent excavations on the site have revealed further violence, from numerous split human bones, fractured in the way animal bones are during marrow extraction, to the bones of three adults and two children, deeply scored with cuts like those in bones from joints of meat. Debates rage about whether the Palaeolithic inhabitants of the cave were cannibals, or whether the scoring of the bones derives from a funerary rite where flesh

▲ Aerial view of Cheddar Gorge, the site of a Time Team dig, showing how the gorge cuts deep into the Mendips. This is where the earliest complete human skeleton in Britain was found.

is removed from the bones before burial.

Nearby Aveline's Hole is another cave in use during the early Stone Age. Between 60 and 100 skeletons were reported to have been discovered in the 18th century, making it the largest Stone Age

◄ *The skeleton of 'Cheddar Man' was found in Gough's Cave and shows that he died as a result of a brutal blow to the face. Evidence of cannibalism adds to the grim picture.*

cemetery in Europe. Although few of the original remains from the site survive, making modern interpretation difficult, the bones that do survive show interesting evidence for the health and lifestyle of those buried in the cave, from the first case of osteoarthritis in Britain to childhood nutritional diseases. It is currently thought that the cave was in use over only a relatively short period of time, between 7100 and 6800BC.

■ **LOCATION** Gough's Cave: B3135 runs through Cheddar Gorge, 7 miles NW of Wells, Somerset. Aveline's Hole: B3134 runs through Burrington Combe, 3 miles N of Cheddar.
■ **ACCESS** Gough's Cave and Cheddar Man: see www.cheddarcaves.co.uk for opening times and other details. Admission charge. Aveline's Hole: see OS Landranger map 182 for location and footpath. Warning: access beyond entrance for experienced cavers only.

NEOLITHIC RITUAL SITE

⓫ Stanton Drew

A tranquil, little-visited site in a bend of the River Chew, in north Somerset, holds an archaeological surprise. The monument proper consists of three major elements: a central large circle (the Great Circle), flanked by two smaller ones, to the south-west and north-east respectively. In addition, a structure known as the Cove, consisting of

three large stones, stands south-west of the main complex in a small paddock close to the church (now part of the garden of the local pub, the Druids' Arms), and a lone outlier, a standing stone called Hautville's Quoit, is sited to the north, on the other side of the river. Both the Great Circle and the smaller north-east circle have short 'avenues' of standing stones leading roughly north-eastwards from them, towards the Chew.

Stanton Drew is one of the largest monuments of its type in Britain. At 112m (368ft) in diameter, the Great

Circle is second only in size to Avebury. Although studied by earlier generations of antiquarians, its secrets remain almost intact, and therefore available to modern, scientific methods of excavation. But its potential significance was revealed in the summer of 1997, when a geophysical survey showed that the interior of the Great Circle was occupied by a complex pattern of pits, each probably over a metre (3⅓ft) in diameter, and arranged in a concentric series of nine rings. It is possible that they are settings for gigantic vertical timber posts, probably over 400 of them, much larger in diameter than telegraph poles. This was a massive wooden monument that preceded the stone circle. This development, the

conversion of a wooden monument to stone, is well known elsewhere, for example at Avebury (see page 38), and most famously at Stonehenge itself (page 42). But the revelation was the sheer size of the new discovery. In the next few years, archaeologists hope that Stanton Drew will form the focus of a major, long-term study.

■ **LOCATION** Stanton Drew village, 6 miles S of Bristol; off B3130, near A37.
■ **ACCESS** Main circle: permitted access on private farmland. Admission charge. The Cove: in the Druids' Arms pub garden.

▼ One of the elements of Stanton Drew is this three-stone structure, known as the Cove, which provides added interest to the pub garden of the Druids' Arms. The local parish church is in the background.

INDUSTRIAL REVOLUTION

⑫ Bristol

The huge impact that Bristol had on the industrial revolution is hardly surprising. By the 1700s, its port was second only to London in prosperity. The wealth bestowed on the city was mainly derived from the triangular slave trade, whereby goods would be exported to Africa in exchange for slaves and ivory. The slaves were then taken to the colonies in the West Indies and America, where they were traded for sugar, rum and tobacco before the ships returned to Bristol. Together with Liverpool, Bristol overtook London's volume of diverse trades, thus ensuring a booming economy for the city.

During the 18th century, revenue derived from glassmaking, tobacco, rope and twine manufacture and brass and iron founding thrust Bristol to the forefront of the industrial revolution. Abraham Darby famously developed methods of casting brass (see Baptist Mills page 31) and later iron, but the impact of industrialization is most evident in the contributions made by Isambard Kingdom Brunel. Brunel designed the Clifton suspension bridge and several magnificent steamships, including the *Great Britain* and the *Great Western*.

However, Brunel's most significant achievement was the Great Western Railway, which linked Bristol to London and allowed Bristol to prosper as an industrial centre. His

work is still evident all along the line, which remains in use today, and includes Bristol Temple Meads station, the Chippenham and Hanwell viaducts and the Box Tunnel near Bath. The GWR line is testament to Brunel's impact on the era.

■ **LOCATION** Bristol.
■ **ACCESS** For opening times and other details of Bristol City Museum, Industrial Museum and Georgian House, search for 'museum' at www.bristol-city.gov.uk; SS Great Britain: see www.ss-great-britain.com; Clifton suspension bridge: see www.clifton-suspension-bridge.org.uk. Admission charges. Bristol Temple Meads is a mainline railway station.

INDUSTRIAL REVOLUTION

⓭ Baptist Mills, Bristol

With the establishment of the Bristol Brass Company at Baptist Mills in 1702, it could be argued that the Industrial Revolution began. Prior to this, London merchants, who imported and re-exported brassware from the Dutch–German border, blocked commercial brass manufacture in Britain. This monopoly was ended by the Mines Royal Act of 1689 and, by 1698, Bristol's foreign, colonial and slave-trade economies had expanded greatly. New markets were stimulated, with brass at the forefront of demand.

In 1700, a group of wealthy Quakers teamed up with Abraham Darby to establish Britain's first brass manufacturers. In 1702 the location at Baptist Mills was chosen because of the proximity of a copperworks, as well as water, coal and zinc supplies. Furthermore, the port and city of Bristol allowed access to thriving trade routes. Encouraged by

◀ *Clifton suspension bridge in Bristol, designed by Isambard Kingdom Brunel, spans the river Avon in dramatic style. Bristol was among the places at the forefront of the industrial revolution.*

the trading of goods and slaves between Africa and the plantations of the West Indian and American colonies, increased demand for brass goods ensured high levels of production, but in 1709 Darby left to establish a joint copper, brass, iron and steel works at Coalbrookdale in Shropshire (see page 124). Nevertheless, Baptist Mills continued to grow through the 18th century until competition arrived from the Birmingham Metal Company in 1781.

Faced with a more modern competitor, Baptist Mills fell into decline until the 5.5-hectare (13½-acre) site was finally abandoned. It was sold off in plots in the mid-1800s. Subsequent development has hidden much of what was, even in the Victorian era, a sprawling industrial centre, but remnants do remain, such as parts of the arch from the Crew's Hole Copper Works and the copper-slag coping blocks used in the building of the Greek Church.

■ **LOCATION** Nothing survives of the Baptist Mills brassworks, but some of the 18th-century Warmley brassworks does: Warmley, South Gloucestershire; off A420.
■ **ACCESS** Kingswood Heritage Centre at the Warmley brassworks, see www.southglos.gov.uk/Museums for opening times and other details.

NEOLITHIC MONUMENT

⓮ The Dorset Cursus, Cranborne Chase

Stretching over 6 miles in length and measuring more than 100m (330ft) across, the gigantic cursus on Cranborne Chase is among the largest and most puzzling of Britain's prehistoric monuments. Dating from the Neolithic period, cursus monuments are exceptionally long and narrow earthwork enclosures and are some of the oldest man-made structures in the world. Archaeologists are fascinated by them because their purpose is still unknown.

On the surface, most cursus monuments in Britain look like marks in the ground made by extensive ploughing, or crop marks. What they all have in common is that their long boundaries consist of an interior bank flanked by an exterior ditch. The parallel banks and ditches of the Dorset Cursus run across perhaps the richest prehistoric landscape in the country. It incorporates several of the surrounding barrows and other Neolithic monuments, suggesting an association with religious rituals and practices.

One theory is that the Dorset Cursus may have been used as a ceremonial processional route; another is that it could have been a proving ground for young men. We may never know the true purpose of the Dorset Cursus. After all, even the word 'cursus' is misleading. It is derived from the Latin word for 'racecourse' because it was originally believed that cursus were ancient racecourses.

■ **LOCATION** NW of Fordingbridge, Dorset; near A345.
■ **ACCESS** Many prehistoric monuments survive as earthworks in this area. See OS Landranger maps 184 and 195 for locations and footpaths.

CIRCULAR EARTHWORKS

⓯ Knowlton Rings

These four ring or circular earthworks lie at the heart of this Neolithic and Bronze Age landscape, approximately 8 miles north of Wimborne. Geophysical surveys reveal that three of the circles (North, Southern and Central) are actually henges. The North Circle was originally a horseshoe-shaped henge with a wide south-eastern entrance while the Southern Circle once measured 230m (750ft) across. Unfortunately, extensive ploughing has damaged both sites.

The rough, rectangular-shaped Central Circle is the best preserved, its outer bank and inner ditch being noticeable. However, the most prominent feature is the medieval church in the middle of the circle. Records show that Knowlton Church, as it is officially known, remained in use up until the mid-17th century, and its construction was possibly intended to 'Christianize' the existing site. The church's chancel and nave date from the 12th century, and it is believed that the north chapel, west tower and south porch were added during the 15th century.

The fourth circle (known as the Old Churchyard) is the least spectacular, also largely as a result of the effect of ploughing, but it is thought that this enclosure once had a southern entrance. Aerial photography of Knowlton Rings and the surrounding area reveals a spectacular array of Bronze Age barrows and ring ditches focusing on these Neolithic henge monuments. Neighbouring fields feature monumental mounds and circular rings that contribute to form a remarkable prehistoric site, which yielded a significant find in 1958 when the remains of Christian-Saxon skeletons were unearthed. Their religion was determined by the lack of personal goods found in the grave, and the fact that their bodies had been laid in an east–west alignment with arms crossed on the chest.

■ **LOCATION** Knowlton, Dorset; 6 miles N of Wimborne Minster, on B3078.
■ **ACCESS** See www.english-heritage. org.uk for details.

ROMAN AQUEDUCT

⓰ Dorchester

Present-day Dorchester is on the site of the Roman town of Durnovaria. Now buried beneath modern urbanization, Durnovaria was established around AD70 and once covered an area of 70–80 acres. The town was a centre for mosaic-making; many have been unearthed and put on display in the town's

Dorset County Museum. Dorchester is blessed with a wealth of archaeological finds dating from the Roman era. These include a wonderfully preserved Roman townhouse, originally excavated in the 1930s, an amphitheatre at Maumbury Rings, and the only remaining section of the Roman defensive wall in the Top O' Town.

However, the most significant Roman find unearthed in the area is the 11-mile-long aqueduct that had supplied Durnovaria's populace with fresh water at an estimated rate of 60 million litres (13 million gallons) a day. Excavations revealed that the aqueduct was constructed before Durnovaria existed and originally supplied water to the legion based at the fort that was near where Dorchester is today. The aqueduct was later diverted to Durnovaria and fed by water from a dammed-up tributary of the River Frome.

A great deal of archaeological investigation has been undertaken in

▲ *Frozen in time – the village school at Tyneham. The whole village was requisitioned by the army in 1943 and it has been in MOD possession ever since. It wasn't only medieval barons who ordered populations around.*

an attempt to trace and understand the aqueduct. First discovered in the late 19th century, it is easily visible on the hillside near Dorchester, but its real purpose was not confirmed until the Roman bathhouse was excavated in 1977.

- **LOCATION** Dorchester, Dorset.
- **ACCESS** Dorset County Museum, High West Street: see www.dorsetcounty museum.org or telephone 01305 262735 for opening times and other details. Admission charge.

SECOND WORLD WAR

⑰ Tyneham

Anything like a ghost town is hard to find in Britain, but that's exactly what you get when you visit Tyneham village. Its origins lie in the medieval era, and until relatively recently Tyneham was a remote and peaceful village tucked away in the fertile downs overlooking the Dorset coast. During the course of the Second World War, in 1943, it was requisitioned by the British army to be used for training the military. An unexpected letter from the War Department informed the villagers that they were to be moved from their homes to help the war effort. Tyneham's residents were led to believe that they would return when the war was over, and a note was pinned to the door of St Mary's Church stating:

'Please treat the church and houses with care; we have given up our homes where many of us lived for generations to help win the war to keep men free. We shall return one day and thank you for treating the village kindly.'

However, the government reneged on its promise in 1948, and Tyneham has remained deserted and the property of the MOD ever since. Now part of a 3,000-hectare (7,500-acre) firing range, Tyneham can be visited on weekends and bank holidays. Most of the houses, including the Tudor manor house, lie in ruins, but the medieval church of St Mary still stands, and the school, preserved exactly as it was left in 1943, is a museum.

- **LOCATION** 6 miles SW of Wareham, Dorset.
- **ACCESS** Tyneham is on Ministry of Defence land, but some access is permitted. See www.defence-estates. mod.uk for opening times and other details.

NORMAN CASTLE

⑱ Corfe Castle

Situated between Wareham and Swanage, Corfe Castle dominates the Purbeck Ridge. In AD978 it was the site of King Edward's alleged murder at the hands of his stepmother, which led to her birth-son (Aethelred the Unready) taking the throne.

The castle itself was rebuilt with local Purbeck stone by the Normans and functioned as an important stronghold, with the keep and inner bailey developed by Henry I during the 12th century. King John made improvements to the accommodation and defences in the 13th century. He also added a hall, chapel and domestic buildings, before Henry VIII under his reign added further walls, towers and gatehouses.

Corfe Castle remained under the ownership of successive monarchs until 1572 when Elizabeth I sold it to her suitor, Sir Christopher Hatton. In turn, the Hatton family sold the castle to Sir John Bankes in 1635, and it was left to Lady Bankes following his death during the outbreak of civil war. Lady Bankes defended the castle through two sieges (in 1643 and 1645) before succumbing, through treachery, to

Parliamentary forces in 1646. Parliament ordered the destruction of Corfe Castle, the result of which is the spectacular ruin we see today.

▼ *Corfe Castle still dominates the local Dorset landscape, despite its ruinous state. The attempts by Parliamentary forces to destroy it in the 17th century did not entirely succeed.*

The fact that Corfe Castle could not be utterly obliterated is testimony to the formidable strength of the Purbeck stone used to build it.

■ **LOCATION** Corfe Castle, 5 miles S of Wareham, Dorset.
■ **ACCESS** See www.nationaltrust.org.uk or telephone 01929 481294 for opening times and other details. Admission charge.

ANGLO-SAXON BURH

⑲ Wareham

In the late 9th century AD, King Alfred the Great and his son Edward the Elder established or refounded a network of strongly fortified towns, called 'burhs', across southern England. These burhs were part of a long-running campaign to defend

the region from attack by Viking armies, and the scale and organization of Alfred's strategy is widely regarded as remarkable. Wareham, in Dorset, is one of the best of the surviving burhs. It was probably a royal and religious centre even before Alfred's time, and it may be that he simply built on existing defences. But whatever their origins, Wareham's well-preserved and impressive circuit of defensive ramparts owes its final form to Alfred.

As Alfred succeeded against the Vikings and the threat faded away, some of the burhs declined, but many, like Wareham, went on to become prosperous towns. As with many Anglo-Saxon towns refounded in this period, Wareham was given a very regular, grid-iron street pattern, and like the defences, this layout is unusually well preserved in the modern town.

■ **LOCATION** Wareham, Dorset; 7 miles W of Poole on A352.
■ **ACCESS** Sections of the defences can be seen W of town. See OS Landranger map 195 for locations and footpaths.

Southern England

The chalk downlands of Wiltshire and Berkshire have an amazing inheritance of monuments from the age of the first farmers, the Neolithic, to the Iron Age and beyond. Stonehenge, Avebury and Silbury Hill all originated in the Neolithic. The stone phase at Stonehenge itself is, of course, the country's greatest Bronze Age monument. Perhaps the most enduring image of this area, however, is the Bronze Age figure of a galloping horse carved into the hillside above Uffington. The Roman period is well represented in southern England. The large, stone-built fort at Portchester in Hampshire was part of a chain of late Roman defences stretching around the eastern and southern coasts. Also representing the region's maritime connection are Henry VIII's flagship the Mary Rose, and Nelson's ship HMS Victory, both preserved at Portsmouth. Evidence of a conflict of much more recent times can be seen at Lepe near the Solent in Hampshire, where some of the concrete pontoons used for the D-Day Mulberry Harbours were built.

N

0   20 m
0   20 k

BANBURY

GLOUCESTER   CHELTENHAM

② Littledean
③ Gloucester Cathedral
④ Chedworth

Lydney ①

A40

A41

AYLESBURY

⑤ Cirencester

M5

A429   A419

⑨ City of Oxford

SWINDON

⑦ ⑧ Uffington White Horse

Wayland's Smithy

M40

A413

SLOUGH

Avebury

M4

⑥ Bradford-on-Avon

A338

READING

M4

Stonehenge

A303

BASINGSTOKE

M3

⑩ Old Sarum

SALISBURY

A36

A31

Southampton ⑪

M27

Portchester Castle

A31

Stone Point Lepe ⑫

⑬ Mary Rose
⑭ HMS Victory

PORTSMOUTH

ISLE OF WIGHT

Avebury and West Kennet
Ceremonial landscape

PHIL CALLS AVEBURY the 'big granddaddy of them all', and although it is Stonehenge that draws the crowds, the henge and stone circles at Avebury are considered by many archaeologists to be more impressive. Avebury is one of the largest structures of its kind in Europe. An immense bank and ditch surrounds the site, containing an area of over 12 hectares (30 acres) – enough space for 15 football pitches. The ditch is now very silted up, and its original depth can best be appreciated by looking at the pictures of Harold St George Gray's excavations in 1910, which show tiers of workmen standing on platforms. (They can be seen in the Alexander Keiller Museum at Avebury.) The amount of labour required originally to dig the ditch of over 7–10m (23–33ft) deep would have been immense. The bank is nearly a mile in circumference, and as you walk around it you get a sense that it may have acted as an observation point – a prehistoric grandstand from which to view events inside.

The stones

The ditch and bank surround one large stone circle – the biggest in Britain – with two smaller ones on the inside. The northern inner circle also had a small group of three stones, called the cove, at its centre. The transport and erection of the stones was a huge task: some weigh up to 50 tons and were brought over from Marlborough Downs to be set up inside the bank and ditch. They are sarsen quartzite sandstone, an incredibly hard material. Unlike at Stonehenge, the stones do not appear to have been worked but seem to have been selected for their natural shape. The main circle consists of alternating column-shaped stones and diamond- or lozenge-shaped ones, which are sometimes interpreted as 'male' and 'female'. They're arranged in four quadrants, between four entrances into the henge. One to look out for in particular is the diamond-shaped stone at the north-north-west entrance. Nearly 5m (16½ft) wide, this diamond shape often appears in stone circles.

Most of the excavation at the site was carried out in the early 1900s by Harold St George Gray and Alexander Keiller. Keiller actually bought much of Avebury, demolishing modern buildings and old

◀ Avebury is one of the largest stone circles in Europe and this aerial photograph shows clearly the vast bank and ditch that surround the site. The henge is criss-crossed by roads and a small village is sited within the circle.

▼ Two stones from the avenue. The opposing straight and diamond-shaped stones that line the way from Avebury to the Sanctuary are thought to represent male and female.

cottages alike and re-erecting many of the fallen stones in the 1930s. Despite his efforts, only 27 of the 98 stones that originally formed the outer circle are still standing, while most of the two inner circles have been destroyed. That's because the village of Avebury grew up inside and around the henge, and many of the stones were deliberately broken up, either to make way for buildings and to use as construction materials, or perhaps because they were considered pagan and 'ungodly'. However, recent geophysical surveys have confirmed the positions of the missing stones, and revealed that several stones remain buried at the site. The surveys have also picked up a possible lost timber circle and other

prehistoric features inside the henge, including a horseshoe-shaped feature that may have looked similar to the inner trilithon at Stonehenge (see page 43), indicating how complex Avebury's development was.

Like Stonehenge, Avebury was created over a long period and had various phases. The best estimates for when the bank was dug centre around 3000BC. The sheer effort required must have been extraordinary. Mike Pitts in his excellent book *Hengeworld* estimates it might have taken three or four hundred people working solidly for over a year. This implies a certain amount of organization,

and the communal resources to have large groups of people engaged in activities other than farming and hunting. The stones themselves were erected after the ditch had been dug, with the smaller inner circle being completed around 2800BC, and the outer circle around 2000BC.

Artefacts and human bones

The 20th-century excavations revealed a wealth of prehistoric artefacts in the ditches, including early Bronze Age Beaker pottery, as well as antler picks and ox bones used for digging. One of the most dramatic discoveries was a

▼ West Kennet long barrow from the air showing its entrance. It has been estimated that more than 400 people have been buried here since its construction. Phil says: 'I have a particular affection for West Kennet – it's a rare long barrow that you can still get inside.'

prehistoric female skeleton, buried in the ditch near one of the entrances and covered in stones. Gray referred to her as a 'dwarf', but although she was undoubtedly short in stature, it's unlikely this was the correct medical term.

This skeleton wasn't the only human body to be discovered at Avebury. In the south-west quadrant of the circle is a stone known as 'the barber-surgeon stone'. Excavations below this stone recovered the skeleton, and professional toolkit, of an unfortunate 14th-century barber-surgeon, who'd clearly been curious enough to explore the pit under the stone, and for his pains was crushed to death.

New discoveries

Avebury sits at the centre of a huge ritual landscape, which, like the henge itself, developed over a long period of time. There are hundreds of prehistoric sites in the countryside around the henge, from Neolithic enclosures and standing stones to Bronze Age barrow cemeteries. Some survive as earthworks, others are known only from survey and excavation. More are being discovered all the time, and their sheer numbers demonstrate the importance of this area.

Two avenues of stones, now mostly disappeared and known only from archaeological work, lead from the henge. One heads south-east towards another stone circle called the Sanctuary, and towards a nearby series of Neolithic enclosures and a long barrow at West Kennet. The other avenue heads south-west towards a recently identified Neolithic enclosure at 'Longstones'. Two other major Neolithic sites lie within a few miles of Avebury as well. Nothing much remains of the massive causewayed enclosure on top of nearby Windmill Hill, but it's hard to miss Silbury Hill, an enigmatic monument, the function of which is difficult to interpret – whatever it might be, you can only marvel at the huge effort required to build it.

New archaeological surveys of the henge itself and the landscape around it have increased our understanding of Avebury a huge amount, but there are still many questions to be answered. However, there's no doubt that it was an incredibly important focus of ritual activity for our prehistoric ancestors.

Time Team

Phil suggests that, like many of our sites, you need to get a larger perspective. Avebury is part of a ceremonial landscape. One way of tackling it might be to start chronologically with Windmill Hill, an early Neolithic settlement famous for its wonderful pottery, go on to West Kennet long barrow, then arrive at Avebury and, if you have time, look at Silbury Hill – the largest man-made mound in Europe.

He goes on to say: 'In West Kennet long barrow, I suggest you look for a specific stone used for grinding axes. As you enter the barrow it is on the left-hand side in the second stone chamber. West Kennet is over 100m (330ft) long and is a vast burial chamber. Inside are five chambers, and it has been estimated that over 400 people have been buried in it since its construction around 3400BC. One of the people was killed in battle or possibly as a sacrifice. Archaeologists found a flint arrow tip in his throat.'

■ **GETTING THERE**
Avebury is 7 miles W of Marlborough, Wiltshire, on the B4003 (off the A4). For Avebury, see www.nationaltrust.org. uk or telephone 01672 539250 for opening times and other details. Admission charge for museum. For West Kennet and Silbury Hill, see www.english-heritage. org.uk for opening times and other details. There is a viewing area at Silbury but no access to hill itself.

■ **OUR VIEW** The vast investment of time and sheer effort over generations makes this one of the most astonishing sites in Britain, and one that we would recommend you visit again and again. Given enough time you should try to walk Phil's route (see above).

Stonehenge
Neolithic vision and ambition

2900–1600BC

Ｌike many of the great sites – and Stonehenge is one of the world's great historic monuments – the amazing stones at its centre need to be seen as part of a wider landscape. Surrounding Stonehenge is a series of ridges including Kings Barrow Ridge and Winterbourne Stoke Down; these are all covered with barrows. It's worth taking a look at the main complex from one of these ridges before heading for the main monument. The barrows are Early Bronze Age –

around 2500BC – and may have been placed in a position from which the later phases of Stonehenge would be visible.

This introduces the other element that is key to understanding Stonehenge: what we see today is only the final phase of a whole set of different versions of 'Stonehenge', which gradually developed over time.

Stonehenge began around 2900BC as a sort of causewayed enclosure – a large circular earthwork. In 2004 Time Team dug a causewayed enclosure with Francis Pryor and found a distinctive ditch with sections left intact that seemed to provide a number of crossing points into the central area. Francis's site was probably a thousand years earlier than

▶ The preparation of stones using mauls carries on while a burial proceeds, probably to be placed on a platform inside the stones. The final stones were in place by around 1600BC.

the first Stonehenge, which is why we said Stonehenge was a 'sort of' causewayed enclosure.

The earliest Stonehenge wasn't stone at all. It consisted of a circular ditch, dug in segments and with a bank on the outside. There were two gaps in this ditch, giving access into the interior. If you stood inside the circular ditch you would see a circle of 56 posts, which were sunk into the ground in the Aubrey Holes; these are marked by concrete. (Aubrey was a 17th-century antiquarian who took advantage of a dry summer to note the parched marks left by the postholes.)

In the next stage, around 2500BC, the posts were removed from the Aubrey Holes and several were filled with cremations. The enclosure ditch was partially filled in, and cremations were added here too. We don't know precisely what was going on, but there were several post-built structures at the centre and in the main north-easterly entranceway. But still there were no stones.

The stones

It's not until the third phase (from 2500 to 1600BC) that we see the appearance of the first stones at Stonehenge. These were the famous 'Bluestones', which were arranged in a circle. They were quarried in the Preseli hills of Pembrokeshire. There were about 80 of these, each about the weight of a family car, and all had to be transported a huge distance: over 200 miles, probably via the sea and up the Avon river.

The third stage of Stonehenge also involved the destruction of this original bluestone circle and the arrival of the massive 30-ton blocks of sarsen stone brought from 20–30 miles away on the Marlborough Downs. Twenty or so of the bluestones were re-erected inside the sarsen stones. There were originally 80 sarsen stones creating an outer circle with a continuous set of lintels on the top, and

inside the five pairs of much larger stones creating a horseshoe shape of trilithons (two upright stones with a lintel). Another huge block of what might be Welsh sandstone was placed at the centre – the 'Altar Stone'. The final phase was completed around 1600BC. This structure is an amazing extension of the ideas of earlier wooden structures and it preserves for us methods of jointing that would have been familiar to Bronze Age carpenters. Tongue-and-groove joints join the sarsen lintels and they in turn are attached to the uprights by mortise and tenon. You can see a bare tenon projecting from one of the uprights. Virtually all the stones have been worked in order to enhance the curve of the circle and the visual appearance of the finished monument. It is likely that the surfaces would have been dressed using massive stone mauls with teams of workers repeatedly dropping them onto the face of the rock.

During this final stage a great processional way known as the Avenue was constructed. It was marked out by ditches and banks, and linked Stonehenge to the river Avon.

▲ You can clearly see here a tenon that would have fitted into the mortise cut into a lintel. Painstaking effort and skill, possibly derived from an earlier woodworking tradition, must have gone into creating the henge.

These are some of the bare facts of Stonehenge, but when you go to the site what is most impressive is its scale and the ambition of those who created it. It is one thing to create a wooden henge monument, but to visualize something that required this amount of labour, skill and organization is hard for us to fathom.

What was it for?

We wanted to ask one of Time Team's Bronze Age experts – Francis Pryor – the obvious question: what was all this effort for? His answer seems to centre on a number of ideas connecting the dead with the living. Stonehenge is surrounded by the dead, housed in the barrows that dot the skyline. In its third phase, around 2500BC, Stonehenge may have been linked with two other huge monuments built at this time – Durrington Walls, which is even larger than Avebury, and Woodhenge. These according to Francis Pryor may have been assembly points for ceremonial activities by the living preparing to make a journey along the river Avon and up the Avenue to Stonehenge.

There is also the matter that the stones seem to correlate with astronomical events, and some archaeologists go even further and suggest that Stonehenge is a vast prehistoric clock for predicting them. This is the kind of thing that makes Mick and Phil uncomfortable, but a great deal of mathematical and astronomical study has now been done on the site and it would appear that either there was a deliberate attempt to create a monument orientated to major solar and lunar events, which could be used to predict lunar eclipses, or you happen to be looking at one of the most bizarre coincidences in archaeology. Certainly what always catches Francis's attention is the way the circle of stones directs your attention up into the sky.

He told us: 'I have had the great privilege of walking around the stones early in the morning, before the visitors begin to arrive, and I was able to appreciate not just the size of the monument, but the contrasting scale of its components. The smaller bluestones are more human in size and it's hard to avoid the impression that they may once have represented individual people – perhaps the shades of the ancestors. The massive trilithons, on the other hand, look down from above in an altogether more ominous and unforgiving fashion.'

For a detailed understanding of the culture that produced Stonehenge, Mick and I recommend *Hengeworld* by Mike Pitts; Julian Richards' recent book *Stonehenge: A History in Photographs*, which includes a good summary of everything up to date, and of course Francis Pryor's *Britain BC*, in which his fascinating ideas on henge monuments

can be studied. This is a monument that deserves a bit of homework being done – there is nothing quite like it.

Excavations

A final note. Stonehenge has been dug into by many people, including the Duke of Buckingham in 1620 'who did cause the middle of Stonehenge to be digged'. The main modern excavations were by Lieutenant Colonel William Hawley in the 1920s and by Professor Richard Atkinson between 1950 and 1964. It is probably true to say that it has been difficult for modern archaeologists

to interpret the findings from past excavations at Stonehenge.

Francis Pryor and others are convinced there is more waiting to be found. In 1966, for example, a series of large pits were uncovered when the car park facilities were expanded, which imply a set of posts erected in the Mesolithic era around 8,000BC – 4,000 years before the first phase of the monument you see today began. When you enter this amazing monument and the landscape around it, you need to bear in mind that you may be walking over secrets that still remain to be uncovered.

▲ *Stonehenge has been an important part of the archaeological landscape for generations. Here the camera lens exaggerates the way the sarsens appear to curve inwards – this may have been the effect the original builders wished to create.*

■ **GETTING THERE** Stonehenge is 2 miles W of Amesbury, Wiltshire, on the A344. See www.english-heritage.org.uk or telephone 01980 624715 for opening times and other details. Admission charge.

■ **OUR VIEW** We recommend you pay two initial visits to Stonehenge – the first to take in the surrounding landscape and to take a look at the structure from the outside. Then return, having filled out the appropriate forms to join a group allowed into the centre. Here you will see and feel the tremendous power of the monument, particularly if you are present at sunset. You will also be able to see the carvings of daggers and look at the detail of the construction.

Portchester
Roman 'Fort of the Saxon Shore'

AD286-1800s

WHEN WE THINK OF the Romans, we tend to have in mind their roads, features such as Hadrian's Wall and sites such as Bath. We are less familiar with the coastal defences and the huge fleet of ships the Romans used to defend our shores.

▼ This aerial shot shows how well Portchester's Roman walls and bastions are preserved. The fort helped control maritime traffic in and out of the harbour.

From the 1st to 4th centuries, the sea between Britain and the continent was a busy place. Cross-Channel imports and exports made piracy an attractive and lucrative operation, and there was the increasing problem of raids by the barbarian tribes from northern Europe. One response by the Romans was to create a line of fortified compounds, which collectively have been given the rather evocative title 'the Forts of the Saxon Shore'. The title is not greatly liked by Time Team's Roman experts,

but it seems to have stuck. Portchester is just one of eleven such forts built; others include Pevensey and Bradwell-on-Sea (see pages 92 and 162).

Portchester is one of the most impressive, however, and both Francis and Mick regard it as important because of the size of the walls and its excellent state of preservation. This is one of the biggest pieces of standing Roman stonework in north-west Europe. And in some stretches of the wall you can see the original Roman towers. The Roman defences appear to have been built some time after AD268 and constitute a massive perimeter wall, some 3m (10ft) thick and 6m (20ft) high, within twin earthwork ditches.

The walls are largely complete with hollow bastions spaced at regular intervals so that defenders on each bastion could protect the towers on either side with artillery fire. The square plan of the fort encloses a huge area of nearly 3.5 hectares (8½ acres). Such strong defences naturally appealed to later generations, and Portchester was reused as a defence against the Vikings. In Norman times a magnificent keep was erected in one corner – it survives intact. In the interior stands a priory church with a wonderful Norman doorway.

Mick recommends a visit to the medieval loos, which are one of the finest examples of their kind. Always keen to ask the obvious questions, we consulted medieval experts on the question of medieval loo paper, and were told that a stick with grass or sponge was the preferred option.

Piracy in the Channel

Portchester's story begins in the second half of the 3rd century. It has been thought that the fort at Portchester (Portus Adurni) might have had a link with Carausius. Carausius was a sailor of Belgian origin serving in the Roman army. He was commissioned by the Romans to rid the Channel of pirates in AD286. Much to the chagrin of the Romans, he was believed to be getting rich from the ill-gotten gains of the Saxon looters. In 286 Carausius declared himself emperor in Britain and ruled until he was murdered in 293. His successor, Allectus, held power in Britain until 296, when he was defeated by a massive Roman fleet and army. Until then Portchester probably served as a power base for the rebel emperors. Excavations indicate that the fort might have been refortified and reoccupied around 340.

Later occupants

The fort finally went into decline by the early 5th century after the Roman withdrawal from Britain, and was subsequently occupied extensively by the Saxons.

Further occupation of the fort saw it emerge as a castle under Norman rule, with an inner bailey and keep being built in the early 1100s. In the middle ages, Portchester became a royal palace. The great tower which forms the keep was built during the reign of Henry I, while Richard II added domestic buildings. Successive monarchs exploited Portchester as a strategic location, but this waned as nearby Portsmouth grew in importance.

Portchester then served in various roles, including that of barracks, hospital and prison, until the 19th century. Porchester is a marvellous site precisely because of its continuity of occupation, and the preservation of the stonework.

■ GETTING THERE Portchester Castle overlooks Portsmouth Harbour in Hampshire. See www.english-heritage.org.uk or telephone 023 9237 8291 for opening times and other details. Admission charge.
■ OUR VIEW Portchester would benefit greatly from an improved visitor centre, but none the less the site is worth spending a whole day on.

Other sites to visit

❶ Lydney

Now part of Lydney Park Estate, the Lydney Roman temple and villa complex dates from around AD364. The remains of the buildings visible today represent only the final phase of what was a successful and long-established settlement.

The temple was built overlooking the Severn estuary, in a landscape dominated by the mining of iron. Excavations in the 1920s uncovered thousands of finds, including inscriptions, mosaics, bronzes, bracelets and more than 8,000 coins, which by their dates indicate continued use of the temple into the 5th century. The temple was part of a larger Roman complex, which appears to have been successively developed into a thriving concern that also prospered into the 5th century.

Rectangular in shape with strong buttresses, the temple measures over 18m by 24m (60ft x 80ft) and contains not one central room but three rooms in the north-western end. It appears, following the discovery of inscriptions, that Lydney was a temple to the god Nodens, a local pagan deity probably adopted and incorporated with the Roman god Mars. This was a common practice. It was allowed by Rome, as a way of accepting and Romanizing native peoples. Nodens must have been popular, as the complex at Lydney is fairly substantial. ·

■ **LOCATION** Lydney Park is ½ mile N of Aylburton, Gloucestershire; off A48. ·
■ **ACCESS** The temple remains are in the Lydney Spring Gardens, which themselves are worth a visit. Both are subject to restricted opening times. For details telephone 01594 842844. Admission charge.

❷ Littledean

Littledean House of Correction was built in the late 18th century by the Georgian prison reformer Sir George Onesiphorus Paul. It still stands today as one of the best examples of a purpose-built prison designed to change damp and unhealthy mixed-occupant gaols into strict, clean and efficient places of correction.

Before the reforms, most criminals were dealt with by deportation, the death penalty or detention in desperate conditions in privately owned lock-ups. Pioneers like Paul created sites where prisoners were separated by sex, given uniforms and often individual cells, and 'improved' by a regimen of hard labour and correctional education.

■ **LOCATION** Littledean, Gloucestershire; on A4151.
■ **ACCESS** No public access. Another of Paul's gaols can be viewed at Northleach, Gloucestershire, strictly by appointment only; telephone 01285 655 611.

❸ Gloucester Cathedral

While the 16th-century dissolution of the monasteries resulted in the destruction of many ancient ecclesiastical buildings, a few survived by being converted into cathedrals to serve new dioceses. The magnificent Gloucester Cathedral was once the Benedictine abbey of St Peter and was saved from destruction by being converted to cathedral status in 1541.

Situated in the centre of the city, the cathedral has impressive large Norman drum pillars in the nave and beautiful 15th-century fan-vaulted cloisters. Apart from the

▶ *The intricate 15th-century fan-vaulted cloisters of Gloucester Cathedral. This beautiful ecclesiastical building was saved from dissolution by being converted to cathedral status in the 16th century.*

magnificent architecture, including some fine tracery, other features of note are the tomb of Edward II (who was killed in 1327 at nearby Berkeley Castle) and the 14th-century east window, which displays scenes from the famous English victory at Crécy, France in 1346. Some of the original 600-year-old stained glass still survives in the window.

■ **LOCATION** Gloucester.
■ **ACCESS** See www.gloucestercathedral. org.uk or telephone 01452 528095 for opening times and other details.

ROMAN VILLA

❹ Chedworth

A classic large Roman villa, Chedworth stands within a beautiful rural setting. This is an exceptionally rich and successful villa with origins in the first half of the 2nd century, which developed into an interesting double-courtyard design by the later stages of the 4th century.

Excavation has revealed the opulence of the site, including a nymphaeum, or water shrine, a second, self-contained duplicate suite of rooms in the north wing, possibly for extended family, extravagant mosaics, extensive hypocaust underfloor heating, and even a double set of baths enabling the patrons to choose either the traditional Turkish style or the more energy-sapping Spartan dry heat sauna-style of cleansing.

Running water was provided by a natural spring that rises in the north-west corner of the site at the nymphaeum. After collection in the shrine basin, the water was then piped to different parts of the villa.

A small early Christian sign has been carved inconspicuously into the stone of the shrine.

Another inscription, roughly carved into a wall at Chedworth, refers to a 'green company'. Some have suggested that this relates to traditional Roman racing colours, and could even indicate that horse- or chariot-racing may have been sponsored by the villa.

■ **LOCATION** 1 mile N of Chedworth, Gloucestershire; off A429.
■ **ACCESS** See www.nationaltrust.org.uk or telephone 01242 890256 for opening times and other details. Admission charge.

ROMAN ADMINISTRATION

❺ Cirencester

Among the wealth of Roman settlements in the Gloucestershire region is the large administrative centre of Cirencester. Its Roman name, Corinium Dobunnorum, incorporated the name of the local tribe, the Dobunni, to distinguish the settlement from others as a centre of local government. As areas of administration were often based upon the pre-Roman tribal domains, the Roman settlement may have developed near or around an earlier centre of power.

The early importance of the settlement is evident in the 2nd-century development of stone gateways and defences, one of which, the Verulamium Gate, is a unique structure within Europe because of its four entrances. The town also features an outstanding amphitheatre, which would have witnessed games and contests together with gladiatorial competitions.

It has been estimated that the town could have had 20,000 inhabitants at its height, and the

◀ *The Roman villa at Chedworth was high status and had underfloor heating, a water shrine and running water from a natural spring. The mosaic, which shows the figure of Spring, would have impressed visitors.*

archaeological evidence points towards a booming and successful economy. Excavation in the town has revealed shops and evidence for a variety of crafts, from monumental stonemasons to a highly successful mosaic school. Over 50 floors in the region are known to have been credited to the craftsmen of this school.

The town may even have had one of the first metropolitan bishops by AD314. This followed the conversion of Emperor Constantine to Christianity two years earlier, whereupon Christianity became the official religion of the empire.

■ **LOCATION** Cirencester, Gloucestershire.
■ **ACCESS** Corinium Museum: see www.cotswold.gov.uk (go to 'Leisure and Culture') or telephone 01285 655611 for opening times and other details. Admission charge. Roman amphitheatre: see www.english-heritage.org.uk for opening times and other details.

ANGLO-SAXON CHAPEL

❻ Bradford-on-Avon

The wonderful later Anglo-Saxon chapel of St Laurence at Bradford-on-Avon displays a wealth of early church architecture.

The chapel remained undiscovered and in private use as a store and cottage until 1856, when the then vicar of Bradford, Canon Jones, recognized what he thought were ancient features while work was being carried out on the property. His research led him to an early 12th-century manuscript written by William of Malmesbury, which recorded a church having been built at Bradford-on-Avon by St Aldhelm in AD705.

Canon Jones was thrilled to have discovered an early ecclesiastical building on his doorstep, but further research suggested that the architecture of the chapel was more in keeping with a later 10th-century style. This dating quandary between the written evidence and the structural style is probably best

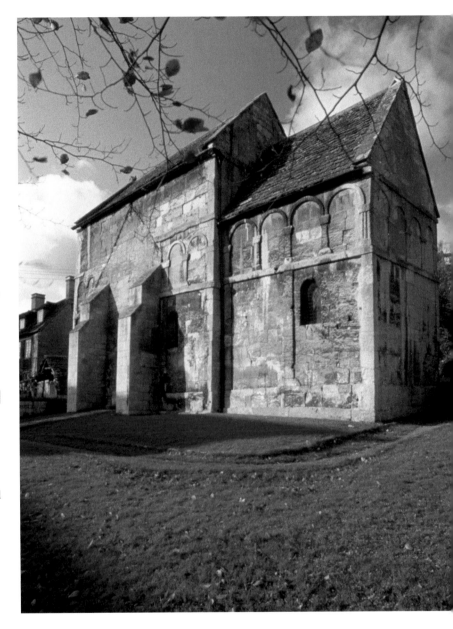

▲ The Anglo-Saxon chapel at Bradford-on-Avon was built by the nuns of Shaftesbury to house the relics of Edward the Martyr, who was killed at Corfe Castle.

explained by assuming that the current building was erected on top of an earlier chapel.

The chapel may be small but it was constructed to an extremely high quality. The 10th-century architectural decoration includes typical late Anglo-Saxon pilaster strips and blanked arcading, set out in a geometric fashion. The stone carved angels on either side of the chancel arch are stylistically dated to around AD950, based on their similarity to Saxon manuscript artwork of that date from Winchester.

■ **LOCATION** Bradford-on-Avon, Wiltshire.
■ **ACCESS** Telephone 01225 713000 for opening times and other details.

◀ *The Neolithic chambered long barrow of Wayland's Smithy was built on the site of an even earlier tomb and is part of a rich multi-period landscape. One of Phil's favourites.*

cutting the turf to reveal the underlying white chalk, but work undertaken in the 1990s suggested that the original design was cut as shallow trenches, which were then filled with compacted chalk.

■ **LOCATION** 5 miles SE of Shrivenham, Oxfordshire; off B4507.
■ **ACCESS** See www.english-heritage.org. uk for opening times and other details.

FOUNDING OF A UNIVERSITY

❾ City of Oxford

In an early historical reference, Oxford is named in the *Anglo-Saxon Chronicles* as Edward the Elder 'takes control' of the strategic settlement on the border between the kingdoms of Wessex and Mercia. The settlement was certainly a fortified Saxon town, or burh, by the 10th century, having grown up around an earlier abbey founded by St Frideswide. Oxford was a thriving community that suffered heavily from the Norman invasion. However, once the new administration was under way, the town had its own castle by 1071.

The 12th century saw a great fire destroy much of the city, which later became the venue for the ongoing struggle between King Stephen and Matilda. During the 13th century the Dominicans, Franciscans, Augustinians and the Carmelite religious orders founded centres of learning, and it's at this time that the university truly became established.

The reformation of the monasteries in the 16th century deprived many of the colleges of their tutors, and the subsequent

MULTI-PERIOD LANDSCAPE

❼ Wayland's Smithy

Found north of the prehistoric Ridgeway trading route, overlooking the Vale of the White Horse, Wayland's Smithy is a Neolithic chambered long barrow. It is part of a fascinating multi-period landscape, which also includes the Uffington White Horse and its associated Iron Age hillfort.

The existing three-chamber structure, complete with four standing stones at the entrance, is some 5,000 years old. Smaller stones mark the outline of the barrow. Excavations in the early 1900s and again in the early 1960s found that the mound had been built over the top of an even earlier tomb around 2800BC.

The site is named after the Saxon god of metalworking, Wayland.

■ **LOCATION** 4 miles SE of Shrivenham, Oxfordshire; off B4507.
■ **ACCESS** See www.english-heritage.org. uk for opening times and other details.

IRON OR BRONZE AGE ART

❽ Uffington White Horse

Situated north of the Ridgeway (see Wayland's Smithy), the Uffington White Horse is a stylized figure. Its design is reminiscent of Iron Age artwork, and it is impossible to ignore the Iron Age hillfort, complete with impressive earthworks, which dominates the hilltop of Whitehorse Hill.

The horse, on the north-western side of the hill, is over 112m (368ft) long. There are no perfect positions from which to view it from the hill or the immediate surrounding landscape, but the design can be clearly seen for up to 20 miles all across the lower ground of the Vale of the White Horse. A clear Iron Age boundary marker for all northern tribes to see? Perhaps, but dating of the underlying soils by optical stimulated luminescence indicates that an earlier Bronze Age date is more likely. The horse was initially thought to have been made by

▶ *The best view of the Uffington White Horse in Oxfordshire is from the air. Though considered typically Iron Age in its artistic style, the latest thinking suggests that it has earlier origins, perhaps in the Bronze Age.*

decline in the university triggered economic depression in the town. The 17th century was a time of great revival and expansion, however, and this was the period that saw the university town develop into one of the greatest seats of learning in the world.

■ **LOCATION** Oxford.

■ **ACCESS** Parking in the city centre is limited. Museum of Oxford: telephone 01865 252761 for opening times and other details.

CENTRE OF ANCIENT POWER

⑩ Old Sarum

The massive 2,500-year-old earthwork defences of Old Sarum create a substantial first impression. Though the site was first used even earlier in the Neolithic period, it's the later, multi-period occupation of the area that illustrates the importance of the site as a centre of power and administration, rich in history.

The site is dominated by the massive motte-and-bailey castle built in 1069, just three years after the Norman invasion. However, it was built on the site of a much earlier settlement, occupied in the Iron Age and throughout the Roman and Saxon periods as well. In 1070, William the Conqueror himself assembled his army here to disband them.

By 1092 the settlement was well established and a Norman cathedral

was completed on the site, only to be destroyed just days later by a severe storm. Development continued and in the early 12th century the castle had a stone keep and Bishop Roger, chancellor to Henry I, built a bishop's palace. By the early 13th century it appears that

▼ *The deserted city of Old Sarum still dominates the landscape. The Norman motte-and-bailey castle stands out, but was built on the site of a much earlier settlement.*

life at Old Sarum had become difficult. Its position was relatively remote and it lacked natural resources, such as a suitable nearby water supply, to support the settlement. People started to move away and settle further south at New Sarum (modern Salisbury). By the 1220s Bishop Poore founded the new cathedral in Salisbury, signifying the end of Old Sarum's reign as the important regional centre.

■ **LOCATION** 2 miles N of Salisbury, Wiltshire; on A345.
■ **ACCESS** See www.english-heritage.org. uk or telephone 01722 335398 for opening times and other details. Admission charge.

COASTAL TRADING CENTRE

⑪ Southampton

Modern Southampton has its origins over the river Itchen to the east of the current city. Around AD700 a Saxon market settlement called Hamwic was established just south of an earlier Roman fort called Clausentum (modern Bitterne), which had been sited to take advantage of the international trading economy.

In Saxon terms the settlement was massive, covering up to 50 hectares (125 acres), and numerous excavations have revealed timber structures, postholes and pits set out along an established grid street plan complete with enclosure ditches. Evidence for metal-working, weaving and leather-working, together with glass and bone crafts and a wealth of continental pottery, illustrate that it was an important settlement and that it traded with European markets.

By the 10th century, Hamwic appears to have fallen into decline, its economy threatened by both Viking raiding and the upcoming development of Winchester. However, the need was still there for a coastal trade centre and so medieval Southampton grew up around a Saxon enclosure called Hamtun, on the periphery of Hamwic.

Following the Norman conquest in 1066, Southampton thrived once again as an economic centre. 1127 saw the foundation of the Augustinian friary at St Denys and the 13th century witnessed the fortification of the town as disputes with the continent ensued.

During the 14th and 15th centuries, Southampton became a centre for luxury goods imports from Italy as well as a great shipbuilding yard in support of the Hundred Years' War. Decline through the 16th century due to plague was overcome and the city became a successful port once again from the mid-1700s.

■ **LOCATION** Southampton.
■ **ACCESS** God's House Tower Museum of Archaeology: see www.southampton. gov.uk (go to 'Leisure', then 'Heritage') or telephone 023 8033 9601 for opening times and other details.

SECOND WORLD WAR

⑫ Stone Point Lepe, Solent

A short walk east along the foreshore from Lepe will take you to the remains of industrial activity at Stone Point where concrete caissons for the famous Mulberry Harbours were constructed ahead of D-Day in 1944.

The formidable fortifications of Hitler's Atlantic Wall, especially around strategic ports on the French coast, made the Allies aware that the possibility of successfully taking a deep-water harbour intact was unlikely. The Allies developed the ingenious concept of building a harbour in Britain and then taking it directly to the beaches in kit-form before assembling it behind the beachhead to supply the advance.

In 1943 construction began on the massive 60m by 18m (200ft x 60ft) hollow steel-reinforced concrete caissons, or Phoenixes. Over 150 of these floating sections were eventually built at different sites across the south coast. For the invasion, in an operation called Corncob, the floating sections were pulled across the Channel by tugboats towards St Laurent and Arromanches. Once in position their sea valves were opened to flood them and drop them to the sea floor, creating two artificial harbours each over a mile long.

Less than a month after completion, two storms severely damaged the harbours and the one at St Laurent was never used again. Remains of the Mulberry Harbour at Arromanches can still be seen today.

■ **LOCATION** Lepe Country Park, 3 miles S of Fawley, Hampshire; off B3053.

■ **ACCESS** See www.hants.gov.uk /countryside/lepe or telephone 023 8089 9108 for opening times and other details. Charges for car parking.

⑬ HMS Victory, Portsmouth Harbour

Though open to the public today, *Victory* remains the oldest commissioned warship in the world, and is still crewed by officers of the Royal Navy. Her career has taken her from construction in 1759 and launch in 1765, through three major campaigns to her active retirement in 1812, and she still continues as the flagship of the Second Sea Lord and Commander-in-Chief Naval Home Command.

The 104-gun first-rate warship was designed by the senior surveyor of the navy, Thomas Slade, and renowned for her outstanding seagoing ability. It's been estimated that over 40 hectares (100 acres) of forest were needed to build her and once complete she could hoist nearly 5,500 square metres (60,000 square feet) of sail. No less than six admirals used *Victory* as their flagship, in campaigns ranging from the American War of Independence to the French Revolution and the Napoleonic wars.

▲ *The* Victory *had perhaps her finest hour at Trafalgar. In her long service, she was the flagship for five admirals besides Nelson.*

One of her finest moments remains the Battle of Trafalgar in October 1805. Admiral Lord Nelson led the British fleet of 27 warships against the Franco-Spanish, who were trying to escape the British blockade of Cadiz with 33 vessels. After hoisting the famous signal, 'England expects every man to do his duty', the ensuing battle saw Nelson steer *Victory* directly through the line of enemy ships to deliver shocking destruction at the expense of over 2,500 rounds of her ammunition and 57 of her crew. At 1.15pm, an hour and three quarters after the battle had commenced, Nelson was hit by a musket ball. He died at 4.30pm, after he had heard news that the battle had been won.

■ **LOCATION** Portsmouth Harbour, Hampshire.

■ **ACCESS** See www.hms-victory.com or telephone 023 9286 1533 for opening times and other details. Admission charge.

⑭ Mary Rose, Portsmouth Harbour

The *Mary Rose*, spectacularly raised from its resting place on the seabed in 1982, is a fascinating example of a 16th-century warship. With his accession to the throne in 1509, the young Henry VIII inherited a small but efficient navy from his father, Henry VII. The international climate at the time was one of French power, and the new king set about building a navy that would enable him to counter the French threat.

The *Mary Rose* offers us a snapshot of a fascinating period of ship-building development and tells us a lot about the life of a sailor in 1545, the year the ship sank with the loss of nearly 500 sailors, soldiers and gunners. Personal possessions such as clothes, games and cutlery show us how they dressed and how they entertained and cared for themselves, while excellently preserved weapons such as cannons and longbows demonstrate the vessel's formidable purpose. The well-preserved barber-surgeon's kit hints at the awful realities of fighting at sea.

The technology used in the ship was the very latest of the day. Probably built around 1510, smooth carvel construction, rather than the traditional overlapping clinker-style planking, enabled watertight gun ports to be installed on the lower decks. This radical concept enabled the *Mary Rose* to deliver a devastating broadside barrage with her multiple guns. However, her constant uploading with increased firepower and crew saw her fighting weight raised by nearly 50 per cent to 700 tons, and her top-heavy loading may have been the reason she took water through the gun ports and rapidly sank while lining up to oppose the French fleet in 1545.

■ **LOCATION** Portsmouth Harbour, Hampshire.

■ **ACCESS** See www.historicdockyard. co.uk or telephone 023 9281 2931 for opening times and other details. Admission charge.

▼ *The remains of the hull of the* Mary Rose *are being conserved today by saturation with chemical agents. The scale of the wreck still impresses.*

Greater London

Like most large towns, London's archaeology is usually only seen through 'windows' during new building work. The city has grown up as well as outwards, so that ground level today is metres above the Roman remains. Geography made it inevitable that London, or a Thames-side site like it, would become an important place after the arrival of the Romans, although once the Roman period was over the area was largely deserted for several centuries. It was King Alfred in the late 9th century who formally re-established it as a fortified town. It may be no coincidence that the old Roman amphitheatre lies under the Guildhall, from where the Saxon and medieval city was governed. From this time on, London became the capital city, and its medieval and post-medieval remains are rich.

British Museum 6

Spitalfields 9

St Paul's Cathedral 7

8

Roman London

St Stephen Walbrook

Tower of London 10

The Rose and the Globe

HMS Belfast 11

Whitehall Palace 5

12

George Inn

Westminster Abbey 4

3

Jewel Tower

2 Thames River Front

River Thames

0 ___ 1 m
0 ___ 1 k

N

HARROW

A1

A12

ILFORD

A40

WEMBLEY

HAMPSTEAD

M4

CITY

STEPNEY

WEST HAM

A13

HAMMERSMITH

WESTMINSTER

M11

M25

13 Greenwich Park

RICHMOND

A316

GREENWICH

A2

TWICKENHAM

WIMBLEDON

STREATHAM

A20

KINGSTON

M3

1 Hampton Court Palace

Merton Abbey Mills

A3

A232

A23

A21

M25

Roman London
The capital of Roman Britain

AD50-450

WHEN YOU ASK THE EXPERTS the standard question, 'What did the Romans do for us?' the answer usually includes creating London as our capital city. Before this, Britain had a number of key centres, but it was only with the development of the Roman province that London emerged as a major city. Its defining feature was the Thames, which, like some of the vast continental rivers, such as the Rhine, provides navigable water deep into the heart of our island.

▼ A marble head of Serapis being excavated in London's mithraeum in 1954. Serapis was an Egyptian god made out of Osiris and Apis and was introduced in Graeco-Roman times. It shows just how cosmopolitan Roman London was.

Boudicca's revolt

London began as a strategic crossing place over the Thames during the Roman conquest of Britain, and around AD50 the first settlement was established there, becoming an important trading centre within ten years. But in AD60, Britain was thrown into turmoil by Boudicca's revolt. As the historian Tacitus vividly describes, the Roman commander Suetonius withdrew the army from London in order to defend the rest of the province, and the fledgling settlement was destroyed by Boudicca's forces.

It is after Boudicca's revolt that London seems to have become the capital of Roman Britain. We have a tombstone from the city, now in the British Museum, of Gaius Julius Alpinus Classicianus, who served as procurator immediately after the revolt, and took care of provincial finances. London was rebuilt in the late 1st century as a planned town surrounded by a defensive wall. At its heart were a range of huge and impressive public buildings: the open courtyard or forum, the administrative basilica where the procurator probably had his offices, a variety of public baths and even an amphitheatre. But as Guy points out, although it had all the features of a civilian town, the archaeology shows it was always a settlement dominated by the army with its own fort, unlike towns such as St Albans.

In the aftermath of the revolt, London's trade also rapidly recovered. It became one of the key ports for Roman ships bringing goods from throughout the Roman world. The Thames would have been crowded with galleys bringing goods from as far afield as Greece and Egypt. When I asked Guy for a key Roman find from London other than the architectural remains, he referred to a late-1st-century flagon from Southwark with the inscription *Londinii ad fanum Isidis*: 'London, at the temple of Isis'. The dedication shows that London in remote Britain was now part of a culture that stretched all the way to the Nile in Egypt.

The Temple of Mithras

Like Guy's flagon, the Temple of Mithras also highlights what a cosmopolitan and exciting place Roman London must have been. Mithraism was an ancient Middle Eastern religion which became popular throughout the Roman Empire, particularly with soldiers. It was a 'mystery cult' and much of what we know about it comes from archaeology – temple remains, inscriptions and artworks – rather than written sources. The accidental unearthing of a 2nd-century Mithraic temple beside the river Walbrook in London in 1954 was thus an important discovery, and an interesting moment in the history of archaeology: it highlights the sometimes difficult relationship between ancient monuments and developers (see also the Rose, on page 64).

Because of the importance of the temple, the remains were moved and re-erected on Queen Victoria Street, EC4. It was an early experiment in preserving ancient architecture, and what you see today doesn't really give you a clear idea of the original temple; Mithraic temples were often built underground to represent a legendary cave where the god Mithras slayed a bull. Statues found inside the temple of Roman gods, including Bacchus and Minerva and a fine head of Serapis (visible in the picture on the facing page), can now be seen in the Museum of London.

Mithraism declined in the face of Christianity; and in the 4th century

▲ The Romans brought a range of cults and religious practices with them to Britain. Here an offering is being made within a temple precinct. Roman gods such as Mithras were the focus of many such activities; cults were also centred upon the emperor.

▲ *Mithras kills the sacred bull and releases the life force. Mithraism was popular among soldiers. This relief, found beside London's mithraeum, was commissioned by a veteran of the II legion, based at Caerleon in Wales.*

Mithraic temples were often destroyed. However, when Time Team were at Ancaster, we excavated a Roman Christian burial that contained a stone inscribed with the name of a pagan god, which had been placed in front of the deceased's face. So it raises the question of how many Roman Britons adopted Christianity in public but continued to follow cults such as Mithraism in private.

London suffered mixed fortunes throughout the Roman period, as the political and economic situation in the province and throughout the empire waxed and waned. Many of its large public buildings and facilities were demolished in the early 4th century, possibly as punishment for rebelling against Roman rule. By this time, Britain had been divided into four provinces, and London was the capital of one of these. Despite these political upheavals, it remained an important trading and financial centre until the 5th century, when the area inside the walls appears to have been gradually abandoned. By 450, it seems to have been deserted.

Visiting Roman London

The Roman settlement covered the area now occupied by the City, London's financial district, and an area of Southwark, south of the river. The layout of the Roman defensive wall, gates and many roads can still be traced in the modern street plan of the City. Although later development has largely destroyed the city wall, some of it can still be seen today. The luxury hotel on 8–10 Coopers Row, EC3, contains a 30m-long (100ft) section. The best section to see, however, is at Tower Hill, in the underpass to the Tower of London. We know that originally London's Roman wall stood approximately 6–7.5m (20–25ft) high, while a portion of the wall base discovered in America Square, EC3, goes down some 6m (20ft) deep.

Guy suggests a visit to Noble Street (EC3), where you will find the corner of the Roman fort wall where it meets the city wall. This was where the garrison of London was based. Soldiers from all round Britain were sent on detachment here (a letter from Vindolanda – see page 220 – shows that some came from there). They served as the governor's guard and also took part in provincial administrative duties.

In 1988, a team of archaeologists from the Museum of London made the exciting discovery of the remains of the Roman amphitheatre in Guildhall Yard. The oval-shaped amphitheatre was around 100m (330ft) in length and 80m (260ft) wide with a seating capacity of about 6,000. The earliest building had been made of timber and was later reconstructed in stone. The find was so significant that the Corporation of London insisted that the amphitheatre be integrated with the new Guildhall Art Gallery, which finally opened to the public in June 2002. The long-lost amphitheatre is regarded as one of London's most important Roman finds.

To see a private Roman house, contact the Museum of London to find out the entry times for Billingsgate Bathhouse.

▲ London Wall. The brick marks medieval and later structures but the original Roman 3rd-century flint and tile courses can be seen in the foreground.

■ **GETTING THERE** For the Museum of London, see www.museumoflondon.org.uk or telephone 0870 444 3852 for opening times and other details. It's on the corner of London Wall and Aldersgate Street, EC1; admission charge.
The Guildhall Art Gallery is at Guildhall Yard, EC2; see

www.cityoflondon.gov.uk (go to 'Leisure and Heritage', then 'Libraries, Archives, Museums and Galleries', then 'Guildhall Art Gallery') or telephone 020 7332 3700 for details. The Temple of Mithras is at the NE end of Queen Victoria Street, EC4, near Bank tube; it's a fenced site and permanently visible.

■ **OUR VIEW** The most useful way to start understanding Roman London is to look at the reconstruction and aerial view in the Museum of London. Seeing Roman remains in London itself requires a bit of planning and persistence. It's well worth consulting the Museum of London for its list of events.

The Rose and the Globe
Elizabethan theatre

1574–1644, and 1987 to the present

ARCHAEOLOGICAL DISCOVERIES rarely spark controversies that hit the national headlines, but in 1989 the remains of the Elizabethan Rose theatre, unearthed during building work on London's Bankside, did just that. The site was due to be developed into offices, but many famous actors and actresses, led by Dame Peggy Ashcroft and Sir Laurence Olivier, felt it should be saved and exposed for public display instead. After much debate and protest, the office block did go ahead, but to a new design which allowed the remains to be preserved beneath a layer of wet sand and concrete under the new building.

What interests me about the Rose is that, like the Newport ship in 2002 (see page 114), it roused such strong feelings in the public. After all, many sites are excavated or reburied in advance of development every year and don't make it anywhere near the headlines. But the Rose is one of the rare sites where archaeology gets personal and gives you a direct insight into familiar historical events and characters. The sight of Dame Judi Dench standing on the spot where Shakespeare's plays were performed during his own lifetime was an extraordinary moment.

Purpose-built theatre

Tudor theatre had an unsavoury reputation, and the City of London banned traditional theatrical performances in pubs in 1574. Entrepreneurs looked for alternative arrangements, and a number of theatres were built in Southwark, a busy district on the southern bank of the river Thames, where disreputable activities such as bearbaiting, cockfighting and prostitution took place. The Rose was the first purpose-built theatre, financed by Elizabethan theatrical impresario Philip Henslowe in 1587, on an old garden that gave it its name.

It was rapidly followed by others. At one point, there were five playhouses lined up along Bankside, one of which was the famous Globe theatre, built in 1597 by the actor Richard Burbage, of Shakespeare's company the Chamberlain's Men. Shakespeare himself was also a member of the syndicate that built the Globe theatre – holding a 10 per cent share of the whole enterprise. *Henry V*, *Hamlet*, *Julius Caesar* and *Twelfth Night* were all written for performance there.

Elizabethan theatres were open to the air, with tiers of galleries around a 'pit' where the majority of the audience would stand to watch the performance. The stage stuck out into the pit. The Rose excavations revealed that the buildings were polygonal, rather than round; enough was found of the Globe to work out that it was twenty-sided. These theatres were really small – the Globe was just 30m (100ft) in diameter for audiences of up to 3,000 people; the Rose was even smaller. The central stage combined with the small size meant that going to an Elizabethan theatre was an intimate experience. No member of the audience was far from an actor on stage.

▼ *Excavations revealed details of the Rose's auditorium, and showed how small Elizabethan theatres were.*

◄ The reconstruction of the Globe. The theatre was recreated using, among other sources, evidence from the Rose.

Recreating the Globe

The lifespan of Elizabethan theatres was short. The Rose was probably pulled down about 20 years after it was built, and the Globe was destroyed in 1613 when stage cannonfire set light to the thatched roof. It was rebuilt but was finally pulled down in 1644 after Oliver Cromwell's government outlawed public theatrical performance during the civil war; its remains lie beneath a 19th-century Grade II listed building. In 1987, work began on the reconstruction. Digging for the new theatre partially uncovered an original auditorium, and this allowed the plans for the new Globe to be altered to reflect more closely the layout of the original.

■ **GETTING THERE** The Rose is at Park Street, SE1, off Southwark Bridge Road. A theme show can be seen by pre-booked tour; go to www.rosetheatre.org.uk or telephone 020 7902 1500 for details. Admission charge. The reconstructed Globe Theatre is at Bankside, SE1. See www.shakespeares-globe.org or telephone 020 7902 1400 for opening times and other details. Admission charge.

■ **OUR VIEW** A performance at the Globe is a wonderful experience. And it's the first thatch-roofed structure built in London for over 300 years – this time with fire proofing!

Merton Abbey Mills
Arts and Crafts movement

1833-1970s

IT IS HARD TO BELIEVE that the delicate business of printing on silk might leave fascinating archaeological remains, but when Time Team went to Merton Abbey Mills in 2002, we discovered a whole range of evidence that brought the Arts and Crafts movement of William Morris and others to life.

When you visit the site today, you will see the Wandle, where Tony Robinson and our other diving archaeologists discovered the small brass pins used to hold the silk in place while it was being dried. I have fond memories of Phil labouring with the wooden blocks to produce silk cloth dyed with a floral pattern. Later we found evidence of the

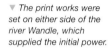
▼ The print works were set on either side of the river Wandle, which supplied the initial power.

small railway tracks that were laid to carry the tables that held the dye.

Merton Abbey Mills is named after an imposing 12th-century Augustinian priory that once stood here. Founded in 1114, Merton Priory flourished for over 400 years before Henry VIII's dissolution of the monasteries. During that time, Merton Priory was host to many important historic occasions, including coronations, parliaments and state visits. Merton was stripped of its great wealth in 1538. Its stone was dismantled and used for the construction of Nonsuch Palace at Cheam. During our excavations we found remnants of medieval buildings under the floor of the printing works.

Liberty prints
During the 1800s, Merton became the factory base for Arthur Liberty, founder of the Liberty shops and influential pioneer of the Victorian Arts and Crafts

movement. Liberty began his career in a 'cloak and shawl emporium' on Regent Street before setting up his own shop. He'd seen how popular the fabrics printed in the far east had become and he wanted to produce the same quality of fabric but make it available to the middle classes. The dresses and frocks he produced were of a less severe style than previous fashions and the new fabrics appealed to women who wanted a softer appearance. Liberty knew many members of the Arts and Crafts movement and he believed in the principles of hand-crafted goods. In effect, he became the shopkeeper to the movement. Many of the designs he produced had been created by William Morris and his fellow artists.

As we were to discover, the process of hand-printing silk is an arduous one. It requires a large supply of material, which has to be washed after each stage. The colours have to be applied individually by craftsmen pressing down wooden blocks by hand. With thousands of yards of fabric to be printed, the process needed a dedicated workforce who required skill and concentration to create the finished product.

The Wandle provided water for washing and for powering machinery. Each part of the site was involved in an element of the process. There had been a factory here since the 18th century; Edmund Littler took over the works in 1833. By the late 19th century most of Littler's factories were producing material for Liberty, and in 1904 Liberty took over the works. As technology developed, machines replaced some of the processes previously done by hand, but printing with blocks on silk continued. Cutting out the blocks itself requires highly developed skills. It took our craftsmen on the Time Team reconstruction nearly 15 hours to carve out just half of one block. And as Phil

◀ *Victor's drawing shows the rail and cart device used to move the paint along the laid-out cloth. The worker in the centre is gently tapping the back of a block to impress the colour pattern onto the material.*

discovered, considerable skill is needed to position each block by hand and eye.

As you walk around the site, spare some time to look into the Wandle, which probably still contains fragments of the original factory. The small pins we found in the silty mud were part of the drying process, but we also located part of what might have been a dock for loading and unloading canal boats.

When we investigated the rest of the site, we found the Victorian factory remains just inches under the surface, and thanks to Stewart Ainsworth's work on old black-and-white photos we were able to locate storage houses and warehouses on the opposite bank of the river and build up a picture of the original Littler works.

It was a memorable moment when we discovered the track marks from an ink cart worn into the floor in the dyeing room. Merton is a fascinating example of the archaeology of an industrial process – not the furnaces and heavy machines we associate with the industrial revolution, but the lighter processes of the Arts and Crafts movement.

■ **GETTING THERE**
Merton Abbey Mills is at Watermill Way, Merton, London SW19 (a mile from the centre of Wimbledon). See www.mertonabbey mills.com or telephone 020 8543 9608 for the Chapter House Museum, or 020 8543 6656 for the Wheelhouse Museum.

■ **OUR VIEW** Merton Abbey Mills remains a focus of activity in the community. The site hosts a busy market, where around 300 people earn their living and many thousands more visit regularly. You can see the still-working waterwheel.

Other sites to visit

❶ Hampton Court Palace

The earliest recorded buildings at Hampton Court date to 1236, when a new religious order called the Knights Hospitallers of St John of Jerusalem purchased a manor to be used as their grange, or estate administration centre. The abbots of St John gradually built the grange into a retreat, which became a popular place for royalty to patronize.

In 1514 a 99-year lease of the property was given to Thomas Wolsey, the chief minister to Henry VIII, yet his sumptuous development of the palace could not guarantee its keeping. By 1528 Wolsey had fallen from grace because he could not gain the consent of the pope to secure Henry's divorce from Catherine of Aragon, and Henry took Hampton Court for himself.

Henry spent a fortune and ten years turning Hampton Court into a palace. Highlights included hunting grounds, tennis courts, colossal kitchens and a huge toilet for 28 people to use at once.

Much of Hampton Court was rebuilt by Sir Christopher Wren in the late 17th century under the enthusiastic eye of William III. However, William died after falling from a horse at Hampton Court Park and never saw his finished apartments.

The palace remained a favourite with royalty, especially for its

hunting, until 1760 when George III inherited the throne and lost interest in the property. Queen Victoria would later go on to open the palace and its grounds to the public.

■ **LOCATION** East Molesey, Surrey.
■ **ACCESS** See www.hrp.org.uk/webcode /hampton_home.asp or telephone 0870 752 7777 for opening times and other details. Admission charge.

▼ *Hampton Court grew from a manor building first recorded in 1236 to a huge palace. Monarchs at different times lavished a fortune on it to turn it into the ultimate fashionable royal residence for their era.*

WATERFRONT OFFERINGS

❷ Thames River Front

The Thames is an instantly recognizable aspect of London's landscape but in its ancient form it was a much wider river, untamed compared to the one we are familiar with today. During the Bronze Age, it was fed by many tributaries and was dotted with small islands or 'eyots'.

Water appears to have featured greatly in ancient rituals and religions, with weapons predominant as symbolic offerings. Before the Time Team dig at Vauxhall, which uncovered a Bronze Age jetty, two Bronze Age spearheads had been discovered. They had been deliberately embedded deep into the foreshore, almost certainly as an offering. The abundance of finds over the years includes Bronze Age pottery, Neolithic flints and tools and an array of Roman and medieval artefacts. Nautical archaeology has led to the discovery of the remnants of at least 30 medieval vessels, several of them foreign in origin.

Probably the most beautiful find to be drawn from the Thames is the Iron Age Battersea shield. The short shield, just over 70cm (28in) in length, is made from a sheet of bronze bound by an edging strip. Three roundels hold red enamel studs set within swirling La Tène decoration. As the shield would have been impractical for warfare, it is believed it was used for display or even specially made as an offering.

Research along the riverfront continues to reveal aspects of London's social, economic and cultural history, contributing to our understanding of how London grew in importance.

■ **LOCATION** Time Team dig was near Vauxhall Bridge, SE1.
■ **ACCESS** There's nothing to be seen at the foreshore. Instead, see www.museum oflondon.org.uk or telephone 0870 444 3852 for opening times and other details of the 'London before London' exhibition. Admission charge.

▲ *The beautiful Iron Age Battersea shield is too small to have been much use in defence. It must have been a status symbol or an offering, or both.*

14TH-CENTURY STRONGHOLD

❸ Jewel Tower, Westminster

The Jewel Tower was constructed around 1365 to house the personal treasures, or King's Privy Wardrobe, of Edward III. As part of the original medieval Palace of Westminster the tower was protected by an additional moat, part of which can still be seen today, together with the remains of the medieval quay.

Along with Westminster Hall, the tower was the only part of the medieval Palace of Westminster to survive the great fire of 1834. In addition to being Edward's stronghold, the tower has also been used to safely store the records of the House of Lords and up until 1938 served as the government's weights and measures office. The site today carries an exhibition about the Houses of Parliament.

■ **LOCATION** Abingdon Street, SW1; near S end of Palace of Westminster.
■ **ACCESS** See www.english-heritage. org.uk or telephone 020 7222 2219 for opening times and other details. Admission charge.

▼ *The vaulted roof of the Jewel Tower, which was originally built as a stronghold for Edward III. It later became the records office of the House of Lords, and today houses an exhibition about the Houses of Parliament.*

❹ Westminster Abbey

Since the crowning of William the Conqueror in 1066, every monarch – other than Edward V and Edward VIII – has been crowned beneath the roof of Westminster Abbey. Its correct name is The Collegiate Church of St Peter, Westminster. More than 3,000 people are buried or memorialized at the abbey, including medieval kings and queens and the Unknown Warrior.

It has been claimed that a church was founded on the site by Serbert, King of the East Saxons. However, the earliest foundations have been attributed to St Dunstan, who established an abbey on a Thames eyot around AD960. A more majestic abbey was founded less than a hundred years later by Edward the Confessor. Very little of the Norman monastery remains, except for features in several monastic buildings, arches and columns around the cloister.

Henry III ordered the abbey to be rebuilt in 1245, but the immense gothic abbey we know today wasn't completed until 1745. The Pyx Chamber contains funeral relics of medieval kings, Roman remains have been found in the abbey precincts, excavations of the cloister undercroft have uncovered evidence of flooding dating to the 11th century, and wall tiles from the 1070s can be found in situ in the abbey.

■ **LOCATION** Deans Yard, SW1.
■ **ACCESS** See www.westminster-abbey.org or telephone 020 7222 5152 for opening times and other details. Admission charge.

❺ Whitehall Palace

From 1530 to 1698, Whitehall Palace was the grandiose London residency of English monarchs. Whitehall is, of course, now the British Government's administrative centre, but over 400 years ago it was the largest palace complex in Europe, an amalgam of buildings, gardens and courtyards that stretched for half a mile along the Thames.

Henry VIII established Whitehall Palace following the confiscation of York House from Cardinal Wolsey in 1530. York House was extensively redesigned to include a bowling green, tennis courts, cockpit and a tiltyard, and given its new name. Successive sovereigns dwelled there until 1698, when a careless maidservant caused a fire that destroyed virtually the entire palace. The only complete building to survive to this day is the Banqueting

House, built for James I by Inigo Jones in 1622. It was intended for state occasions and to house plays and masques; its architecture reflects the classical Renaissance and Roman influence. The Banqueting House was the venue for the execution of King Charles the First.

It used to be claimed that secret passages riddled much of Whitehall. What archaeological investigation of the former Whitehall Palace area has revealed is the remains of Henry VIII's personal Turkish steam bath, evidence of his continental lifestyle tastes.

■ **LOCATION** Whitehall, SW1; from Parliament Square to Trafalgar Square.
■ **ACCESS** Most surviving parts are within government buildings. No public access, except Banqueting House: see www.hrp. org.uk/webcode/home.asp or telephone 0870 751 5178 for opening times and other details. Admission charge.

▲ *The magnificent dome of St Paul's is one of the highlights of the largest cathedral in England. This is how the dome looks from inside as you stand dead centre beneath it.*

MUSEUM

❻ British Museum

Parliament established the British Museum in 1753 after a debate about what to do with over 71,000 objects left to George II by the enthusiastic collector Sir Hans Sloane, who died that year. The culture of the British Museum was one of equality and public space. Prior to its foundation most museums were the domain of academics and the aristocracy, but the British Museum belonged to the nation and was free to all who were 'studious and curious'.

During the 18th and 19th centuries, the collections expanded with thousands of objects from across the British Empire and beyond. Famous artefacts on display include the beautiful and intriguing Rosetta Stone, key to deciphering Egyptian hieroglyphics, and the Elgin Marbles, whose housing in this museum is contentious.

Finds from British archaeology are particularly well represented in the prehistory, Roman and medieval galleries, where artefacts from many classic sites are on display. Other galleries explore the archaeology of Africa and Asia, and in addition there is a rotating programme of regular specialist exhibitions.

■ **LOCATION** Great Russell Street, WC1.
■ **ACCESS** See www.thebritishmuseum. ac.uk or telephone 020 7323 8000 for opening times and other details.

WREN'S MASTERPIECES

❼ St Paul's Cathedral

St Paul's is the most famous and innovative example of Sir Christopher Wren's architectural and artistic talents and is the largest cathedral in England. A cathedral dedicated to St Paul had been an integral part of London since AD604, but Wren's version was built after the Great Fire of London obliterated its predecessor. It was Wren's third design in 1675 that was finally given royal approval, and St Paul's Cathedral was completed in 1710. However, the first service at the cathedral was held on 2 December 1697, while visitor charges were introduced in 1709.

During rebuilding, Wren and his team discovered the remains of Roman cremation vessels and pots. Later investigations revealed evidence of industrial pottery production. Moreover, excavation work in 1830 unearthed a Roman stone altar, indicating that a temple once stood on the same site.

For 70 years after its completion no monuments were permitted in the cathedral, but the main body has since been adorned with effigies to commemorate great national figures. St Paul's suffered serious damage during the Second World War but came to be regarded as a symbol of resistance, remembrance and rejoicing.

St Paul's itself is an archaeological paradise. Medieval stone fragments can be found in the crypt, the wrought-iron gates from 1700 remain and the organ, dating from 1695, is still in use.

■ **LOCATION** St Paul's Churchyard, EC4.
■ **ACCESS** See www.stpauls.co.uk or telephone 020 7246 8357 for opening times and other details. Admission charge.

St Stephen Walbrook, flooded with light. The church is often regarded as a rehearsal for Sir Christopher Wren's design of St Paul's Cathedral.

architect of St Paul's Cathedral, but in the interim he designed other buildings and churches, including St Stephen Walbrook.

Regarded as a rehearsal for St Paul's, St Stephen Walbrook incorporates a central dome housed above a traditional English church with beautiful interior design. Reputed the world over as one of Wren's masterpieces, St Stephen Walbrook was badly damaged during the Blitz. Fortunately, many of the 17th-century fittings escaped serious harm. Complete with aisles, chancel and crossing transepts, the church is full of light and space, but is also renowned for being the place where the Samaritans was founded by the Reverend Dr Chad Varah in 1953.

■ **LOCATION** 39 Walbrook, EC4; near Bank tube.
■ **ACCESS** St Stephen is a working church; telephone 020 7626 8242 for opening times and other details.

WREN'S MASTERPIECES

➑ St Stephen Walbrook

It is believed that a 7th-century church first stood on the site now occupied by St Stephen Walbrook. It was built on the banks of a Thames tributary, the river Walbrook, which now runs through an underground pipe. The Great Fire of London destroyed the original St Stephen Walbrook in 1666.

The fire started at Thomas Farrinor's bakery in Pudding Lane and halted at Pye Corner, leaving the city devastated. Sir Christopher Wren, an Oxford scholar and founding member of the Royal Society, was commissioned to rebuild the city. Wren was, of course, the

MEDIEVAL CEMETERY

❾ Spitalfields

In the centre of an ancient sprawling metropolis like London the archaeology runs deep, as centuries of building and rebuilding gradually bury the past. Through the late 1990s, in advance of a new office complex, archaeologists from the Museum of London conducted an assessment of a typical central urban area at Spitalfields. Records indicated that the medieval hospital of St Mary Spital had once stood on the site, together with a priory. The remarkable excavation revealed a huge cemetery, together with mass burial pits, containing the remains of over 8,600 individuals dating to around the beginning of the 14th century, as well as earlier Roman burials.

A large part of the priory church was discovered, with an additional chapel complete with a cellar charnel house loaded with bones. The charnel house has been dated to some 20 years after the substantial burial pits, which leads to the

assumption that it was constructed to hold the large numbers of disturbed bones from the packed and overflowing cemetery. It is believed that the concentrated interments in the pits are the result of a disaster such as a famine.

Innovative plans for the site include incorporating a viewing area for the charnel house in the basement of the office complex. The majority of the remains are held in the Museum of London.

■ **LOCATION** Spitalfields, E1.
■ **ACCESS** The excavation site was off Spital Square, but there's nothing to see now. Finds are in the Museum of London; see www.museumoflondon.org.uk or telephone 0870 444 3852 for opening times and other details. Admission charge.

FAMOUS LANDMARK

❿ Tower of London

In 1066–7, following the Norman invasion, William the Conqueror founded one of the capital's most famous landmarks, the Tower of London. In the Tower's 900-year

history it has served as a royal palace, fortress, prison, place of execution, royal mint, arsenal, menagerie and treasury.

Between 1190 and 1285 two curtain-walls and a moat followed the initial completion of the White Tower, which was built in the late 1070s. The Tower of London functioned as a royal power base and refuge during times of civil upheaval. A long line of subsequent monarchs embarked on numerous building campaigns, with Edward III creating a vault over the gate passage and Henry VII adding a private chamber, library, lay gallery (a function room) and garden.

Notably famous for being the permanent home of the Crown Jewels, the Tower of London was also a notorious venue for imprisonment and execution. The moat, long since drained and filled, has attracted

▼ *The imposing facade of the Tower of London. The Tower was a royal power base across the centuries and saw subsequent monarchs add to its architecture in numerous building campaigns.*

much archaeological interest. Early excavations unearthed the well-preserved skulls of two lions and a leopard, which were probably features of the royal menagerie. A 16th-century wicker fishing basket was found in the clay at the moat's bottom, while early evidence of 13th-century bridges were found 1996.

- **LOCATION** Lower Thames Street, EC3.
- **ACCESS** See www.hrp.org.uk/webcode/tower_home.asp or telephone 0870 756 6060 for opening times and other details. Admission charge.

BATTLESHIP

⑪ HMS Belfast

HMS *Belfast* was built in 1936 at the Harland and Wolff shipyard in Belfast. Nearly 30 years of active service would see her involved in the destruction of the German cruiser *Scharnhorst* in 1943 and supporting the Allied landings on D-Day the next year. She also performed during the Korean War, and spent many years representing Britain across the world before being opened to the public in London in 1971. Her operational life has seen her travel nearly half a million miles.

HMS *Belfast* is a classic example of a six-inch cruiser, so called because she holds twelve six-inch guns among her armament and is built to cruise independently from the fleet. Her design represents the pinnacle of the lengthy development of fast fighting ships, from sail and wood to steam and steel, and she epitomizes the powerful warships of her era.

- **LOCATION** Morgan's Lane, Tooley Street, SE1.
- **ACCESS** See www.hmsbelfast.iwm.org.uk or telephone 020 7940 6300. Admission charge.

◄ *HMS* Belfast *at rest by Tower Bridge. With thirty years of active service to her credit, she was one of the most powerful warships of her era and remains as a monument to the Second World War.*

COACHING INN

⑫ George Inn

The George Inn, south of the Thames by London Bridge, is the last remaining galleried 17th-century coaching inn in London. The galleries act as partitioned private drinking compartments, which in their day would have served as cosy and intriguing dens. The pub is mentioned by Dickens in *Little Dorrit* and the panelled interior and open fires found today would certainly have been familiar to him.

As you enter the courtyard from the High Street it's not hard to imagine the inn packed with travellers in the past. Though partly demolished to make way for the Great Northern Railway, the building still retains many of its original features, including windows and exposed beams, and the bedchambers which are now a restaurant.

The inn, owned by the National Trust, serves a variety of beers such as Old Speckled Hen, Caledonian Old and the dependable London Pride. There is also a house beer called George Ale.

■ **LOCATION** 77 Borough High Street, Southwark, SE1.
■ **ACCESS** A working pub. See www.nationaltrust.org.uk or telephone 020 7407 2056 for opening times and other details.

▼ *Time has still not been called at Southwark's George Inn, which has been serving ale since the 17th century. It is the last remaining galleried coaching inn of that era.*

OLD LONDON

⑬ Greenwich Park

There is a rich history to the World Heritage Site of Greenwich Park and a great deal to see in the area. Greenwich Park is the oldest enclosed park in London and covers more than 28 hectares (70 acres). The site includes a Roman temple complex (excavated by Time Team), an Anglo-Saxon barrow cemetery and a variety of historic buildings, such as the Royal Naval College, National Maritime Museum, the Old Royal Observatory and the Prime Meridian Clock.

The parkland itself has always been a favourite with royalty. Henry IV dated his will at 'Greenwich Manor' in 1408, and Henry VIII was born in the upgraded Greenwich Palace in 1491. Henry VIII later introduced deer to the park. His daughters, Mary and Elizabeth, were also born here, and on the south bank of the Thames he held the tournaments that were renowned throughout Europe. In the 17th century James I gave the park to his wife Queen Anne, who had the Queens House, now part of the National Maritime Museum, built by the architect Inigo Jones.

In 1675 the Royal Observatory was founded by Charles II and built by Sir Christopher Wren. Astronomer Royal John Flamsteed then set about perfecting the art of navigation and finding longitude (your position east and west). His reference point of Longitude Zero can be seen on the ground at the observatory, where you can step from the eastern to the western hemisphere.

Another historic attraction is the 1869 tea clipper *Cutty Sark*. In her day *Cutty Sark* was the fastest ship making the lucrative run from China to England with precious cargoes of tea. She was famous for her continuous races against the Aberdeen ship *Thermopylae*, and in 1885 smashed all records by sailing from Australia to England in an incredible 73 days.

■ **LOCATION** Greenwich, SE10.
■ **ACCESS** See www.royalparks.gov.uk /parks/greenwich_park or telephone 020 7298 2000 for opening times and other details.

▶ *Aerial view of Greenwich Park looking north towards the observatory (centre left), the National Maritime Museum and the river.*

South-east England

The south-east has, at Boxgrove and Swanscombe, given us some of our earliest human remains. The area's proximity to the English Channel also means that maritime links with the continent are evident here, from the prehistoric, such as the Dover boat, to post-medieval and more recent archaeology. It was in this area that the Romans first landed, and the Roman remains include Fishbourne. Canterbury was first a Roman settlement, then became one of the most important medieval towns in Britain. William of Normandy landed in this region; castles such as Dover are part of the Norman legacy. The south-east has, it seems, always borne the brunt of invading forces. In the first half of the 20th century, the area became crucial in the defence of the country once more.

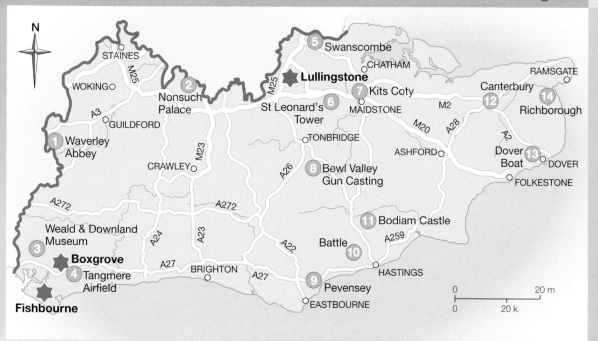

N

STAINES

M25

WOKING

Nonsuch
Palace

A3

GUILDFORD

1 Waverley
Abbey

M23

CRAWLEY

A272

Weald & Downland
Museum

3 Boxgrove

4 Tangmere
Airfield

Fishbourne

2

A24

A23

A27

BRIGHTON

A272

A26

A22

A27

5 Swanscombe

CHATHAM

Lullingstone

St Leonard's
Tower

7 Kits Coty

6 MAIDSTONE

M25

TONBRIDGE

8 Bewl Valley
Gun Casting

11 Bodiam Castle

Battle

10

9 Pevensey

EASTBOURNE

HASTINGS

A259

RAMSGATE

Canterbury

12 14 Richborough

M2

M20 A28

ASHFORD

A2

Dover
Boat 13 DOVER

FOLKESTONE

0   20 m
0   20 k

Boxgrove
Palaeolithic game-hunters

500,000BC

BOXGROVE, NEAR CHICHESTER in Sussex, is in some ways a rather perverse inclusion because there is little to be seen, but its importance in British archaeology and Phil's interest in the site means that we've decided to include it prominently.

The site is, without doubt, one of the most important Palaeolithic or 'Old Stone Age' discoveries in the country. It has produced by far the oldest in situ archaeological deposits anywhere in Britain, dating from 500,000 years ago. These deposits include the world's oldest non-stone tools: these are extraordinary antler 'hammers'. As Phil puts it: 'I've held many stone axes in my time but to hold the oldest tools that were actually used to make them is amazing.'

Game-hunter's paradise

Since the 1980s, gravel quarrying at Boxgrove has revealed a buried Palaeolithic landscape, and evidence for our early ancestors. From this, archaeologists have been able to reconstruct what the area was like half a million years ago, and the way of life of these hominids. Environmental and geological evidence shows that the Boxgrove area was on a 'raised beach' – a huge open area of wet grassland and shrub – at the base of a long cliff, which lay 7 miles north of where the south English coast is now. A watering hole attracted a wide range of animals, from elephant and rhinoceros to lions, bears and hyenas and herds of horses and deer, providing an attractive game-hunting area for early hominids.

Most of the evidence for the hominids at Boxgrove comes in the form of stone tools and animal bones that show butchery marks. It seems that the site was somewhere that our early ancestors returned to repeatedly, and it is likely that they operated in teams of hunters and killed the animals with wooden spears – we're at a time before the invention of the bow and arrow – then butchered the meat with hand-axes. One of the discoveries at Boxgrove captured a unique moment in the Palaeolithic past. The team of archaeologists, led by project director Mark Roberts, found a place where the body of a horse had been butchered. They exposed the area and found both the horse bones and the axes used for the job – lying exactly as they'd been left 500,000 years ago.

Stone tool technology

The hand-axe was the key tool of the Palaeolithic and at Boxgrove over 150 have been discovered. On Time Team, we have filmed Phil creating a hand-axe – it is an incredible art to get the balance and the shape right, and requires the knapper to imagine the kind of shape he wants before he begins to remove chunks from the core to leave the intended shape behind.

Phil's reproductions are used at Boxgrove to illustrate just how effective a tool a stone hand-axe could be. He has great admiration for his tool-making ancestors. When he first held one of the original axes, he was impressed by how sharp the edges were. 'I'd just knapped some axes for a demonstration and in terms of sharpness and "freshness" you couldn't tell the difference between the two.' One of the fascinations of Boxgrove for Phil is the evidence for axes having been made on the spot. In particular, he likes the evidence from one location where the spread of waste flakes, mapped by archaeologists, reveals exactly how they fell between the knapper's legs as the axe was made. One of the famous antler

▲ *This is an idealized landscape of hunter-gatherers, which is based on the Time Team site at Elvedon.*

hammers from Boxgrove also had flint chips embedded in it, which showed that it had been repeatedly used to create hand-axes.

Boxgrove hominids

Despite Phil's excitement about the antler hammers and the hand-axes, Boxgrove is most famous as the home of the oldest hominid bones in Britain. A bit of lower leg bone and two teeth might not seem much to get excited about, but in terms of British archaeology, finds like this from the Palaeolithic are incredibly rare.

The hominid remains from Boxgrove predate the arrival of recognizably modern humans in Britain by hundreds of thousands of years, which gives you some idea of how lucky we are still to have the evidence preserved at Boxgrove. They're vital for giving us clues to how our early ancestors developed. Current thinking suggests that the remains at Boxgrove belonged to *Homo heidelbergensis*, a powerfully built species that might not necessarily link directly to modern humans, but might be an ancestor of the Neanderthals. Nonetheless, the hunters at Boxgrove were beginning to engage in activities that were the start of what we think of as human, and that's why sites like Boxgrove are so important. The Palaeolithic might seem very remote, but as Phil always points out, it was the longest period of human evolution so far!

■ **GETTING THERE** Boxgrove is 4 miles NE of Chichester, West Sussex, off the A27. See www.ucl.ac.uk/boxgrove, and www.english-heritage.org.uk for details; currently no public access to the excavation site. ■ **OUR VIEW** English Heritage has purchased the quarry site at Boxgrove to save it for the nation, and there are major plans to restore the site and resume excavations. In the meantime, casts of the bone can be seen at the Natural History Museum, and you can see a good display of Palaeolithic hand-axes at the Museum of London and the British Museum.

Lullingstone
Life in a Roman villa

1st–5th centuries AD

OMAN VILLAS ARE a popular and fascinating subject for us on Time Team – we get more letters from the public about them than any other type of site. The artefacts, construction features, decorative floors and plasterwork give you a real sense of getting close to the people who once occupied the villas. From an archaeological point of view, the large quantities of building materials and domestic goods that were used at villas survive very well and produce a range of valuable debris that enables them to be located more easily – and makes them more impressive to look at – than at many sites, and this is one of the reasons why they generate so much interest.

Lullingstone is one of the most famous Roman villas in Britain. This isn't because it's particularly large, but because the evidence found there for the lifestyle and changing beliefs of its inhabitants is so good. The villa was discovered before the Second World War, and excavated between 1949 and 1961 by a team of archaeologists, students and volunteers. Lullingstone was the location that so entranced a 14-year-old Guy de la Bédoyère that it began his interest in all things Roman and made him decide, some weeks after his first visit with his parents, to get on his bike and ride all the way back here from Wimbledon in south London for a second look.

▶ *Lullingstone's beautiful 4th-century mosaic being excavated in the 1950s. In the foreground is a scene from mythology, showing Europa being abducted by Jupiter in the guise of a bull.*

A country retreat

The Lullingstone villa began its life in the late 1st century. A small winged building was built on an artificial terrace overlooking the river in the Darent valley, an area popular with villa builders. Close to the main road from London to Richborough, it was perhaps the country retreat of a wealthy city dweller. From about AD200 the villa owners allowed the house to fall into disrepair. In about 275 things looked up again and the villa was rebuilt. The late 3rd and 4th centuries were what might be described as the golden age of villa building, and villa owners, like those at Lullingstone, spent large amounts of money on sophisticated alterations and mosaic floors, with underfloor heating systems called hypocausts. Villas weren't just impressive homes, they were the centre of farm estates as well, and a large granary was also added at Lullingstone.

Much of the walls and architecture of the villa can still be seen at Lullingstone today, and when you look at it you realize, as Guy always says, what a difference there was between Roman masonry buildings and the Iron Age roundhouses that had gone before. Its solidity represents part of a whole Roman 'package' that was on offer. To those British tribes willing to cooperate, the Romans offered stability and security, which, regardless of our sense that it went with a fair bit of oppression, we can still regard as attractive. I remember sitting with Phil and Mick with our feet on the floor of a Roman villa – a Time Team reconstruction – feeling the

◄ *This geometric panel from Lullingstone's mosaic floor marked the division between hall and dining room. At the bottom are two lines in Latin verse referring to the Europa scene, which can be seen in the facing picture.*

underfloor heat radiating up and thinking how good this must have felt to our predecessors during a cold British winter. Romanization brought creature comforts, as well as stability and access to new goods from throughout the empire.

Religious beliefs

It is relatively unusual in archaeology to find clear evidence of people's thoughts and religious beliefs actually in their homes, but at Lullingstone, the excavations have revealed some remarkable and rare insights. The late 2nd-century villa had a cellar in one wing, and archaeologists made a unique discovery down here: two marble busts, indicating a shrine to the household gods, where the villa inhabitants would go to worship them and leave offerings.

The cellar shrine might have been hidden from general view, but the occupants of the later villa weren't afraid to show off their culture and religion. About AD300, a circular mausoleum was built on the terrace behind the house, containing a male and female skeleton, each in a lead coffin, buried with many grave goods. About 60 years later, an elaborate mosaic was installed in the dining room, depicting the classical myth of Jupiter carrying off Europa, and including two lines in Latin referring to the episode in the style of famous Roman poets. As Guy says, it's rather like one of us putting Shakespeare quotations on our walls to impress dinner guests with our learning!

By the time the mosaic was installed, the classical myths were probably more about culture than belief, because there is evidence that by then the villa inhabitants had become Christian. During excavation, fragments of plasterwork from a collapsed upstairs room were collected and then painstakingly reassembled to reveal beautiful wall paintings depicting people in the ancient attitude of prayer

combined with Christian symbols. (These can be seen in the British Museum today.) To make such a public commitment to their new faith was significant, and to do so on wall paintings clearly demonstrated dedication to the new religion. This room may have been a sacred space in which the owners worshipped, and it's rare to uncover this in Britain – or, in fact, anywhere in the Roman Empire. It's some of the earliest evidence for Christianity in this country.

It is worth noting that initially Christian worship tended to be a private event conducted in these kinds of house chapels; churches were to come later. Interestingly, the villa at Lullingstone, judging from the archaeological evidence, appears to have burnt down in the 5th century, but a small Saxon chapel was built over the remains of the mausoleum.

▲ Lullingstone today. Lullingstone is the only villa in Britain completely exposed and under cover. The view is south across the Deep Room (see facing page) towards the main range.

■ **GETTING THERE** Lullingstone is ½ mile SW of Eynsford, Kent, off the A225. See www.english-heritage.org.uk or telephone 01322 863467 for opening times and other details. Admission charge.

■ **OUR VIEW** For the site itself, Guy must have the last word: 'Whenever I visit the place I always feel that I've come somewhere that is still magical, and I know that in my own life and interest in Roman Britain, Lullingstone played a big part in influencing me, more than any other site that I can think of.'

◄ Lullingstone's Deep Room started life as a cellar grain store. Later it became an underground shrine. This painting of water nymphs was later blocked up, protecting the images – perhaps when the Christian church was installed.

Fishbourne
Romano-British palace

1st-3rd centuries AD

▼ *This 2nd-century mosaic from Fishbourne is perhaps the best known and most beautiful of what is the largest collection of in-situ mosaics visible in Britain today. According to experts, this was made from over 360,000 individual tesserae.*

OVER THE YEARS Time Team has dug many Roman villa sites, including some with mosaics. Indeed, villas are some of the most common buildings archaeologists find – and yet none has matched the vast and unusual complex at Fishbourne. Most of Roman Britain's impressive villas belong to the 'golden age' of villa building in the 3rd and 4th centuries. But Fishbourne started life long before, in the middle of the 1st century, and soon became the biggest villa so far recorded in Britain. Although some experts hedge their bets, this building was surely the closest Britain came to a Roman palace.

This was a palace built to impress. As you enter through the main gate you are standing where Roman visitors must have waited, awed by what they saw.

Over 50 mosaics lined the rooms; 12m-high (40ft) reception halls led into rooms that bounded a courtyard surrounded by dozens of slim columns. A garden awaited you, laid out with piped water supplying fountains, statues, formal lawns and flowerbeds. In the south wing the owner would have shown you views towards Fishbourne harbour while you admired another spectacular mosaic. Of all the British sites this is one where you can most believe the toga-clad inhabitants sat enjoying their wine. It was a palace unashamedly influenced by the Mediterranean style of the great Roman villas of Italy. Many of the floors and decorated plaster may well have been created by Italian or possibly Gaulish craftsmen who had access to imported marble and other building materials from as far afield as Turkey.

Loyalty to Rome

The wealth and power symbolized by Fishbourne may be a measure of what became available to those British who

sought to make an allegiance with the
Romans. Although we do not know for
certain, one likely candidate for the
owner of Fishbourne was Tiberius
Claudius Cogidubnus. Tacitus, the
Roman historian, calls Cogidubnus a
British king who was loyal to Rome.
Indeed, Cogidubnus was probably the
British leader of the Atrebates tribe, made
a Roman citizen by the emperor
Claudius. He may have been educated at
Rome and groomed as the puppet ruler
of part of southern Britain after the
invasion, to create a kind of buffer state.

Nearby Chichester was developing as a
major town where several inscriptions
record declarations of loyalty to the
emperor Nero (54–68). One theory is
that the kingdom of Cogidubnus and his
palace at Fishbourne provided the
Romans with a key base during the
process of conquest, as the Romans faced
a series of rebellions, culminating with
Boudicca's revolt in AD60. However,
there's no conclusive proof of who owned
Fishbourne, and not all archaeologists
agree about it.

Chance discovery

This amazing building was discovered by
chance in 1960, although as long ago as
1806 it was known that Roman remains
were present on the site. In 1960 a
workman digging a mains water trench
discovered a pile of ancient building
material and pottery. Believing the
accidental finds were of some significance,
the workman reported what he had
found and the British Museum was then
contacted. An archaeological investigation
team was dispatched to the site and
excavation work was soon under way.

The buildings you see today were
begun in the late 1st century, replacing
earlier timber structures. However, it went
through many alterations over the next
200 years. By the late 3rd century, just
as Roman Britain's other villas were

entering their finest phase, the old palace
at Fishbourne was a ruin, destroyed by
fire. It was ransacked for building
materials, some probably finding their
way to a nearby fort at Portchester (see
page 46). In Saxon times, bodies were
buried among the ruins and the site was
completely forgotten until modern times.

The identity of the builders and
owners of Fishbourne will probably
never be known, but whoever they were,
the remains stand as a good reminder
that we shouldn't always think of the
Roman conquest of Britain as a forced
invasion. For many people, particularly in
the south, the Roman Empire was a
familiar and welcome neighbour before
the invasion, and there were many
benefits to be enjoyed from it, including
luxury villas with beautiful gardens.

▲ *Fishbourne underwent many modifications. This hypocaust (underfloor heating system) was still being installed when the palace burned down at the end of the 3rd century, and was never put to use.*

■ **GETTING THERE**
Fishbourne is 1 mile
W of Chichester, West
Sussex, off the A259.
See www.sussexpast.
co.uk or telephone
01243 785859 for
opening times and
other details.
Admission charge.

■ **OUR VIEW** Fishbourne
has become the
centre for a wide
range of educational
activities and it is
possible to see
demonstrations of
Roman technology
and learn about
Roman horticulture
and mosaic
construction. Like
many of Britain's
Roman sites it has
become a struggle to
keep it viable. We
hope that Fishbourne
will be able to continue
displaying its amazing
finds into the future.

Other sites to visit

❶ Waverley Abbey

Beside the river Wey, 3 miles south of Farnham, is Waverley Abbey, the first Cistercian monastery to be built in Britain. It was founded in 1128 by the Bishop of Winchester and colonized by French monks, who followed the Cistercian rule of a strict liturgy combined with manual work. In contrast to the other major Cistercian houses, such as Tintern, Fountains and Rievaulx (see pages 116, 207 and 202), which were built on a grand scale and in an architecturally striking style, Waverley is basic and reserved in appearance.

Little of the church can be seen, apart from a section of the south chancel, but the undercroft of the lay brothers' refectory has a fine 13th-century vaulted ceiling and the south gable still extends to its full height. The gable has two pairs of lancet windows with larger windows above each set. A central round window crowns the apex.

The abbey proved successful during the 14th century but was closed by the reformation in 1536. Much of the stone stolen from the abbey was used in local buildings.

■ **LOCATION** 2 miles SE of Farnham, Surrey; off B3001.
■ **ACCESS** See www.waverley.gov.uk /abbey or telephone 01252 715094 for opening times and other details.

❷ Nonsuch Palace

Started in 1538, Nonsuch Palace was Henry VIII's last great building project. Though the palace was demolished in 1682 by its then owner, Countess of Castlemaine Barbara Villiers, to pay off her gambling debts, excavations at the Sutton site in 1959 revealed the splendour and grand scale of this palace, which has such a fine reputation in the historical record.

The palace was built at a time when Henry had just had a son whom he believed would be his heir. The palace was of the highest fashion and was designed to proclaim to all the power and influence of the Tudor dynasty. The design was based around a double courtyard. The first was enclosed by stone and brick walls with a turreted gatehouse typical of the period. The second, inner courtyard was enclosed with stone walls, which were topped by timber framing covered in gilded slate. This fantastic gold framework held high-relief mouldings of gods and goddesses. The royal apartments were divided between the east and west of this court, and two massive five-storey octagonal towers, again covered in gilded slate, held the southern corners. Such opulence could rarely have been seen and Nonsuch was surely one of the most eccentric and indulgent buildings of the period.

■ **LOCATION** SW area of Nonsuch Park, Cheam, Surrey.
■ **ACCESS** Park open all year round. Nothing survives of the palace.

❸ Weald and Downland Museum

Seven miles from Chichester in 20 hectares (50 acres) of picturesque Sussex countryside, the Weald and Downland Museum is considered to be England's finest museum of ancient buildings and historic rural life. The museum was established in 1967 for the purpose of rescuing and conserving buildings from south-east England's historic past. It opened to the public in 1971 and has grown considerably from the seven buildings that originally occupied the site.

The open-air museum now has a collection of nearly 50 buildings, which range from prehistoric reconstructions through to rescued buildings of the 19th century. 'Rescued' buildings are saved from

▼ *The illustration of Queen Elizabeth I's royal procession towards Nonsuch Palace in 1582 also shows the opulence indulged in by the Tudor dynasty, where stone walls gave way to wooden structures faced with gilded slate.*

PALATIVM REGIVM IN ANGLIÆ REGNO APPELLATVM NONCIVTZ, *Hoc est nusquam simile.*

Titchfield Market Hall – one of nearly fifty buildings rescued for posterity and painstakingly restored at the Sussex Weald and Downland Museum.

demolition by being painstakingly dismantled then moved from their original locations in Kent, Sussex, Surrey and Hampshire and rebuilt on the museum site.

Recreations are as historically accurate as possible, and many of the interiors have also been furnished to show the way the original owners might have lived in them or used them. Each day a working 17th-century water mill produces stone-ground flour for sale in the museum shop. A Victorian school shows what education was like in that era, and a Tudor farmhouse demonstrates traditional farming methods of an earlier time.

The museum also demonstrates early construction skills and runs courses in building conservation and rural trades.

■ **LOCATION** 7 miles N of Chichester, West Sussex; on A286.
■ **ACCESS** See www.wealddown.co.uk or telephone 01243 811363 for opening times and other details. Admission charge.

WORLD WAR AIRFIELD

❹ Tangmere Airfield

The area of Tangmere is steeped in the history of flight. It was first spotted as an ideal place for an airfield by a stricken pilot who made a forced landing here in 1916. Two years later the War Office had constructed an airfield on the site as a training base for Handley Page bombers. The end of the First World War saw the base briefly close, only to open again in 1925 to house fighter squadrons.

The Second World War saw the trusty Hurricane and the iconic Supermarine Spitfire based at the airfield. Additions to the base at this time included blast pens, high earthen banks built around aircraft-holding areas to protect the aircraft against the flying debris of a bombing raid. The base was subsequently bombed heavily by the Germans in August 1940, but the

fighters of Tangmere proved themselves repeatedly during the Battle of Britain.

Other wartime activity on the base included actions by the secret Special Operations Executive (SOE), who ran agents into and out of France, while during the preparations for D-Day the airfield was home to many Canadian airmen.

The post-war years were not quiet. Tangmere hosted many speed record-breaking attempts by the RAF and repeated testing of new jets, but in 1970 the airfield was finally decommissioned. Many nationalities have flown out of Tangmere over the years and their history and actions are recorded in the fascinating museum here.

■ **LOCATION** 4 miles NE of Chichester, West Sussex; off A27.
■ **ACCESS** Tangmere Military Aviation Museum: see www.aeroflight.co.uk (go to 'Museums', then 'UK Aviation Museums', then 'Tangmere') or telephone 01243 775223. Admission charge.

▲ *The 'must-have' stone tools of the Palaeolithic period. These flint hand-axes from Swanscombe in Kent would have been used for cutting and chopping.*

PALAEOLITHIC PEOPLE

❺ Swanscombe

Excavations at Swanscombe have uncovered evidence for our Palaeolithic ancestors, who lived some 400,000 years ago. Environmental evidence has proved the key to reconstructing life in the distant past. Floral and faunal samples showed that the hunter-gatherers who lived here on a seasonal basis existed in what were then reed swamp and lightly wooded surroundings. Animals sharing the natural resources at the time would have included rhinoceros, straight-tusked elephants and wild ox.

Primitive stone tool sets belonging to the basic Clactonian type (so named because of the type was originally found at Clacton) and the later more diverse Acheulian type were found in a series of lower gravel beds. These tool sets illustrate the development of stone tools from rough worked flakes into the beautiful egg-shaped hand-axes of the Acheulian style. The site also revealed three fragments of early hominid skull, which appear to fit within the transition from *Homo erectus* to modern humans.

■ **LOCATION** Swanscombe, Kent; on A226.
■ **ACCESS** There is nothing to see at the Barnfield Pit excavation site. The majority of finds from the site are at the Natural History Museum, London, but are not currently on display.

NORMAN BUILDING

❻ St Leonard's Tower

The Kentish hamlet of West Malling has a fine Norman defensive structure in St Leonard's Tower. Standing approximately 18m (60ft) high, it is an excellent example of a tower keep. It is believed to have been named after the chapel dedicated to St Leonard (the patron saint of prisoners) that once stood near by.

◀ *Three magnificent upright stones supporting a large capstone are all that remain of the barrow, Kits Coty House.*

Gundulf, Bishop of Rochester and architect to William the Conqueror, constructed the tower keep out of coarse Kentish ragstone between 1077 and 1108. Some of the zigzag 'herringbone' stonework with additional carved stone dressings of tufa ashlar is visible, as are two low stretches of medieval walling, which were later incorporated into a garden boundary wall.

Very little is known of the tower's history, and its actual function is debatable since it has a ground-floor entrance and no bailey, which means that it was either a poor defensive design or that it had some alternative use. Most Norman keeps retain a defensive bailey or curtain wall and have the entrance on the first floor accessed by steps. Some suggest that it was merely a bell tower built in the form of a keep.

■ **LOCATION** ½ mile S of West Malling, Kent; W of A228.
■ **ACCESS** See www.english-heritage. org.uk or telephone 01732 870872. Internal access by prior arrangement only.

NEOLITHIC LONG BARROW

❼ Kits Coty House

This fascinating Neolithic tomb lies 2 miles north-east of Aylesford village. It was once a chambered long barrow measuring some 70m (230ft) in length, but as the mound has been excavated away, the site now consists of just the three upright stones supporting the large capstone of the main chamber. Some of the original stones, used for an outline kerb and a terminal stone at the far end of the barrow, have been removed in the last hundred years, and others were destroyed in the 1800s to enable ploughing. Today the remains are surrounded by a rather ungainly iron railing, which unfortunately doesn't keep out those

determined to deface the stones with graffiti. This is not a new problem, however, as you can still see where the stones were defaced in the 1800s.

Just over a mile south of Kits Coty House is Little Kits Coty House, or the 'Countless Stones'. This jumbled collection of 21 stones of mixed size is possibly the remains of another tomb, but there is currently no generally accepted idea of what the original site looked like. Kits Coty House and its cousin are both the remains of prehistoric burial mounds, which were once prominent in the landscape. Though they are now in ruins, they still capture the imagination.

■ **LOCATION** 2 miles N of Maidstone, Kent; W of A229.
■ **ACCESS** Open all year round.

WAR INDUSTRY

❽ Bewl Valley Gun Casting

Many villages in the Bewl valley, a beautiful area along the Kent and Sussex border south-east of Royal Tunbridge Wells, have a history based on iron-working. One of the most well-known iron resources in the area is the village of Wadhurst, where for centuries iron ore was mined out of the underlying clay by digging large pits. Foundries such as those at Brightling and Robertsbridge then made the area famous for the production of guns, cannons and shot over a period of nearly 300 years.

Several families became wealthy and influential in the area by making and supplying guns for the navy and the government, most of which would have been tested, or 'proved', at the Woolwich Arsenal in London. At one time over ten furnaces were working in the valley at once; the last to close was Ashburnham in the early 19th century.

■ **LOCATION** Wadhurst, 6 miles SE of Tunbridge Wells, Kent; on B2099.
■ **ACCESS** Valley accessible all year round. Nothing survives of the furnaces.

SHORE FORT

❾ Pevensey

Pevensey Castle is one of Britain's oldest and most significant strongholds. It dates back to the Roman period, when invading forces initially settled in the area.

They named it Anderida, and around AD290 built a fort on the site. Roman forts were typically rectangular but the Anderida fort was oval, built to conform to the shape of the peninsula it was sited on.

After the Roman withdrawal the fort lay derelict until the Normans landed near Pevensey in 1066. Before marching for Hastings, William the Conqueror set up camp within the fort walls. He then handed Pevensey to his half-brother, Robert de Mortain, who built the castle within the remains of the fort, where it gradually developed over

the centuries despite periods of decline.

The castle remained occupied up until the time it served as a state prison in the 15th century, but was left to decay between the 16th and 20th centuries. In 1925, it was rescued and presented to the state by

◀ *Mist rises from the moat of Bodiam Castle. Its towers, built from golden-cream stone, are reflected in the water, exaggerating its impression of impenetrability.*

the Duke of Devonshire, and during the Second World War it was refortified with machine-gun posts and billets.

Part of what makes Pevensey Castle so fascinating is that it covers three distinct periods. Two-thirds of the Roman fort walls remain standing, there are extensive remains of the medieval castle, such as the curtain wall, and the Second World War pillboxes are also still evident.

■ **LOCATION** Pevensey, East Sussex; off A259.

■ **ACCESS** Pevensey Castle: see www.english-heritage.org.uk or telephone 01323 762604 for opening times and other details. Admission charge.

❿ Battle

Battle is the actual site of the Battle of Hastings (Hastings itself is some 6 miles south), the famous conflict between the last Saxon king, Harold, and the Norman invader, William the Conqueror, in 1066.

The site marks a pivotal moment in history. In the mid-11th century, England faced enemies, uprising and invasion from Norway, Wales and France. In January 1066 Edward the Confessor died and Harold was elected king, but his throne was soon under threat. Harold was already renowned as a good leader and diplomat, but his diplomacy and tactical skills were shortly to be severely tested.

During the summer Harold prepared for an impending Norman invasion. In September he charged north to fight off an invasion party from Norway, which landed in Northumbria, then a race to the south was needed in order to combat the Normans, who had finally arrived.

Harold's exhausted army encamped and stood with their shield wall at the high ground of what is now Battle. Successive attacks and Norman cavalry charges were beaten off until a feint by the invaders drew the Saxons away from the wall. A Norman counterattack succeeded in breaking the wall and Harold was killed, possibly by an arrow in the eye.

The next year (1067), William founded Battle Abbey, with the altar reputedly over the place where Harold fell. This was one of the first post-conquest monastic houses to be established in England following a vow by William to atone for the loss of lives during his campaign.

■ **LOCATION** Battle, East Sussex; off A21.

■ **ACCESS** Abbey and battlefield, see www.english-heritage.org.uk or telephone 01424 773721. Admission charge.

⓫ Bodiam Castle

This castle is a good quarter of a mile from its car park, located 3 miles south of Hawkhurst, but it's well worth the walk. Majestic within its moat, the beautiful symmetrical design in golden cream stone looks like a children's storybook castle. Historically the architecture represents the dynamic heights of fashionable castle design in the late 14th century.

The highly successful and bombastic knight Sir Edward Dalyngrigge returned from France a wealthy and influential man after freelancing in the Hundred Years' War. He married Elizabeth Wardeux in 1378 and in doing so gained Bodiam Manor. Further threats from the French meant that seven years later he was given permission by Richard II to 'crenellate his house' and the building of the present castle began.

Rather than reinforce the old manor, Dalyngrigge selected a more suitable site and incorporated his experience in warfare into the design of a new castle. Though in plan a basic rectangle, the castle has great drum towers on the corners together with a complicated approach through three successive drawbridges, each offset at an angle to the next. After this a substantial barbican had to be overcome to gain entry to the castle. Even inside further protection was provided by a self-contained hall.

Various appointments kept Dalyngrigge from his new castle but he did return to live there for a short while before his death in 1395. The castle later featured in history during a siege by Richard III, and later still saw a short assault during the English Civil War, but the castle has remained remarkably intact.

■ **LOCATION** 3 miles S of Hawkhurst, East Sussex; off B2244.

■ **ACCESS** See www.nationaltrust.org.uk or telephone 01580 830436 for opening times and other details. Admission charge.

ADMINISTRATIVE POWER

⑫ Canterbury

During the Iron Age, much of the Canterbury region was controlled by the Cantii tribe. The invading Romans of the 1st century named their settlement Durovernum Cantiacorum, or 'walled place by the marsh of the Cantii'.

This was obviously an important tribal centre at the time and the Romans incorporated this into their designation of Canterbury as a *civitas* capital, or administrative centre of the region. This further established the town as a powerful centre of influence throughout the area.

Canterbury was a thriving town protected by a stone wall. Though many Roman walled towns later incorporated bastion towers butted against their defences, Canterbury appears to have had its bastions bonded into the original build, indicating the early need for substantial defence. Some of the town wall was incorporated into the building of the later medieval church

of St Mary, Northgate, and you can still see the Roman crenellations preserved in the stone courses.

Excavation at Canterbury has uncovered the site of a Roman theatre and two Roman churches, reused in the 6th century by St Augustine. Evidence for trade and economy has also been uncovered with various shops and even a flour mill, complete with mule-driven millstones.

Some of the most intriguing evidence is for the continued use of Canterbury as a settlement following the Roman withdrawal. While many towns fell into complete disuse and decay, early Saxon pottery finds and subsequent mid-Saxon structures built over Roman remains illustrate the settlement's continued importance.

■ **LOCATION** Canterbury, Kent.

■ **ACCESS** Museum of Canterbury: see www.canterbury.gov.uk (go to 'Enjoying', then 'Museums and Galleries', then 'Museum of Canterbury') or telephone 01227 475202 for opening times and other details. Canterbury Roman Museum: see www.canterbury.gov.uk (go to 'Enjoying', then 'Museums and Galleries', then 'Canterbury Roman Museum') or telephone 01227 785575. Admission charges at both museums.

BRONZE AGE BOAT

⑬ Dover

During the construction of the Dover to Folkestone link road in 1992, the remarkable remains of a 3,000-year-old Bronze Age boat were uncovered. This incredible find was so well preserved because the boat had been covered with silt soon after it was abandoned, sealing its wooden hull from the natural bacteria that decay and destroy timber.

In a huge rescue-archaeology challenge, the majority of the boat was recovered in poor weather and under pressure from both development delays and vital conservation demands. Over 9m (30ft) long and nearly 2.5m (8ft)

wide, the boat was lifted in sections before undergoing a conservation ordeal which included saturating the soaked timbers with a wax solution and then freeze-drying them. The boat is now on display in Dover Museum.

Close examination of the remains gives us a unique insight into Bronze Age carpentry and boat construction. The basic structure is of six large

◀ *Richborough Castle in Kent. It has some of the best-preserved Roman walls in England, and as a successful port it acted as the main entry point for Roman troops pouring into Britain after AD43. The 3rd-century triple ditches can be clearly seen, as can the later stone rampart of the Saxon Shore fort.*

ROMAN INVASION

⑭ Richborough

In AD43, under the orders of Emperor Claudius, four Roman legions consisting of around 40,000 men sailed for Britain. The fortified beachhead at Richborough has been traditionally identified as the prime landing site, although this is a very contentious issue and there were probably many landing places in the south east.

Richborough (Rutupiae) became a successful port and the 'main gate' into Britain from the continent. A massive marble monument was constructed on the site to signify entry to the province and mark the beginning of the road to London. A large civil settlement also existed in the surrounding area, but the present site was dominated by the military works.

The remains of the marble monument foundation are surrounded by an impressive triple set of ditches which belong to an early 3rd-century fort, and this itself is enclosed by a later stone rampart of a Saxon Shore fort (see page 46), constructed in the late 3rd century.

Excavations at the site have revealed that Richborough was an important supply and trading base, with finds such as marked amphorae (jars) for expensive imported wine. Further investigation has also identified the location of an early 5th-century Christian church and font.

oak timbers lashed together with twisted yew ties, with moss hammered into the joints. A central rail acts as the keel and the hull is supported and fixed using wedges, cleats and lengths of oak reinforcing. This is similar to other examples, such as those discovered at North Ferriby (see page 213).

Some people believe that the Dover boat would have been suitable for crossing the Channel under the power of 18 paddlers, which gives us some tantalizing clues to prehistoric international trade.

■ **LOCATION** Dover, Kent.
■ **ACCESS** Dover Museum: see www.dover.gov.uk/museum or telephone 01304 201066 for opening times and other details. Free admission for Dover residents; admission charge for non-residents.

■ **LOCATION** 1 mile NW of Sandwich, Kent; off A256.
■ **ACCESS** See www.english-heritage. org.uk or telephone 01304 612013 for opening times and other details. Admission charge to Roman Fort.

Wales

Wales gives little away to its larger neighbour in the range and quality of its archaeology. It has one of the most intriguing, and early, human burial sites in Britain – the Paviland Cave on the Gower Peninsula. Wales has always been rich in natural resources, which have been exploited throughout the past: copper from the mines at Great Orme, stone from the Preseli Hills (which was taken to Stonehenge), gold (mined by the Romans), and in the post-medieval era, iron and coal. Monastic sites such as Tintern are part of the important Christian tradition. Wales also has some of the greatest medieval fortifications in Europe, to be seen in castles such as Conwy and Beaumaris. Wales's rich industrial heritage has recently been recognized: Blaenavon is now a World Heritage site.

N

0   20 m
0   20 k

HOLYHEAD

Llyn Cerrig
Bach
1

Great Orme
3
RHYL   PRESTATYN
LLANDUDNO   A55

Llys Rhosyr
2

BANGOR

Conwy
Castle

A5

Pontnewydd
Cave
4

A487

A470

WREXHAM

Pontcysyllte
Aqueduct
5

A494

A458

WELSHPOOL

A470

A470

A483

ABERYSTWYTH   A44

A487

Castell Henllys

Carreg Coetan
7
A487

A482

A483

6 St Davids

A485

A40

Llangorse

A40   A40

CARMARTHEN

A477

MERTHYR
TYDFIL

Blaenavon
Ironworks

A465

Tintern Abbey
13

SWANSEA

Caerleon
10

12
Caerwent

8

M4

NEWPORT   11
The Newport Ship   9   Caerwent
Goldcliff

Paviland
Cave

CARDIFF

Castell Henllys
Iron Age hillfort

500–100BC

MICK AND I BOTH think that Pembrokeshire has a number of interesting sites, including this one, which would be worth visiting over a couple of days.

Situated between Newport and Cardigan, Castell Henllys is an Iron Age inland promontory fort, which has been excavated for over 20 years. In fact, the site is one of the most intensively studied hillforts in Britain and has a continuing programme of research and excavation, run to train the archaeology students at York University. The hillfort consists of a natural headland with steep scarps to the east, south and west, augmented by a bank. To the north of the site, where the entrance was, there are significant earthworks in the shape of several ditches and banks. Inside these fortifications, archaeologists have found evidence for numerous Iron Age roundhouses dating to between 500 and 100BC. Adjacent to the fort they discovered a farmstead settlement, which is believed to have been occupied throughout the Romano-British period.

Defended communities
There are a large number of Iron Age hillforts in west Wales. These are generally much smaller than their counterparts in England – Castell Henllys covers an area of less than half a hectare (just over one

▼ *Aerial view of the Pembrokeshire hillfort showing the area of the excavations together with the reconstructed roundhouses.*

acre), compared to 19 hectares (47) acres at Maiden Castle in Dorset, for example – but far more numerous. Hillforts such as Castell Henllys were probably home to a community of extended families, maybe up to 150 people, and building and maintaining the site would have been a big commitment for the inhabitants. Excavation of the defences has shown how massive and complex they were, particularly at the gateway end, going through many phases of rebuilding and construction. This may show that Welsh Iron Age society was violent, and that's why so many communities were prepared to invest in hillforts.

A large slingshot hoard – a rare find for Britain – was discovered behind the rampart at Castell Henllys, suggesting the defences were ready for use. Alternatively, or additionally, it might suggest that these hillforts were high-status sites, where the inhabitants used the massive and elaborate defences to demonstrate to observers that they could afford to spend labour and resources on building them. Interestingly, one of the original motivations for excavating the site was the name: the '*llys*' part means 'palace' or 'court' and this name is associated with high-status locations in the early medieval period.

One of the most unusual defensive discoveries at Castell Henllys was made by archaeologist Harold Mytum. Below one of the outer banks of the hillfort he discovered a 'chevaux-de-frise' (see page 305), what Mick refers to as a 'sort of prehistoric barbed wire'. It was particularly effective at stopping cavalry and chariots, and that's why it extends in a band outside the gateway area, so attackers would become entangled at the point where they were in slingshot range. This feature is common in France and Spain, but relatively unknown in Britain. Before Harold Mytum's excavation no one knew that these stones existed at Castell Henllys, and it

makes you wonder how many others are waiting to be found at other sites.

Roundhouse reconstruction

A large portion of the interior of the hillfort has been excavated, and this has produced detailed information about the layout of the site and the lifestyle of its inhabitants – so much so that a number of roundhouses and a granary have been recreated on the exact location of the original Iron Age structures. The granary and one of the old roundhouses are the oldest reconstructed prehistoric buildings in Britain. The first roundhouse (Roundhouse One) was excavated in 1981 and is located to the south-east of the site. Reconstructed the following year, it has a diameter of 10m (33ft) and is unique in that it has an inner ring of timber posts. Roundhouse Two is a smaller building (6m/20ft in diameter), while Roundhouse Three is roughly the same size as Roundhouse One but, unlike its counterpart, it did not have an inner ring of wooden posts.

As well as the roundhouses, the site contained deposits such as carbonized bone, charcoal, grain, several iron objects, pieces of pottery, glass beads and a few spindle whorls. Mick particularly likes the fact that although the site is Iron Age, only a few iron objects have been found there, such as a small hunting spearhead and a sickle blade. This indicates what a highly valued commodity iron was, and that it was never needlessly discarded but was probably carefully recycled instead.

■ **GETTING THERE** Castell Henllys is 6 miles SW of Cardigan, off the A487. See www.castellhenllys. com or telephone 01239 891319 for opening times and other details. Admission charge.

■ **OUR VIEW** Castell Henllys has a good visitor centre, and there are beautiful trails through the surrounding woodland (complete with prehistoric pigs). Don't miss the recreated Iron Age ritual area with its wooden fertility figures, which has been adopted by New Age enthusiasts as though it really was an ancient feature. But then, it's always nice to see people taking an interest in the past!

Llangorse
Royal fortress in a Welsh lake

AD890-916

LANGORSE IS IN SOME ways an odd site to include but it has frankly rather nostalgic associations for Mick and me as it was the site of an early Time Team dig – and one of our most challenging reconstructions, which involved creating a log boat out of an oak trunk in just three days. However, the other reason for its inclusion is to show you the kind of place we don't normally associate with high-status sites in this country: a crannog, or settlement on a man-made island. Crannogs tend to be common in Ireland and Scotland (see page 238), and more are being discovered all the time; they might be more widespread in the rest of Britain than we think. However, Llangorse remains the only known crannog in Wales.

Living on a man-made island like Llangorse is an experience we no longer can easily relate to, but for many communities in the past this was an ideal location with many advantages. It offered a vital combination of security and defence, a wide variety of good food and resources – from fish, eels and waterfowl

to plants and building materials – and a natural system of waste disposal. Crannogs are known as far back as the Stone Age and right through to the end of the medieval period.

A royal fortress

The crannog at Llangorse was first discovered in the 19th century, and was originally thought to be Iron Age. But ring-dating of oak planks from the site suggests that it was an early medieval settlement, erected between AD889 and 893. It seems likely that it was built as a defended royal centre for the Welsh kingdom of Brycheiniog, which roughly corresponded to the area of Brecknockshire. It was a time of conflict between neighbouring kingdoms, and the island, created from layers of rocks and brushwood shored up by timber stakes, would have been a haven. Access would have been by causeways that were often concealed just beneath the surface of the water as a deterrent against would-be intruders. But despite these advantages, the Llangorse crannog was short-lived. Excavations between 1989 and 1993 (including the early Time Team dig) revealed that the site came to a fiery end just twenty or so years after it was built – it seems that the royal fortress may have been attacked by an English army. There is an account in the *Anglo-Saxon*

▼ The crannog today – the only example of such a structure in Wales.

Chronicle of a Mercian force destroying a Welsh site in this area in 916, and that site was probably Llangorse.

Archaeology of crannogs

Time Team has now worked on three crannog sites and they are fascinating places for archaeologists. Because of the muddy, watery environment, you get good preservation of organic material around the edges of the island, and this enables information to be gathered on diet, agriculture and other aspects of life, which tend to disappear on dryer sites. As well as the timber for ring-dating, at Llangorse we found wattles from buildings still preserved in the mud. The archaeological teams from the National Museums and Galleries of Wales and Cardiff University, who worked at the site for many years, collected a remarkable range of finds that show what a high-status settlement it was. Highlights include a section of an embroidered tunic and part of an enamelled case for storing religious relics. The most famous discovery from Llangorse Lake, however, was made by a local carpenter in 1925: a massive log boat constructed from a single oak tree. Radiocarbon dating has shown that it

▲ Iron Age log boat made from a single oak tree, discovered in 1925 by a local carpenter.

was built in a similar period to the crannog, and doubtless many more of these essential vessels came to rest in the muddy depths of the lake.

Analysing and conserving such a range of finds takes years. Archaeologists working on the Llangorse material believe they have found the bones of early Corgi-type dogs at the site, possibly the first known from Wales. Corgis were originally used for herding cattle, the bones of which have also been found at the crannog, but perhaps the kings of Brycheiniog were as partial to the breed as their modern counterparts!

■ **GETTING THERE** Llangorse Lake is 8 miles SE of Brecon, Powys, off the B4560. See www.brecon-beacons.com or telephone 01874 622485 for details. No buildings survive, but the island can be viewed from the lake shore.

■ **OUR VIEW** The lake is in the Brecon Beacons National Park and a beautiful spot to visit. It's worth a trip to Brecknock Museum in nearby Brecon to see the massive log boat from the lake.

Conwy Castle
The Welsh castles of Edward I

1283-1655

THE 13TH CENTURY was a great period for castle construction. Stone masons became increasingly skilled at building huge structures that often used ideas taken from Crusader castles in the Middle East. However, the expense of building and equipping castles meant that eventually only the king could afford them, and even then only just. It has been estimated that Edward I's construction of major castles in Wales in the late 13th century cost him over £75,000 – a modern equivalent would be around £75 million.

Edward I and Llywelyn ap Gruffudd

After the Norman Conquest, a large area of Wales had come under the control of Anglo-Norman lords. However it was never fully conquered – north Wales, in particular, remained independent to some degree – and during the 12th and 13th centuries there was continual conflict and political wrangling between Welsh rulers and the English monarch. When Edward I came to the English throne in 1274, the powerful north Welsh prince Llywelyn ap Gruffudd refused to pay him homage, and so two years later the king launched a massive invasion of Wales to subdue Llywelyn and his supporters. By 1283, Llywelyn was dead, and Edward had completed a vicious campaign to stamp out rebellion in Wales.

Edward was a seasoned military campaigner, and knew he needed a strong network of castles across Wales to secure his conquests. In some locations, such as Carmarthen, Montgomery and Cardigan, he refortified and updated existing castles, but in others he built

▶ *Aerial view of Conwy Castle and the fortified town. The two bailey areas inside the castle walls are surrounded by eight enormous towers. This view shows how access to the sea was essential for supplying the castle.*

new castles from scratch. He particularly focused his construction efforts on creating an 'iron ring' of fortresses around north-west Wales that were designed to prevent further rebellion in this troublesome region, and to this day they are recognized as one of the most spectacular and ambitious military systems in medieval Europe. Edward began with Flint and Rhuddlan castles, and the ring eventually extended as far south as Aberystwyth, but the most famous castles are undoubtedly Harlech, Caenarvon, Conwy and Beaumaris (on Anglesey). Beaumaris was the last in the line and failed to be finished. Caenarvon is sometimes regarded as the finest, but Mick is most keen on Conwy, regarding it as 'brilliant', and for breathtaking views and imposing architecture, I think it is hard to beat.

Master James of St George

The most fascinating aspect of Edward's castles is that we know the name of the Italian architect he used to create his vision of the perfect fortification: Master James of St George. Both Edward and his architect were familiar with Crusader castles, and they employed the latest in state-of-the-art military design when building the Welsh castles – and you can see this at Conwy. The best way to understand the castle's magnificent design is to climb to the top of one of the round towers. From here, you will be able to see the ring of defensive works that made the castle virtually impregnable. There are over 1,200m (1,300yds) of wall at Conwy, much of which is an astonishing 6–8m (20–26ft) thick. As Mick says, Conwy was a more straightforward structure than some of Edward's other fortresses, and very workmanlike – 'a real working castle'. It consists of one massive curtain wall with eight vast circular towers around the perimeter and two bailey areas inside, containing the living

▶ Safe in the knowledge that Conwy was the best fortified castle in the region, Edward's troops could exert their control over the Welsh.

quarters, king's chamber and great hall. The genius of the design is that every section of the curtain wall can be seen and defended from elsewhere, making it very difficult to attack.

Mick points out that Conwy has a rather unusual and charming feature tucked into the eastern end of all this war-like architecture – a small garden. It's a reminder that medieval castles were royal residences as well as fortresses, and a garden would doubtless have provided a haven of peace for the king when he was campaigning from here.

When you look at the view from the tower, the incredibly strong position of the castle, perched on top of a rocky outcrop looking down over the town and harbour, also strikes you. Conwy, like most of Edward's Welsh castles, was placed so it could be supplied by ship. In the event of the castle being besieged by land, this provided – given Edward's command of the sea – a secure source of reinforcement via a fortified quayside.

Conwy town walls

As well as building the network of castles, Edward created a fortified town to go with each to enable him to introduce English settlers to the region. At Conwy, the town defences are pretty much intact, and it is reckoned to be one of the finest medieval defended towns in Europe. The town walls stand 9m (30ft) high, with 21 circular towers along the three-quarter-mile route and three fortified gateways. Like the castle, they display cutting-edge military design. Each tower contained a wooden bridge that linked the walkways

along the top of each section of wall. Removing the bridges enabled each section of wall to be isolated if attackers had managed to scale it. The 480 firing positions around the town are carefully located to ensure a perfect, uninterrupted view of attackers outside the walls.

Mick also recommends a visit to the parish church. It has a typically English look but is in fact the church of what was a Cistercian abbey, which Edward had moved when laying out the town.

▲ The massive towers that guard the perimeter wall still dominate the landscape today.

■ **GETTING THERE** Conwy Castle is in Gwynedd, north Wales. See www.cadw.wales.gov.uk or telephone 01492 592358 for opening times and other details. There is an admission charge.

■ **OUR VIEW** Test out Edward's military design by visiting Tower 13 on the town walls. It's the highest point on the circuit and set forward from the walls so when you look down you get a clear firing view of the gate and the stretches of wall adjacent. For a bit of a contrast, Mick is particularly fond of Robert Stephenson's Victorian railway bridge, right next to the castle, built with dramatic mock fortifications.

Blaenavon
Industrial revolution ironworks

1789-1902

WHEN MICK FIRST SAW the massive arches of the water balance tower at Blaenavon, he said it reminded him of a Mayan temple, and I knew exactly what he meant. The tower is on a truly monumental scale and is just one of the many elements that make the 18th- and 19th-century ironworks at Blaenavon so impressive and important. It was one of the biggest ironworks in the world when it was built, and it remains today the best-preserved complex of its type anywhere. The founders took advantage of the latest technology available and from the start the works were equipped with steam-operated, coke-fired blast furnaces. The water balance tower which so impressed Mick was revolutionary when it was built in 1839 – it used water as a counterweight to lift trucks and wagons up to the higher levels of the complex.

The founders of the ironworks chose Blaenavon because the landscape around contains all the resources needed to produce iron: coal, iron ore, limestone and water. Producing pig iron in the blast furnaces was just one stage of a complex industrial process which began with quarrying and mining the necessary raw materials, then transporting and treating them. One of the many reasons why Blaenavon is so special is that evidence of all these processes survives in the landscape around the ironworks.

At the ironworks themselves, you see how cleverly they have been built to take advantage of the natural contours of the landscape. Up on the hillsides above the furnaces was the system of railway lines that brought materials from the quarries to be prepared in ancillary ovens and kilns before being tipped into the top of the furnaces. The pig iron then ran out of the bottom into casting houses, and the ingots were lifted from the production houses to transport them away across the valley.

Lost viaduct
When Time Team excavated at Blaenavon in 2001, we worked with local archaeologists to find one very specific feature relating to the ironworks. In 1790, the first arched railway viaduct in the world was built there to carry coal to the top of the blast furnaces. Twenty-five years later it had totally disappeared.

▼ The water balance tower, which enabled iron production to be carried out on a massive scale.

We had only a few old maps and one illustration to guide us, and it was one of our most tense investigations – we had no idea whether the viaduct had been destroyed, and few clues as to whether we were even looking in the right place.

In the end, radar and GPS triumphed. We dug our biggest hole ever, and at the end of the third day discovered the viaduct 15m (50ft) down. As Phil and I looked into the hole, he reminded me that we were looking at the *top* of the viaduct, which stretched many more metres down below that into a valley now totally buried by slag tipping. It brought home to me what a powerful force the industrial revolution was. It changed people's lives, and at places like Blaenavon, it completely altered the landscape itself in just 200 years.

The workers

As well as the industrial landscape, an incredible amount of evidence for the social conditions at Blaenavon survives. There are preserved remains of the first workers' houses on the site, and we excavated some more lost ones on Time Team too. There was little local population to draw on when the works were built, so the owners had to bring skilled labour from elsewhere and build accommodation for them. As the works developed, more and more workers were needed, and the accommodation became more and more cramped.

The town of Blaenavon grew up around the works as they became larger and more successful, and although it has a rather forlorn air these days, it's well worth a stroll around the streets. It's one of very few south Wales industrial towns that has largely escaped modern

development. My favourite building is St Peter's Church – built in 1804 with cast-iron pillars, font and gravestones, it's a monument to the local industry.

During Time Team, we watched some casting of iron on a small scale, and the heat and noise generated by the process made us realize what the site must have been like in its heyday, in operation 24 hours a day, with roaring furnaces, clanking trucks and red-hot molten iron flowing into moulds.

The Blaenavon site was just one of many ironworks in the area, and together they made south Wales the leading producer of iron and coal in the world during the 19th century. It was here that many technological advances were put into the large-scale production that would fuel the industrial revolution.

Iron from south Wales was transported to other industrial areas of Britain to be turned into machines and consumer goods, and was used to create the rails, bridges and other structures that were exported throughout the growing British Empire.

▲ *Engine Row, Stack Square – a row of workers' houses which has been preserved. Workers would have been able to see the furnaces from their front doors.*

■ **GETTING THERE** Blaenavon is 6 miles N of Pontypool, Gwent, off the B4246. See www.cadw.wales.gov.uk or telephone 01495 792615 for opening times and other details. Admission charge.

■ **OUR VIEW** If you have time, don't just go to the ironworks, but head out into the beautiful hills surrounding them to appreciate the site in its context. www.world-heritage-blaenavon.org.uk/ has many fascinating aerial photographs and maps.

Other sites to visit

❶ Llyn Cerrig Bach

The island of Anglesey in north Wales has, in Llyn Cerrig Bach, one of the most important ritual sites in Britain. At one time a natural lake, the site is now boggy; it was discovered during the Second World War when RAF engineers were building a runway to service the nearby airforce base.

Llyn Cerrig Bach is a spectacular site on an island already renowned for prehistoric artefacts. The excavations in 1943 uncovered a multitude of Iron Age deposits. Archaeologists found weapons, chariot fittings, tools, cauldrons, horse bridles, currency bars and slave chains.

It is unlikely that items of such prestige would have been needlessly discarded, and so it is believed that the objects were purposefully deposited in the lake as religious offerings to lake-dwelling deities. Furthermore, the practice of casting such objects into watery sites is typical of Iron Age custom, with many similar finds evident throughout Europe.

Recent radiocarbon dating suggests that the finds originate from 500BC to around AD100: a late Bronze Age and Iron Age date range.

■ **LOCATION** 1 mile S of Caergeiliog, Anglesey; off A5.

■ **ACCESS** Only a small part of lake survives; on MOD property. Finds on display at the National Museum of Wales, Cardiff: see www.nmgw.ac.uk or telephone 029 2039 7951 for opening times and other details.

A circular plaque with an embossed Celtic design and a well-preserved bridle bit from the hoard at Llyn Cerrig Bach. The plaque was probably a chariot fitting, and the bridle bit once part of a chariot pair. The bridle bit, in particular, demonstrates the skills of the Iron Age bronze-workers.

❷ Llys Rhosyr

Lying on the periphery of Niwbwrch (Newborough) on Anglesey, Llys Rhosyr (*llys* indicates royal court) has been the recent subject of archaeological investigation attempting to find out more about the golden age of Welsh independence. Llys Rhosyr was one of the royal courts of the Princes of Gwynedd during the 13th century, and the epicentre of Welsh rule in the middle ages.

In 1282–3, this rule was brought to an abrupt halt by the invading English forces led by Edward I. This resulted in the death of Llywelyn ap Gruffudd, the last true monarch of Wales. Llys Rhosyr was of no use to Edward and, over the centuries, it was allowed to become buried by sand blown in from the coast.

The result of its abandonment to sand was that, after careful excavation, Llys Rhosyr was discovered to be quite well preserved, with long stretches of the perimeter wall and several major buildings remaining. It was found that the original layout incorporated a series of disconnected rooms. Evidence that the individual rooms were in the process of being linked up suggests that a large-scale expansion had been under way before the English invasion.

None the less, the architecture was essentially simple, and it is believed that the royal lifestyle at Rhosyr was curiously unluxurious. The discovery of modest ring brooches, pottery and a few coins doesn't indicate great affluence, but the Palace in the Sand remains a fascinating relic from the era of Welsh royalty.

■ **LOCATION** Newborough, SW Anglesey; off A4080.

■ **ACCESS** Site now in a field; visit audiovisual display at Prichard Jones Institute in Newborough: telephone 01248 440888 for opening times and other details.

▷ *A caver examining one of the impressive chambers in the Great Orme copper mines. These Bronze Age mines can be visited by members of the public.*

BRONZE AGE MINES

❸ Great Orme

The picturesque Great Orme country park in north Wales is home to the largest Bronze Age copper mine in the world that can be visited by the public. Positioned a mere mile from the centre of Llandudno, the Great Orme copper mines have been excavated by archaeologists since 1987.

Since that year, 100,000 tonnes of waste left over from 18th- and 19th-century mining have been removed to reveal entranceways into a network of ancient mines, while surface archaeology uncovered a remarkable prehistoric landscape. Archaeologists have surveyed 5 miles of tunnels that date from between 1860BC and 900BC. One large cavern was seen to have been mined over 3,500 years ago.

What is believed to be one of the world's largest collections of prehistoric tools has been found in the mines – over 3,000 stone hammers and 30,000 bone tools have been unearthed so far. It is estimated that nearly 1,800 tonnes of copper metal was mined at Great Orme during the Bronze Age, making it almost certainly one of the predominant copper sources for Britain during this period.

■ **LOCATION** Great Orme Country Park, Llandudno, Conwy.
■ **ACCESS** See www.greatormemines.info or telephone 01492 870447 for opening times and other details. Admission charge.

NEANDERTHAL PRESENCE

❹ Pontnewydd Cave

The most widely known cave in the 'Denbighshire cluster', Pontnewydd Cave is on the side of the Elwy valley in north-east Wales. Digs have been carried out here since the 1800s but it was when the cave was used as an ammunitions store during the Second World War that its true archaeological worth was uncovered – for within it lay the evidence of the earliest human presence in Wales.

Excavations at Pontnewydd, including those by the National Museum of Wales between 1978 and 1995, have yielded an array of important stone artefacts and animal bones. However, it was the discovery of human teeth and bone fragments that was of most significance. These findings revealed that the cave had been used by Neanderthal hunter-gatherers some 225,000 years ago.

It is believed that the Neanderthals sheltered for warmth in the cave. A study of the teeth found at Pontnewydd showed that they all had taurodontism, a characteristic short-rooted feature common in Neanderthal teeth. The tooth and bone fragments came from a range of ages, from young children to adults, and were discovered alongside stone tools including hand-axes knapped from volcanic rock and flint flakes manufactured using the 'Levallois' technique, a style of flint-working that attempted to remove identical-sized flakes from a flint core.

Animal bones found at the site indicate the wildlife in the area and, therefore, the diet of this early human species. Horse, deer and rhinoceros may have been hunted for food, while the skull of a brown bear found at the site indicates that the cave was an ideal shelter.

■ **LOCATION** Pontnewydd, Denbighshire, 6 miles NW of Denbigh; off B5382.
■ **ACCESS** No public access.

INDUSTRIAL ENGINEERING

❺ Pontcysyllte Aqueduct

The 41 miles of the Llangollen Canal take you from Nantwich in Cheshire, across Shropshire and into the Llangollen valley of Wales. Work began in 1793 to create a canal to connect the river Severn with the river Dee. Construction of the waterway required some considerable engineering feats, including the

Ellesmere tunnel and Chirk tunnel and aqueduct, but by far the most incredible achievement is the Pontcysyllte aqueduct over the river Dee, which took ten years to build and completed the canal in 1805.

Built out of 19 interconnecting cast-iron trough sections, each just over 3m (11ft) wide, the aqueduct stands at over 36m (120ft) high on stone supports. On one side is a narrow towpath complete with handrail, while the opposite side finishes in a small lip just inches above the waterline. This gives the canal-boat passenger an almost unreal feeling of floating across the valley in the sky. The Pontcysyllte aqueduct is a masterful and iconic piece of engineering by the pioneering civil engineer Thomas Telford.

■ **LOCATION** 5 miles E of Llangollen, Denbighshire; off A5 or A542.
■ **ACCESS** Public access to towpath across aqueduct. See www.waterscape. com and search for 'Pontcysyllte' for further details.

ECCLESIASTICAL STATUS

❻ St Davids

St Davids is the smallest city in Britain, granted city status in 1995. In essence it's a small village that fences the magnificent cathedral of St David and the impressive ruins of the Bishop's Palace on their eastern and southern sides.

Founded as a monastery on the Pembrokeshire coast, possibly as early as the 6th century, St Davids has witnessed Viking raids, earthquakes, vandalism by parliamentary soldiers and pilgrimage by thousands of visitors. The core of the cathedral that can be seen today is the huge 12th-century nave of the cruciform church originally built in 1176. Successive development, particularly

◀ *This view of the Pontcysyllte aqueduct from the river Dee demonstrates the determination and skill of the canal builders of the industrial revolution.*

through the 13th and 14th centuries, has resulted in an impressive building that is a dramatic sight when approached from the village.

A reminder of the power of St Davids' bishops can be seen in the imposing ruins of the Bishop's Palace. This bold work was largely developed under the influential bishop Henry de Gower in the 14th century as a symbol of status worthy of receiving important guests. Of particular note are the round window in the east gable of the great hall and the chequered pattern of stone courses in the upper sections of the walls.

■ **LOCATION** St Davids, Pembrokeshire; on A487.
■ **ACCESS** For the Bishop's Palace, see www.cadw.wales.gov.uk or telephone 01437 720517 for opening times and other details. Admission charge.

▼ *View from the top of St David's Cathedral down onto the opulent remains of the Bishop's Palace. Henry de Gower's magnificent great hall is in the background.*

BURIAL MONUMENT
❼ Carreg Coetan

Surrounded by a housing estate on the outskirts of Newport, Pembrokeshire, Carreg Coetan is a fine example of an early Neolithic portal-dolmen monument. The portal-dolmen is a mortuary-monument style favoured in this region, consisting of a large stone slab held aloft by standing stone pillars.

Contrary to the early antiquarians' belief that these monuments were once covered with a mound, current archaeological thinking is that they were chambers with their contents open to the elements. This goes some way towards explaining the scarcity of finds associated with them.

Carreg Coetan holds a capstone measuring 3.2m (10ft 6in) long and 2.7m (9ft) wide. Experimental archaeology has recently shown that, although the capstone is of great weight, only a small number of people are needed to lift it when

wedges and levers are properly employed, by gradually easing up the stone and packing the cavity. This leads to the consideration that portal-dolmen could have been family monuments rather than larger community affairs. Excavations at the site in the late 1970s and early 1980s uncovered fragments of Neolithic pottery and cremated human bone.

■ **LOCATION** 2 miles E of Newport (Trefdraeth), Pembrokeshire; off A487.
■ **ACCESS** Pedestrian access to stones from housing estate.

EARLY HUMAN BURIAL
❽ Paviland Cave

Excavations at Paviland Cave in the Gower peninsula in the 1820s resulted in an outstanding set of finds. Thousands of flint tools and items of worked bone identified the site as an Upper Palaeolithic occupation area dating back some 30,000 years, a time when modern humans were establishing themselves as the dominant species.

As one of the richest sites of its kind in Europe, the cave also held a remarkable secret: the remains of an early human burial. When the remains were discovered in 1823 it was thought they belonged to a woman because of the associated grave goods of bone and shell bracelets and pendants. The ceremonial burial was also covered in red ochre, which had stained the remains and grave goods red. However, later analysis revealed that the 'Red Lady of Paviland' was in fact a man of around 21 years of age.

This incredible find is a window into a very early phase of human development, a time when the UK was still part of the same continent as Europe and mammoths roamed the landscape. The very fact that the remains were buried and then adorned with colour and trinkets is proof of care by others within the group at the time of death. This indication of a sense of purpose, or appreciation of an afterlife, is an early sign of the development of conscious thought in humans.

■ **LOCATION** 2 miles SE of Middleton, Gower peninsula, West Glamorgan; off B4247.

■ **ACCESS** No public access to cave, which is very dangerous. 'Red Lady': Oxford University Natural History Museum. See www.oum.ox.ac.uk or telephone 01865 272950 for opening times and other details.

▲ ▶ *The dramatic view out to sea from the interior of Paviland Cave in the Gower, and an artist's impression of the prehistoric burial in red ochre that was discovered to have taken place in the same spot.*

MEDIEVAL SEAFARING

❾ Newport Ship

Affectionately christened the 'Welsh Mary Rose', the Newport Ship is a wonderfully preserved example of medieval maritime history. It was discovered accidentally in 2002 when excavation works for a new arts centre were under way on the banks of the Usk in central Newport. Following its discovery the ship was very nearly lost again until a massive public outcry and campaign ensured its safety for further study and the city council agreed to the construction of a dedicated conservation centre.

Amazingly, the hull of the ship is largely intact and ring-dating indicates that the timber came from trees felled between September 1465 and April 1466. Uniquely, some of the rigging had survived. The true length of the ship has been estimated at 25m (82ft) and certain characteristic features resemble those attributed to Viking longships. The construction of the hull involved overlapping a series of oak planks before inserting timber 'ribs' to strengthen the frame.

Archaeologists have determined that the ship had been trading with Spain and Portugal, following the discovery of coins, pottery, clothing, lumps of cork and engraved brass straps originating from those countries.

■ **LOCATION** Newport, Gwent; on M48.
■ **ACCESS** Site is now an arts centre with an audiovisual display about the ship. No public access to timbers. Arts Centre: www.newport.gov.uk or telephone 01633 656757.

ROMAN LEGIONARY LIFE

❿ Caerleon

Caerleon needs little introduction, as it is arguably one of the most important and varied Roman sites in Britain. It was strategically significant to the Roman Empire in their fight to quell the stubborn resistance of the powerful Silurian tribe.

▲ The impressive oval-shaped Roman amphitheatre at Caerleon contained eight sections of tiered seating that could hold up to 6,000 spectators.

Known as Isca to the Romans, Caerleon was a formidable fortress and permanent home of the Second Legion Augusta (*Legio II Augusta*), which boasted a force of 5,500–6,000 men and guarded the region for over 200 years. The fortress was built on this location because it was defendable against attack and was close to the Usk estuary. In 1909, the first formal excavations were carried out, and in 1926–7 30,000 tons of soil were removed to unearth the impressive amphitheatre that could hold up to 6,000 spectators and was used for military display and sporting competition.

The 20-hectare (50-acre) Caerleon site is rectangular in shape and at one time was protected by a deep ditch and timber palisade, before the erection of a fortified stone wall (*c.* AD100). It reveals a great deal about how the legion lived, with the remains of legionary life still clearly visible today, including ruins of barrack blocks and communal latrines. Excavations have also shown that the legionaries enjoyed the conveniences of a substantial bathhouse and leisure complex – such were the innovations of the Roman Empire.

■ **LOCATION** 1 mile NE of Newport, Gwent; off M48.
■ **ACCESS** See www.cadw.wales.gov.uk or telephone 029 2050 0200 for opening times and other details.

MESOLITHIC FOOTPRINTS

⓫ Goldcliff

Goldcliff is located on the Gwent levels near Caldicot in Monmouthshire, on the north side of the Severn estuary. Archaeological excavation and survey have revealed an evolution of the land that can be traced back to Mesolithic times. The discovery of stratified Roman pottery and animal bones suggests

and charred grains, but even these are overshadowed by the discovery of 8,000-year-old footprints preserved in the Goldcliff clay. The footprints are those of an array of adults, teenagers and children, and provide an affecting snapshot of a moment in Mesolithic life.

■ **LOCATION** 3 miles SE of Newport, Gwent; off A455.
■ **ACCESS** Open coastal site, accessible all year round.

ROMAN TOWN

⑫ Caerwent

Known to the Romans as Venta Silurum, Caerwent is one of Britain's most significant Roman sites. The Latin name is a reference to the local tribe of Silures, who ferociously opposed the Roman advance into south Wales. The locals were eventually suppressed (around AD75), subsequently 'romanized' and left to manage their own affairs, establishing Caerwent as their capital.

Although relatively small, Caerwent was prosperous and quite wealthy with substantial stone-built town walls (a 5m-high (17ft) section survives today), commercial buildings, houses, basilica, courtyards and a small Romano-Celtic temple. At the height of its power, Caerwent could house 3,000 people – the largest concentration of civilian population in Wales. This number was neither matched nor surpassed for 1,500 years.

Caerwent is a small, tranquil village today, but as a thriving market town about two millennia ago it was a fine example of the influence of the Roman occupation on ancient Britain.

■ **LOCATION** 1 mile NW of Caldicot, Monmouthshire; off A48.
■ **ACCESS** See www.cadw.wales.gov.uk or telephone 029 2050 0200 for opening times and other details.

that the salt marshes around this area were first drained by the Romans (possibly from nearby Caerleon) to increase the amount of agricultural land.

Further study has revealed timber structures (among which are eight rectangular buildings) preserved since the Iron Age, while human skull deposition and wooden structures dating to the Bronze Age have also been found. However, the most exciting finds in recent years have been those related to the Mesolithic period. Painstaking work has unearthed tiny flint tools (microliths)

◀ *The well-preserved bastions of the Caerwent curtain wall are particularly fine on the south side and still retain their Roman facing stone.*

⓭ Tintern Abbey

Set deep in the Wye valley, Tintern Abbey precinct is a remarkably complete and in many ways classic example of a medieval monastic ruin. Walter de Clare, Earl of Chepstow, founded the abbey in 1131, as a 'daughter' house to the l'Aumone abbey in France, and it was run by Cistercian monks for around 400 years. It became one of the wealthiest monasteries in Wales thanks to rich patrons bestowing lavish gifts.

The present remains date from the late 13th and early 14th centuries – the abbey was expanded and rebuilt between 1270 and 1301. In 1349, the Black Death impinged on life at the abbey but it continued to function for a further 200 years until Tintern was surrendered to the ownership of Henry VIII during the dissolution of the monasteries. In time, the lead was plundered from the roof and the abbey was left to decay. Overrun with ivy, the architecture was saved in 1782, and thanks in particular to the writings of Wordsworth and the paintings of Turner, visitors soon swarmed to Tintern to view the abbey.

The abbey's consummate construction has ensured the survival of towering moulded arches, intricate carvings and delicate traceried windows. The surrounding landscape is impressively framed by lancet windows at either side of the chapel. Now under the care of Cadw, Tintern Abbey is one of Britain's outstanding historical architectural achievements.

■ **LOCATION** 6 miles N of Chepstow, Monmouthshire; on A466.
■ **ACCESS** See www.cadw.wales.gov.uk or telephone 029 2050 0200 for opening times and other details. Admission charge.

▶ *Tintern Abbey viewed from St Mary's church. Cistercian monks all over Europe chose remote valleys to site their monasteries in. The Wye valley provided a perfect setting.*

Heart of England

Within this relatively small central region is a range of sites representing an extraordinary cross-section of archaeological survival. They vary from the vast Roman remains of Wroxeter to Iron Age hillforts and the earthworks of Offa's Dyke, and major medieval monuments such as Kenilworth and Warwick castles. There are also some of the country's most beautiful cathedrals, such as Worcester, and from more recent times the Coalbrookdale and Ironbridge Gorge sites, which, along with Birmingham canals and early manufacturing sites such as Soho, are part of a rich legacy from the industrial revolution.

N

1 Oswestry
2 Offa's Dyke
3 Richard's Castle
4 Stokesay
5 Wroxeter / Ironbridge / Wrekin
6 Wedgwood Factory
7 Castle Ring
8 Boulton and Watt Factory / Birmingham
9 Back to Backs
10 Avoncroft Museum
11 City of Coventry
12 Lunt Roman Fort
13 Warwick Castle
14 Wasperton
15 Goodrich

STOKE-ON-TRENT

STAFFORD

SHREWSBURY

Kenilworth Castle and Priory

WARWICK

LEAMINGTON SPA

HEREFORD

A53
M6
A49
A5
A518
A34
M54
M6 (Toll)
M42
A442
A456
A44
A49
M40
A46
M5
M6

0   20 m
0   20 k

Wroxeter
Lost Roman city

1st to 5th centuries AD

THE ROMAN CITY of Wroxeter is an unusual site. Unlike many other Roman cities, such as London or Colchester, its successor, Shrewsbury, grew on a different site so Wroxeter has largely escaped modern development, which means it's incredibly well preserved. It still has some of the largest sections of standing Roman stonework in Britain, and Guy de la Bédoyère recommends a visit particularly to see these remains.

Like many Roman settlements, Wroxeter developed on the site of a former Roman fort. There was a timber legionary fortress there by the mid-1st century, located near to the Wrekin – a strategically important Iron Age hillfort, and tribal centre for the Cornovii. By AD87 the fort had been replaced by an urban settlement, partly populated by retired soldiers and taking its name – Viroconium Cornoviorum – from the local tribe. From this, Wroxeter grew to become the fourth largest city in Roman Britain. From the 1st to 3rd centuries it would have been an important administrative site controlling a range of local government functions, including taxation and land ownership.

Wroxeter has been known about for a long time, but most of the evidence for what it was like has come from archaeological investigations by Roger White and Philip Barker, begun in 1966 and continued today by Birmingham University. Because the city isn't buried beneath modern buildings but fields instead, it's a rare chance to look at the layout and development of the city. As Time Team's own Mr Geophizz, Chris Gaffney, says: 'Wroxeter is in my top ten sites list. It was the first ever complete gradiometer survey of a Roman town anywhere. Wonderful geophysics.'

The city lay next to the river Severn, and the Roman road Watling Street ran from London to Wroxeter. The earthwork ramparts that surrounded the city can still be seen in the fields today, and inside this, a grid plan of streets was laid out.

When you visit the site, it's hard to imagine a bustling city of 5,000 people where the fields are now, but the excavations have shown how densely populated Wroxeter was, and the standing masonry gives the best clue to how impressive its buildings must have been. The main area you can visit today represents one block at the heart of the city, where the magnificent 2nd-century public baths were located. What really catches the eye is the 'Old Work'. This huge archway originally divided the exercise hall from the bath complex and its facade would have been richly decorated. The city aqueduct and sophisticated timber and lead pipes could supply millions of gallons of water to its occupants, where it was available in the bath facilities and public fountains.

Under Hadrian, around 130, the public forum and basilica were dedicated. An inscription commemorates the event, and it may be that Hadrian visited Wroxeter when he came to Britain about 122 and ordered the building work. Excavation has shown that the forum burnt down in the late 2nd century.

All around the public buildings would have been houses, commercial and industrial districts and trading stalls. Guy de la Bédoyère points out that the inhabitants of the city had access to a whole range of sophisticated trading goods, and the recent discovery of a harbour on the Severn suggests that these were arriving by boat as well as along Watling Street.

◄ The 'Old Work' at Wroxeter is one of Roman Britain's largest pieces of upstanding masonry. It marks the doorway from the baths (foreground) into the vast covered exercise hall beyond.

The end of the city

Wroxeter is a good example of how Roman towns and cities thrived and declined according to political and economic conditions. During the early (Flavian) period, the city baths were begun but never finished. When the city's development speeded up under Hadrian, the new public baths that survive today were created and Wroxeter began to expand. Similarly, one of the most exciting archaeological revelations was the discovery that formal buildings of timber were erected after the deterioration of the stone buildings in the 5th and 6th centuries, in and around the ruins of the town baths. By this time, many Roman settlements, such as Bath, appear to have been abandoned, but Wroxeter seems to have continued.

However, Guy de la Bédoyère points out that although there is evidence for timber buildings it is probably something of an exaggeration to imply that there was continuity of sophisticated Roman life after the 4th century. In some way these timber buildings were a poor substitute for the Roman architecture that preceded them, and at Wroxeter the remains of the baths are a testament to the skills of the builders of the 2nd and 3rd centuries.

■ **GETTING THERE**
Wroxeter is 5 miles SE of Shrewsbury, Shropshire, off the B4380. See www.english-heritage.org.uk or telephone 01743 761330 for opening times and other details. Admission charge.

■ **OUR VIEW**
Wroxeter isn't that far from Ironbridge, and its peaceful atmosphere is a good contrast to the crowds there. English Heritage has a small museum at Wroxeter which includes multimedia reconstructions of the city's past, and artefacts found during the excavations. The village of Wroxeter itself, which lies just by the Roman city, is an attractive place to visit.

Kenilworth
England's largest castle ruins

12th to 17th centuries

THERE ARE FEW medieval castles in England as impressive as Kenilworth, and Mick is one of its biggest fans, partly because he likes its ruinous state and partly, as he puts it, 'you can tell what's going on'.

Geoffrey de Clinton founded an Augustinian priory at Kenilworth at the same time as the castle. The king had given him a manor, called originally Kenelphsworth, and he built the castle on this estate. It started out as a modest motte-and-bailey timber castle, located to take advantage of a peninsula of land overlooking a low-lying marsh, and you can still see the large mound of earth that formed the base of the motte.

Within a few decades, the castle had become a powerful stronghold – too powerful to remain outside royal control, and Henry II confiscated it, and began a process of alteration and rebuilding that was to last for hundreds of years. As you enter the castle today you will be aware of the number of gatehouses, ditches and defensive buildings in different styles you have to cross to get into the central area. Castles, and improving them, became an obsession with their owners and came near to bankrupting even the richest.

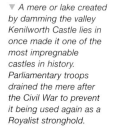
▼ A mere or lake created by damming the valley once made it one of the most impregnable castles in history. Parliamentary troops drained the mere after the Civil War to prevent it being used again as a Royalist stronghold.

Kenilworth Castle lies in

Henry II was responsible for the massive keep which still dominates the site today, while King John spent in excess of £1,000 – a huge amount of money – on developing and enhancing the defences, including an outer wall which was built according to the most up-to-date ideas of castle construction.

The siege of Kenilworth

In the 13th century, the castle was granted to Simon de Montfort, Earl of Leicester and brother-in-law of Henry III. He made a number of improvements to the fortifications, including strengthening the water defences that made Kenilworth virtually impregnable. However, de Montfort became the leader of a group of barons who rebelled against the king and was killed in battle in 1265. His son and supporters holed up at Kenilworth the following year, and the longest siege in English history ensued. The castle was so well fortified that the rebels held out against royal forces for six months, only being finally defeated by the king cutting off their supplies of food.

Although the buildings are impressive, the castle's most dramatic feature was the huge lake or mere that surrounded it, which has now disappeared. It was one of the crucial defences, but it must also have been a grand sight seeing the castle reflected in the water. The lake was created early on in the castle's history by damming the valley the castle lies in, and covered a vast area. The best way to appreciate this is to climb the stairs near the great hall. From the top, a large proportion of the fields you can see behind the castle were once underwater. In the distance, at the other end of the mere, was 'the pleasance', a moated island built in 1414 as a retreat and place of entertainment for the king and his visitors. It was a convenient and discreet boat ride away from the castle and had a dock to receive large boats.

Queen Elizabeth's visit

In the Tudor period, the castle became the seat of Robert Dudley, Earl of Leicester, one of Queen Elizabeth I's favourites. Leicester spent lavishly, modernizing the medieval castle to turn it into a fashionable Tudor palace in anticipation of Queen Elizabeth's visits. Her final stay at Kenilworth, in 1575, complete with an entourage of several hundred, has become legendary. She was entertained with lavish displays on the mere, which included the building of a mock floating island, and fireworks and music – the festivities are said to have been the inspiration for Shakespeare's *A Midsummer Night's Dream*. They cost Leicester an incredible amount of money, and nearly reduced him to penury.

Kenilworth was an important royalist stronghold during the civil war, but couldn't withstand long-range cannons. It was eventually partially dismantled by parliamentary troops to prevent it being used again. Sadly, the mere was drained at the same time.

The priory that Geoffrey de Clinton had founded at Kenilworth at the same time as the castle flourished throughout the middle ages but was largely demolished during Henry VIII's dissolution in the 16th century. Most of the stone was used by Robert Dudley to build extensions at the castle. Mick recommends a visit to the priory and the town parish church which has a rather fine Norman porch.

■ **GETTING THERE**: Kenilworth, Warwickshire; on the A452. For the castle, see www.english-heritage.org.uk or telephone 01926 852078 for opening times and other details. Admission charge. The abbey gatehouse survives in the public park.

■ **OUR VIEW** A marked trail goes across the fields behind the castle – the fields are the site of the great lake and it can still be muddy at times. It's worth persevering, though, as it takes you to the surviving earthworks of the pleasance, and you get the best views of the castle from here. Mick, along with other archaeologists, would like to see the mere reflooded!

Ironbridge Gorge and Coalbrookdale

Industrial revolution birthplace

18th and 19th centuries

I F YOU ASKED MICK where you should go to experience one of Britain's most unique and telling contributions to world history and development, you might be surprised if he suggested this backwater of Shropshire as a starting point. And yet the Ironbridge and Coalbrookdale area was the site of the important transition from individual craftsmanship to industrialized production that characterized the industrial revolution of the 18th century.

In fact, the vital resources of the Coalbrookdale area on the river Severn were being exploited long before the 18th century. Coalmining and quarrying for limestone and clay had been carried out since the medieval period, and by

the 16th and 17th century there was a flourishing water-powered iron-smelting industry, albeit on a small scale. Mick likes to point out that medieval monasteries were good at exploiting local resources, and that many of the industrial growth spots in this country seem to have had monasteries near them. The Cistercian abbey of Buildwas is near Ironbridge, and perhaps an entrepreneurial spirit sprang up locally with the need to supply bits of metalwork for the abbey.

Innovation

A combination of new discoveries in the early 18th century launched the massive success of the Ironbridge and Coalbrookdale area. Industrial pioneer Abraham Darby began experimenting with using coke (made from coal) instead of charcoal to smelt iron, and his Coalbrookdale Company blast furnaces were producing coke-smelted pig iron by 1715. When Time Team investigated

▼ By the 18th century these water wheels were being replaced by steam engines.

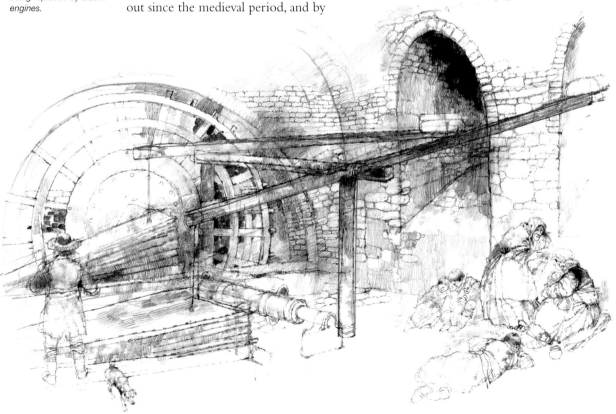

◄ *The area gradually expanded throughout the 1700s to include small factories producing a wide range of products.*

an early blast furnace at Leighton, near Ironbridge, a few years ago, Phil tried his hand at making charcoal the traditional way, and after witnessing the laborious and chancy process of producing charcoal, and the relatively easy production of coke in comparison, it emphasized for me the improvements that the new technology offered. Making charcoal is incredibly labour- and timber-intensive, making it an expensive fuel and hard to procure in large amounts. Meanwhile Mick had had a chance to look at iron-working and tried his hand at producing cannon balls, and came away deeply impressed by the skill of the iron-casters.

At the start of the 18th century, steam was also beginning to replace water as a major source of power. Steam engines were first used in the Coalbrookdale area to pump water from coalmines and recycle water at the ironworks, and, later, to directly power the blast furnaces and

other ironworking machines themselves. By 1800, there were about 200 steam engines working in the area.

In the course of 100 years, the Coalbrookdale and Ironbridge area totally changed, and by the second half of the 18th century it had become one of the leading suppliers of iron goods in the world. Factories, furnaces and mining operations spread throughout the valleys near by. Ironworking was constantly being improved by the introduction of new technologies, and cast iron was used to create millions of goods. The main importance of the area lies in the inventive solutions its pioneers had to mass production problems, which ultimately led to the modern industrial world. Domestic and agricultural items such as guns, cooking pots and scythes could be produced in vast numbers, but iron was also used in other new technologies: the Coalbrookdale

▲ One of the best views of the Ironbridge, showing the way individual iron components were built to form the structure.

Company supplied cylinders for the new steam engines, and was a major player in the development of railway transport, making iron rails.

The iron bridge

The iron bridge, which spans the river Severn and gives the area its name today, was the brainchild of a local architect, Thomas Farnolls Pritchard, and its component parts were cast at Darby's Coalbrookdale Works. Built between 1777 and 1781, it was the first iron bridge in the world, and was designed as a showpiece for the iron industry. As soon as it was finished, it drew admiring visitors from all over the globe, and continues to do so today. The best way to look at it is not from above, but from below. Although this is a cast-iron structure, it still has the look of something made from pieces that 100 years earlier could have been made of timber. Here we have the sense of transition – the form is similar but the material has changed, and it demonstrates the ability of the industrial process to produce endless numbers of a similar strength and shape.

to, eventually made this unviable. By the Second World War, much of the ironworks was derelict, but in 1963 an innovative trust was launched to save the evidence of this industry, and in 1986 Ironbridge became Britain's first World Heritage Site.

Today the area has ten museums dedicated to its industrial past, and if you have the stamina you can see every aspect of life at the birthplace of the industrial revolution, from the early ironworks in Coalbrookdale, to the houses of the industry owners and workers, and the canals and warehouses that serviced the factories. However, you have to use your imagination to conjure up the atmosphere. The quiet, almost rural scene you see today at Ironbridge suggests more what the area was like before Abraham Darby arrived, before it was transformed into the 'dark satanic mills' of the 18th and 19th century, with furnaces belching smoke and flame.

▲ The design of the bridge also included aesthetic elements to enhance its appearance.

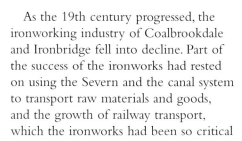

As the 19th century progressed, the ironworking industry of Coalbrookdale and Ironbridge fell into decline. Part of the success of the ironworks had rested on using the Severn and the canal system to transport raw materials and goods, and the growth of railway transport, which the ironworks had been so critical

■ **GETTING THERE**: Ironbridge is 2 miles W of Madeley in Shropshire, on the B4373. See www.ironbridge.org.uk or telephone 01952 884391 for opening times and other details. Admission charges to museums.

■ **OUR VIEW** The iron bridge itself, in Ironbridge Gorge, is the most popular spot, but don't miss the Museum of Iron and other attractions in neighbouring Coalbrookdale, where Abraham Darby started out.

Birmingham Canals
Arteries of early industry

1767-1930s

THESE DAYS, FREIGHT transport in Britain is dominated by road and rail, but before the advent of the railways, water transport was the only way to move the huge tonnage of raw and finished goods that the increased production of the industrial revolution generated. For a relatively brief but vitally important

period from the middle of the 18th century onwards, a complex canal system was built and became the lifeblood of the British economy, linking new centres of industry and expanding cities like London, Birmingham and Manchester.

Canal-building in Britain took off in the second half of the 18th century, and by the end of the century had reached the peak often referred to as 'canal mania' because of the large number of canals being built. They were seen as a good speculation and business opportunity, and many different routes were proposed and

▶ This canal-side complex in the centre of Birmingham would have been teeming with activity in the 18th and 19th centuries.

built. Canal-building was a rather chaotic industry, with a variety of companies and investors responsible for building different stretches piecemeal and negotiating with other canal owners to join up with them and agreeing tolls. While the major canals became essential arteries of the industrial revolution, many others weren't successful at all, built on inadvisable routes or suffering from heavy competition or business problems. Anyone wanting to build a new canal required permission by Act of Parliament before beginning construction.

Navigation company

Birmingham was located in a key place for water transport, at the natural crossroads of many of the longer river and canal routes, from Manchester, Liverpool and the north-east, to Bristol and London in the south. In addition, it lay in the 'Black Country' – some of the most important areas of mineral resources and production during the early industrial revolution. In 1767, the Birmingham Canal Navigation Company was formed, and the first stretches of canal were completed within a few years. The system

▶ *Gas Street Basin was where many canals met. From here routes headed south to London and north to Manchester.*

grew over many years, as piecemeal construction by different companies resulted in the Birmingham area being served by five major, and many other smaller, linked canal routes. Hundreds of wharves and private stretches were added to link businesses into the system, and overall it consisted of about 160 miles of canal, some open-air, some in tunnels, making it the most extensive urban waterway in the world.

Birmingham lies on a high plateau, and getting so many canal routes across this high ground at all required serious engineering. Complex locks were used to transport water and vessels up and down the canals, but each opening and closing of the 200 locks involved some loss of water from the system, so rivalry and negotiations about building new

canals was fierce as existing owners tried to ensure that their water supply, as well as trade share, wasn't compromised. Huge reservoirs were needed to keep the water supply going for the whole network and some still survive today. The famous engineer Thomas Telford made major additions to the system in the early 19th century to carry the increasingly large amount of traffic, dropping the level of the canals by 6m (20ft), and creating much straighter, more efficient cuttings, as well as building the Edgbaston reservoir to serve new stretches of canal.

Originally many of the canal boats were horse-drawn, and when the long canal-tunnel system needed to be navigated, the boatmen would 'work' the boats by lying on their backs and treading on the tunnel roofs to push the

Gas Street Basin

The key convergence point for two of the biggest Birmingham canals – the Worcester and Birmingham Canal and the Birmingham Canal Main Line – was the Gas Street Basin (so named because it was the first road in the city to have gas lighting installed), and it was in many ways the heart of the canal network for the whole country. Today, the canals there survive, although most of the industrial buildings around have been lost to modern development, and as Mick points out, what you can see there today looks a lot different from the dirty, smoky and busy place it would have been in its heyday.

If you go there, look out for the Worcester Bar. This was the barrier that separated the two canals and prevented one losing water to the other. All goods had to be unloaded and transported over the bar to continue their journey, until a narrow passage was created to allow the boats through.

The growth of the railways in the mid-19th century signalled the end for the canals, which couldn't compete with them commercially over long distances. The Birmingham Navigations survived longer than most because local industry was dependent on them, but the system slipped into a steady decline, with commercial transport largely finished by the 1930s.

Today, there has been a renaissance in the canals as leisure and water resources, but their future is far from secure. These canal systems are unique: evidence for the sheer power of the industrial revolution and its ability to transform working and the management of resources.

boats along. However, with the advent of steam engines and steam pumps to move the water and vessels around, the whole system became more efficient. At its height the canal complex was working 24 hours a day carrying heavy bulk goods such as coal, grain, stone and lime. Over 100 boats a day passed through Birmingham alone, and it was possible to send large consignments of goods from Manchester in the north to London in the south. The Birmingham canals were essential to local industry as well, moving huge amounts of coal from the collieries around the region.

■ **GETTING THERE**
Gas Street Canal Basin, Birmingham B1, is especially recommended. For other details, telephone the Canal Information Centre on 0121 632 6845.
■ **OUR VIEW** Steam power was crucial to the development of the canal system, where it was used to pump water. It is well worth visiting some of Birmingham's excellent industrial museums to see contemporary steam engines at work.

Other sites to visit

IRON AGE HILLFORT

❶ Oswestry

A mile north of Oswestry, this outstanding Iron Age hillfort is one of the best examples of its type in the country. The complicated western entrance is supported by an incredible seven sets of ramparts, which thin down to a further five sets constructed around the low hill. The complete defences enclose more than 6 hectares (15 acres).

This imposing feature of the landscape was probably first settled in the Bronze Age, but later 6th-century defences led to repeated phases of development until the formidable site was finally abandoned as a permanent settlement after Roman invasion. An interesting feature are the earthworks integrated into the western entrance. Their purpose is unknown but it has been suggested that they were either for the storage of water or the result of quarrying.

■ **LOCATION** 1 mile N of Oswestry, Shropshire; off A483.
■ **ACCESS** See www.english-heritage. org.uk for opening times and other details.

▲ *Seven sets of ramparts were built to defend Oswestry Iron Age hillfort. It remains a dominant feature of its local Shropshire landscape.*

CONTENTIOUS EARTHWORK

❷ Offa's Dyke

King Offa ruled the western kingdom of Mercia from AD757 to 796. According to Bishop Asser, who wrote the *Life of King Alfred* in 893, during his fiery reign Offa ordered the construction of a defensive feature to guard Mercia from the Welsh.

The lengthy earthwork that can be seen today, running 182 miles from Sedbury near Chepstow to Prestatyn in the north, is commonly known as Offa's Dyke, but archaeological research has shown that this mixed continuous and broken line is in fact several different defensive features. Work by the University of Manchester has identified the Offa's Dyke turf-cut bank and ditch as running for 64 miles from Rushock Hill near Hereford to Treuddyn south-west of Chester.

The defences leading the path to the sea further north belong to what is now known as the Whitford Dyke, a self-contained defence with its own double-ditched style. The patchy defences south of Rushock Hill, though probably contemporary, appear to be more broken in their plan. However, the river Wye provides a natural obstacle from north of Hereford to the Severn, so the odd sections of bank and ditch could simply represent the strengthening of weak points rather than a separate

▶ *The earthwork feature known as Offa's Dyke runs for an impressive 182 miles and was originally built to defend the western kingdom of Mercia against the Welsh.*

feature altogether. The dating of the complete monument is not easy and it continues to be a matter of contention.

■ **LOCATION** 3-mile section, 3 miles NE of Chepstow, Monmouthshire; off B4228.
■ **ACCESS** See OS Landranger map 162 for footpaths. Visitor centre at Knighton; www.offasdyke.demon.co.uk or telephone 01547 528753 for opening times and other details.

PRE-NORMAN CASTLE

❸ Richard's Castle

The modern village of Richard's Castle on the Shropshire–Herefordshire border has a history that dates from before the Norman invasion of 1066. The castle from which the village takes its name stands in a ruinous state on a hill to the east of the village. Excavations in the 1960s suggested that the original motte-and-bailey site could date to 1050, making it one of the very few pre-Norman castles in Britain.

The position of the castle takes advantage of the natural topography to require a 27-metre (88ft) climb from ditch to motte plateau on the western side. A south-eastern entrance to the bailey is provided by a causeway across the ditch. During the 12th century, an octagonal stone tower was constructed on the motte and St Bartholomew's church was founded outside the bailey.

Though in the hands of the influential de Mortimer family for nearly 200 years, Richard's Castle was always liable to take second place against the larger local seats of Wigmore and Ludlow. However, by the late 14th century the castle held over 100 burgage plots (building plots leased from the local lord) and a regular market.

The compact plan of castle, church and village at Richard's Castle are a classic unspoilt site, probably because the economic and geographical position of the settlement didn't allow it to develop further into a town like nearby Ludlow.

■ **LOCATION** ½ mile NW of Richard's Castle, Shropshire; off B4361.
■ **ACCESS** No public access but can be viewed from church.

FORTIFIED MANOR HOUSE

❹ Stokesay

This manor house in the village of Stokesay, near Ludlow, is the best-preserved fortified manor house in Britain and a fine example of how the upper classes modified and remodelled their homes to fulfil

their aspirations of greater social standing.

By the 13th and 14th centuries it became common for lords and earls to apply to the king for a 'licence to crenellate', which bestowed permission to fortify manors and houses with defences as security against potential intruders. These licences were highly sought after, as it was both an honour and a privilege to crenellate your home and it reflected a high status within the community.

In 1291, permission to crenellate Stokesay Manor was granted to Laurence of Ludlow, a rich wool merchant who had purchased the property ten years earlier. Ludlow successfully combined a comfortable residence with defensive structures that have altered remarkably little since the late 13th century and even escaped destruction during the Civil War. Among the many features that have survived to this day are the Great Hall with gabled windows and original wooden staircase, the timber-framed Jacobean gatehouse that was added in 1640, and the solar chamber that contains a large fireplace with an intricately carved overmantle. Stokesay Manor was restored in the 19th century and further repairs were carried out by English Heritage in the 1980s.

■ **LOCATION** 2 miles S of Craven Arms, Shropshire; off A49.
■ **ACCESS** See www.english-heritage. org.uk or telephone 01588 672544 for opening times and other details. Admission charge.

HILLFORT

❺ Wrekin

The Wrekin is a 407-metre (1334ft) hill that dominates the landscape between Shrewsbury and Telford and is the most distinctive landmark in

▶ *Stokesay was awarded the 'licence to crenellate' in 1291, allowing the manor house to be fortified. This was a mark of status for its owner.*

Shropshire. Past belief claimed that the Wrekin was an extinct volcano, while local legend would have it that a giant was responsible for its presence. Neither is true!

The ridged summit of the Wrekin holds the remains of a large hillfort that was begun in the Bronze Age and completed by the Celtic Cornovii tribe in the Iron Age. Up until the 1st century AD, the Cornovii used the hillfort as a base of administration, a trading centre and as an obvious place of refuge at times of conflict. In general, hillfort design ensured that they were difficult to capture, as the Romans found when they laid siege to the Cornovii's Wrekin stronghold.

Natural geological defences were supplemented by massive earthen ramparts supporting wooden palisades, while solid gates on top of a steep slope defended against unwelcome access from the enemy. Nevertheless, the Cornovii were eventually defeated and relocated near to the fort at Viroconium – present-day Wroxeter (see page 120).

The prominent earthworks of the hillfort are evident in the form of the inner and outer lines of defence that were so typical of Iron Age defensive sites. In addition, excavations have revealed that the fort had been occupied some three to four centuries before the arrival of the Romans.

■ **LOCATION** SW of Wellington; 2 miles NW of Little Wenlock, Shropshire.
■ **ACCESS** See OS Landranger map 127 for footpaths around the fort.

WORLD-FAMOUS POTTER

❻ Wedgwood Factory

Burslem is just one of the six old towns that make up Stoke-on-Trent in the heart of the Potteries region. It's also the birthplace of world-famous potter Josiah Wedgwood.

In 1998 Time Team opened a number of archaeological trenches outside the Old Town Hall, finding the site of Wedgwood's Ivy House pottery and also uncovering evidence belonging to the man who produced some of the most exquisite china in the world.

The team's digging confirmed the historical record. In 1758 Josiah became a master potter when he leased the Ivy House pottery from his cousins, Long John and Thomas, who were themselves famous for producing salt-glazed stoneware. With a small group of workers Josiah experimented on a variety of glazes in his huge bottle kilns. While still in his late twenties he developed the beautiful cream-coloured earthenware for which he became famous. The trenches not only uncovered masses of pottery but also the base of a Wedgwood bottle kiln.

■ **LOCATION** Burslem, Stoke-on-Trent, Staffordshire; on A50.
■ **ACCESS** Wedgwood Museum: www.wedgwoodmuseum.org.uk or telephone 01782 282818 for opening times and other details. Museum galleries closed until 2006 for refurbishment. Admission charge.

▼ Huge bottle kilns at the Wedgwood Etruria factory. Josiah Wedgwood put beautiful earthenware within reach of many people for the first time.

❼ Castle Ring

Castle Ring is an Iron Age hillfort that holds a prominent position north of Burntwood, next to the Heart of England Way. Its striking location provides outstanding views across the Trent Valley and the diverse natural environment of Cannock Chase. The hillfort is five-sided and the construction of the banks and ditches has been dictated by the topography of the landscape. The more vulnerable south and south-eastern sides are protected by up to five banks and ditches, whereas the western and northern sides have only two because of their naturally steep position.

The original entrance is to the east where there is a break in the bank. Parts of the earthwork defences still stand to 4m (13ft) high and the whole enclosure covers some 3.2 hectares (8 acres).

■ **LOCATION** 3 miles N of Burntwood, Staffordshire.
■ **ACCESS** See OS Landranger map 125 for footpaths around the fort.

❽ Boulton and Watt Factory

In 1761, next to the Hockley Brook in Handsworth, Birmingham, Matthew Boulton established a small factory for coin making, which he called the Soho Manufactory. Time Team excavated the site as part of the 1997 broadcast series, and the archaeology uncovered there marked a fascinating phase of the industrial revolution.

In 1773 Boulton went into partnership with engineer and inventor James Watt and the steady production of Watt's steam engines commenced at the site. Watt's design was incredibly efficient and his engine was used to pump water out of coal and tin mines at a rate higher than any other manufacturer's model could. Watt soon developed his basic

machine into a much more versatile rotary steam engine. Before long the Boulton and Watt engines were installed in over 500 factories and mines, fuelling the industrial revolution. By 1786 Boulton even powered his coin machines by steam.

■ **LOCATION** Handsworth, Birmingham.
■ **ACCESS** Nothing survives of factory. Matthew Boulton's Soho House is open to the public. See www.birmingham. gov.uk or telephone 0121 554 9122 for opening times and other details.

❾ Back to Backs Museum

The Back to Backs museum in Birmingham is a homage to the way thousands of working people lived in the industrial centres of the 19th century. Back-to-back houses, as the name suggests, were built backing on to each other around tiny courtyards and often consisted of only three small rooms. People were effectively packed into these houses, creating densely populated areas to feed the insatiable growth of the factories.

Many of the houses, though overpopulated with extended families, also turned a room over for a wage-earning workshop. The living

▲ *Workers and their families were packed into back-to-back houses in cities like Birmingham. A museum commemorates the way the workers of the industrial revolution lived.*

conditions were cramped and unsanitary with few amenities, and it would have been almost impossible for the inhabitants to prevent them becoming sites of squalor and disease. This type of inadequate housing was banned in 1876.

Business tenancies enabled Court 15 in Hurst Street to survive demolition and these, the last three remaining back-to-back houses in Birmingham, have been painstakingly restored by the National Trust and the Birmingham Conservation Trust. The expert restoration has divided the housing into four different periods, each reflecting the people and the cultures that lived in the area from 1840 to the late 1970s. Visitors walking through the rooms can also learn about what it was like to live in the houses from the first-hand accounts of people who lived there.

■ **LOCATION** Inge Street and Hurst Street, Birmingham B5.
■ **ACCESS** See www.nationaltrust.org.uk or telephone 0121 666 7671 for opening times and other details. Admission charge.

❿ Avoncroft Museum

Two miles south of Bromsgrove in the heart of the Worcestershire countryside, the Avoncroft Museum of Historic Buildings has earned a reputation as one of the best open-air museums in the country.

The museum opened in 1967 following the eleventh-hour rescue of the timbers from a 15th-century house in Bromsgrove which had been scheduled for destruction. This timber-framed Merchants House became the first building to be repaired and then re-erected on the 6-hectare (15-acre) site where the museum now stands.

Since then, the Avoncroft museum has saved, restored and rebuilt over 25 buildings, which include a working 19th-century windmill, a rural Victorian toll cottage and a Victorian gaol. Most of the buildings are from the Midlands region and together they offer an architectural, social and historical outlook that spans 700 years. There is even a 1940s prefabricated house to be seen, and the museum is also home to the National Telephone Kiosk collection.

■ **LOCATION** 2 miles S of Bromsgrove, Worcestershire; off A38 bypass.
■ **ACCESS** See www.avoncroft.org.uk or telephone 01905 763888. Admission charge.

⓫ Coventry

Following the heavy bombing of Coventry during the Second World War, large areas of the city were gutted and to a great extent the surviving medieval origins of the city were destroyed. The new city centre was constructed after the war, but with archaeological excavation, historical records and survey of the surviving old buildings, a picture of Coventry's medieval past can be put together.

Starting out around the 10th century as a small Saxon woodland settlement with a few surrounding communities, the area began to develop with the founding of a Benedictine priory by Leofric, Earl of Mercia, in the early 11th century. At the beginning of the 12th century the administration of the growing settlement was split in half between the prior and the earl, and this led to continuing disputes between the two. At this stage the cloth trade became the staple economy of Coventry.

The bustling town was becoming a centre of industry, and 12th- and 13th-century deeds record that Spon Street was home to countless woaders, dyers, fullers and tanners – all particularly unpleasant-smelling jobs. The finer trades of tailors and weavers were conducted around Earl Street. By the 1400s the town had become the fourth-biggest producer of cloth in the country.

Buildings of particular note to be seen today include the ruins of St

▼ *The beautiful medieval meeting room of St Mary's Guildhall in Coventry with its antique furnishings and middle ages glass window.*

Michael's Cathedral, destroyed by bombing in 1940, and the beautiful St Mary's Guildhall just a short distance away, which was first established in 1342.

- **LOCATION** Coventry, West Midlands.
- **ACCESS** Cathedral: www.coventry cathedral.org.uk or telephone 024 7652 1200; St Mary's Guildhall: www.coventry museum.org.uk or telephone 024 7683 2565 for opening times and other details.

ROMAN CAVALRY

⑫ Lunt Roman Fort

Lunt Roman fort at Baginton dates to AD60 and was established at this location near Coventry after the Boudiccan revolt. Excavations at the site through the 1960s and 1970s uncovered a large gyrus, or enclosed ring, possibly for the training of horses. As these are rare in other Roman fort designs it has been suggested that Lunt could have acted as a central training depot for the Roman cavalry, who would have forwarded the trained horses to other units.

The position of the gyrus on the eastern side also affects the shape of the fort, which does not follow the standard 'playing card' pattern. Archaeological excavation has also highlighted some of the phases of the fort. It appears that the site was developed over three phases during its early years before it was abandoned for some time, then reconstituted in the 3rd century.

Today the site displays a reconstruction of a timber gateway copied from depictions on Trajan's column in Rome, together with a granary (the site's museum) and the gyrus. The foundations of other buildings within the fort, including the headquarters or *principia*, can also be seen.

- **LOCATION** Baginton, Coventry, West Midlands.
- **ACCESS** See www.coventrymuseum. org.uk or telephone 024 7683 2565 for opening times and other details. Admission charge.

▲ Aerial view of Warwick Castle with its impressive stone defences. It was originally built as a timber motte-and-bailey fortification, then rebuilt and strengthened many times in its history.

MEDIEVAL CASTLE

⑬ Warwick Castle

Warwick Castle, one of England's finest medieval castles, was originally built as a timber motte–and–bailey fortification by William the Conqueror in 1068. It stood on a sandstone bluff overlooking a bend in the river Avon, defended by the steep river cliffs on one side and a dry moat around the rest. Its critical strategic and defensive position in the heart of England meant the castle was rebuilt and strengthened many times in its history. In the 14th century, Thomas, the 12th Earl of Warwick, completed the impressive stone defences that still dominate the castle today, including Caesar's Tower, the gatehouse and barbican, and Guy's Tower. The earls of Warwick were supremely powerful landowners and politicians in the middle ages, the 15th-century earl

Richard Neville earning the title 'Warwick the Kingmaker' for his vital influence on the Crown during the Wars of the Roses.

As the military importance of the castle declined, the castle was remodelled by the earls as a palatial residence. In the 17th century, Fulke Greville rebuilt parts of the 14th-century castle, including the Great Hall, to suit Jacobean tastes, and many of the Victorian interiors, created after a devastating fire in 1871, survive today.

- **LOCATION** Warwick.
- **ACCESS** See www.warwick-castle. co.uk or telephone 0870 442 2000 for opening times and other details. Admission charge.

⑭ Wasperton

Excavations in the 1980s at Wasperton, south of Warwick, in advance of a gravel-extraction programme, uncovered a fascinating cemetery.

The period of the Romano-British to Anglo-Saxon transition in the 5th century is often regarded as being shrouded in the sort of confusion that would inevitably be caused by the withdrawal of an efficient administration and the filling in of the vacuum by the remaining locals, along with the influence of newly settling peoples from the continent. However, the term Dark Ages reflects more our lack of understanding of this time than the reality, which seems to be that of a thriving culture in some areas. Archaeologists are constantly re-evaluating the evidence of the time, and sites like Wasperton have been invaluable.

A total of 182 burials were discovered on the site, together with 25 cremations, providing evidence for continued use of the cemetery from the Roman period through to the Anglo-Saxon. Of the burials recovered, 36 are of Roman date, while 137 are Saxon. The material is still being studied but Wasperton appears to offer us an insight into the transition from Roman to Saxon periods. Both cultures practised burial with grave goods, and some of the remains are of individuals who were buried wearing Roman-style hobnailed sandals but accompanied by Saxon personal items.

■ **LOCATION** 4 miles S of Warwick; off A429.
■ **ACCESS** Nothing survives of site. Some of the finds are displayed in Warwickshire County Museum: www.warwick-uk.co.uk or telephone 01926 412500 for opening times and other details.

▶ *Historic Goodrich Castle, photographed in the last light of a winter's evening. Documents reveal the lifestyle of the Marshal family at the castle some 700 years ago.*

⑮ Goodrich

A note in the Domesday Book mentions a Godric Mappeston who held the Goodrich Castle area in 1086. Though this could have been the first fortification here, the only surviving early defence is the later 12th-century keep, a particularly fine example with a first-floor doorway (later turned into a 15th-century window) and a chevron-styled projecting course two-thirds of the way up.

The 13th century saw the construction of the main body of the castle, complete with three heavy drum towers and the chapel tower, gatehouse and solar chamber, by

William Marshal and his sons. The castle passed to William de Valence in 1247 when he married Joan, heiress to the Marshal family estates. A late-13th-century manuscript recording her expenses provides us with a snapshot of her lifestyle some 700 years ago, including her fondness for fish and the well-stocked wine cellar she kept for entertaining.

In the 14th century the castle passed to the Talbot family and another phase of development resulted in the outer ward walls and the barbican entrance. The Talbot family also established an Augustinian priory near the castle.

During the Civil War (1642–8) the castle was occupied at different times by both the Royalists and the Parliamentarians and was eventually made uninhabitable as a precaution against it being used for further defence.

■ **LOCATION** 5 miles S of Ross-on-Wye, Herefordshire; off A40.
■ **ACCESS** See www.english-heritage. org.uk or telephone 01600 890538 for opening times and other details. Admission charge.

East of England

Between 300,000 and 200,000 years ago, Clacton-on-Sea in Essex was the site of early stone-tool production. A yew spear-point found here is also the country's only surviving wooden artefact of this period. Production on an almost industrial scale also occurred much later, in Neolithic times, at Grimes Graves in Norfolk. Eastern England's low-lying landscape gave rise to one of our best-known Bronze Age sites: Flag Fen. In the Iron Age, Norfolk was the heartland of Queen Boudicca of the Iceni. After the Roman period, eastern England saw incursions from the Germanic countries, and East Anglia contains our highest density of early (400–500s AD) Anglo-Saxon remains. Sutton Hoo in Suffolk has revealed what is almost certainly an Anglo-Saxon royal burial of the early 7th century, in a ship, the dead man surrounded by the most spectacular collection of artefacts known from this period.

N

2 Snettisham
A148
KING'S LYNN
3 Castle Acre Priory
A140
NORWICH
GREAT YARMOUTH
A47
4 Norwich Castle
PETERBOROUGH
1 Fengate
Flag Fen
A141
A10
A11
Grimes Graves
A1
Isleham Priory Church
5
West Stow
A140
6 Moulton
A14
CAMBRIDGE
A14
BEDFORD
A505
Sutton Hoo
14
MILTON KEYNES
M1
IPSWICH
Orford Ness
A12
A6
M11
LUTON
A1
Colchester
12
7 St Albans
10 Cressing
13 Clacton-on-Sea
WATFORD
8 Waltham Abbey Gunpowder Mills
CHELMSFORD
A12
0   20 m
0   20 k
M25
11 Bradwell-on-Sea
A130
Tilbury Fort
9
SOUTHEND-ON-SEA

Grimes Graves
Stone Age flint mine

4000-2500BC

IF YOU'D VISITED Grimes Graves in the 19th century, you would have had trouble interpreting what was going on. The strange pockmarked landscape attracted a wide range of interest, and the first excavations were carried out in 1868 by Canon Greenwell. These revealed the existence of deep shafts dug into the chalk to the point where they exposed black bands of flint.

One hundred and four years later, the Reverend Greenwell's trench was exposed again by one Phil Harding Esquire, and as you might expect this is one of Phil's favourite sites. Phil tells the story of Greenwell digging the site using a group of Cornish miners, whose skills and familiarity with mining geology enabled them to get to the base of the shaft from where, we now know, galleries

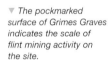
▼ The pockmarked surface of Grimes Graves indicates the scale of flint mining activity on the site.

radiate out into the seams of flint. Having reached the gallery level, as Phil puts it, 'the somewhat infirm canon was lowered down and shown the galleries by the miners. They then winched the old B up and filled the hole back in.' Greenwell's lack of persistence meant that Phil and his team were able to excavate the galleries and work in areas not visited since the Neolithic period. They found grooved-ware pottery and dozens of antler picks.

Early technology

An antler pick is the key piece of technology used in digging Neolithic mines, and their strength, and the skills required to use them, are impressive. Around 300 or so antlers were found at Grimes Graves; providing them must have been a major cottage industry at the time. They were used both as picks to extract the flint and as hammers to create axes. Having seen Phil at work with an antler on a piece of flint, I know how amazingly durable and effective it can be. In the case of Grimes Graves, the antlers

were often trimmed to produce one strong main point that was used to prise out the flint and undermine the lower level of chalk and clay, causing the stone to collapse under its own weight.

The team which included Phil was not the only group of archaeologists to go shaft digging at Grimes Graves. Over 35 of the shafts have been excavated, including some by a group of unemployed Dutch miners.

Floorstone

When you visit the landscape of Grimes Graves today you enter a strange lunar–like area marked with vast burrows and shafts, and when you go down a shaft you should be able to see a band of black 'floorstone' rather like a skirting board. Phil describes it as 'black as your hat', and you can still see the scoring marks where they removed the clay to undermine the flint. Floorstone was a highly desirable type of flint, in part perhaps because of its deep black hue, but also because it flaked easily and was less flawed than other types of flint.

Surprisingly little evidence has been found around the site to suggest the complete processing of axes and other implements. It seems that they would have selected the best bits, carried them to the surface and then processed them, possibly into a roughed-out form. Tools called discoidal axes were also being made, and in some cases these have been found polished and ground. Many of these axes had to be given a haft, and it was likely that they were taken and traded in their roughed-out form, and finished and hafted nearer to the point of use.

The flint from Grimes Graves is of an incredibly high quality. This means that it has relatively few impurities and is very high in silica. If there was one object I would like you to be able to hold it would be a Neolithic polished and ground axe. To produce these takes a

◀ The gallery level shows the main areas where the flint was mined.

great deal of time, and they have an intrinsic beauty that takes them across the boundary from utilitarian object into minor work of art. They are, however, incredibly effective. Phil, for a Time Team programme, felled a tree with one, and this kind of thing makes you realize that bands of Neolithic farmers would have needed little time to clear a forest to plant their crops.

Grimes Graves is the biggest flint mine site in the country; it looks like our first 'industrialized' mining landscape. As Phil says, 'When you think of all the human endeavour that went into shifting that chalk to get at the flint, you can't help but be impressed by it, and by the Neolithic workers' knowledge of mining techniques and geology.' The business of excavating on this scale only serves to emphasize the skills of the early workers. A wide range of knowledge and abilities were needed for deep mining. It's impressive that this was achieved with antler picks as the main tool.

■ **GETTING THERE** Grimes Graves is 7 miles NW of Thetford, Norfolk, off the A134. See www.english-heritage.org.uk or telephone 01842 810656 for opening times and other details. Admission charge.

■ **OUR VIEW** Grimes Graves could be better presented – it deserves better. Local people remember walking along the galleries as kids, but now it is unsafe to do so. You can go down the path and look along the gallery, and you might be able to imagine the Neolithic miners hacking away at the chalk and finding the raw material that to them was the key part of technology. Flint mines were the oil wells of their day.

Flag Fen
Understanding the Bronze Age

2300–700BC

FLAG FEN IS ONE of Time Team's favourite sites and combines for me two magical qualities: organic preservation and ritually deposited bronze objects. We filmed at the site in 1999 and my abiding memory is of staring down at a group of our diggers covered in black organic mud, excavating in a sea of branches, logs and other wooden remains.

The site was discovered by Francis Pryor in 1982. Francis is a long-standing contributor to Time Team and he tells me that he first noticed something of interest when he tripped over a log while walking the Fens. Further inspection convinced him that it was ancient: part of the top layer of a huge amount of timber associated with a Bronze Age settlement. In terms of archaeological evidence, this is rare material.

It has been estimated that over 80 per cent of potential archaeological evidence is lost because it is made of organic material that simply rots in the ground and leaves little trace. Archaeologists are left to build their assumptions on the 20 per cent that is left. At Flag Fen you will get a chance to see what you have been missing on other sites, including pre-Roman in-situ timber.

▶ A view along Flag Fen causeway about 1000BC, with people making offerings of broken weapons to the spirits of their ancestors below the water.

The creation of bronze

Before you head out across the Fens it may be useful to get an idea of what you can expect from a Bronze Age site. We are talking of a period between 2300 and 700BC where a key piece of technology has been developed – the ability to make an alloy of copper and tin in order to create bronze. Flint is still around and Bronze Age flint arrowheads are some of the most beautiful objects of prehistory – but metal is beginning to appear, and this is being combined with skills in working wood.

Archaeologists have given the name Beaker to the distinctive set of objects found dating from around this time. The objects include pottery, knives, arrowheads and distinctive buttons, which seem to suggest an influx of either people or technical and cultural influence from the continent. This exchange of ideas may have been stimulated by the trade in the raw products needed to make bronze. It is likely that tin from Cornwall, copper from Wales and possibly gold from Ireland were all being traded and some of it was ending up at Flag Fen.

As part of the Time Team shoot we brought in an expert in ancient technology to demonstrate the casting of a bronze axe. This brought us much closer to an understanding of the process and the way both the technology and its end products have a more than utilitarian quality.

These objects would have been revered – their production carried out by a high-status minority, a secular priesthood of

▼ Francis and his team let a half-size replica of the Bronze Age causeway collapse to see what Flag Fen was like in the Iron Age.

▲ *A Late Bronze Age (9th century BC) bronze socketed spearhead found hidden among the timbers at Flag Fen.*

▶ *British houses in the Bronze and Iron Ages were round. Such houses at Flag Fen would have had reed thatch.*

skilled craftsmen who guarded their secrets. Francis talks about these objects having a birth on the casting floor and then a ritual death where they are broken and carefully deposited in the water of the marsh. It's likely that important objects may have been given names and would have existed in a world where they had a sacred magical connotation that in our time of mass production is difficult to appreciate. It may be that there is an echo of this in the traditional legends associated with Arthur, his sword Excalibur and its eventual resting place in a lake.

Around 1300BC craftsmen would have been making axes at Flag Fen, casting them in moulds and creating the wooden hafts that turn them into a workable tool. Flag Fen axes are in general socketed axes, and when you see them in the presentation centre it is worth remembering the woodworking skills that were needed to create the hafts and secure the axehead to them.

Meeting of land and water

At an early stage in the excavation Francis and his team used metal detectors and wonderful objects started appearing. Francis reckons that these may eventually run into the thousands; many can already be seen in the presentation centre. As you walk around outside, if

you are lucky you should be able to see some of the current excavation work. The reedy, marshy surroundings might not look much but you have to keep reminding yourself that this is one of the most important Bronze Age sites in northern Europe.

When you first arrive at the site, it's a good idea to get a concept of the geography of the whole area. Although the fens appear flat as you drive through them, they aren't. There are areas of slightly higher land – you could hardly call them a hill, but in this kind of landscape small differences in level are important. When it floods, or in the damper parts of the year, locals have a very clear idea where they can keep their feet dry, and to our prehistoric Bronze Age ancestors this was a critical bit of information. The places where land and water met were also important to their rituals, and it was in the water that they deposited the artefacts that Francis and his team began to discover. Having got an idea of the external geography, head towards the presentation centre where you will be able to see some of the objects they found.

Look out for one find in particular – a Bronze Age dagger from around 1000BC that was unearthed with its blade lying on top of an antler hilt; nearby were found the small oak wedges that secured

the blade into the socket. Remember that most of this material would have disappeared on drier sites. The lack of oxygen deep in the peat probably helped to preserve this dagger, and the fact that it had been deliberately pulled apart. What fascinated Francis about Flag Fen was the evidence not of grandiose gestures, but of small-scale rituals like this, where a knife was separated into its components and laid to rest in a shallow wet pool at the edge of a lake.

This was one of the essential clues for the archaeologists working at the site to understanding how Flag Fen functioned – it was a place where small groups of people came together to deposit the important personal items of someone who had died.

Another critical thing to remember as you look around the objects is that they did not come just from Britain. This society was successful and buoyant enough to draw in luxury goods including gold and jewellery from France, Austria, Switzerland and northern Italy. Here were found some of the earliest tin artefacts to be discovered in Britain, possibly from the Alps. Near by the remains of the boats that would have carried this trade have been uncovered, so this was obviously a society that was capable of contact and movement over a wide area.

Pre-Roman timber

Next stop is the preservation hall where you will see a site that is unique in the world – pre-Roman in-situ timber. Every few minutes, water containing a biocide is sprayed over the timbers, and this will hopefully preserve them for

▲ The posts of the Flag Fen causeway during excavation. It crossed wet ground, and was used from 1400 to 900BC.

another 20 years or so. Francis and his partner Maisie Taylor, who has provided her skills in ancient woodwork and conservation on many Time Teams, devised this method of preserving the ancient timber and it is not in use anywhere else. With the support of English Heritage, they have enabled you to see wood that was being constructed before the Romans landed.

The other side of Flag Fen's work has been to match up ancient tools with the timber raw material. I remember the pleasure of feeling the axe-shaped scrapes taken out of the timber, and at Flag Fen, Francis, Maisie and their team have created an amazing library of Bronze Age wood matched to the Bronze Age tools that created the structures.

More is waiting to be found at Flag Fen and Francis tells me that near to where Time Team put their last trench, a Bronze Age scabbard and a harness fitting may be pointing the way to new and exciting areas of potential excavation.

■ **GETTING THERE:** Flag Fen Bronze Age Centre is east of the City of Peterborough. See www.flagfen.com or telephone 01733 313414 for opening times and other details. Admission charge.

■ **OUR VIEW:** There's something worth seeing at any time of year. Since no two visits are likely to be the same, it's a good idea to visit more than once. If you want to understand the Bronze Age, Flag Fen should be at the top of your list of places to visit.

Sutton Hoo
Burial place of pagan kings

AD600–700

ACCORDING TO MICK, one of the most unforgettable images of British archaeology is the Sutton Hoo helmet. Not only is it a technical tour de force and a work of art, it's also a serious piece of equipment for fighting. The Anglo-Saxons had great skills in the arts of warfare. Historically, from somewhat dubious sources, we first hear of them as mercenaries employed by the British to keep other invaders at bay. Once they had begun to settle, they created their own kingdoms, and one of the greatest was in East Anglia.

In the 9th century, an Anglo-Saxon lineage was written down which included Anglo-Saxon kings going back to a founding line beginning with Woden. The lineage also has a reference to Caesar – it's worth noting that the Anglo-Saxons were influenced by the Romans, whose land they occupied, particularly in the 9th century. East Anglia was a rich agricultural area which some archaeologists consider to have been dominated between 300 and 400 by huge Roman estates. The Anglo-Saxons were able to take advantage of this rich legacy, and they were also influenced by

Roman and other continental art. It is likely that the chaotic conditions that prevailed after the departure of the Romans began to settle down around 470–80. Areas like East Anglia were settled by people whose technological skills and artistic mastery could perhaps be seen as coming to a pinnacle in the evidence at Sutton Hoo.

Saved from robbers

In order to get a better understanding of this amazing monument, we talked to Helen Geake, Time Team's Anglo-Saxon expert, who dug there in the period from 1987 to 1991 with Martin Carver's excavation, which aimed to re-evaluate some of the evidence from previous excavations. Sutton Hoo is more than one mound – it's a vast site, and the excitement of the finds at Mound One can easily obscure the fact that there are a number of other burial mounds, some of which have yet to be excavated.

The first excavations were carried out by Mrs Pretty, the owner, with a team led by Basil Brown in 1939. With war approaching, the circumstances were not ideal: many archaeologists were being called up to apply their skills to interpreting aerial photography.

Some of the mounds had been attacked by robbers, but a singular piece of luck preserved Mound One at Sutton Hoo. A medieval field boundary went over the

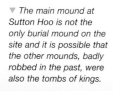
▼ The main mound at Sutton Hoo is not the only burial mound on the site and it is possible that the other mounds, badly robbed in the past, were also the tombs of kings.

◀ *The final journey of the king's boat, as interpreted by Victor.*

main mound and, by altering the shape of the barrow, made the centre appear to be some distance from its true position. A robber pit had been dug but little had been found because it was off-centre.

Nothing else like it

Helen suggests taking advantage of the visitor centre and the guided tour. The main thing to see is the reconstruction of the burial itself. This was the Anglo-Saxon equivalent of the Tutankhamen burial. A wonderfully rich tomb indicates the power and connections of the deceased, together with a range of objects including spears, bowls, gold ornaments, food and textiles, all of the finest quality. This is the most impressive set of grave goods from anywhere in Europe for this period; as an assemblage of Anglo-Saxon

objects it is unique. Helen says that Sutton Hoo is especially interesting not only for its splendour, but because it blends traditional 6th-century Anglo-Saxon influences with elements of Roman, Byzantine and Scandinavian culture. The bowl is Coptic; some of the fabrics are from Syria. The person who was buried here – and we have no evidence of his bones – had access to an amazingly wide range of contacts. We are looking at something that feels like an experiment. Archaeologists notice a package of evidence and behaviour that seems to break the mould – and doesn't particularly seem to catch on. Sutton Hoo has this quality and it stands alone in many ways. Burial in ships did not become the height of fashion, although this may have been for purely pragmatic reasons. It adds up to Sutton Hoo perhaps being something of a one-off.

▶ *An attractive and unforgettable object but also, according to Mick, a serious piece of military hardware – the Sutton Hoo helmet.*

◄ The gold buckle from Sutton Hoo. Nearly a pound of pure gold was turned into this work of art by Anglo-Saxon goldsmiths.

Anglo-Saxon decoration

The society that created the means whereby this burial could take place was clearly wealthy – it had probably inherited the Roman agricultural potential of the rich soils and large estates – and it chose to spend its money not on spectacular stone buildings but on works of personal art. All the materials and objects at Sutton Hoo are of the highest technical standard. Sutton Hoo has some of the best gold and precious stone work in Europe, and the designs suggest an artistic school of the highest standards working in East Anglia.

This richness came as a revelation, and showed that the wonderful descriptions of decoration and ornament in Anglo-Saxon literature such as *Beowulf* were not just imaginative flights of fancy. If you are lucky the gold buckle will be on one of its rare visits from the British Museum; otherwise, you will have to make do with a reproduction. This artefact ranks in many of the Time Team experts' lists as 'most amazing object'. It is nearly a whole pound of gold, and

every detail from the twirling beasts to the tiny dog biting its own leg is crafted meticulously. As a buckle it would have been unwieldy and required the support of a huge leather strap. This was an object of status, part of regalia worn on rare occasions – but by whom?

Likely candidates include Raedwald – the richest and highest-status king that East Anglia ever produced, who died around 624/5, which is right for Sutton Hoo's main range of dates, although Helen points to something of an enigma. The artwork is perhaps too well developed for such an early date, and there appears to be a strong Christian influence at work in the imagery.

The intriguing possibility is that Mounds One and Two relate to two kings who died in the same battle – Sigabert and Edric. Although Mound Two was badly robbed, some metalwork exists that appears to be by the same workshop as Mound One. If this is the case, one wonders if other kings are buried in the earlier mounds and an entire lineage is represented at Sutton Hoo.

■ **GETTING THERE** ½ mile E of Woodbridge, Suffolk, off the B1083. For site and visitor centre see www.nationaltrust.org.uk or telephone 01394 389714 for opening times and other details. Admission charge.
■ **OUR VIEW** When you visit Sutton Hoo, you are seeing one of the greatest archaeological discoveries in Europe and some of its finest objects. You can very easily imagine the excitement that Basil Brown and his team must have experienced when they brushed away the soil from the golden buckle and helmet.

West Stow
Anglo-Saxon village

AD420–650

ANGLO-SAXON EXPERT Helen Geake makes the point that before West Stow was excavated, we knew relatively little about the kind of houses Anglo-Saxons occupied in this country. The excavations at West Stow were meticulous and made the most of the good survival of materials on the site. The fine sand that had engulfed the area in the 13th century preserved organic remains, and thorough analysis produced detailed information about construction, diet and artefacts such as textiles.

Reconstruction and long-term experiments in archaeological technology have added to the interpretation of the site. Helen suggests reading through the guidebooks before you step into the village – although it is not a village in the picture-postcard sense. In this way it feels unusual in its arrangement of houses. There is no focus like a church or a village green. Helen compares it to the kind of layout you might see in a modern African village – there are no clear boundaries. Basil Brown, whose name is closely connected with Sutton Hoo, was the first archaeologist to recognize its importance.

The group of people who lived here were in the process of creating what we might call the first 'English' settlements. These early Anglo-Saxons grew crops, raised pigs, sheep and cattle and were largely self-sufficient. They were non-Christian and were buried with their possessions, symbols of their wealth and power, in a cemetery close to the village. West Stow in its structure and the kind of buildings being created was very different from the Roman predecessors – the language and artefacts, which included combs and bronze brooches, were early evidence of a society that would be an important founding element of what became England.

▶ *The exterior of a reconstructed Anglo-Saxon hut. Like much of Anglo-Saxon building, reconstruction has to be based on interpretation of limited evidence.*

Anglo-Saxon life

Along with sites like Mucking in Essex and West Heslerton in Yorkshire, West Stow helps to build a picture of typical early Anglo-Saxon dwellings. This process was helped by the fact that two of the houses had been burnt, and the charred timbers had survived better than the unburnt wood of other buildings. Of particular interest was that what had once been thought of as pits in Anglo-Saxon villages now began to look more like cellars beneath suspended floors.

It is important to note that many of the interpretations of Anglo-Saxon buildings are based on fairly slender evidence. Time Team have excavated a number of Anglo-Saxon sites and there is often a frustrating business involved in interpreting stains and postholes in the ground. Exactly what happened a few feet above them is usually conjecture. The same set of holes can give rise to a humble hall or something with elaborate carvings and woodwork in the grand Anglo-Saxon/Germanic style. We can see, however, that these structures created a significantly large space and in some we can imagine the grand feasts of Anglo-Saxon celebration taking place.

Finds around the area of the huts show that cattle were a main source of food. Quern stones for grinding corn, made from lava and originating in the Rhineland, emphasized the importance of bread in the diet.

△ *The interior of an Anglo-Saxon hut. West Stow has an excellent set of reconstructions and other resources that increase our understanding and enhance the enjoyment to be had from the site.*

■ **GETTING THERE** West Stow is 7 miles SE of Mildenhall, Suffolk, off the A1101. For the West Stow country park and visitor centre, see www.stedmundsbury. gov.uk/weststow or telephone 01284 728718 for opening times and other details. Admission charge.

■ **OUR VIEW** West Stow's visitor centre is also the entrance to the Anglo-Saxon village. It has exhibits and audio-visual displays and a shop. The excellent resources are suitable for a wide age range. There is also a good chance of seeing demonstrations of Anglo-Saxon technology and the occasional re-enactor dressed up as an Anglo-Saxon.

Other sites to visit

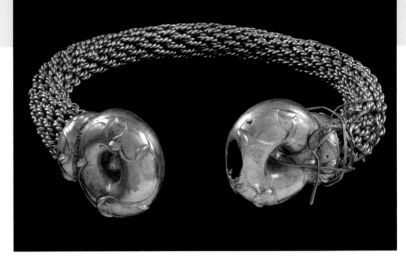

▲ *This Iron Age silver torc from around 75BC is one of many gold, silver and bronze items found in a field in Snettisham after a chance discovery during ploughing.*

PREHISTORIC SETTLEMENT

❶ Fengate

The Fengate excavations, conducted by regular Time Team specialist Dr Francis Pryor in the 1970s, shed new light on prehistoric use of the Fens. Little was known about how they were used before the work of Francis and his team uncovered evidence for established settlement throughout prehistory. A variety of excavations, including the classic Fengate farming settlement, enabled understanding of the seasonally changing Fens and how they were exploited.

Together with house platforms Francis uncovered Bronze Age land divisions in the form of an established system of field boundaries enclosing areas thought to have been used for animal husbandry. The excavations highlighted that, rather than being inhospitable bogs, the Fens presented Bronze Age and Iron Age settlers with seasonally dry lush meadows ideally suited for animal grazing. The principal site for visitors in the area today is nearby Flag Fen (see page 146), which has the reconstruction of an Iron Age roundhouse found at Fengate.

■ **LOCATION** 6 miles E of Peterborough, Cambridgeshire; off B1040.
■ **ACCESS** See www.flagfen.com or telephone 01733 313 414 for opening times and other details. Admission charge.

IRON AGE TREASURE TROVE

❷ Snettisham

A field in Snettisham, Norfolk is the site of one of the richest Iron Age treasure hoards so far discovered in Britain. The field was being ploughed deeper than usual in 1948 when the chance discovery was made of a curious piece of metal, which turned out to be a gold torc. Excavations followed and further discoveries of torcs together with coins and metal ingots were made in 1950, 1964, 1968 and 1973. It was assumed that there was nothing left to discover until a metal-detector enthusiast was granted permission to sweep the field.

Little was found at first, but in August 1990 the metal detectorist came across a large pile of scrap metal in a bronze container. The British Museum was called in and discovered a further five hoards. Greater investigation yielded a still more exciting find: seven silver and bronze torcs in a shallow pit. A larger and richer pit was also found with two bronze bracelets, two silver torcs and, most remarkable of all, ten gold torcs.

Originally thought to be a refugee hoard from Caesar's time, there is now the suggestion that the finds could be an Iceni tribal treasury. The British Museum produced an authoritative catalogue of the hoard in 1997.

■ **LOCATION** 2 miles S of Heacham, Norfolk; off A149.
■ **ACCESS** Nothing to see at excavation sites. Finds on display in the British Museum; see www.thebritishmuseum. ac.uk or telephone 020 7323 8299 for opening times and other details.

"TIS ONLY AN ACRE!"

❸ Castle Acre Priory

The village of Castle Acre, 5 miles north of Swaffham, stands on the ancient Peddars Way trail and boasts some of the best-preserved Cluniac priory ruins in the country. Castle Acre was an outstanding example of Norman town planning. It was originally built as a fortified town defended by a large bank with a ditch and gateways protecting the entrances.

Domesday reports that Castle Acre was held by William de Warenne, the 1st Earl of Surrey and close ally to William the Conqueror. De Warenne was inspired by the Cluny monastery in France – the priory at Castle Acre was constructed with this influence in mind.

The priory became a stopover for pilgrims travelling the route to Thetford, Bromholm Priory and Walsingham, and was home to a community of monks until dissolution in 1537. The 700-year-old priory ruins include a 12th-century church and a 15th-century gatehouse, and the remains of

▼ *The ruins of Castle Acre Priory are some of the best-preserved Cluniac remains in the country. The priory was once a stopover for travelling pilgrims.*

external walls are evident around the 30m (100ft) square cloister.

The priory ruins and the double-moated motte-and-bailey castle changed ownership several times until its purchase in 1615 by Sir Edward Cokes. His retort when challenged by King James (who showed concern over Cokes's growing estates) became infamous: ''Tis only an Acre I have acquired!' The Castle Acre ruins remain the property of Cokes' descendants and under the care of English Heritage.

■ **LOCATION** 5 miles N of Swaffham, Norfolk; off A1065.
■ **ACCESS** See www.english-heritage. org.uk or telephone 01760 755394 for opening times and other details. Admission charge.

NORMAN POWER

❹ Norwich Castle

The motte-and-bailey fortress that is Norwich Castle is one of many built under the Normans to subjugate the local people, and it survives as a symbol of their military and political power. Norwich Castle was built between 1066 and 1074 by Ralph de Guader, the Earl of the East and follower of William the Conqueror. Until 1165, Norwich possessed the only royal castle in Norfolk and Suffolk. The Norman keep is one of the largest in the country and was originally made up of garrison quarters, pantry, kitchen, latrines, chapel, and a private room for when the king paid a visit.

Traces of the Norman construction are still evident, such as the apse of the chapel and the fireplace in the Great Chamber. Parts of the original flint and Caen stone walling are visible too.

The castle declined in importance as a defensive site as the area became

more secure during Norwich's dominance of medieval East Anglia. The keep served as the county gaol for 650 years. During this time the stone exterior of the keep was replaced with Bath stone, eliminating some of the original texture, while the number of battlements on each side was reduced from thirteen to nine. In 1887 the gaol was closed, and in 1894 the keep was opened as a museum and art gallery, which remain open today.

■ **LOCATION** Norwich, Norfolk.
■ **ACCESS** See www.museums.norfolk. gov.uk and go to 'Norwich Castle', or telephone 01603 493625 for opening times and other details. Admission charge.

BENEDICTINE PRIORY

❺ Isleham Priory Church

Isleham Priory is an early Norman church that remains remarkably original and intact even after being converted into a barn: a process that in fact saved it from further ecclesiastical development.

The Benedictine priory was established in the late 11th century and administered under the abbey of

▶ *View from the north of Isleham Priory, an early Norman church. Its history includes being used as a barn, which in fact helped preserve it. Today it is managed as a historical site.*

St Jacut in Brittany. In the building you can see some particularly fine herringbone stonework and window details in local clunch and barnack stone. The south wall now contains a large doorway, inserted possibly as early as the 16th century to make the building suitable for use as a tithe barn. The building was used as a barn until the 1800s. Today Isleham Priory is managed by English Heritage.

■ **LOCATION** 16 miles NE of Cambridge; on B1104.

■ **ACCESS** See www.english-heritage. org.uk for opening times and other details.

PACKHORSE BRIDGE

❻ Moulton

Four miles east of Newmarket, the Moulton packhorse bridge over the

▲ *Moulton packhorse bridge was built of flint in the middle of the 15th century, and was designed with low parapets to allow loaded horses to cross easily.*

river Kennett dates from the middle of the 15th century. Belonging to the old road from Bury St Edmunds to Cambridge, the four-arched bridge made of flint includes a low parapet to allow packs of loaded horses to cross. Before this humpback design, bridges tended to be built in timber or to follow the more basic 'clapper bridge' style of stone slabs resting on piers. The Moulton bridge is one of few surviving examples of its type.

■ **LOCATION** 4 miles E of Newmarket, Suffolk; on B1085.

■ **ACCESS** See www.english-heritage. org.uk for details.

❼ St Albans

The original town of St Albans was founded on the west bank of the Ver river some time during the 1st century BC as an Iron Age settlement named Verlamion. The conquering Romans soon established their own town on the site, which became known as Verulamium. Built mainly of wood, it was severely damaged when it succumbed to Boudicca's forces in AD61. Nevertheless, the town was rebuilt and Roman occupation continued.

Around AD304, a Roman named Alban sheltered a Christian priest and subsequently converted to Christianity himself. Executed on the banks of the Ver for his crime, Alban became a martyr. In 793, King Offa of Mercia founded an abbey church on what was believed to be the execution site and the town was renamed St Albans. The stone-built St Albans abbey church was founded on the site of Offa's church in 1077.

The abbey fell victim to Henry VIII's dissolution policy and closed in 1539. From the mid-16th century, the abbey church became a school. Reverting to church use in 1870, the church was granted cathedral status in 1877 when the diocese of St Albans was created. One of the church's most fascinating aspects is that you can still see how plundered Roman brickwork was used to build it.

■ **LOCATION** St Albans, Hertfordshire.
■ **ACCESS** St Alban's Abbey and Cathedral: www.stalbanscathedral.org.uk or telephone 01727 860780. Verulamium Museum: www.stalbansmuseums.org.uk or telephone 01727 751810. Admission charge.

❽ Waltham Abbey Gunpowder Mills

In 1540, Waltham Abbey, lying on the Hertfordshire border, became the last abbey in Britain to be dissolved by Henry VIII – but the

area is far better known as being the home of the Royal Gunpowder Mills. By the time of the dissolution, the area around Waltham Abbey had developed into a market town, and 16th- and 17th-century timber buildings, such as the Welsh Harp Inn and Sun Inn, survive to this day.

The establishment of the gunpowder mills in the 17th century, however, brought industry and wealth to the town. The Crown acquired the mills in 1787 shortly before the Napoleonic Wars, which inevitably

caused a surge in demand. By the outbreak of the First World War, the Royal Gunpowder Mills employed 5,000 workers and production had progressed to technologically advanced explosives.

Production ceased in 1943 but the mills became an important research centre, and remained so until their closure in 1991. The 80-hectare (200-acre) site has 21 English Heritage listed buildings and structures, but there are also the remains of over 400 buildings. Some buildings dating

from the 1870s were designed with blast-resistant walls because of the obvious danger of working with explosives. It is believed that the gunpowder used by Guy Fawkes and the explosives used by the Dambusters were both from Waltham Abbey. Today the site has an excellent visitor centre.

■ **LOCATION** ½ mile E of Cheshunt, Hertfordshire; on B194.
■ **ACCESS** See www.royalgunpowder mills.com or telephone 01992 707370 for opening times and other details. Admission charge.

❾ Tilbury Fort

Henry VIII built the first blockhouse fort on this site to protect London from a naval attack via the Thames. However, the fort that can be seen today is a later 17th-century design and represents the very latest thinking of its day in defensive structures.

In an age of artillery, standard castle walls proved inadequate against prolonged assault. The clever 1672 design used deep earth embankments

▲ *Tilbury Fort in Essex. Built by Henry VIII to protect London, the fort's ingenious design enabled it to withstand repeated impacts from artillery.*

constructed behind low stone walls set at indirect angles to the river. This enabled the walls to receive repeated impacts with little damage.

Tilbury Fort had most of its heavy guns ranged over the Thames, but the land-facing sides were also protected by a moat and had a bastion plan to provide covering fire between emplacements. The garrison of Tilbury had a quiet time except during the First World War, when they shot down a Zeppelin airship with their anti-aircraft guns, and again in the Second World War when the fort suffered from bombing.

■ **LOCATION** ½ mile E of Tilbury, Essex; off A126.
■ **ACCESS** see www.english-heritage. org.uk or telephone 01375 858489 for opening times and other details. Admission charge.

TEMPLAR BARNS

⑩ Cressing

Cressing, between the Essex towns of Witham and Braintree, houses probably the best-preserved examples of medieval timber-framed barns in Britain. Archaeological investigation has also unearthed Bronze Age pottery fragments and flintwork, while traces of Iron Age features show that the site was in use for

nearly 2,000 years before even the surviving structures were built.

The 13th-century Barley and Wheat barns were built after Queen Matilda, wife of King Stephen, presented the land to the Knights Templar in 1137. In addition to the Barns, a stone-lined well built by the Knights Templar can be found inside the Well House. The Templars were a religious-military order of knights with a reputation for valour and fighting skills. They became powerful and wealthy, which is why Cressing flourished under their control.

With the aid of ring-dating, archaeologists have found that the Barley Barn was built from trees felled between 1205 and 1235, while the Wheat Barn followed later,

▼ The interior of Barley Barn at Cressing, a restored medieval timber-framed barn and probably the best example of its type in Britain.

around 1259 to 1280. The Templars were suppressed in 1312 by order of Pope Clement V, and the Cressing Estate was handed to their successors – the Knights Hospitaller. The barns were believed to have suffered during the Peasants Revolt and the Civil War, but there is no evidence of serious damage.

■ **LOCATION** 2 miles SE of Braintree, Essex; off B1018.
■ **ACCESS** See www.cressingtemple. org.uk or telephone 01376 584903 for opening times and other details. Admission charge.

SAXON CHURCH

⑪ Bradwell-on-Sea

Bradwell-on-Sea is the site of an interesting combination of ancient Saxon church and Roman fort site. The Chapel of St Peter-on-the-Wall is a rare example of a piece of intact Anglo-Saxon stone architecture, and the interior still has an air of sanctity

about it. The fort, originally called Othona, was built by the Romans to defend the coast against Saxon invaders, and you can still see the remains of the walls and traces of the towers.

It is quite a trek to reach the site. Its relative isolation appealed to early Christian monks who, under the leadership of St Cedd, set up a monastery here around AD650. Cedd had been a pupil at the great monastic centre of Lindisfarne, and he set out to convert the East Saxons from there, setting up a monastic site at Bradwell-on-Sea. He eventually left the church to head further north to found another monastery at Lastingham, where he and many of his followers died of the plague in 664.

The chapel is dedicated to St Peter and claims to be one of the oldest churches in England. For many years it was used as a barn; it was restored to a chapel in 1920. There is a lively interest in retaining the worship of Christianity here.

■ **LOCATION** 8 miles N of Burnham on Crouch, Essex; off B1021.
■ **ACCESS** Nothing to see of the Roman fort. The chapel is a working church but is open for viewing during the day all year round: www.bradwellchapel.org or telephone 01621 776203 for further details.

ROMAN TOWN

⑫ Colchester

Colchester is one of the oldest recorded towns in Britain and, from an archaeological perspective, incredibly complex. Colchester was the capital of the Trinovantes tribe until the land was seized in AD43 by the invading Romans under the personal supervision of Emperor Claudius, and made capital of Britannia. So important and significant was this capture that on his return to Rome Claudius declared himself Conqueror of Britain. A fortress was immediately built and, by AD49, Colchester – or

Camulodunum – had become established as a town and capital. This was the first time bricks and mortar were used for building in Britain.

On the death of Claudius in AD54, a temple was built to honour his memory. The locals were taxed heavily and used as slaves to build the huge temple before being forced to worship there. Colchester was already the focus of the Britons' anger, and the Temple of Claudius, and the manner in which it was built, only served to feed resentment against the Romans. The Boudiccan revolt razed Camulodunum to the ground and burnt the temple with many people still trapped inside. The remains of the enormous temple formed the foundations of Colchester Castle, founded by William the Conqueror, and consequently one of the largest Norman castles in Britain.

■ **LOCATION** Colchester, Essex.
■ **ACCESS** See www.colchestermuseums.org.uk or telephone 01206 282939 for opening times and other details. Admission charge.

CLACTON SPEAR

⑬ Clacton-on-Sea

In 1911, Clacton-on-Sea became established on the archaeological map after the discovery of one of the oldest wooden objects in Britain. The Clacton Spear, fashioned from yew, was found on the foreshore among early Hoxnian (inter-glacial) deposits in the clay cliffs.

Measuring 36.7cm (15in) in length, the artefact is around 400,000 years old, and its discovery was all the more surprising given that very few wooden objects survive the test of time unless sealed by exceptional environmental conditions and preserved from bacterial decay. The spear tip has been interpreted as a thrusting spear, ice probe or multipurpose tool, but was most likely used for hunting.

The riverside locations that appear to have been favoured by early

humans in this area are also renowned for their distinctive flint-flake tools, named Clactonian tools by archaeologists. Environmental sampling (microscopic examination, usually of soil) has indicated that bison, horse, rhinoceros and elephant were all hunted or scavenged by early inhabitants here.

■ **LOCATION** Clacton, Essex; on A133.
■ **ACCESS** Nothing to see at sites. Clactonian artefacts on display at the Castle Museum, Colchester: www.colchestermuseums.org.uk or telephone 01206 282939 for opening times and other details. Admission charge. The Clacton Spear is at the British Museum: www.thebritishmuseum.ac.uk or telephone 020 7323 8299 for opening times and other details.

WORLD WARS

⑭ Orford Ness

Orford Ness is a wonderful area of nature conservation, but it wasn't always that way. The shingle of Orford was once a secret military testing station that specialized in work from parachute testing in the First World War to the very latest developments in rockets and radar in the Second World War and atomic weapons in the 1950s.

Now under the management of the National Trust, many buildings and areas of the site can be accessed so that you can see at first-hand some of the structures that tell the story of Orford's fascinating past. From 1935 Robert Watson-Watt and his team undertook some of the most important work here in developing what was to become radar.

The site of Orford Ness also has a 19th-century Martello tower near Aldeburgh, part of a series of towers built across the east coast in the early 1800s for coastal defence against a feared French invasion.

■ **LOCATION** 12 miles E of Woodbridge, Suffolk; on B1084.
■ **ACCESS** See www.nationaltrust.org.uk or telephone 01394 450900 for opening times and other details. Admission charge.

East Midlands

This region covers some of the most varied terrain of any in England, from the heights of the Derbyshire peaks to the fens of Lincolnshire, some of which are below sea level. One of the East Midlands sites with the earliest signs of human activity is also one of the most important in the country for its period: the caves at Creswell Crags. The East Midlands bear as strong a stamp of Romanization as any other area of lowland England. Lincoln was founded originally as a legionary fortress in the 60s AD. Leicester was founded as the region's main Roman town and still has substantial Roman remains. From the middle of the 9th century, almost the whole region came under Viking sway.

Barton-upon-Humber ①

SCUNTHORPE
M180
GRIMSBY
A15
A46
A16
A158

Peveril Castle ②

A619

Creswell Crags ⭐

LINCOLN ⭐ **Lincoln Cathedral**

Stanton Moor ③
Arbor Low ⭐
Masson Mills ④

Bolsover Castle ⑤
MANSFIELD
A617

A15

A17

NOTTINGHAM
DERBY
M1
A607

Shardlow ⑦
Repton ⑥
A42

A1
A15
A52

A606

City of Leicester ⑧
Jewry Wall ⑨
M69

STAMFORD

M1

Rockingham Castle ⑩

Naseby ⑪

Raunds
Stanwick ⑬⑭

Brixworth ⑫
Stanwick
WELLINGBOROUGH

NORTHAMPTON

N

0   20 m
0   20 k

Creswell Crags
Prehistoric art

12,000BC

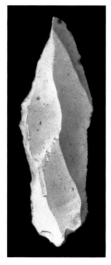

▲ *A distinctive flint tool from the Creswell site.*

THE CRESWELL HERITAGE AREA runs from Mansfield to Doncaster in the southern Pennines, squeezed between the Peak District National Park and Sherwood Forest. Within the area is Creswell Crags, a limestone gorge packed with fissures and caves with names like Mother Grundy's Parlour and Robin Hood's Cave. It's an attractive venue that has about 30,000 visitors a year.

Evidence of settlement before the last Ice Age has been found in the form of tools made from flint and quartzite, which have been dated to between 60,000 and 40,000 years of age. By 12,000BC, the ice caps from the last glaciations had retreated and Britain was once again suitable for settlement. The caves at Creswell Crags were reoccupied by prehistoric hunter-gatherers around this period, and it seems that our ancient ancestors used them for quite some time.

▶ *The occupiers of Creswell caves produced some of the earliest art in Britain and Ireland. The drawings may have been a means of sharing knowledge of hunting and of the animals they pursued.*

Human prehistory

Phil Harding visited Creswell when Time Team were digging at the nearby Carsington Caves. Being a fan of prehistory, the site had always been on his list to visit. 'As a prehistorian I like the very beginnings of our story, and this is where our roots really are. This was occupied by our early ancestors – *Homo sapiens sapiens*, not Neanderthals – and what is here represents what our species introduced, in particular stone tools and the earliest "art".'

The people who lived in the caves were from the period we call the Upper Palaeolithic – about 14,000 years ago – and evidence of them is fairly rare in Britain and Ireland. You have to come here or to places such as Cheddar and Kents Cavern (see pages 27 and 24) to find evidence of these communities. The technology they used included the creation of blades from flint, and as Phil points out this was a very efficient use of the raw material. It creates a number of cutting edges and often leaves behind a distinctive core. The flint came from a variety of sources, some of them clear evidence of long-distance trading.

The first archaeological investigation at Creswell Crags was carried out during the 1870s. Unfortunately, although the excavations were extensive, the Victorian archaeologists removed a great deal of evidence from the caves without the advantages of modern methodology to help them record their finds. However, continued investigation has uncovered a substantial collection of evidence, including the remains of various species of ancient animal.

The typical 'Creswellian' tool set includes bone and antler in addition to the usual stone materials. Barbed harpoon points and bone needles are of particular note. Excavations at the mouth of Robin Hood's Cave uncovered a hearth near the opening and an area used for meat processing further to the rear.

Cave art

Phil was fascinated by the evidence of an early form of symbolic art at Creswell in the form of engravings in the stone. This is fairly basic when compared to the wall painting of Lascaux, but it is clearly art, and as Phil points out climatic conditions in Britain and Ireland were a lot tougher than in the countries to the south. The community who lived in these caves were surviving in an environment still influenced by retreating glaciers. Skilled hunting was vital to their existence. Much of the artwork portrays their animal prey. A bone from Robin Hood's Cave was found engraved with a horse design. Further explorations of the caves have uncovered more than 80 carvings depicting bison, deer, bear and birds.

The discovery of this cave art is one of the most significant finds from early British prehistory. The initial discovery was made in 2003. Before this, it had been widely accepted that no evidence of Ice Age cave art existed in Britain. A 13,000-year-old carving discovered in July 2004 is said to be a naked woman. If so, this would qualify it as the earliest nude in the history of British art.

The carvings were unidentified for so long because they are not clearly visible unless viewed by the trained eye under certain lighting conditions. This is the most northerly art of its kind known in Britain at this time, and Creswell Crags is believed to be the furthest north that ancient man ventured in this country.

▲ *Creswell Crags, prehistoric hunting grounds.*

■ **GETTING THERE** Creswell Crags are 4 miles SW of Worksop, Nottinghamshire, off the B6042. See www.creswell-crags. org.uk or telephone 01909 720378 for opening times and other details. Admission charge.

■ **OUR VIEW** For Phil, a visit to Creswell Crags is an essential act of respect for our earliest ancestors. Much of the best carving is in Church Hole cave. You'll have to make up your own mind about the nude 'engraving'!

Arbor Low
Henge monument

2800-1500BC

Sometimes described as the 'Stonehenge of the north', Arbor Low is an impressive henge monument in Derbyshire's Peak District National Park. It's a spectacular site to visit because of its geographical location on a limestone plateau at more than 335m (1100ft) above sea level. Once you're standing on the massive 2-m high (6½ ft) bank, you get a 360-degree view for miles across moorland countryside.

The original construction of Arbor Low was probably in around 2800BC, during the Neolithic period, but like many henges, it's likely that the monument developed over time in a number of phases, and that this prominent location had long been important to local people. The name is a corruption of an Old English word meaning 'earthwork mound', showing that it was still a landmark thousands of years after it was built.

The oval bank and internal ditch of the henge survives, nearly 67m (220ft) in diameter, with two entrances into it. Inside the ditch a circle of 50 or so stones surrounds a 'cove', a smaller U-shaped group of seven stones. As at Stonehenge, these stones were probably erected later than the bank and ditch. Pretty much all the Arbor Low stones are recumbent, giving the circle a very distinctive atmosphere. It was thought

▼ Arbor Low from the air. The bank is over 2m (6½ ft) in height and 67m (220ft) in diameter.

that the stones were always intended to lie down, after excavations at the site in 1903 failed to find any socket holes for them to stand in. However, if you look at the stones, you'll see that many of them are fragments, and it's likely that the original circle was composed of a smaller number of upright stones, which fell and broke.

The most interesting find in the 1903 excavations was a human burial near the cove – reportedly a male skeleton with a smashed skull – but many pottery shards and flints were also recovered.

Just as at Stonehenge and Avebury, the henge at Arbor Low is part of a wider ritual complex. Arbor Low is connected by a curving earthwork bank and ditch to the mound at Gib Hill, a couple of hundred yards away on a sloping ridge. If you look carefully at Gib Hill in profile, you can see that it is in fact two mounds on top of each other. It's probable that it began as a Neolithic long barrow containing cremations. The bank and ditch were built as a ceremonial avenue at some point to connect the barrow to Arbor Low when the henge was created.

The antiquarian

In the Bronze Age, a round barrow was built on top of the Neolithic mound at Gib Hill, and another one constructed across the bank and ditch near the south-east entrance of the henge. The barrows at both Arbor Low and Gib Hill were to fall victim to one of Derbyshire's early and interesting archaeological characters, Thomas Bateman. A local landowner and antiquarian, he began excavating sites on his estate and creating his own personal museum. In the 1840s and 1850s, he expanded his activities across northern England and dug nearly 200 sites, many of them barrows like these.

His grasp on archaeological techniques was crude compared to modern ideas, but he did leave descriptions and illustrations of what he found at the sites, and his collection of notes and objects is now in Sheffield City's museum. One sketch shows his workmen digging a tunnel into the lower mound at Gib Hill. Not a method approved of by modern archaeologists, the tunnel came to an unfortunate end. Unknown to Bateman, the overlying Bronze Age barrow contained a burial in a stone chamber, which fell through the roof of his tunnel. He reportedly carted off the stones and re-erected the chamber in his garden, but they were returned to the site in 1938, and can still be seen today.

Not much is known about Arbor Low archaeologically, except for these early excavations. English Heritage recently tried to remedy this with a geophysical survey of the henge and barrow complex, but poor ground conditions meant it revealed little: no signs of lost ditches or posts for wooden holes, like those at Stanton Drew (see page 28). For me, though, Arbor Low is one of those sites where it doesn't seem to matter how much or little is known. If you want to visit a henge, it's a great one to choose. For Carenza, it's one of the best sites in the country. 'Arbor Low was the first stone circle I ever saw; as a small child I was fascinated. As an undergraduate, I was still impressed. It's a monument of its landscape. It's worth also making the trip up to Thor's Cave. In places the path is precipitous, but a visit here will get the landscape of Arbor Low under your skin.'

■ **GETTING THERE** Arbow Low is 2 miles S of Monyash, Derbyshire; 1⁄2 mile W of the A515. See www.english-heritage.org.uk or telephone 01629 816200 for opening times and other details. Admission charge at discretion of landowner. OS Landranger map 119.

■ **OUR VIEW** Arbor Low has a distinctive atmosphere and, unlike its more famous and busy southern neighbours, you're far more likely to get ten minutes to yourself, soaking up the spectacular view.

Lincoln
Roman and ecclesiastical city
AD60 to the present

THE ROMANS ESTABLISHED a legionary fortress at Lincoln soon after their invasion, probably by AD60. The fort would have played a key role in subduing the territory of the local Corieltauvi tribe, and would also have been part of a network of defences for securing control of the major river valley routes of the east: the Trent, the Humber, and the Witham, which Lincoln lies on.

By the end of the 1st century AD, Lincoln had become one of a handful of *colonia* in Britain. These were towns populated with ex-soldiers, and were the highest-status settlements in the province outside London. Lincoln grew into a thriving city: an administrative capital at the heart of a network of roads, including the Fosse Way and Ermine

Street, and an important inland port on the Witham.

There are a staggering 27 visible Roman monuments surviving in Lincoln today. Local limestone quarries provided much of the building stone for the Roman city, and the surviving masonry gives a good idea of how impressive it must have been. Many were part of the city defences and walls. The most complete section is the famous Newport Arch, which still spans a road today, and was part of the gate that faced Ermine Street. However, at nearly 6m (20ft) tall and 21m (70ft) long, the highlight of Roman Lincoln is the Mint Wall. This wasn't a defensive wall, but part of the basilica, the civic building at the heart of every Roman city.

For me, the most interesting aspect of Lincoln's archaeology is that it gives us a rare view into what was happening during the controversial centuries at the end of the Roman period in Britain. It seems that Lincoln was still flourishing

▼ It's easy to see why the Romans picked Lincoln for a legionary fortress. With commanding views across the countryside, the hilltop was the perfect place from which to control the newly acquired territory, and had excellent road and river communications.

in the 4th and even 5th centuries AD, when most towns and cities were in serious decline (such as London; see page 62). Archaeological excavations have shown that here, houses remained occupied, coins were still in use, and the waterfront was being maintained. A large cache of butchered animal bones discovered several years ago even showed that industrial-scale meat processing was going on into the late 4th century.

Arrival of Christianity

In religious terms, it's not clear how far Christianity had penetrated into Britain in the Roman period, and Lincoln is important because it's one of the few cities where there appears to be evidence for a Christian community in late Roman and early post-Roman times. Lincoln was one of three British places that sent a bishop to a religious council meeting at Arles in AD314 – only one year after Christianity had become the official religion of the Roman Empire.

Excavations at the church of St Paul-in-the-Bail suggest there was probably a timber church and cemetery on the site of the Roman forum at Lincoln by the 5th century, if not earlier. Paulinus, a missionary who later became Archbishop of York, is said to have founded a church in Lincoln around AD672, and this was probably St Paul-in-the-Bail.

St Paul-in-the-Bail was overtaken in prominence after the Norman Conquest by Lincoln Cathedral. Constructed from the same local limestone as the Roman city, it was first consecrated as a cathedral in 1092 by Remigius, a monk in William the Conqueror's following, but grew over the centuries to become one of the

▲ *Much of the classical architecture that gives the cathedral its character today was constructed in the 14th century, when the towers were heightened and the extraordinary nave with its stained-glass windows was developed.*

largest in England. Repairs were needed in 1141 when the cathedral was ravaged by fire and again in 1185 when it was damaged by an earthquake. By 1192, a drastic phase of rebuilding was under way in the new delicate gothic style of architecture, with huge flying buttresses and vaulted ceilings. Like many medieval cathedrals, the builders were working at the limits of contemporary engineering, and Lincoln suffered some setbacks. Two collapses of the central tower occurred in the 13th century. Incredibly, with a central spire estimated at 160m (525ft) high, medieval Lincoln Cathedral was the first building to exceed the height of the Great Pyramid of Giza, and remained the tallest building in the world until the spire came down in storms in 1549.

■ **GETTING THERE** The town wall is visible at various locations in Lincoln; telephone tourist information on 01522 873213 for more details. For the cathedral, see www.lincolncathedral.com or telephone 01522 544544.

■ **OUR VIEW** Lincoln has extraordinary Roman remains, with the Mint Wall the only part of a Roman basilica still standing in Britain. Some Roman masonry was used in the rebuilding of Lincoln Cathedral in the 13th century.

Other sites to visit

❶ St Peter's Church, Barton-upon-Humber

St Peter's Church at Barton-upon-Humber has been the focus of a dedicated archaeological research project since the late 1970s. Excavation and recording of the standing building has revealed activity on the site dating from the Anglo-Saxon period. As the main parish church for the village from the medieval period until 1970, the work carried out here by archaeologists has proved fascinating, and given us an insight to the congregational and burial practices of the community over the period of more than 1,000 years, including the transition from Saxon to Norman periods.

Excavation uncovered more than 2,800 burials, dating from the mid-9th to the 19th century, both inside and outside the church building. A Saxon enclosure ditch from an earlier phase of the cemetery provided a waterlogged environment that enabled some 30 complete Saxon and Norman coffins to be preserved and then safely lifted.

The in-depth investigation of the site has allowed archaeologists to fully interpret the phases of church building. Following the initial enclosure it appears that the first church was built around AD970. The 11th century witnessed a rebuild in several phases which continually incorporated the existing tower. The church continued to have additions through the 13th, 14th and 15th centuries, including a south aisle, vestry and the placing of upper windows. The site is managed by English Heritage.

■ **LOCATION** Barton-upon-Humber, Lincolnshire; on B1218, off A15.
■ **ACCESS** See www.english-heritage. org.uk or telephone 01652 632516 for opening times and other details. Admission charges on EH event days.

❷ Peveril Castle

High above the small town of Castleton stands Peveril Castle, built by one of William the Conqueror's right-hand men, William Peveril, in the 11th century. The castle was probably constructed fairly soon after the Norman invasion of 1066 to protect and control the Peak

▼ *St Peter's Church. For us on Time Team, this represents an ideal combination: an attractive medieval church with excellent archaeological evidence.*

Forest area. Henry II further developed the site in the 12th century, including building the impressive and imposing square tower which still stands to its original height on top of the naturally high ground.

The site is looked after by English Heritage, who have recently made some first-floor areas accessible. You can enjoy views across the Peak District and also see earthworks that were part of defences extended to protect the medieval town.

■ **LOCATION** 7 miles E of Chapel-en-le-Frith, Derbyshire.
■ **ACCESS** See www.english-heritage. org.uk or telephone 01433 620613 for opening times and other details. Admission charge.

❸ Stanton Moor

Stanton Moor in the Peak District of Derbyshire, 2 miles north-west of Matlock, contains what archaeologists term a dispersed cemetery of Bronze Age barrows. Barrows are usually sited in small clusters, often on the crests of hills or ridges. These prominent positions are thought to represent boundary markers which, by their presence, clearly state the ownership of an area by rights of the ancestors who inhabited the land before.

The interesting point about dispersed cemeteries is that they indicate a large area of land given over to funerary practice. Here a selection of monuments, including a stone circle called the Nine Ladies, stretches across the moor in a disrupted line north to south for over a mile. Either side of this line over 70 prehistoric burials and mounds are scattered in what appears to be a random distribution pattern with the odd clustering of

▶ *This impressive tower, part of Peveril Castle, benefited from Henry II's investment. It was originally built by the Normans to help control the Peak District.*

groups of small cairns. The commanding views across the Derwent Valley below the natural heights of this 4-square-mile patch of moorland may well have been partially responsible for this area being the location for so many prehistoric burials.

At the beginning of the 20th century, a local family called the Heathcotes excavated a large number of the barrows on the moor and many of the finds from these excavations can be seen in Sheffield's museum, Weston Park.

■ **LOCATION** 2 miles NW of Matlock, Derbyshire; off B5056.
■ **ACCESS** Peak District National Park: see www.peakdistrict.org or telephone 01629 816200.

ARKWRIGHT'S REVOLUTION

❹ Masson Mills

Masson Mills at Matlock Bath are part of the Derwent Valley Mills World Heritage Site. Built by the inventor and entrepreneur Sir Richard Arkwright in 1783, these cotton mills represent the height of technology for factory-based manufacturing in the 18th century.

Arkwright was the son of a labourer who, with the help of his cousin, became literate. Trained as a barber, he soon started to build on an entrepreneurial nature and developed hair dyes to boost his wig-making business. When wigs began to go out of fashion, Arkwright turned his attention to the cotton industry and speculated on a new cotton-carding device, patented in 1775. As his business empire grew, Arkwright invested in horse-, water- and finally steam-powered mills designed for the most efficient production of cloth.

The site at Masson Mills is in many ways a classic Arkwright factory

▶ *Masson Mills in Derbyshire. Sir Richard Arkwright's mill represented the peak of 18th-century technology in the cotton trade.*

with a fantastic array of working machinery and associated collections of artefacts related to the trade.

■ **LOCATION** Matlock, Derbyshire.
■ **ACCESS** Derwent Valley Mills World Heritage Site: see www.derby.gov.uk and do a search on 'Derwent Valley Mills', or telephone 01332 255061 for opening times and other details.

ELIZABETHAN HOUSE

❺ Bolsover Castle

Bolsover was originally built by William Peveril (as in Peveril Castle) in the 12th century. However, hardly anything remains of the original

works as the site was heavily developed in the 17th century. Today it is an unspoilt example of a typical Elizabethan house built for fun and pleasure.

The 16th century saw the castle in the hands of Sir George Talbot, but by the turn of the century he had fallen on harder times as his funds were seriously depleted by the burden of being the keeper responsible for Mary Queen of Scots in exile. He leased the castle to Sir Charles Cavendish, who later bought it and began work on his 'Little Castle' dream home in 1612. In 1616 William Cavendish

inherited the house and embarked on further development, including a terrace range and rather grandiose stables.

In 1644, the Civil War saw the Royalist Sir William forced into exile and the Parliamentarians took control of the castle. His return sixteen years later found the castle in ruin. He spent the rest of his life dedicated to rebuilding it to its former glory.

■ **LOCATION** Bolsover, Derbyshire.
■ **ACCESS** See www.english-heritage. org.uk or telephone 01246 822844 for opening times and other details. Admission charge.

❻ Repton

St Wystan's church in Repton, a few miles south-west of Derby, has an archaeologically intriguing past. The church itself contains an extremely rare Saxon crypt dating back to an earlier monastery, which occupied the site around AD653 and was subsequently destroyed by the Vikings. As Repton was an important centre of the Saxon Mercian domain, several kings were buried here, including Ethelbald (AD757) and Wiglaf (AD840).

The most fascinating aspect of the

site is a twin-celled semi-sunken building to the west of the church, which is often associated with the late-9th-century occupation of the area by the Vikings. After the initial discovery of the cairn by interested antiquarians, the site was properly excavated in the 1980s and revealed as a mass grave. The bones from around 250 individuals had been collected together and stored within the mausoleum-type structure. The excavators suggested that the remains could be the ritual burial of Viking bones brought together at Repton from other areas.

Later work revealed that these are unlikely to be Viking warriors because of the lack of trauma evidence on the bones. The remains of fighting men would normally be expected to show signs of injury. Radiocarbon dating suggests they lived between the 8th and 10th centuries. This intriguing mass grave could represent Viking pagan practice in the face of Christianity, and will undoubtedly remain a subject of debate.

■ **LOCATION** Repton, Derbyshire.
■ **ACCESS** St Wystan's Church: www.reptonchurch.org.uk or telephone 01283 703317 for opening times and other details.

❼ Shardlow

The small village of Shardlow is famous for its boatbuilding heritage, tied to the River Trent. In 1998 the discovery of a Bronze Age boat during extraction in the local quarry took that heritage back nearly 3,500 years. The log boat and an associated stone and wood platform were found under 3m (10ft) of gravel in what was once an ancient river course connected to the Trent.

Made of oak and estimated to have originally been nearly 14m (46ft) in length, the boat still contained its prehistoric cargo of quarried stone. The flat sandstone

blocks, uncovered in situ packed along the hull of the vessel, match those that can still be found 2 miles upstream. Archaeologists believe the boat was carrying its cargo down to the platform, which was possibly under construction in this then shallow part of the river. There's also the possibility that the boat was deliberately sunk as an offering. Information about the boat can be found in the village Heritage Centre and also at Derby Museum, where the boat is now housed.

■ **LOCATION** Shardlow, Derbyshire.
■ **ACCESS** Heritage Centre: http://home pages.which.net/~shardlow.heritage; Derby Museum: www.derby.gov.uk, go to 'Leisure', then 'Derby Museum and Art Gallery' or telephone 01332 716659 for opening times and other details.

WEALTH OF MUSEUMS

❽ City of Leicester

Leicester has a rich and colourful history embodied in a good selection of museums. The New Walk Museum exhibits dinosaur remains and 600-million-year-old rocks from Leicestershire's geology, and traces the history of the ancient Egyptians. The Jewry Wall Museum houses local prehistoric, Roman and medieval artefacts. The Jewry Wall itself is a surviving example of a 1,850-year-old Roman wall. It was originally part of Leicester's Roman baths and dates from around AD150.

Leicester's social history from the past 500 years is represented by Wygston's Chantry House and Skeffington House, both of which were built in the 1500s and now comprise the Newarke Houses Museum. In addition, Leicester's Guildhall is one of the best-preserved timber-framed buildings in Britain

◀ *Leicester's surviving chunk of 1,850-year-old Roman brickwork, known as the Jewry Wall. Standing Roman architecture of this size is something of a rarity and well worth seeking out.*

and dates back to the 14th century. The Guildhall had many guises, including that of a meeting place for the Guild of Corpus Christi, a town library and a courtroom.

Science and technology are explored at the Abbey Pumping Station, which contains the largest working steam beam engines in the country, together with an exhibition that tells the history of the development of the toilet. The contrasting lifestyles of 18th-century upper-middle-class families and their servants are displayed at the Belgrave Hall and Gardens, while the Great Hall of Leicester Castle retains its original aisle-posts dating from the 1150s.

■ **LOCATION** Leicester.
■ **ACCESS** Leicester City Museums: www.leicestermuseums.ac.uk or telephone 0116 225 4900 for opening times and other details.

STANDING ROMAN REMAINS

❾ Jewry Wall

Possibly named after the Jewish community of Leicester, who were expelled from the medieval town by charter in 1250, the Jewry Wall has Roman origins. At over 9m (30ft) high, it's one of Leicester's most famous ancient landmarks, and has a particularly fine example of Roman walling with tile- and brick-banded courses of stone.

The Roman town (then called Ratae) had its public baths, constructed around the middle of the 2nd century and following the typical custom of the day with a warm, hot and cold succession of treatments, and the surviving piece of wall would have once separated these areas from an adjoining exercise hall. The exercise hall would have provided a covered space for ball games and sporting activities such as running, boxing and wrestling, while the baths would have supplied a more relaxed social gathering place. The large scale of this site hints at the popularity of the

venue for Romano-Britons with leisure time.

■ **LOCATION** Leicester.
■ **ACCESS** See www.leicestermuseums. ac.uk or telephone 0116 225 4900 for opening times and other details.

NORMAN TO TUDOR

❿ Rockingham Castle

This Norman castle nestles in the Welland valley overlooking the village of Rockingham. The site was occupied during the Iron Age, Roman and Saxon periods, before William the Conqueror ordered the construction of the castle during the 11th century. This commanding location became a centre of administration under Norman rule. One of the first recorded assemblies of state was held here in 1095 when the Great Council of Rockingham met under William II to discuss the Church's allegiance to the pope and king.

Rockingham Castle entertained many kings over the centuries; the surrounding forest was an important royal hunting ground and a popular venue for kingly sortieing trips. The castle could accommodate up to 3,000 people, and developed from the typical Norman design of a motte-and-bailey castle when a shell keep of 30m (100ft) in diameter was added in the 12th century. A twin-towered gatehouse followed this in 1275.

Eventually the seat of power shifted to London and the castle was neglected by royalty, until Henry VIII leased it to Edward Watson in 1530. Watson converted the castle into a plush Tudor house and it remains the home of his descendants today. During the 19th century, Charles Dickens was a frequent visitor to Rockingham and it provided him with the inspiration for his novel *Bleak House*.

What is apparent today is the Tudor influence within Norman walls, and virtually every century since the 14th is represented by architecture, furniture and art, which trace the castle's nigh-on continuous habitation for over 900 years.

■ **LOCATION** 2 miles N of Corby, Northamptonshire; off A6003.
■ **ACCESS** Telephone 01536 770240 for opening times and other details. Admission charge.

CIVIL WAR BATTLE SITE

⑪ Naseby

Naseby in Northamptonshire was the site of a decisive battle between the Parliamentarian (Roundhead) and Royalist armies, which ended the first phase of the English Civil War. On 14 June 1645, the commander-in-chief of the Royalist forces, Prince Rupert, made a last-ditch attempt to break the Parliamentarian hold on the north of England, but was routed by the larger Roundhead army lead by Sir Thomas Fairfax and Oliver Cromwell. The Roundheads captured significant Royalist supplies, leaders and papers in the aftermath of the battle, which effectively marked the end of King Charles I's chance of winning the Civil War.

The modern-day landscape of the battle site is known to have changed since the 17th century, when it mainly consisted of poorly drained heathland and ploughed fields of narrow strip-holdings. Naseby, like many battlefields, has been targeted by metal detectorists looking for military debris over many years. Now a recent archaeological study has drawn upon the data collected by metal detectorists to provide new information about the battle.

By mapping the concentrations of lead shot recovered from the topsoil, archaeologists have been able to re-evaluate the battle site and increase its overall size by more than a mile. Further analysis of the types of shot gathered from the site has also allowed the original position of troops on the field of battle to be reconstructed with greater accuracy.

■ **LOCATION** Battlefield: 1 mile NW of Naseby, Northamptonshire; off A14.
■ **ACCESS** See OS Landranger map 141 for rights of way. Currently little interpretation on site. See www.battle fieldstrust.com, go to 'UK Battlefields' then 'Search for a Battle' or telephone 01508 558145 for further details.

▲ An artist's idea of the carnage at Naseby. Recent archaeological research, including the work of metal detectorists, has provided new and detailed information about the battle.

▼ The peaceful calm of Naseby today, complete with monument. Finds by metal detectorists have helped determine troop positions during the fighting.

ANGLO-SAXON CHURCH

⑫ Brixworth

The 12th-century history called the *Peterborough Chronicle* states that in AD675 a man named Sexwulf became Bishop of Mercia and one of his monks called Cuthbald inherited the post he left behind to become Abbot of Peterborough. There then followed a period of expansion, which included monasteries at 'Brixworth and at many other places'. This historical reference gives the church at Brixworth a late-7th-century date.

As a fine piece of Anglo-Saxon architecture, the Church of All Saints is constructed mainly of brick but also has reused Roman material in the west end. Historical records also hint at Viking raids damaging the church in the 10th century, and some evidence of rebuilding can be seen where local stone replaces the Roman tile.

Excavations in the 1980s uncovered a Saxon ditch, thought to be associated with the original monastery boundary. More recent work has focused on analysis of the stone of the walls and has suggested that the Saxon church may have been connected with Leicester, from where much of the early phase stone originates, rather than Peterborough. Wherever the monastic influence came from, this is a rare and fine example of an Anglo-Saxon ecclesiastical building and makes an interesting comparison with the Chapel of St Laurence in Bradford-on-Avon (see page 51).

■ **LOCATION** 6 miles N of Northampton; off A508.
■ **ACCESS** See http://freespace.virgin.net /jd.brixworth or telephone 01604 880915 for opening times and other details.

IRON AGE TO ROMAN

⓭ Stanwick

The lowland settlement of Stanwick was once a centre of activity for the Iron Age Brigantes group of tribes. An initial enclosure dating from around 400BC was later developed into a vast hillfort and defensive network enclosing over 240 hectares (600 acres). It is thought that this work was undertaken by the Brigantian leader Venutius before his subjugation to the Romans. The client king later suffered under the Roman administration when his wife, Cartimandua, divorced him with the support of Rome.

Excavations at Stanwick have revealed a landscape of settlement from the Iron Age through to extensive Roman occupation. It appears that the area has long been a centre of the agricultural economy, from small Iron Age farming zones to larger established Roman farmsteads. One of these farmsteads developed into a large Roman complex which matured by the late 4th century into a successful villa complete with extra accommodation in additional wings.

■ **LOCATION** 3 miles NE of Higham Ferrers, Northamptonshire; off A45.
■ **ACCESS** Site has been partly destroyed by quarry. Finds not yet on public display, but there are plenty of earthworks and a good church to visit.

MULTI-PERIOD FIELD SYSTEM

⓮ Raunds

A massive research project in the Raunds area of the Nene valley has provided extraordinary insight into the local archaeology. The Raunds Area Project undertook a range of excavations in advance of gravel extraction and road-building plans. Work around Stanwick, West Cotton and Irthlingborough in particular has been particularly fruitful, especially for the prehistoric periods.

With evidence recovered going back over 8,000 years to the time of hunter-gatherer groups and their later clearing of the landscape in preparation for settlement, the most remarkable findings have been from the Neolithic and Bronze Age. Fourteen monuments ranging from mounds and circular enclosures to linear monuments and mortuary sites have been excavated.

Other archaeological methods, such as field walking and geophysical survey, have highlighted other sites, and thorough environmental sampling has helped archaeologists to increase their understanding of Bronze Age field systems.

■ **LOCATION** 4 miles NE of Rushden, Northamptonshire; on B663, off A605.
■ **ACCESS** Sites now mainly residential areas or private land. See www.northants archaeology.co.uk or telephone 01604 700493/4 for further details.

North-west England

This area is perhaps less well known than other areas for its archaeology, although one find has become famous – Lindow Man, whose body, possibly an Iron Age sacrifice, was found preserved in peat in 1984. Other sites deserve more recognition than they get, including the rich Neolithic landscape of the Isle of Man, and the fascinating area of Meols in the Wirral, which thrived in the Viking period. At Chester the Romans had one of their most important centres in the country. From the medieval and post-medieval period, the region includes a fascinating series of monastic remains. The industrial landscape around Liverpool is nationally important and focuses on the Albert Dock, which has one of the largest groups of Grade I listed buildings in Britain.

ISLE OF MAN

DOUGLAS ○

Billown
(13)

N

○ LANCASTER

A683

M6

○ BLACKPOOL

M55

A59

Whalley
Abbey
(2)
✦ **Ribchester**

BURNLEY ○

PRESTON ○
✦ **Cuerdale**
Walton-le-Dale
(1)

M65

○ BLACKBURN

A565

A59

M61

ROCHDALE ○   M62

A58

○ OLDHAM

M58   WIGAN ○

City of
Manchester
(3)

M6

A580

○ ST HELENS

Meols
(5)
✦ **Liverpool Docks**
○ LIVERPOOL
BIRKENHEAD ○

M62

○ WARRINGTON

Lindow
Man
(4)

M53

(7) M56

Norton
Priory

A537

A523

MACCLESFIELD ○

Eddisbury
(8)

M6

Bridestones
(11)

(6) Chester

Sandbach
Crosses
(10)

(12)

Beeston
(9)

CREWE ○

Little Moreton
Hall

0 _____ 20 m
0 _____ 20 k

Ribchester
Roman fort

AD72–200s

RIBCHESTER WAS ONE of Time Team's first Roman sites. The programme included a memorable sequence featuring re-enactors from the Ermine Street Guard. Dressed in full armour they laboured to dig a series of defensive ditches, and their efforts conveyed a sense of just what these legionaries must have gone through in the remote wilds of Britain, attempting to establish a foothold and build forts while under threat of attack from local tribes.

During Roman occupation the village of Ribchester was known as Bremetennacum Veteranorum, and today it is home to the only specialist Roman museum in Lancashire.

The museum is built on the site of a Roman fort that was established about AD72. Set in Lancashire's Ribble valley, Ribchester Roman fort was of strategic importance because it was located where Roman roads converged to cross the Ribble. It was also on a supply route to Hadrian's Wall.

The 1st-century timber forts were succeeded in the early 2nd century by a robust stone construction that was garrisoned with several different auxiliary units during the Roman occupation of Britain. In the 2nd century the garrisons consisted primarily of soldiers and cavalrymen from Spain, and in the 3rd century possibly some from Hungary (one of the units was called the Ala Sarmaturum, the Sarmatian Cavalry Wing). As with most Roman forts, this military presence encouraged the formation of a civilian settlement or vicus beside the fort. These included

▼ The discovery of Roman granaries at Ribchester helped to build up the picture of a thriving military settlement.

what might be called military retirement homes, which often helped to consolidate a settlement. The vicus was laid out in an organized fashion.

A series of excavations gradually revealed the fort's original defences, which had consisted of a stout turf rampart and three V-shaped ditches. The ramparts were later cut into with the construction of stone fortifications. Furthermore, evidence indicates that the fort had what appears to be a cavalry practice hall, which was quite rare and unusual for a Roman fort in Britain. A number of stone walls, furnaces and tiled floors were uncovered following excavations in the 1920s and 1960s. Study of the roundwood (small logs) found in the fort's exterior ditches provided evidence of coppicing, showing that the local woodlands were being managed.

The museum

The recently modernized Ribchester Roman Museum, near the church, was founded in 1914 and opened in 1915. Displayed in the museum are artefacts unearthed over the past 100 years that show varying aspects of Roman domestic and military life at the fort and around, including coins, pottery, woodwork, leather and carved stone inscriptions. One of the most significant finds was discovered in 1796: a bronze cavalry helmet decorated with battle scenes and classical figures, which was probably worn at parades or sporting events. A replica is on display at Ribchester Museum; the original is in the British Museum in London. Guy de la Bédoyère makes the point that this helmet was typical of the

kind of ostentation the Roman auxiliary cavalry enjoyed displaying. Also found at Ribchester were more mundane pieces of evidence, including leatherwork associated with cavalry.

Towards the rear of the museum, the remains of the Roman granaries are visible. The ruins of a bathhouse, first discovered by labourers in 1837, can be seen near Ribchester's White Bull pub. The fort originally covered an area of almost 3 hectares (7 acres) but a large portion has been washed away by erosion from the river. Indeed, the fort's Roman name means 'roaring river'.

▲ The magnificent auxiliary cavalryman's bronze helmet, found near the river in 1796. It would have been used in special performances of horsemanship and in re-enacted battles.

■ **GETTING THERE** Ribchester is 4 miles N of Blackburn, Lancashire, on the B6245. For Ribchester Roman Museum see www.ribchestermuseum.org or telephone 01254 878261 for opening times and further details. Admission charge.
■ **OUR VIEW** As you visit the White Bull en route from the museum, take a look at the columns supporting the pub's porch – they were almost certainly pilfered from one of the Roman buildings!

The Cuerdale Hoard
Viking treasure

AD900s

HOARDS SUCH AS Cuerdale – one of the largest surviving collections of Viking material in Britain and Ireland – can provide a unique insight into the culture to which they belonged. Mick points out that there are many of these hoards in Scandinavian countries, which was the ultimate destination of much of this material. Finds like this are very rare in Britain. It is sometimes hard to look past the glittering surface value and see the archaeology beneath. But as archaeologists begin to look at the detailed content, information about 10th-century coinage, silver ornament styles and trade routes emerges. It's likely that the main origin for the majority of the silver content was Arabian; these were the sources being exploited at this time. The silver in the hoard was essentially bullion that was likely to be melted down. It would have been a considerable loss to its owners, which suggests that only a catastrophe could have led to it being abandoned. We asked Helen Geake, Time Team's Anglo-Saxon expert and someone who has worked closely with the Portable Antiquities Scheme, for some details of this remarkable discovery.

▼ One of the richest Viking hoards found in Britain. The Cuerdale silver included coins, jewellery and ornaments, some of Arabian origin.

Helen's view

The Cuerdale hoard was found in 1840. Workmen repairing the bank of the river Ribble at Cuerdale, near Preston, found that they were digging up coins, not earth. They began to stuff their pockets, but were discovered and forced to give up the loot. Of course, plenty went missing straight away, and because of this, no one can be sure exactly what was found. There were probably about 7,500 silver coins: Anglo-Saxon, Carolingian, Byzantine and Arabic, but most from Viking York. Among the hundreds of pieces of 'hack-silver' – bits of cut-up brooches, arm-rings and so on – are many of Irish manufacture. The whole hoard weighed about 40kg (90lb). The hoard can be coin-dated to between 901 and 911, and would have been worth approaching half a million pounds today.

▲ *If the hoard had a single owner, it would have been a person of considerable substance who could have expected, after death, to have been buried in some style, along with his silver and other possessions and his boat.*

Something exceptional must have happened for the hoard to be assembled in the first place, and something terrible must have happened to stop it being recovered – all who knew where the hoard was buried must have died. What events might have been responsible?

In 902 the Vikings were expelled from Dublin. Maybe the Vikings from Ireland and York were collaborating in an attempt to re-take Dublin, and the Cuerdale hoard was their war chest.

We don't know why the hoard was not recovered, but its loss seems not to have been wholly disastrous, as within another dozen years Viking rule was re-established in Dublin.

Viking hoards aren't just dry data. They are a tantalizing snapshot of past lives. We can see the Vikings' distant travels and their interest in money. But an unrecovered hoard represents human tragedy: who would have known about this hoard, and what caused their deaths?

■ **GETTING THERE** The find site is 3 miles E of Preston in Lancashire, off the B6320. Most of the finds themselves, however, are in the British Museum; see www.thebritish museum.ac.uk or telephone 020 7323 8000. Some coins are on display at Harris Museum, Preston; telephone 01772 905414 for opening times and further details. There's nothing to see at the find site itself.

■ **OUR VIEW** The Cuerdale find emphasizes the importance of archaeological overview of any hoard material and the need to keep it together if possible.

Liverpool docks and railway
British Empire economy

1700s–1800s

WITH WATERBORNE trading origins that go back to the 13th century, Liverpool had become established as one of the busiest maritime centres in the world by the 19th century. This massive expansion was boosted by the industrial revolution, when merchants realized that profits could be greatly enhanced by embracing the new, super-efficient railway transport. The story of one is inextricably linked to the other. With a quest for ever-higher margins of profit, and a pioneering spirit to explore new markets, Liverpool became a powerhouse in the economy of the British Empire.

Probably best known for its Albert Docks, which contained fireproof 'bonded' warehouses to protect stock (now turned into shops, galleries and exclusive housing), the river Mersey actually has some 40 different docks, created to deal with the wide variety of materials traded from across the world.

During the middle to late 18th century, over 50 per cent of trade from

Liverpool was connected with the Slave Triangle, so called because of the trade route shape over the Atlantic Ocean. Ships left Liverpool for West Africa carrying firearms and linen. This was traded in areas such as Senegal and The Gambia for captured slaves. The ships then sailed from Africa to the Americas heavily laden with their human cargo in extremely poor conditions, the crossing often taking up to two months. The ships would then return to England carrying tobacco, sugar, coffee and cocoa. Though other ports, such as Bristol, were involved in this cruel and lucrative business, over 60 per cent of the slave trade was handled by Liverpool. With the abolition of slavery in 1807, the merchants moved into other markets. The thriving docks received and exported palm oil, cotton, tea, sugar, fruit, nitrates used in the manufacture of gunpowder, and timber from as far away as Canada and China. The 19th century witnessed the development of steam-powered ships, and it was the demand for coal at the docks that helped the growth of another industry: the railway.

Stephenson's railway
With trade between the neighbouring cities of Liverpool and Manchester at an all-time high, elsewhere, in the north-east, merchant Edward Pease invested in

▼ *The Albert Docks in their time were one of the most advanced dock systems in the world.*

As the railways became more and more popular, the route between Manchester and Liverpool thrived, and the docks benefited.

a railway between Stockton and Darlington with the help of a master engine-builder called George Stephenson. Stephenson opened the railway in 1825 with the first railway locomotive, called *Locomotion*, pulling 36 wagons nine miles in two hours. Horse-drawn movement of coal was made redundant overnight, and the canals faced a serious threat.

Seeing the potential for increasing profits while transporting the raw materials for textiles to Manchester and the finished linen back to the port of Liverpool, businessman James Sandars set about establishing the Liverpool to Manchester Railway. Again, George Stephenson was a driving force. Some serious engineering feats were needed to achieve the 31-mile-long double line, not least the crossing of a marsh and substantial cuttings through rock. The Liverpool to Manchester Railway was opened in 1830 and ran with the flagship *Rocket* steam locomotive, built by Stephenson and his son Robert. The success of the railway signalled a change in the future of transport. Not only did the railway transform the way industry worked in this pioneering age, but it also transformed people's lives by giving them affordable mobility. In the first year of operation, half a million people travelled on the Liverpool to Manchester Railway.

■ **GETTING THERE**: The docks are in Liverpool L3. For the revitalized Albert Dock and details of how to get there, see www.albertdock. com, telephone 0151 708 7334. See also www.liver poolmuseums.org. uk or telephone 0151 478 4499 for further museum details. For the railway exhibition at Manchester Museum of Science and Industry, see www.msim.org.uk or telephone 0161 832 2244 for opening times and further details.

■ **OUR VIEW** It can take a while to value industrial archaeology, but this site would be a great place to start.

Other sites to visit

ROMAN MILITARY SUPPLIES

❶ Walton-le-Dale

Excavations at an area in Walton-le-Dale, south of Preston, indicate that the Romans used the site on Watery Lane as a military supply base and industrial centre. Precious little is known of Roman military supply networks, but the fact that this complex site lies near to convenient land, river and sea transport links lends weight to the theory. Furthermore, there is no direct evidence of a conventional Roman fortress or settlement at Walton-le-Dale, but the site reveals a clear Roman military influence.

The Walton-le-Dale site has much in common with supply depots found at Red House, Corbridge and South Shields, and is dated from Hadrian's reign to the late AD200s. Evidence of organized and systematic construction of large timber buildings has been found, each containing an industrial fire hearth/pit, while a ditch stored water and was linked to a nearby reservoir.

Walton-le-Dale lies on a tidal estuary feeding the Irish Sea and it is possible that the site could have been a port where the Romans kept and repaired ships. Further evidence of large-scale production suggests that the site could have been a location where goods were imported, exported, stored and redistributed.

■ **LOCATION** 2 miles S of Preston, Lancashire; off A6.
■ **ACCESS** There is nothing to see at the excavation site.

CISTERCIAN MONASTERY

❷ Whalley Abbey

Cistercian monks originally based at the monastery in Stanlow, Cheshire, were so distraught by the unsound conditions and regular flooding of their ill-chosen settlement that they decided to move to a new site. They settled here at Whalley in 1296. Most of the abbey building was done during the 14th century and architectural features associated with that period can be seen in the ruins today.

Abbot Paslew of Whalley Abbey is famous for being a member of the Pilgrimage of Grace, an ecclesiastical uprising that took place in the north in 1536, in a dispute over Henry VIII's policy of reformation of the monasteries. Abbot Paslew was tried, convicted of treason and executed in 1537.

The abbey was later sold and the abbot's quarters were developed into a house which incorporated additions right up to the late 17th century.

■ **LOCATION** 6 miles NE of Blackburn, Lancashire; off A59.
■ **ACCESS** Abbey Gatehouse: www.english-heritage.org.uk. Abbey and grounds: 01254 828400 for opening times and further details. Admission charge.

ROMAN ORIGINS

❸ Manchester

Around AD79 a legionary fort was built on a hill between the Irwell and Medlock rivers. Because the shape of the hill resembled a breast, the fort was named Mamucium. With major roads to the north, south and west, it wasn't long before a vicus settlement grew (the smallest unit of Roman administration). Evidence for this has been found to the north of the fort, and today you can see a reconstructed entrance at Castlefield. A fragment of 2nd-century Roman pottery found during excavation had a Christian symbol scratched into it, one of the earliest signs of Christianity in Roman Britain.

It appears that much of the fort and associated settlement were abandoned around the beginning of the 5th century. During the Anglo-Saxon period, Mamucium, possibly then called Mamecester, was in the disputed region between the kingdoms of Northumbria and Mercia. The 9th century witnessed some Viking settlement, reflected in place names such as Davyhulme and Urmston, which are derived from Norse personal names.

The Domesday records of 1086 record the settlement now known as Manchester as having a parish church. During the medieval period the settlement gradually grew into a successful market town. The 14th to 16th centuries saw the increased development of the church, alongside the development of a considerable trade in the production of cloth.

Manchester made the move from prosperous market town to industrial powerhouse in the 18th century. In 1761 the Bridgewater canal was opened, allowing cheap coal to be transported at huge profits to feed the growing cotton industry. The spinning jenny (which enabled a weaver to use 16 thread spindles at once) and steam-powered mills were to follow, and by the mid-1800s the city was home to over 180,000 people. The turn of the century saw the horse-drawn trams replaced with an electrified system (trams returned to the centre in 1992).

Manchester was still at the forefront of modern technology in the 1940s when the university designed the first memory computer, nicknamed 'Baby'.

■ **LOCATION** Manchester.
■ **ACCESS** Manchester Museum: http://museum.man.ac.uk or telephone 0161 275 2634 for opening times and other details.

THE BODY IN THE BOG

❹ Lindow Man

For a long time, Lindow Moss was simply an unassuming peat bog in the Wilmslow area of Cheshire. However, in the early 1980s a number of gruesome yet important archaeological discoveries were made. In 1983, peat diggers discovered a human female head, and the following year a human leg was unearthed. These finds were overshadowed in August 1984 when local worker Andy Mould came across the preserved head and torso of a man while digging in the peat.

The 'Lindow Man' was removed for examination, whereupon it was

▼ *In spite of extensive tests, Lindow Man still holds on to the secret of why he met such a violent death.*

discovered that he had met with a violent end. He'd received three blows to the head before being garrotted and having his throat slit. He was then placed face down and naked (apart from a fox-fur bracelet) in the bog pool. His death is believed to have occurred around 2,000 years ago, and it's thought that he was around 25 years of age when he died. His brown/ginger hair and whiskers had had the benefit of being cut by scissors or shears, and his manicured fingernails indicated that he was not a manual worker.

There is a possibility that he was ritually sacrificed, especially since poisonous mistletoe pollen was found in his stomach. However, opinion is divided over the circumstances of Lindow Man's demise. Some claim that he could have been murdered by unknown assailants or executed for a crime.

■ **LOCATION** 1 mile NW of Wilmslow, Cheshire; off A538.
■ **ACCESS** There is nothing to see at the site. The body is on display at the British Museum: www.thebritishmuseum.ac.uk or telephone 020 7323 8000 for opening times and other details.

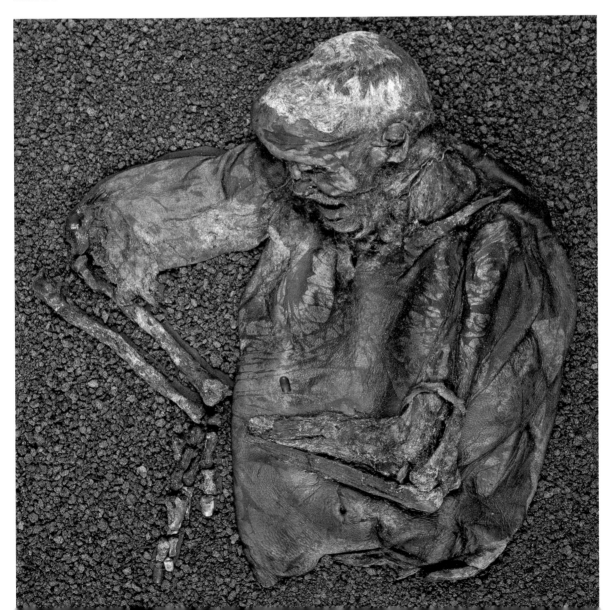

ANCIENT PORT

❺ Meols

Derived from the Norse term *meir* meaning 'sand dune' or 'sandbank', Meols functioned as a Roman, Viking and medieval port. The site is important for what it reveals about coastal settlement and trade during these periods, and it is particularly abundant in finds. Over 3,000 objects dating from between the Mesolithic and post-medieval eras were discovered during the 19th century.

Coastal erosion revealed the remains of an ancient forest, together with an array of unstratified objects (those disturbed from their resting places), which have indicated trade links with places as far apart as Ireland, Scandinavia and the Mediterranean. The ancient port was eventually abandoned during the 1500s when sand dunes gradually enveloped the village. The inhabitants moved inland to establish a village where Meols stands today.

Erosion meant that the original port was lost to the Irish Sea, and 19th-century antiquarians seemed more concerned with collecting artefacts than recording any structures or layers within their excavations. Luckily, a few antiquarians did make some field observations, which included house structures with stone-wall footings that are typical of Iron Age, Romano-British and medieval structures. The collection of finds from Meols is considered to be one of the most important outside of London, providing evidence of a beach market with associated port and settlement that was in continuous use for thousands of years.

■ **LOCATION** 1 mile E of Hoylake, Wirral, Merseyside; off A553.
■ **ACCESS** Nothing to see at the site. Finds are scattered; best single collection at Grosvenor Museum, Chester: www.chester.gov.uk (go to 'Tourism and Leisure', then 'Grosvenor Museum') or telephone 01244 402008 for opening times and other details.

ROMAN AMPHITHEATRE

❻ Chester

The first indication that Chester had an amphitheatre came in 1929 when a large curved wall became apparent during the construction of an underground boiler room at Dee House. Excavations at Caerleon (see page 114) in 1926–7 had stimulated interest in Chester's amphitheatre and further trenches confirmed its identity.

Subsequent excavations revealed that the amphitheatre formed part of the Roman settlement based at the strategic fortress of Chester, known to the Romans as Deva. When the amphitheatre opened to the public in 1972, study into the structure continued. Further investigation confirmed that much of the amphitheatre's stonework had been removed, recycled and incorporated into several of Chester's buildings.

The original timber-framed buildings went up in the late AD70s but were rebuilt in stone to become the entertainment venue and military-training complex for the Deva-based Legion XX. Excavation by English Heritage in conjunction with Chester City Council began

▲ *The Roman amphitheatre at Chester formed part of the settlement known as Deva. Much of its stonework was subsequently recycled into Chester's buildings.*

anew in 2004, attempting to understand how the amphitheatre related to the rest of the city's Roman remains.

Notable findings so far include a 'make-up' spoon, tableware and glass, all dating from the Roman era.

■ **LOCATION** Chester.
■ **ACCESS** Castle and Roman amphitheatre: www.english-heritage. org.uk or telephone 01244 402111 for opening times and other details.

MONASTIC SITE

❼ Norton Priory

In 1115, a priory was founded at Runcorn and became home for a community of Augustinian canons. The priory moved to Norton in 1134 and in 1391 had its status elevated to that of mitred abbey – where the abbot was permitted to wear a mitre – before its dissolution by Henry VIII in 1536. Sir Richard Brooke purchased the abbey and estate in 1545 and built a house incorporating several of the monastic buildings on the site. The house was rebuilt and renamed Norton Priory in 1750, and the remaining abbey buildings were demolished.

The Brooke family left Norton in 1922 and the mansion was subsequently dismantled. The abbey remains were left and the site became overgrown until excavations began in 1970, resulting in one of the most thorough archaeological investigations of a monastic site in Britain.

Archaeologists uncovered one of the largest examples of a mosaic-tiled church floor in the nave of the priory church, and learned of an elaborate water supply and drainage system. The priory's undercroft still stood, and the remains of the domestic buildings that had housed the canons were uncovered.

The remains of a 13th-century bell mould were also excavated, and in 1977 a replica bell was cast, which chimes hauntingly for the public today at Norton Priory and museum.

■ **LOCATION** 3 miles E of Runcorn, Cheshire; off A558.
■ **ACCESS** Priory and Museum: www.nortonpriory.org or telephone 01928 569895 for opening times and other details. Admission charge.

DEFENDED SITE

❽ Eddisbury

Eddisbury hillfort is an Iron Age defended site with outstanding views across the Delaware forest on the Cheshire Ridge. Originally constructed over 2,500 years ago in the domain of the Cornovii tribe, the site marked a boundary near the territory of the larger northern Brigantes group. The Cornovii are an unusual and little understood tribe, who do not appear to have used the distinctive Iron Age coinage or pottery their contemporaries did.

The site appears to have been damaged by the invading Romans in the 1st century, but the most renowned events relate to the early 10th century when the earthworks were revived by Ethelflaed, Lady of the Mercians, and Eddisbury became a defended fort once more.

Ethelflaed was the daughter of Alfred the Great, and was married to Aethelred of Mercia in AD887 to create an alliance. She became governor of Mercia when Aethelred died in 911 and did much to aid the development of the early stages of a unified England. Her work at Eddisbury was a continuation of her father's plan to create strongholds, or burhs, in the path of marauding Vikings.

Ethelflaed was active in military campaigns and negotiated the submission of the Vikings of Jorvik (York) before her death in 918.

■ **LOCATION** 8 miles SW of Northwich, Cheshire; off B5152.
■ **ACCESS** No public access. See OS Landranger map 117 for public rights of way and other hillforts in the area.

13TH-CENTURY CASTLE

❾ Beeston

Beeston Castle sits on a rocky crag 150 metres above the surrounding Cheshire countryside. Excavation has shown that there was prehistoric activity on the site including a possible Iron Age hillfort, but it's in 1225 that the major activity began. The 6th Earl of Chester and crusader Ranulf Blondeville had Beeston Castle built as a symbol of his power in the region. The design featured an innovative style contrary

to the popular keep and curtain wall. Ranulf built an inner and outer bailey protected by walls with intermittent towers, designed to protect each other with covering fire. Instead of a keep, the castle featured massive gatehouses protecting the vulnerable entrances.

When the 7th Earl (John) died without an heir in 1237, the castle passed to Henry III who used the stronghold as a base for actions against the Welsh. By the mid-13th century, Beeston had been given to Henry's son Edward who, after inheriting the throne in 1272, managed to subdue the Welsh and secure the Cheshire area.

The castle saw action again in the Civil War when it was occupied by Parliamentarians. A battle in 1643 saw Royalists take the site only to be

◀ Part of the inner bailey at Beeston Castle. The castle was built by Ranulf Blondeville, 6th Earl of Chester, to demonstrate his substance as well as to defend his power in the region.

under siege for nearly a year before surrender. At the end of the war Beeston Castle defences were destroyed to prevent them from being used in the future.

■ **LOCATION** 1 mile NW of Beeston, Cheshire; off A49.
■ **ACCESS** See www.english-heritage. org.uk or telephone 01244 402111 for opening times and other details. Admission charge.

EARLY CHRISTIANITY

⑩ Sandbach Crosses

Standing in the market place of Sandbach, these two huge carved stone crosses are thought to date from the 9th century. They are carved with biblical scenes, including the nativity and crucifixion, together with various

▼ The stone crosses of Sandbach, carved with biblical scenes, stand freely in the square of this market town, but they have not always been safe from unwelcome interest.

animal representations. High stone crosses dating from the early development of Christianity can be seen all over the country, but these two particularly well-preserved examples are thought to relate specifically to the acceptance of the religion by the kingdom of Mercia in central England. The pagan king Penda who died in the mid-7th century left nine children, who all adopted the Christian religion.

Both crosses were damaged by Puritans in the 17th century and restored to their present position in the early 1800s. Recent work has looked into the iconography of the monuments and tried to assess their purpose as symbols of Christianity in the fascinating phase of its early development in Britain.

■ **LOCATION** Sandbach, Cheshire.
■ **ACCESS** Full public access to Market Square.

MORTUARY CHAMBER

⑪ Bridestones

The Bridestones at Cloud Hill near Congleton are the remains of a Neolithic burial chamber, with two impressive large frontal monoliths measuring over 3m (10ft) tall. Behind the monoliths a large 1.5m by 4.5m (5ft x 15ft) east–west aligned stone-slab chamber is divided into two by a low transect stone. This fascinating monument was probably once used as a chamber for the interment of human remains. This well-built example is of particular interest because megalithic sites of this nature are rare in the Cheshire region.

■ **LOCATION** 2 miles E of Congleton, Cheshire; on minor roads E of A52.
■ **ACCESS** See OS Landranger map 118 for location and public rights of way.

TIMBER-FRAMED HOUSE

⑫ Little Moreton Hall

Little Moreton Hall is probably the most famous timber-framed building in Britain. The incredibly ostentatious

close timber style, which displays a vast amount of unnecessary structural timber, boasts the tremendous wealth of the Moreton family, who started building the moated manor in the mid-15th century. Over 100 years later the manor was complete, with a prominent Elizabethan long gallery in the upper stories. The construction uses multiple jetties of timber work to increase the size of the upper floors. The manor also has a great hall and a number of fine wall paintings.

The southern side of the front shows a remarkable degree of movement over the years, typical in ancient timber-framed structures. Now in the care of the National Trust, Little Moreton Hall also has a cobbled courtyard, garden and chapel typical of the Tudor and Elizabethan periods.

■ **LOCATION** 4 miles SW of Congleton, Cheshire; on A34.
■ **ACCESS** See www.nationaltrust.org.uk or telephone 01260 272018 for opening times and other details. Admission charge.

NEOLITHIC LANDSCAPE

⑬ Billown

Billown lies on the southern part of the Isle of Man, just north of Castletown, and is the location for a joint archaeological venture between Bournemouth University and Manx National Heritage. The Billown Neolithic Landscape Project began in 1995, two years after the discovery of Early and Middle Neolithic pottery, charcoal and flintwork on land reserved for stone quarrying.

Billown has archaeological remains that include four round barrows, eight standing stones, a stone circle and an enclosure comprising several ditches. It's believed that the site was active, albeit not continuously, from about 5000BC to AD600. Mesolithic

▶ *A Ronaldsway jar. Many such jars were used in association with cremation burials. They were often decorated with dots stamped into the wet clay using a pointed tool or quill.*

▶ *Little Moreton Hall, perhaps the most famous timber-framed building in the country. Its use of timber is ostentatious as well as structural – it was done to show off wealth.*

triangular microliths (tiny flint tools, *c.* 5000–4000BC) were found, while the earliest Neolithic deposits seem to be three shallow oval-shaped pots.

Neolithic pottery and leaf-shaped arrowheads were uncovered in several ditches, which also yielded evidence of reworked flint. Another area revealed three heavy round-bottomed basic pottery vessels known as Ronaldsway jars, which had been buried with their rims level with the top of the subsoil. Some of the Neolithic features did not survive as earthworks because of the later restructuring of the landscape. But it is clear that the Billown Neolithic landscape saw much activity over a long period of time.

■ **LOCATION** 1 mile N of Castletown, Isle of Man; off A7.
■ **ACCESS** No public access; site of excavation now a quarry. There is a prehistoric Isle of Man exhibition at the Manx Museum: see www.gov.im/mnh (go to 'Museums'), or telephone 01624 648000 for opening times and other details.

Yorkshire

Yorkshire is a treasure-house of sites, including some of the most important in Britain. At Star Carr, waterlogged conditions have preserved organic Mesolithic artefacts. York itself, also thanks to waterlogging, has produced some of the best evidence of Roman and Viking Britain. The Iron Age is unusual in British prehistory in that we know of relatively few burials and cemeteries – yet spread across south and east Yorkshire are a number of Iron Age cemeteries and single burials. Battlefield archaeology is a new subject of study and Yorkshire is at its forefront as a result of the major discovery of a war grave from 1461 in Towton. This region also contains some of the country's first medieval abbeys, and, from the period of the industrial revolution, important mill and factory sites.

City of York
Key strategic site

YORK HAS MANY memories for me because in 1999 it was home to the third Time Team live broadcast – without a doubt, the most ambitious project we'd ever tackled, in both archaeological and television terms. We had a team of nearly two hundred people working on the programmes, and it was a weekend of sheer excitement and amazing discoveries, but a lot of exhaustion as well, as the live broadcasts came and went.

Because York has such a long and varied history, we'd decided to tackle not one, but three archaeological sites across the city simultaneously, each representing a different period in the city's occupation. It was under the unlikely location of the Royal York Hotel lawn, next to the railway station, that we came face to face with three of the city's Roman inhabitants as we excavated one of its cemeteries.

Changing name
During the Iron Age, the area occupied by present-day York had belonged to a tribal group called the Brigantes. But by AD71 the Roman army was pushing

north into this territory to establish a more permanent presence in the north of England. They built a fort at the junction of the Foss and Ouse rivers, and the settlement of Eboracum or York was born. Because of its strategic significance, controlling routes across the rivers, it grew to become one of the most important cities in Roman Britain. Parts of the impressive military headquarters were discovered during repair work under York Minster, and some sections of the famous city walls that can still be seen today are Roman in origin.

The 5th century saw Eboracum renamed Eoferwic under Anglian rule. In AD627 the Anglian King of Northumbria, Edwin, was converted to Christianity and built a small church at York, traditionally considered the first York Minster.

In 866, the Vikings captured York and gave it the name Jorvik, and it is its Viking Age archaeology that the city is famed for. Excavations in Coppergate in the 1970s dramatically revealed part of a 10th-century street, with workshops, houses, yards, even latrines. Because of the unusual waterlogged conditions, evidence was recovered that wouldn't normally have been preserved.

Jorvik Viking Centre
It rapidly became clear that the archaeologists were dealing with an exceptional site at Coppergate. The wet conditions meant that tens of thousands of objects had been perfectly preserved, from the timber walls and fences of the buildings, to clothing, leather, wooden objects, plant and animal remains. For the five years the dig went on, it captured public interest in an unprecedented way, and visitors came from all over the world to watch the archaeologists at work. And so in 1984, York Archaeological Trust opened the Jorvik Viking Centre – an exhibition centre that used the evidence from the dig to recreate part of the

▼ *Roman glassware from York, one of many high-status finds.*

▲ The Jorvik Centre is one of Britain's most vivid archaeological sites. The recreated buildings and street scenes are based on the exceptionally well-preserved archaeology.

Viking town, as well as giving visitors the opportunity to see real objects and understand how the reconstruction had been achieved.

Carenza says, 'The excavations of the Viking levels are one of the grade-A sites of archaeology, single-handedly changing people's perceptions of the Vikings from raiders and pillagers to decent domestic townspeople. The archaeology is now either dug out or covered over and so the site can't be visited like many others in this book, but for me a visit to the Jorvik Centre, where you travel through a reconstruction of the town in the Viking period, is even better.'

The centre has been so successful, and has so many imitators across the world, that it's easy to forget just how groundbreaking it was. Visitors travel along the streets of Viking York in a small fairground-style car, watching, listening to and even smelling the inhabitants and buildings of the town. Each detail, from the construction methods for the houses, to the food and domestic items on the tables, the rubbish in the streets and the dialects and languages being spoken, was faithfully recreated from the excavated evidence or the latest research. Visiting the centre gives you a real sense of what Viking Jorvik might have been like, and shows just how powerful archaeology can be in bringing the past to life.

Our second Time Team dig site was a similar Viking street, Walmgate, and it

made me realize for the first time how exciting it must have been to work at Coppergate. Finding a unique glass bead, bits of amber, and even nuts and seeds from a thousand-year-old dinner was a rare snapshot of life in a thriving city. Jorvik, along with Dublin, was one of the great trade centres of the Viking Age, with strong international links across Europe and a booming home economy with lots of highly skilled craft workshops.

Medieval city

The last Viking king of York, the gorily named Eric Bloodaxe, was killed in AD954, but it didn't stop Viking and Anglo-Saxon feuding in northern England. Indeed, the Battle of Stamford Bridge in 1066, when the English King Harold defeated Norwegian warrior Harald Hardrada, happened just 8 miles from York. Shortly afterwards, of course, Harold was himself killed at Hastings, and William the Conqueror marched north to subdue the region.

The famous landmark Clifford's Tower is built on top of one of two motte-and-bailey castles William erected when he made York his northern base. York remained an important city throughout the medieval period, and its castles and city walls were repeatedly strengthened and rebuilt – it's pretty much the only place in Britain where you can still walk the original circuit.

Inside the walls, the medieval city was dominated by York Minster. Most of the Gothic cathedral you see today dates from the 13th–15th centuries, when the Archbishops of York decided to rebuild the Norman church to rival Canterbury.

There were many other churches and religious institutions in medieval York as well as the minster, and for our final live site, we chose the Hospital of St Leonard, once the biggest in England. After watching medical historian Carol

Rawcliffe apply leeches and demonstrate other medieval medical techniques, I felt glad to be digging the hospital up rather than having been an inmate at the time.

It was a challenging site, but we did make a good start at tracking down the remains of the hospital, and York Archaeological Trust have been running an innovative public excavation there ever since, carrying on where Time Team left off and revealing the history and layout of the hospital.

We discovered something no one was expecting at the hospital site: an

◄ *York Minster has dominated the city since the middle ages. It was built over the Roman fortress headquarters because the Church knew, as the Romans had done, that York was the secret to power in the north.*

underground public air-raid shelter from the Second World War. It was a small reminder that the city suffered during the war because of its long history. York was bombed in 1942 during the so-called 'Baedeker air raids': bombing raids named after a popular German tourist guidebook, which were designed to destroy Britain's morale by flattening her historic cities. After devastating raids, including one in which the railway station took a direct hit, it's amazing that so much of the city's unique history and architecture survives.

■ **GETTING THERE** York's historic city centre is unsuitable for cars. For the Jorvik Viking Centre, visit www.jorvik-viking-centre.co.uk or telephone 01904 543403 for opening times and other details.

Admission charge. For other sites, try York Tourist Office: www.york-tourism.co.uk or telephone 01904 621756 for further details.

■ **OUR VIEW** Carenza suggests a walk around the medieval city walls as a way to begin getting orientated to the historic theme park that is York. And of course the Jorvik Centre is absolutely unmissable.

Rievaulx Abbey
Cistercian monastery

RIEVAULX IS ONE OF Mick's favourite sites. The beautiful location on the banks of the river Rye in Yorkshire was initially chosen because of its relative isolation, which appealed to the monastic ideal of living outside society.

Rievaulx was founded in 1132 by a group of monks from Clairvaux in France, on land given by a nobleman called Walter Espec. They were Cistercians, sometimes known as the 'white monks' after their distinctive white habit with black scapular over the

▼ Rievaulx is one of the most complete Cistercian monasteries we have.

shoulders. They were keen to recover the austerity and frugality of early Christian monasticism, which they felt had been undermined. In an age when those who sinned could redeem their souls by making gifts of land and money to the church, many monks had taken what the Cistercians regarded as an unhealthy interest in the trappings of wealth. The Cistercians, inspired and led by the charismatic Bernard of Clairvaux, turned their back on any contact with personal or architectural decoration. Gold altar vessels, elaborate stonework and stained glass were frowned upon. In the northern location of Rievaulx, however, they must have found the prohibition against cloaks, fur boots and warm personal undergarments rather hard!

When you first walk around Rievaulx you may notice the plainness of style, and yet the scale and design create an impression of great beauty. The builders had to adjust to the topography of the site, which slopes steeply to the east. The normal orientation for the altar end of a church is east; at Rievaulx it faces south.

Apart from the odd orientation, the plan of Rievaulx conforms to a standard Cistercian layout. As Mick points out: 'The idea was that if you took a blind Cistercian monk from Poland and popped him into a monastery anywhere else, he could still find his way around.'

All this wonderful structure was not built overnight. Rievaulx was added to and altered over time. It is one of the fascinations of the abbey that it shows the changes in architectural style that occurred over the hundreds of years it was being built. Mick suggests you find the lower walls of the transepts – the 'arms' of the church, to see the changes in style. The lower windows and stonework are 12th century; above these you should then be able to see a change from the plainer style to a different look that features more pointed arches in a lighter stone – the start of what architects call English Gothic. In some parts of the monastery you can see where one stone has run out and another quarry has been exploited.

Material success

This architectural activity clearly cost a lot of money. It is ironic that despite their desire for a purer monasticism, the Cistercians became very rich. Their initial willingness to accept only land from their benefactors turned into a money-spinner as they began to farm sheep. By the end of the 12th century, Rievaulx was flourishing. During the time of Ailred, abbot between 1147 and 1167, there were over 140 monks and 600 lay brothers. There was a strict division between monks and lay brothers, whom Mick describes as the 'worker ants' of the community. At this time the monastery and the surrounding landscape would have been a hive of activity, as farming and small-scale industry in the valley supported the spiritual activity of the monks. Rievaulx was so successful that it started up over 30 daughter houses across the country.

The head of the whole community was the abbot, and in the case of Ailred we have a biography written by a fellow monk that gives us many details of his life. He was well connected with Scottish nobility and a confidant of Henry II. As he became old he suffered from arthritis and other ailments and had to take many baths to ease his aches and pains – a rare luxury at this time. At Rievaulx, elaborate structures exist underground to carry spring water around the site. Mick suggests you find the location of the longhouse built for Ailred conveniently between the infirmary and the church. In the chapter house is the stone coffin said to be Ailred's last resting place, and a remarkable shrine to St William, another revered abbot.

Rievaulx continued to expand into the 13th and 14th centuries and often acquired land at the expense of local villages, which was not guaranteed to make them popular with the locals. The larger the establishment, the more lay brothers were required, and when the Black Death hit the local population this may have triggered Rievaulx's decline. By the time of the dissolution in 1538, there were only 21 monks here.

■ **GETTING THERE** Rievaulx Abbey is 3 miles NE of Helmsley, North Yorkshire; off the B1257. See www.english-heritage. org.uk or telephone 01439 798228 for opening times and other details. Admission charge.

■ **OUR VIEW** As you walk round the buildings, you might like to imagine not only the spiritual activities at the centre – the prayer and services – but also all the support activity going on in the surrounding fields.

Wharram Percy
Deserted medieval village

WHEN WEALTHY AND powerful nobility discovers that land occupied by flocks of sheep is more profitable than villagers growing arable crops, commercial realities can take over and what was once a thriving village can disappear back into the landscape. Other economic changes, and to a lesser extent events like the Black Death, can also take their toll. Many of Britain's fields contain the traces of deserted medieval villages (DMVs), and this has become an area of great interest for archaeologists, with Maurice Bereford's book on the subject a landmark publication. It has been established that there might be 2,000 to 3,000 deserted villages in Britain – there is likely to be one in your local area.

Like many of them, Wharram Percy was closed down by the landowners in the 16th century. Only the church remains of the medieval village, which you can see today. Excavations have shown it to have Saxon origins. If the local landowners considered the village of no importance, a later group saw it in a very different light. In the 1950s, the Deserted Medieval Research Group adopted Wharram Percy and have intensively investigated it ever since. It was one of the longest-running excavations in Britain. From the homes of the peasants to the church and manor house, the minute details of life have been recorded.

Time capsule
Excavations of houses from the 15th century revealed typical medieval longhouses with people and animals occupying the same building. There was a hearth in the central area with a simple hole in the roof for the smoke. We even know that they kept their houses tidy, with rubbish and discarded pottery being swept out into the fields. Wharram Percy has become like a time capsule of medieval life. As Mick puts it, 'It was the archaeology of the average medieval peasant.' Before this a lot of work had been done on castles, palaces and abbeys, but at Wharram Percy here was a quite well-preserved medieval village: the sort of place most of us in this period would have lived in.

Time Team dug on a deserted medieval village site at High Worsall (also in North Yorkshire) in 1997. Like many DMVs, aerial photography played a key role in its discovery. It was the ultimate 'lumps and bumps' programme. In many ways it was Wharram Percy where this kind of archaeology first began to be appreciated.

For Mick this site is one of the places where archaeologists began to accumulate some of the details of everyday life in small villages: where the animals lived, the lockable chest for prize possessions, metal locks on the doors, the thick pottery with probably a rich green glaze. When you wander among the lumps and bumps, you might like to close your eyes and imagine the sounds and smells of the place. The animals being moved out of their byres, sharing the same roof as their human occupants, the bustle and the smells of a small village, the conversation in words we would recognize today.

Birth and death of a village
Wharram Percy has a long village green down the middle, homes on each side, a church and at least one manor house. There is also a mill, and a mill fish pond, so it has all the components of what we think of as a medieval village, and yet as Mick points out Wharram Percy was a village for a brief period of only 500 or so years. Before that it was an area farmed from just two or three centres,

during the Bronze Age, Iron Age, Roman and Saxon period. In the post-medieval period it was farmland again, with two or three farms as centres.

What made the people gather together to form a village? Mick suggests a number of factors – single farms were not producing enough as new demands were made by the growth of markets and towns. Military obligations imposed by William the Conqueror meant that tenants had to support knights; Mick describes knights as the Exocet missiles of the medieval period: highly expensive to run. The medieval war machine absorbed a lot of wealth, so people had to come together to support each other's efforts. As groups of people farm together, land becomes more productive, and they find it convenient to live near each other.

Decades of excavation at Wharram Percy have given the site a unique place in British archaeology. We have a very detailed survey of a specific area, and the number of buildings and where they were located has gradually become clear. A key thing to remember is that this did not happen overnight: villages did not spring up with the arrival of the Saxons. 'Ye Olde Village Green' and the village that we take for granted as such a central part of country life is an odd coming together of factors.

Wharram Percy declined in part because of the Black Death. Half the villagers died and this made it difficult for those that were left to carry on farming in the traditional manner. In the end it became easier to enclose the land and evict the villagers.

▲ The landscape of small houses each with their own small fields surrounding a church and an adjacent manor house began to establish our idea of what a village should be. This landscape lasted in its village form for over 500 years.

■ **GETTING THERE** Wharram Percy is 6 miles SE of Malton, North Yorkshire, off the B1248. See www.english-heritage.org.uk for opening times and other details.

■ **OUR VIEW** It is worth remembering that the fields you can see today were once the homes of medieval families to whom eviction must have come as a great sadness. Like many DMVs it is a good idea to visit it when the sun is fairly low in the sky so that you can make out the shadows of the lumps and bumps.

Other sites to visit

❶ Whitby Abbey

Whitby Abbey is sited on a bleak headland overlooking the North Sea. Excavation in the 1920s, and more recently following the threat to the site from coastal erosion, has highlighted what was once a thriving monastic community and associated settlement.

Founded in AD657 by Hild (later St Hilda), the abbey may have been built on the site of an earlier Roman signalling post. Excavation has revealed monks' cells, workshops and other buildings, which help reveal the day-to-day existence of those who once lived here. We're further reminded of the importance of Whitby by recorded events such as the synod (council meeting) of the church held in 664 to discuss the type of monasticism to be practised by the Northumbrian church. Roman was chosen over Celtic.

The abbey attracted many monks and nuns and enjoyed widespread influence. However, the site was destroyed in 867 by Viking raiders. The abbey was rebuilt in fine style following the Norman invasion in the 11th century, yet after the dissolution of the monasteries 500 years later only a small church was retained for the local parishioners from the remarkable complex, while materials from the abbey were stolen to help in the construction of a manor house.

▼ St Hilda's abbey at Whitby, overlooking the north sea. The abbey might have been established on the site of an earlier Roman signalling post.

■ **LOCATION** Whitby, North Yorkshire.
■ **ACCESS** See www.english-heritage. org.uk or telephone 01947 603568 for opening times and other details. Admission charge.

❷ Mount Grace Priory

The ruins of Mount Grace Priory at Saddle Bridge, Northallerton, are all that remains of a Carthusian monastery founded in 1398.

The captivating aspect of the Carthusian order was the austere and hermit-like existence of the monks. Where other orders worshipped and lived as a community, the Carthusians existed as individuals within the monastery. This is reflected in the typical arrangement of their sites, where separate monks' cells surround a large cloister.

Within the remains of the church at Mount Grace is an almost complete tower. The cloister and foundations of 23 cells can also be identified, together with secondary buildings including farm buildings and guest accommodation (converted to a house in the 1600s), and a mill and leat, which reveal the working life of the monastery. An interesting feature is the water

◄ *Thornborough Circles in the Dales, extending for nearly 7 miles across the countryside. They are best appreciated in an aerial shot – a view their creators never had.*

❹ Ripon

Two miles east of the beautiful Fountains Abbey (see below) lies the cathedral city of Ripon, which itself has an intriguing ecclesiastical past. The powerful and imposing architecture of the cathedral you see today dates mainly from the 13th and 16th centuries, an impressive piece of reconstruction work that masks an ancient history.

The first Abbot of Ripon was the Northumbrian bishop Wilfrid who also founded Hexham (see page 233). He started building a minster church here in 672; a small crypt, under the present cathedral, is the only survivor of that date. Viking raiders destroyed Wilfrid's church in 950, and although a replacement was built on the site, it only lasted 100 years before being destroyed by the invading Normans, who reached Ripon by 1069. In 1080 the Normans, with their great tradition of church building, started work on a third church, which became incorporated into the present structure by the grandiose refurbishments of later centuries.

■ **LOCATION** Ripon, North Yorkshire.
■ **ACCESS** See www.riponcathedral.org.uk or telephone 01765 603462 for opening times and other details.

❺ Fountains Abbey

Fountains Abbey, so called because of the abundant springs that cover the site, is one of the most beautiful monasteries in Britain, with a history that reads like a medieval crime story.

Around 1132, a group of Benedictine monks at St Mary's Abbey in York decided that things had become too lax for their spiritual good and determined to

system, supplied by nearby springs. Channels direct water around the gardens to the latrines.

The plan of Carthusian monasteries tends to be less conventional than other orders, and Mount Grace gives us a glimpse of this obscure group who held only a handful of monasteries in Britain. A reconstructed cell and garden can also be seen on the site.

■ **LOCATION** 6 miles NE of Northallerton; on A19.
■ **ACCESS** See www.english-heritage. org.uk or telephone 01609 883494 for opening times and other details. Admission charge.

❸ Thornborough Circles

The Thornborough Circles near Ripon represent the largest Neolithic henge monument complex in the north of England and the biggest site of its type between the Orkney islands and Stonehenge. The three main henges at Thornborough act as focal points along a series of earthworks and causeways that mark an ancient sacred landscape some 5,000 years old. The henges and their associated features, including barrows, extend for nearly 7 miles across the landscape.

Henges are regarded as non-defensive sites because their bank and ditch enclosures feature the ditch on the inside. The Thornborough henges appear to have been in use all around the same time, which makes the area probably one of the most active ritual landscapes of the period. Though the sites are scheduled by English Heritage, the landscape continues to face threats from the demands of gravel extraction in the region.

■ **LOCATION** 6 miles N of Ripon, North Yorkshire; off B6267.
■ **ACCESS** See OS Landranger map 99 for footpaths and location.

▶ *Fountains Abbey is one of the most beautiful monasteries in Britain, and at one time was among the richest.*

branch out on their own. Their desire to begin a new life would have come to nothing had they not found a benefactor in the shape of Archbishop Thurston of York, who granted them some land in the valley of the river Skell. Here they created a set of simple wooden buildings, the precursor of the magnificent ruins you see today.

In 1133 they joined the Cistercians and were again supported by another wealthy benefactor from York, who provided more land and additional funds. Gradually the community grew. By 1150 Fountains Abbey had acquired stone buildings and a growing reputation, and had successfully sent its monks out to found other abbeys throughout England.

When Thurston died, his successor William Fitzherbert was less sympathetic to the abbey, and the abbey found itself caught up in political battles that eventually resulted in it being attacked by Fitzherbert's followers. Much of the abbey was burnt and many buildings damaged. Fitzherbert would eventually die in suspicious circumstances, and after the fire Fountains was rebuilt with a sense of renewed optimism. The beautiful Chapel of Nine Altars was part of the rebuilding in the 13th century, and this and the picturesque Huby's Tower – built around 1500, and a rarity in a Cistercian abbey – are two of the key features to see. The cellarium, the main storage area of the monastery, is a unique survival from the 12th century. It is over 90m (300ft) long, and its ribbed vaulting with 22 bays is in excellent condition – testament to the skills of the medieval builders.

At the time of the dissolution, Fountains Abbey had become one of the richest abbeys in the county, owning vast amounts of Yorkshire.

Like many Cistercian monasteries, it was a hive of activity with small-scale industrial works and thriving agricultural businesses. The mill in the abbey precinct is one of the best preserved of this date in western Europe.

One of the reasons Fountains Abbey survived was that it was adopted as a sort of decorative garden folly by the Studley Royal Estate; the excellent gardens of the adjoining stately home are well worth a visit.

■ **LOCATION** 4 miles W of Ripon, North Yorkshire; off B6265.

■ **ACCESS** See www.english-heritage. org.uk or telephone 01765 608888 for opening times and other details. Admission charge.

❻ Addingham

The industrial revolution saw nearly 2,000 mills established in the Yorkshire regions. Many towns and villages thrived under the new manufacturing processes, and one such place is Addingham.

Weaving machines such as Richard Arkwright's water frame and Crompton's mules, powered by water or steam, allowed for yards of fabric to be produced in a fraction of the time taken to produce them by hand. In the late 18th century John Cunliffe and John Cockshott established their spinning factory at Low Mill using water power to drive a wheel by the wharf. Their products helped fuel the worsted yarn markets of Bradford, and soon Addingham had other mills developing around the growing town.

Low Mill was a main employer, important in the local economy. When it briefly closed in the early 1800s the population of the town diminished in response. The 20th century saw Addingham driving no

There has been some contention over the date of the road. It's generally assumed to be Roman because of the extremely high quality of construction – so good, in fact, that roads of a similar standard would not be built again in Britain until 1,300 years after the Romans had withdrawn.

■ **LOCATION** 3 miles E of Littleborough, Lancashire; off A58.
■ **ACCESS** See OS Landranger maps 109 and 110 for 'Roman' road and other footpaths in the area.

❽ Sandal Castle

Sandal Castle lies 2 miles south of Wakefield in a prominent position overlooking the river Calder. This outstanding mid-12th-century motte-and-bailey stronghold had its original wooden structures upgraded to stone during the 12th and 13th centuries. Excavated during the 1960s and 1970s, the castle has revealed some interesting features, including an unusual inner barbican within the main bailey complete with its own substantial ditch. Both the motte and bailey contain the stone remains of several phases of building. Foundations of a hall and towers are clearly defined for the visitor to see.

The 14th century saw the castle passed to Edward III, who gave the estate to his son Edmund, Earl of Cambridge (later Duke of York under Richard II). During the 15th century the castle witnessed the Battle of Wakefield (1460) and remained undamaged. This battle, where the Lancastrians fought the Yorkists for control of the throne, gave birth to the 'Grand Old Duke of York' rhyme.

Later that century plans for conversion into a royal house under Richard III were abandoned when Richard fell at Bosworth in 1485, his death signalling the end of the Wars of the Roses. Development of the castle ceased almost before it had

less than five textile mills. Many of the factory buildings and workers' houses can be easily identified today.

■ **LOCATION** 4 miles NW of Ilkley, West Yorkshire; off A65.
■ **ACCESS** Mills and workers' houses can be viewed from public streets.

❼ Blackstone Edge

A fine surviving section of a Roman road can be seen at Blackstone Edge near Littleborough on the Yorkshire/Lancashire border. The original route would probably have run over the Pennines from Rochdale to Halifax, and it's from the A58 Rochdale road

▲ *What is believed to be a surviving stretch of Roman road at Blackstone Edge in the Pennines. The central channel is for drainage.*

(by the White House Inn) that you can access the site.

Roman roads were generally built with a central camber in three main layers of graded stone, with drainage ditches running along the sides. The Blackstone Edge section, well known to walkers of the Pennine Way, is of a particularly high quality and incorporates drainage channels within the cobbled surface. Well-worn grooves caused by wheeled carts can be seen on the surface of what was once a busy road.

started. During the Civil War it was used briefly for defence and was then made unusable by decree of Parliament in 1646.

■ **LOCATION** 2 miles S of Wakefield, West Yorkshire; off A61.
■ **ACCESS** Visitor centre and site: telephone 01924 305795 for opening times and other details.

ROMAN LEATHERWORK

❾ Castleford

The ancient history of ex-mining town Castleford starts with the Roman occupation of the 1st century. Practically no trace of the town's Roman history survives above the ground and it was only rediscovered in the Victorian era when the area was extensively

developed. A series of excavations uncovered the remarkable Roman heritage of the town, which lies alongside a major Roman road.

The pattern of settlement is of a Roman fort and supply base established around AD70, followed by a second-phase fort built perhaps just ten years later. A civilian settlement grew around the fort and by the 2nd century, after the military had moved elsewhere, it expanded into the area occupied by the fort. By the 4th century the town, which appears to have enjoyed a continuing success, became fortified once more, probably as a result of the unsettled closing stages of the Roman period.

Archaeological work within the town has brought to light some extraordinary finds. The waterlogged

conditions have preserved leatherwork in the form of shoes, military tent material and, particularly remarkable, a saddle cover and a protective shield cover.

■ **LOCATION** Castleford, West Yorkshire.
■ **ACCESS** Nothing to see at excavation sites. Finds from Roman Castleford on display at Wakefield Museum: www.wakefield.gov.uk, go to 'Culture and Leisure' then 'Museums', or telephone 01924 305351 for opening times and other details. Roman Castleford exhibition at Castleford Library and Museum: telephone 01977 722085 for opening times and other details.

BLOODY BATTLEFIELD

❿ Towton

In March 1461, the Wars of the Roses, which saw Edward IV's Yorkists vying for power against Henry VI's Lancastrians, reached a bloody peak at the Battle of Towton. Day-long brutal hand-to-hand fighting, which saw the fortunes of each side sway under the developing mêlée, left an estimated 28,000 dead on the battlefield. Though the Yorkists won the day, the wars were far from over. Both sides endured another ten years of erratic fighting before the deciding battle at Tewkesbury in 1471 saw Edward able to rule in relative peace.

Towton remains one of the bloodiest battles to be fought in Britain, and in 1996 a mass burial pit from the battle was discovered by builders working near the site of the fighting. The remains of 43 men, stripped and entangled, were excavated from a shallow pit. Careful recording and subsequent computer analysis of the distribution of bones allowed archaeologists to piece together the remains. Bones specialists working together with the Royal Armouries and the excavators managed to establish that many of the individuals had healed wounds from

◀ *Towton battlefield, silent witness to the deaths of an estimated 28,000 people in one of the bloodiest battles fought in Britain.*

medieval weapons, indicating that they were experienced fighters. The remains also showed evidence of strong muscle growth and premature development, which suggests heavy training in their youth.

The mortal wounds were of a particularly brutal kind, involving severe trauma to the head and face. The relatively minor abrasions to the rest of the body suggest that they may have been wearing armour at the time of death. In many respects the Towton grave illustrates the true horror of medieval warfare – and it is a far cry from the chivalrous and posturing picture often portrayed.

■ **LOCATION** 4 miles S of Tadcaster, North Yorkshire; on A162.
■ **ACCESS** See www.towton.org.uk for further details. OS Landranger map 105 for footpaths around the battlefield and village.

⑪ Star Carr

First excavated in 1949–51, Star Carr is still one of the best examples of a Mesolithic camp known in the UK. The Mesolithic period (8000–4000BC) saw bands of hunter-gatherers roaming the landscape, often with seasonal or one-off opportune camps providing their homes. The nature of their lifestyle means that they travelled light and in this age, before humans even used pottery, finds can be thin on the ground.

The site at Star Carr was based around a constructed birchwood platform that originally stood on the edge of a lagoon and appeared to have acted as a centre for the community. The site's unusual wealth of finds provides a glimpse into Mesolithic life. Animal remains indicate that wildfowl, red deer, wild pig and cattle were staple foods. Many of the unwanted heavy and less useful parts of a carcass (spine and pelvis) were not found at the site, which indicates the efficient butchery of animals elsewhere.

Nearly 200 barbed antler points, similar to harpoons, and 240 tiny flint microlith weapons also give us an idea of the scale of the operation. Grahame Clarke, who excavated the site, estimated that a group of around 25 members could have lived here.

Possibly the most intriguing finds are 21 red-deer skull parts with antlers. They appear to have been trimmed to size using flint tools, and some have holes made through their edges. Many of the antlers are broken down and thinned. One theory is that the skulls were used as headdress for disguise and camouflage during hunting; another is that they were part of everyday wear for the group, or necessary for ritual practice.

■ **LOCATION** 2 miles S of Seamer, North Yorkshire; off A64.
■ **ACCESS** Nothing to see at excavation site, no public access. Selection of finds on display at the British Museum: www.thebritishmuseum.ac.uk or telephone 020 7323 8299 for opening times and other details.

⑫ Wetwang

Interesting Iron Age barrows enclosed with square ditches can be found in isolation and also grouped in cemeteries all over the East Yorkshire area. It's not just their shape that makes them unusual. A few have been found to contain the remains of dismantled two-wheeled carts, each containing the crouched body of a dead person. These so-called 'chariot burials' represent a local tradition for which there are parallel discoveries in the Mosel area of Germany and the Ardennes region of France.

The Yorkshire group has been named the Arras culture by archaeologists. Excavations during the 1970s and 1980s at Wetwang Slack quarry and nearby Garton Slack uncovered four chariot burials within a landscape bustling with Iron Age settlements. The most recent chariot burial was discovered in

2000 in the village of Wetwang, when an archaeological assessment was being conducted in advance of a new housing development. At 10m (33ft) in diameter, the barrow site was fairly large, and its isolated position on a ridge suggested the burial of an important figure. After weeks of careful excavation, the remains of an Iron Age woman were uncovered, together with her dismantled cart, a bronze hand mirror and a selection of beads, all dating to around 300BC.

■ **LOCATION** 6 miles W of Driffield, East Yorkshire; on A166.
■ **ACCESS** Nothing to see at excavation sites. Exhibition including Wetwang finds at Hull and East Riding Museum: www.hullcc.gov.uk/museums or telephone 01482 613902 for opening times and other details.

⑬ Rudston

The Rudston area has an enthralling Neolithic past. The most obvious relic from prehistory is the huge monolith that stands alone at over 7.5m (20ft) high in the graveyard of All Saints Church within the village. The single piece of upright stone might have been quarried from the North Riding over 10 miles away.

The Rudston area also contains a variety of barrows and at least four obscure cursus monuments. Cursus generally take the form of twin straight ditches with banks on the interior side built up from the excavated ditch material, often stretching for great distances. Their purpose isn't known to us (though their name tells us they were once thought to be racecourses), but a great deal of effort would have been expended in building them, so their significance must have been considerable. Some archaeologists suggest they were the routes of ritual procession, while other believe they mark out the boundaries of sacred landscapes. The cursus at Rudston have largely been identified through

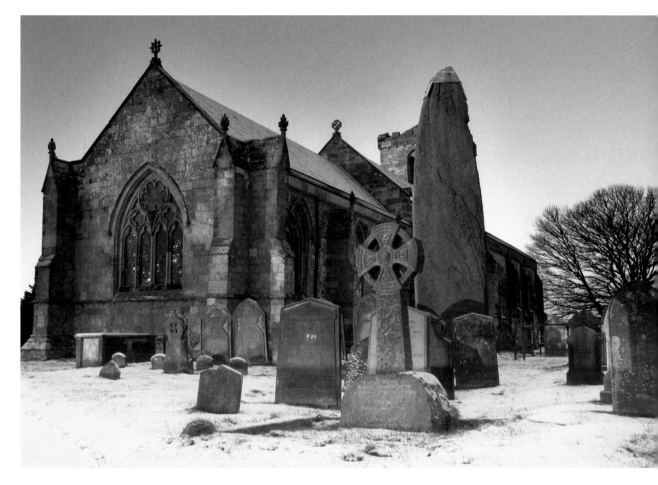

▲ *The unmissable prehistoric monolith in the graveyard of All Saints Church at Rudston in East Yorkshire.*

landscape survey and aerial photography – hardly anything survives above ground.

■ **LOCATION** 6 miles W of Bridlington, East Yorkshire; off B1253.
■ **ACCESS** Cursus are not visible on the ground. Monolith on view in churchyard of All Saints Church. See OS Landranger map 101 for footpaths and other monuments in the area.

⑭ Humber Estuary

From the early 1930s, local man Ted Wright regularly searched the foreshore at North Ferriby for finds. It was in 1937 that he spotted the

ends of three planks of oak jutting from the clay and instantly recognized them as parts of a boat. Subsequent excavations revealed the remains of a Bronze Age boat some 13m (43ft) long and nearly 1.7m (6ft) wide. Three years later he discovered the remains of a second, less well-preserved boat, and excavations were carried out in full after the war.

The construction of the boats was mainly established by the largely intact first find. A succession of long single planks up to 20cm (8in) thick were tied together via bracing timbers with yew withies (flexible strips of wood or branch shoot used like rope) to form the flat-bottomed hull of the boat. The joins were caulked with moss and covered with oak laths to ensure the hull was

watertight. It has been estimated that the boats could have carried 4½ tons of cargo and made over 6 knots under the power of 18 paddlers. There is even some suggestion that they could have been sail-powered and suitable for coastal waters. The archaeological evidence in Bronze Age Britain for artefacts with continental origins hints intriguingly at vessels like the Ferriby boats being used for early foreign trade.

■ **LOCATION** North Ferriby, 5 miles W of Hull, East Yorkshire; off B1231.
■ **ACCESS** Nothing to see at sites. See OS Landranger map 106 for footpaths. Estuary coast and tides can be extremely dangerous. Finds on display at Hull and East Riding Museum: www.hullcc.gov.uk /museums or telephone 01482 613902 for opening times and other details.

North of England

Our northern region includes some of the wildest, most rugged and also most beautiful landscapes of any in England, where in many areas a sparse population occupies small, thinly scattered settlements. Often because of this very isolation, the northern counties preserve a rich inheritance of historic and archaeological sites. From the prehistoric legacy of the Langdale axe factory and stone circles such as Castlerigg and Long Meg, to medieval monuments such as Lindisfarne, Jarrow and Durham Cathedral, the north has a wealth of historic remains, many of which are of national importance and figure prominently in events that had an impact far outside the region.

N

BERWICK-UPON-TWEED

Lindisfarne

Old Berwick
Moor

A1

A697

(2)

(1) Dunstanburgh
Castle

A1

A68

Lanercost
Priory

(9)

A69

Vindolanda

Hadrians Wall

Holy Jesus
Hospital (13) NEWCASTLE

(14) Jarrow

(10)

Carlisle (8)

Hexham

Harperley (11)(12)

Beamish

SUNDERLAND

A596

M6

Long Meg and
Her Daughters

(7)

A689

A68

DURHAM

Durham
Cathedral (15)

A66

Castlerigg (5)

(6) Mayburgh

A19

HARTLEPOOL

(4) Langdale Axe Factory

A66

A1(M)

MIDDLESBROUGH

(3) Ravenglass

KENDAL

A590

DARLINGTON

0   20 m
0   20 k

**Furness
Abbey**

Hadrian's Wall
Rome's furthest line of defence

AD122 into the 3rd century

WHEN TIME TEAM excavated at Birdoswald Fort on Hadrian's Wall, the weather was not wonderful. With rain running down the back of our necks and horizontal gale-force winds, I remember wondering, as we uncovered the remains of cremations, burials and pieces of Samian pot with rather naughty designs, why a successful Mediterranean empire, brought up in the warm sun, with long summers and endless supplies of wine, would want to end up here? Even today a journey up the M6 can seem like a lifetime, and yet not only did the Romans push up to what was the northernmost part of the empire, but they built huge structures to hang on to it.

In search of answers and looking for advice on where best to go to understand Hadrian's Wall, I talked to Guy de la Bédoyère – Time Team's Roman expert.

The empire's frontier
Guy stressed that expansion was one of the driving forces of the Roman Empire. As expansion took place it provided more

▼ The Romans were brilliant at exploiting the landscape. Hadrian's Wall was built along the top of crags wherever possible, presenting a formidable challenge to anyone who fancied a fight with the Roman army.

resources to support the empire and satisfied the Roman belief that their destiny was to rule the world. But as the empire grew it also became harder to manage those resources and defend the frontiers. This was particularly so in areas like northern Britain, where there was no tradition of accepting the benefits of Roman patronage. This meant the Romans could not rely on local people to adopt Roman ways and do much of the government work themselves.

Rome existed by offering support to local tribes in return for peace and all the benefits of the Roman system, and in many parts of Britain both sides

benefited. Up in the north there were fewer major centres of power and a more diffuse system. The result was a greater need for purely defensive structures that demarcated a line between the civilized and – as far as the Romans were concerned – barbarian world.

To begin with just a road called the Stanegate marked the northern frontier in Britain by Trajan's reign (AD98–117). It ran from Carlisle to Corbridge, and probably continued further east. Forts along the road held the garrisons.

Hadrian decided to fix the empire's boundaries. He ordered fortifications to be built in many parts of the empire. In Britain he ordered a wall, and construction began in about AD122.

Exploring the wall

Half a mile west of Housesteads Fort is Milecastle 37, a typical structure representing many that were strung out along the wall. Guy recommends visiting this to get an idea of how the wall functioned. Milecastles were fortified gateways with a small garrison. They did not prevent people from crossing the wall but controlled the movement. Between each milecastle were two lookout turrets. A ditch forward of the wall protected it from assault. To the south a ditch and mound system protected the wall zone.

Milecastle 37's north gate and walls are substantially complete. If you stand there on a cold wet day, you get a sense of the isolation the Roman auxiliaries who garrisoned the wall must have felt. You look north across forbidding moorland and south over rolling hills with little to comfort the eye, unless you're a sheep farmer. This was a narrow ribbon of power in the wilderness, and in the 2nd and 3rd centuries the forested areas just beyond the hills would have contained a selection of locals unimpressed by the delights of Roman civilization and just awaiting a chance to do a bit of damage.

Building the wall

In one of our first reconstructions of a Roman ditched site, at the fort in Ribchester (see page 182), the re-enactors wore full military armour and the steel plates chafed painfully at their arms as they dug. This was the start of an occupation that must have never been easy. The locals were anything but friendly.

Guy refers to the design of the wall as a textbook plan that had to be adapted to local realities. The original 10-Roman-feet-wide wall was scaled down to 8 feet. If you look carefully, at some places you can see a larger foundation supporting the smaller wall. Initially there were no forts, then the decision was taken to build them on the wall itself, even if that meant demolishing sections of wall that had only just been built. The forts at Birdoswald and Housesteads today are two of the best preserved.

The amount of stone used was colossal, and the work would have been done by legionaries on detachment from their fortresses further south. Roman soldiers were builders as well as fighters and Hadrian knew that large numbers of troops with nothing to do became fractious. Guy refers to the wall as partly a job-creation scheme, with different centuries (units of 80 men) being given sections to build – probably with an element of competition to spur them on. Having completed a length of around 15 metres (50ft) or so, each century would install an inscription to mark the achievement and also allow the officers to check on work done. The teamwork and competition would have helped unite the soldiers. One inscription, from Milecastle 38 and dated to about 122–4, records Hadrian's name and the governor who built the wall for him: Aulus Platorius Nepos.

It is worth noting that in its first phase, the western sector of Hadrian's Wall was built not of stone but of turf. The Romans used turf of a size laid down by Vegetius in his manual of military building for those locations where stone was scarce. This turf wall ran from the river Irthing to the Solway Firth in the west, while the stone wall ran from Newcastle to the Irthing. The wall was soon extended east to Wallsend, and by the late 2nd century the turf wall had been rebuilt in stone.

Living on the wall

At places like Birdoswald where Time Team excavated, an adjacent civilian settlement has been discovered, which seemed to provide the facilities of a small town for the troops. There may have been as many as 1,000 auxiliaries or 500 cavalry stationed in these kinds of places, and they would have had to be prepared to make attacks to the north using the gateways in the forts.

Hadrian's Wall was mothballed soon after it was built. With the construction of the Antonine Wall (see page 244) in

▼ *Every fort, as here at Housesteads, had granaries to make sure the garrisons were fed. The pillars raised the floor to protect the grain from rodents, and the massive buttresses stopped the settling grain from pushing the walls out.*

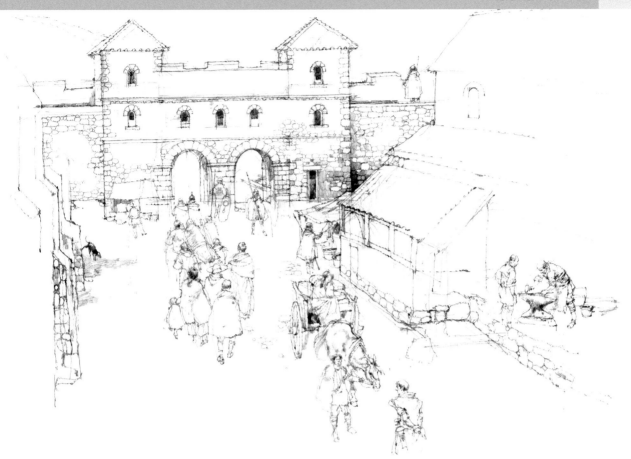

about 139–43, a move was made to push the frontier further north. It is likely that the number of soldiers occupying the forts on Hadrian's Wall was reduced. But the Antonine Wall was permanently abandoned in the 160s. Hadrian's Wall was reoccupied and repaired under Marcus Aurelius (161–80), who faced further threats from the northern barbarians. The wall was later repaired and rebuilt by the emperor Septimius Severus around 205.

From the letters found at Vindolanda (see page 220) on the Stanegate road, dating to the beginning of the 2nd century, you get a sense of many of the Roman soldiers who occupied these sites as being ordinary people, far away from home, in an unpleasant and dangerous situation.

Another site we suggest you take a look at is Arbeia at South Shields, where

Time Team worked in 2004. Here the west gate of a fort has been rebuilt, and it's a good opportunity to get a sense of the scale of Roman military architecture. There are massive wooden doors with towers on each side and a section of the fort wall. There were dozens of these forts along the wall, attempting to preserve Rome's far-flung ambition at the edge of the empire.

▲ Life could go on in relative safety behind the fort gate, and Victor's drawing shows what one of these fort gates might have looked like in its heyday. But no one knows for sure how high they were, or whether the towers had roofs.

■ **GETTING THERE** The wall runs W from Wallsend, Newcastle upon Tyne, to Carlisle and beyond. See www.english-heritage. org.uk. Admission charges may apply depending on site. Birdoswald Fort is 3 miles W of Greenhead, off the B6318. See the English Heritage website or telephone 01697 747602 for opening times and other details. Admission charge. The wall is covered by OS Landranger maps 85, 86, 87, 88.

■ **OUR VIEW** The image that I will always associate with the wall is of the groups of legionaries in the acute discomfort of full armour, maybe in the wind and the rain, constructing this monument that has lasted into our own time, and it is a tribute to their extraordinary skills and the skills of the surveyors who laid it out that we are still able to trace its route today, 1900 years later.

Vindolanda
Letters from the Romans

OUR KNOWLEDGE OF WHAT Roman Britain was like is very dependent on archaeology, because we, unlike many other parts of the Roman Empire, don't have much surviving documentation. And, as Guy de la Bédoyère is always reminding me, that means there are many areas of Romano-British life we don't understand very well, because they don't leave physical traces: like how the administration of the province worked, and what its inhabitants liked and disliked about living here.

Vindolanda is a Roman fort that formed part of the Hadrian's Wall defences, although, as you see when you get there, it's actually two miles south of the wall itself – for the simple reason

that it was part of the Stanegate line (see page 217) and existed before the wall was built. Thirty years later it was rebuilt in stone and incorporated into Hadrian's defence system. The visible remains you see today at Vindolanda are from the 3rd and 4th centuries AD; underlying them are earlier forts, rebuilt many times.

The site would be just another fort along Hadrian's Wall if it hadn't been for the 'Vindolanda letters'. Beginning in 1973 and ever since, excavations at the fort have uncovered hundreds of fragments of handwritten documents left by the inhabitants of Vindolanda. These documents were largely written before the building of Hadrian's Wall. Most of them were written in ink on thin sheets of birch and alder wood, some as slim as 2mm, and about the size of postcards. Many had been thrown out on rubbish dumps, some burnt in a bonfire. Preserved because of exceptional anaerobic soil conditions, they are fragile

▼ Straggling civilian settlements, such as this one hugging the road outside Vindolanda, grew up outside almost every Roman fort. Here soldiers, traders, travellers, women and children created thriving communities on the frontier.

and require careful conservation, and the use of infra-red photography before they can be read – although some remain illegible and can't be deciphered at all.

'Wretched Britons'

What's exciting about the Vindolanda tablets is that they're not epic works by famous authors, but the kind of reports, personal notes and everyday letters that people like you or me might leave behind. Written by the fort's officers, their families, soldiers and servants, they provide an incredible amount of detail about the military routine of the fort, but also give personal insights into the day-to-day concerns of ordinary people.

They reveal that the soldiers stationed at the fort – Tungrians and Batavians – were from the area of modern Belgium and Germany, and there's even a strength report listing how many of the soldiers were fit for duty, stationed elsewhere, or sick at one particular time. An intelligence memo describes the 'wretched Britons' and their fighting habits (see caption, right). One work report shows the soldiers were building themselves a bathhouse at the fort.

The prefect of the Batavian cohort, Flavius Cerealis, features heavily in the letters, some of which are addressed to him and some of which he wrote himself, arranging meetings and dealing with business. One of his officers even writes to request more beer for the soldiers. Perhaps the most famous letter is to Flavius's wife, Sulpicia Lepidina, from a friend inviting her to a birthday party. Although the letter is written by a scribe, the friend adds her own

postscript – 'I shall expect you, sister. Farewell, sister, my dearest soul, as I hope to prosper, and hail' – one of the first Latin texts written by a woman.

▲ This document is a memorandum describing the Britons' manner of warfare. The frustrated writer says the numerous cavalry did not use swords, and that the 'wretched Britons' did not mount in order to throw javelins.

Doing deals

Lots of the documents are about money and supplies, and they really give you an idea why *vici*, the towns outside the fort like the one we dug at Birdoswald, grew up so rapidly, when there was such good business to be done supplying the army with all kinds of items.

The longest letter discovered so far is from an enterprising character, Octavius, to his business partner Candidus, and it's easy to imagine Octavius at Vindolanda, masterminding deals to buy and sell animal products; the note mentions sinew, hides and leather. Octavius has laid out a 300-denarii deposit and begs Candidus to send him more money before he loses it. Clearly Roman roads weren't always as good as we think they were. One lot has gone uncollected because Octavius 'did not care to injure the animals while the roads are bad'.

■ **GETTING THERE** Vindolanda Roman fort is 1¼ miles SE of Twice Brewed, off the B6318. See www.english-heritage. org.uk or telephone 01434 344277 for details. Admission charge. The letters are on display in the British Museum: www.thebritishmuseum.ac.uk or telephone 020 7323 8000 for opening times and other details.

■ **OUR VIEW** Vindolanda was the first site Carenza ever dug, at a time when it was still buzzing from the discovery of the letters. She says: 'The reconstructions are well worth a visit. I was there for a month, and spent a lot of time working on the left bit of the main street as you walk down towards the museum – so have a good look at that bit!'

Lindisfarne
Celtic Christianity

AD635-1537

TIME TEAM EXCAVATED on Lindisfarne in 2000. We were looking at a site near the edge of the island that provided warehousing for the monastery and might have been used to brew ale. Like many modern excavations on the island, this was outside the main church area, but our visit there gave us a chance to look at all the remains of this remarkable site. The isolation of these island sites attracted early Christian monks, and the places have a real magic about them – down to the sound of the seals singing.

Lindisfarne was founded by St Aidan in 635, from the monastic base of Iona. Iona was one of the most important sites of Celtic Christianity and inspired many other monasteries (see page 258). Lindisfarne had connections with the royal palace of Bamburgh, and under the patronage of King Oswald this remote site became a major force in Christianity. Most of what you see today is a medieval Benedictine priory, re-founded in the 11th century, but underneath it are probably the remains of a Celtic Christian site with an enclosure that held stone-walled houses for individual monks.

The main influences on the early life here would have been Columba and Aidan – great saints in the Celtic tradition who sought to search for God

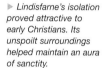

▶ *Lindisfarne's isolation proved attractive to early Christians. Its unspoilt surroundings helped maintain an aura of sanctity.*

in remote wildernesses. Although ascetic and saintly characters, many of these monks had a powerful influence on the local leaders and their presence was associated with miracles, even after their death. Cuthbert, one of Lindisfarne's most famous abbots, who lived here from 634 to 687, was particularly venerated. His skull, his possessions, and even his bones were considered holy.

Defenceless monks

On 8 June 793 the monastery was ransacked by Vikings, the monks murdered or taken into slavery and all the treasures stolen. It was a horrific event that shook the whole of Christian Britain. Alcuin of York, recording the event, referred to 'the church of St Cuthbert's spattered with the blood of the priests of God, despoiled of all its ornaments'. From this point on, any monastic settlement was vulnerable. The monks had little defence against invaders. Eventually, in 875, having endured enough, the monks removed St Cuthbert's remains from the shrine, abandoned the monastery and settled in Durham (see page 235).

It was the Bishop of Durham who rebuilt the priory on the island in 1081. Cloistral buildings were added later but the priory was dissolved in 1537 by Henry VIII. The monastery decayed and much was demolished before excavation work began in 1888. Visible remains today include traces of the cloister, the well-preserved ruins of the church and the remains of the presbytery.

Exploring the site

Mick suggests that you start with the north wall of the nave of the church, which is largely 12th century and gives you some idea of the scale of the building, originally over 50m (160ft) long. At the west end you can see typically Norman chevrons on the doorway. The main stone is a wonderful red colour, best

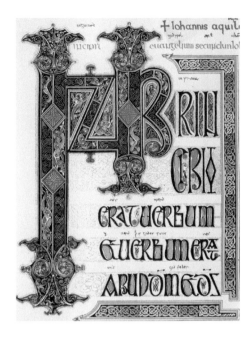

◄ The Lindisfarne Gospels in the British Museum are an amazing example of monastic skill and devotion. The visitor centre in Lindisfarne Castle usually has a display illustrating their history.

seen at sunset. Lindisfarne has always been vulnerable to attack and elements of the buildings you can see today are clearly defensive.

Worth a visit, if you can get to it at low tide, is St Cuthbert's Isle, with its chapel where the great man retreated when monastic affairs became too busy.

An area near the monastry has recently been excavated by Deirdre O'Sullivan. She found evidence of vellum processing and small-scale metal-working, probably connected with manuscript production. But the main area of Lindisfarne is largely unexcavated, and its early history hidden.

■ **GETTING THERE** The island is 10 miles down the coast from Berwick-upon-Tweed, off the A1. It is reachable at low tide across the causeway. For Lindisfarne Priory, see www.english-heritage.org.uk or telephone 01289 389200 for opening times and other details. Admission charge. For Lindisfarne Castle, see www.nationaltrust.org.uk or telephone 01289 389244 for opening times and other details. Admission charge.

■ **OUR VIEW** The last excavations in the central area of the island were in 1888, so we have very little evidence from modern excavation for activity from Cuthbert's time, but the site is perhaps best visited for its atmosphere and the way it still retains the ambience of an early monastic settlement cut off from the world. The causeway is subject to tides, so you have to be careful not to get stuck on the island – as Mick and his campervan did.

Furness Abbey
Cistercian isolation

1127–1500s

FURNESS ABBEY, like many of the Cistercian sites, was founded in a place that guaranteed its isolation from the world at large. The remains you see today are set between the wilds of the Lake District and Morecambe Bay, an area which, when the abbey was founded, was a lot less accessible than it is today. The abbey established itself in this position in 1127 after trying Tulketh near Preston and finding it unsatisfactory.

The abbey's original founder, Stephen, Count of Blois, was to become King of England, and his abbey of St Mary at Furness was to become incredibly wealthy. It owned land throughout the Lake District and the north of England, and much of this was used for sheep farming. Furness began life as part of the order of Savigny but changed its monastic leadership to the Cistercians. Mick describes this move as not having been popular with the founding monks.

Savigny is on the borders of Normandy and Brittany, and began as an order founded by a group of hermits who, like the Cistercians, sought a simpler and purer form of monasticism. The pope brought the Savignac order into the Cistercian order around 1147, and Furness unwillingly made the transition.

Furness is an excellent example of the high level of civil engineering skills required to set up an abbey. Water was of critical importance, and the large community needed effective systems for the removal of waste. You can see the main drain that brings in the water to a point where a set of sluice gates, like carved stone shutters, enables it to be diverted in various directions: to the kitchens, the infirmary and the toilets.

One of the key skills when selecting a site is the availability of water and a topography that enables it to swiftly drain away – nothing gets in the way of holy thoughts more than a ripe smell issuing from the sewers, and in this way abbeys were often better equipped in terms of plumbing than the great palaces and manor houses.

At Furness there are, in addition to the water systems, other excellent remains which enable you to get an idea of the key buildings connected with monastic life. Mick recommends what he calls the 'standard route' for viewing abbey sites. Start in the church at the high altar. This was where the choir stalls stood and it was the heart of the monastery, where the monks would spend over half their day. From here go through the day door into the cloister. The cloister was an important part of the monks' life and was the enclosed area within which they could safely exist, cut off from the outside world. From the cloister find your way into the chapterhouse in the east wing, where every day around nine o'clock in the morning there would be a communal meeting. Traditionally this was the place where a chapter from St Benedict's rules would be read out – hence its name – but

▼ The imposing cloister arch entrance to the chapter house.

it was also the place where much of the daily business and duties of the monks were carried out. Next door is the day room, where Mick likes to imagine the monks having a cup of cocoa and mending their socks! Next in the cloister is the southern range – the lavatorium, refectory and kitchens, and the warming house, which in winter would have had a good fire blazing in the fireplace.

In the 14th century a new infirmary was built for the care of sick monks. In an abbey the infirmary was more than just a hospital – ill health was both a physical and spiritual matter and great care was taken in the construction of these buildings. You may be able to find the recesses where each monk's bed was located. The adjacent chapel is now a museum, which is worth a visit.

Riches from wool

When you wander round the site, which is nicely tidied up and covered with mown grass, it's worth remembering that Furness is another abbey that wasn't really excavated. All the ruined stonework and rubble that lay around the walls was cleared away by local workmen, which often meant any archaeological stratigraphy got removed as well. There is often, on an old site, a location where a great pile of stonework is dumped. This, when correctly analysed, can reveal all sorts of archaeological changes that the standing remains don't. Like most abbeys, Furness was frequently subject to rebuilding, and at various times was damaged by invading Scottish rebels. There were, for example, at least four phases of frater (refectory) built at various times to feed the lay brothers.

What is clear from the vast amount of building work carried out is that Furness was very wealthy. This wealth was based largely on wool. It has been estimated that the great abbeys like Furness and Rievaulx had over 10,000 sheep on their land. Lay brothers looked after the flocks and prepared the fleeces for market. Records still exist for the vast number of fleeces these abbeys produced. With the dissolution the abbey lost its lands to Thomas Cromwell's Commissioners and gradually fell into ruin, but at its height it was one of the richest abbeys in Britain, and its abbot had the power and status of a great baron or lord.

▲ Five arches in the east wall of the abbey. Furness Abbey was subject to many rebuilds. The sheer volume of building is evidence of its wealth.

■ **GETTING THERE** Furness Abbey is 1½ miles N of Barrow-in-Furness, Cumbria, off the A590. See www.english-heritage.org.uk or telephone 01229 823420 for opening times and other details. Admission charge.
■ **OUR VIEW** Underpinning all this magnificent architecture – and typical of monastic sites – is a cleverly engineered plumbing system. Look for traces of it as you go round the abbey.

Other sites to visit

❶ Dunstanburgh Castle

Standing high on a cliff along a stretch of Northumberland's coastline, Dunstanburgh Castle dominates the remote landscape. It was built in 1314 for Thomas, Earl of Lancaster, a nephew of Edward II and the second richest man in Britain. The relationship between the king and his nephew was strained and culminated in Thomas's death in 1322 for rebelling against the monarch.

Towards the end of the 14th century ownership of the castle passed to John of Gaunt who carried out substantial alterations (of which little remain today), including converting the original gatehouse into a keep and building a second gatehouse further along the curtain wall. By the 16th century, the castle had become neglected and was left to decay – its design and structure were no longer suitable defence against the gunpowder-fuelled artillery of the day.

Archaeological surveying in 2003 revealed that Dunstanburgh had housed a radar station in the early days of the Second World War: an example of archaeological investigation providing unbiased confirmation of what had been in living recollection. The remains of Mediterranean terraced gardens belonging to homesick Italian POWs were also discovered. Study of the castle indicated that, more so than in most castles, Dunstanburgh's main purpose was to symbolize Thomas's wealth, power and status, rather than bear any strategic significance. Evidence of shallow lakes suggest that reflections of parts of the castle, such as the gatehouse and the Liliburn Tower, would have been used to augment the aesthetic value of the structure. Interestingly, much of the stonework was removed to construct buildings elsewhere but the best towers were left standing, perhaps to preserve the dramatic landscape.

■ **LOCATION** 8 miles NE of Alnwick, Northumberland; then 1½ mile walk from Craster or Embleton.
■ **ACCESS** See www.english-heritage. org.uk or telephone 01665 576231 for opening times and other details. Admission charge.

❷ Old Berwick Moor

Old Berwick Moor, north of Alnwick on the eastern edge of the Northumberland National Park, is a beautiful area with an astonishing prehistoric landscape. A large sandstone block to the east of Old Berwick village, deposited on the landscape during the last ice age, was first recognized in the 1820s as a piece of rock art. It depicts a variety of cup-and-ring designs, painstakingly engraved into its surface possibly some 5,000 years ago. The geometric shapes of concentric rings surrounding dots linked by straight lines certainly required a great deal of effort to create and would have been clear for passers-by to read, though today their meaning is lost.

Berwick hillfort dominates the horizon of Berwick Hill. This interesting Iron Age (or possibly older) enclosure follows a double plan of two parallel sets of defensive works, one that is not known anywhere else in the country. House platforms are also evident within the enclosed areas. To the east a further smaller hillfort can be seen at Corby Crags on Harehope Burn.

The importance of the landscape to our ancestors is compounded by the Blawearie cairns. This Bronze Age cemetery is centred on a large stone 12m (40ft) wide, and a rubble cairn with impressive kerb stones and burial cist chambers within. The main cairn is surrounded by a number of smaller monuments. This bleak and angular landscape is

▶ *The stark ruins of Dunstanburgh Castle, seen here from the north-west, give little impression of what a sophisticated medieval residence it was, with elaborate water gardens surrounding the fortress.*

a good walk on a fine day and an indulgence in unspoilt prehistoric archaeology.

■ **LOCATION** 7 miles NW of Alnwick, Northumberland; off B6346.
■ **ACCESS** See www.northumberland-national-park.org.uk or telephone 01434 605555 for details.

❸ Ravenglass

Ravenglass is in a remarkable position where the Mite, Irt and Esk rivers meet on the western Cumbrian coast. Named as Glannaventa by the Romans, Ravenglass was a vital naval base in the 2nd century, and also served as a fort and supply base for the north-west. Occupied with a garrison for some 300 years, the original fort was established in AD130.

The most prominent remains of the fort are the bathhouses, which still have walls standing up to 4m (13ft) high and cover an area of over 12m by 27m (40ft x 90ft). The baths follow the traditional plan of three stages of bathing.

A lead seal found at the fort gives us an indication of who garrisoned the base. It carried the inscription '*Cohors I Aelia Classica*': the First Cohort of the Aelian Fleet. The Aelian Fleet are also referred to in the early 5th century *Notitia Dignitatum*, a document recording the distribution of Roman military resources, as being based at another local fort called Tunnocelum, and possibly near Calder Bridge.

■ **LOCATION** ¼ mile E of Ravenglass, Cumbria; off A595.
■ **ACCESS** See www.english-heritage.org.uk for opening times and other details.

❹ Langdale Axe Factory

Great Langdale in Cumbria's Lake District is a remote location for one of Britain's first industries. Nevertheless, a Neolithic axe factory existed on the Langdale Pikes and it seems that axe production thrived from around 5500 to 4000BC. Cast-off axes, manufacturing debris and rough-outs (unfinished axe blanks) were discovered in the area by archaeologists, but the most significant aspect is the use by the manufacturers of 'greenstone'. Greenstone comes from an intrusion in the volcanic rocks of Langdale and would have made a highly efficient axe.

How Neolithic peoples came to discover greenstone as the perfect material from which to fashion sharp axes is unclear, but it is believed they would have been skilled at recognizing quality usable stone. Langdale axes have been found far afield in sites all over Britain and Ireland – 15 were found in the Thames – indicating that the 'factory' was the basis for a thriving export market. The axes were produced and traded as blanks – they would have been honed and finished later by the individual who obtained them.

These highly prized axes were ideal for hunting and woodcutting. They are believed also to have served as offerings in ancient water rituals: many have been found in wet areas.

■ **LOCATION** 4 miles W of Grasmere, Cumbria; off B5343.
■ **ACCESS** Various sites around Langdale Pikes. Steep scree slopes, access difficult and dangerous. See OS Landranger map 89 for footpaths.

STONE CIRCLE

❺ Castlerigg

Castlerigg Stone Circle near Keswick in Cumbria is believed to have been built sometime around 3000BC during the Neolithic period.

The 'circle' is in fact pear-shaped. It measures 30m (100ft) in diameter at its longest point and consists of 38 unhewn chunks of Borrowdale volcanic rock – 33 of which remain standing – with an average height of 1m (3½ft). Two larger stones flank a gap resembling an entrance on the northern side, while an outlier stands to the south-west of the circle.

A further ten stones form a rectangular enclosure or cove within the eastern side of the circle, the purpose of which is unknown. Castlerigg is believed to be one of the earliest examples of a stone circle in Europe but its origins remain a mystery. It could have been used for religious or ceremonial practices. Castlerigg is maintained by English Heritage on land owned by the National Trust.

■ **LOCATION** 1½ miles E of Keswick, Cumbria; off A66.
■ **ACCESS** See www.english-heritage. org.uk for details.

HENGE MONUMENT

❻ Mayburgh

The Mayburgh henge is a fine example of early monument building. The henge, a non-defensive monument probably used in ritual practice, measures over 90m (300ft) across and contains a single entrance by way of a break in the bank that provides a causeway to the interior. The banks still exist up to 4.5m (14½ft) high in places, and were constructed out of pebble deposits.

Estimated to have been built around 4,000 years ago, the interior space of the henge measures over 6,000 square metres (64,500 sq ft). A single stone remains standing at a height of 2.8m (9ft) on the plateau within the banks. The famous 18th-century antiquarian William Stukely recorded the existence of a further four stones within the monument, which were later destroyed.

■ **LOCATION** 1 mile S of Penrith; off A6.
■ **ACCESS** See www.english-heritage. org.uk for details.

STONE CIRCLE

❼ Long Meg and her Daughters

Long Meg and her Daughters is the folklore name given to a prehistoric stone circle in the Eden valley of northern Cumbria. The stone

▶ *The red sandstone pillar of 'Long Meg' in the foreground, with her 'daughters' in the distance. You need to get close to the stone to see the carvings on its north-west face.*

known as Long Meg is 3.6m (12ft) high; her daughters are represented by the oval-shaped circle of 59 stones. Only 27 stones still stand but the circle was thought to number over 70 stones at one time. The circle measures around 110m by 90m (360ft x 300ft) and the weight of the heaviest stone is in the region of 30 tons.

Unlike her 'daughters', which were constructed from local porphyritic stone, Long Meg was quarried out of

▼ *It's easy to see why the builders of Castlerigg Stone Circle chose this location. The impressive views of Derwentwater and Borrowdale make it one of Britain's most attractive prehistoric monuments.*

red sandstone from the banks of the river Eden over a mile away. The north-west face of the Long Meg megalith has been decorated with spiral and cup-and-ring marks together with half-completed concentric circles. Long Meg's position in the south-west aligns with the midwinter sun when viewed from within the circle, indicating the importance to the early Bronze and Iron Age farming communities of understanding the seasonal changes.

■ **LOCATION** 6 miles NE of Penrith, Cumbria; off A686.
■ **ACCESS** Public access. See OS Landranger map 91 for footpaths.

FORTIFIED TOWN

❽ Carlisle

Over many centuries, Carlisle was subject to numerous sieges and the scene of countless conflicts. The Romans named it Luguvallum and regarded it as an important frontier town. The Scots burnt Luguvallum

down on one occasion, leading the town to erect fortifications to prevent further invasions from the Scots and attacks from the Picts. After the Romans departed, Carlisle did fall to its persecutors and, apart from the fortifications, was virtually destroyed.

The city was rebuilt in the 7th century but was again destroyed by Danish Vikings around 876. It lay desolate until the Normans arrived nearly 200 years later. Once again the city was rebuilt with refortified walls, a castle and stone keep. Regardless of these defences, Carlisle was besieged many times over the centuries as a consequence of Anglo-Scottish conflicts and periods

of Civil War. During the English Civil War the Royalist Carlisle Castle came under siege by Parliamentarians. The siege lasted eight months (October 1644 to June 1645) and only ended when the inhabitants had exhausted their food supply and, facing starvation, surrendered.

The castle's most famous detainee was Mary Queen of Scots, who was incarcerated in 1568 after her abdication. Carlisle Castle remains a poignant symbol of the city's border-town past, while the local Tullie House Museum tells of Carlisle's history of invasions and border disputes.

■ **LOCATION** Carlisle, Cumbria.
■ **ACCESS** Carlisle Castle: www.english-heritage.org.uk or telephone 01228 591922 for opening times and other details. Admission charge. Carlisle Museum (Tullie House): www.carlisle. gov.uk (go to 'Leisure', then 'Museums'), or telephone 01228 534781 for opening times and other details. Admission charge.

AUGUSTINIAN PRIORY

❾ Lanercost Priory

The Vaux family founded Lanercost Priory in the mid-12th century and populated it with Augustinian monks, who were probably from a monastery at Pentney in Norfolk, where Vaux also held lands. Running for almost 400 years, the priory appears to have had relatively peaceful beginnings in its Borders position until it faced war during the 14th century as Scotland brewed the uprisings of Robert the Bruce and William Wallace.

Following Henry VIII's widespread campaign, Lanercost was dissolved as a monastery in 1536 and handed to Thomas Dacre of Naworth Castle. Dacre converted some of the buildings for private use while the rest of the site fell into disrepair.

◄ *The roofless remains of the priory in the parish graveyard at Lanercost in Cumbria. The priory nave was restored and that building is still in use as the parish church.*

In the mid-18th century the roof was restored on the priory nave and the building reused as the parish church. Though the parish church is still in use, the surrounding priory ruins are in the care of English Heritage. The remains of the transepts, choir and sanctuary are of particular note, as is the early western front of the church.

■ **LOCATION** 2 miles NE of Brampton, Cumbria; off minor road.
■ **ACCESS** See www.english-heritage. org.uk or telephone 01697 73030 for opening times and other details. Admission charge.

SAXON ABBEY

⑩ Hexham

With few prehistoric or Roman finds to date, it appears that the town of Hexham developed around the time of its earliest historical reference: the foundation of an abbey in AD674 by the Northumbrian Bishop Wilfrid, who also founded the abbey at Ripon (see page 207).

Sent out from the island of Lindisfarne to introduce St Benedict to Northumbria, Wilfrid built a fine stone abbey church at Hexham, which retains its rare Saxon crypt to this day. Some of the stone used in the construction was taken from the nearby Roman fort at Corbridge and from Hadrian's Wall.

Though the abbey was largely destroyed by the Viking raids of Halfdene the Dane in 875 and then rebuilt, the site is best known for its skirmishes in the Scottish uprisings of the 13th and 14th centuries. An artefact of note is the Saxon stone Frith stool, which would have been the bishop's throne or possibly even the crowning seat of Northumbrian kings.

■ **LOCATION** Hexham, Northumberland.
■ **ACCESS** Hexham Abbey: www.hexham abbey.org.uk for details.

◀ *Hexham Abbey chancel. The Frith stool has probably had an important symbolic function since before the Norman Conquest.*

POW CAMP

⑪ Harperley

Harperley (otherwise known as Camp 93) was built in 1943 on requisitioned farmland in Weardale, County Durham, to house Italian prisoners of war. It was later used to house up to 900 German prisoners of war categorized as 'low risk'. There were over 1,500 POW camps in Britain in operation during and after the Second World War, of which around a hundred were purpose-built camps like Harperley. Like many other 'base-camps', Harperley parented other POW hostels in the area, from which the prisoners would go out every day to work as labourers on local farms and businesses. The contribution made by the estimated 100,000 POWs interned at camps such as Harperley across the country was vital to the British war effort.

Harperley was in the hands of a single owner from 1948 to 2002, and is one of only five intact camps now surviving in England. Despite much of the camp having been used after the war for agricultural storage and chicken sheds, Harperley still contains most of its original buildings intact, including some unique interior fittings, such as a canteen complete with ten mural wall paintings and even a theatre, all created by the prisoners themselves. The survival and legal protection of Harperley was ensured in July 2002 when it was made a Scheduled Ancient Monument.

■ **LOCATION** 7 miles W of Chester-le-Street, County Durham; off B6168.
■ **ACCESS** Telephone 01388 767098 for opening times and other details.

OPEN-AIR MUSEUM

⑫ Beamish

With 350,000 visitors a year, the Beamish Museum is a huge success. As an open-air site the museum offers the visitor a living history experience that details how people lived and worked in the north of England during the 19th and 20th centuries. Displays are based in buildings either native to the site or reconstructed after rescue from important rural and industrial locations in the north.

Pockerly Manor and Railway reconstruct life in the early 1800s and boast one of the oldest steam engines still running. The defended manor has fine gardens and also working horses. A reconstructed town, colliery and farm take you into the 1900s. The style at the museum is interactive, and the visitor is surrounded in a bustling and active environment by hundreds of original period artefacts.

■ **LOCATION** 8 miles SW of Newcastle on Tyne; on A693.
■ **ACCESS** See www.beamish.org.uk or telephone 0191 370 4000 for opening times and other details. Admission charge.

SURVIVING ARCHITECTURE

⑬ Holy Jesus Hospital

Holy Jesus Hospital in Newcastle stands in stark contrast to its surroundings, its stone and brick caged in by 1960s concrete development. The earliest part of the existing building is the tower from a 13th-century Augustinian friary. In the 17th century the Corporation of Newcastle built the hospital as a hostel for 'pilgrims and travellers' with rooms for 39 people.

Interesting features of the hospital are the brick round-topped arches of the frontal arcade facing onto a stone fountain. The most striking view is from across the road where you can see the 17th-century hospital and 13th-century friary tower stubbornly standing against the 1960s Manors multi-storey car park. The building is now in the care of the National Trust.

■ **LOCATION** City Road, Newcastle upon Tyne NE1.
■ **ACCESS** See www.nationaltrust.org.uk or telephone 0191 261 7383 for opening times and other details.

⓮ Jarrow

St Paul's Monastery in Jarrow is of Anglo-Saxon origin and was founded in AD681–2 by Benedict Biscop. A few years earlier (674), Biscop had founded St Peter's Monastery in Wearmouth, but both were built on the understanding that they would function as one institution. Influenced by Roman architecture, Biscop's monasteries were among the first stone buildings in the region since the Roman occupation.

The twin monastery is renowned for being the home of the Venerable Bede. St Bede was born in 673 and educated at the monastery from the age of seven, and lived there until his death in 735. Regarded as the founder of medieval historical writing, Bede compiled the first recorded account of English life in *The Ecclesiastical History of the English People*, using the AD dating system for the first time.

Archaeological research suggests that after Bede, life at the monastery was disrupted by fire between the 9th and 11th centuries. Vikings were the most likely culprits but some attacks have been attributed to Scottish raiders. The monastery was rebuilt to a Benedictine layout under the Normans. It was dissolved in 1537, although the monastic church was retained to serve the parish,

▲ *The Sanctuary Knocker.*

◄ *This view of Durham Cathedral captures its dominant position in the surrounding landscape. It is one of the most enduring symbols of the power of the medieval Church.*

of the Nine Altars (to accommodate throngs of pilgrims) were built later. The architecture of the cathedral and associated buildings is predominantly Romanesque, although the Chapel of the Nine Altars is distinctly Early English Gothic in style.

During the middle ages, Durham Cathedral was a place of sanctuary. Fugitives would use the lion-like Sanctuary Knocker on the north door to gain entry and receive refuge for a maximum of 37 days. The original knocker is on display in the cathedral museum and an exact replica has adorned the north door since 1980.

Durham Cathedral famously holds the remains of St Cuthbert of Lindisfarne and St Bede of Jarrow-Wearmouth, while the cathedral muniments are rich medieval archives, holding original charters, documents, account rolls and letters. Many examples from the archive have retained their original seals. For over 900 years, Durham Cathedral has stood without falling victim to invasive rebuilding work, making it one of the least altered cathedrals in Europe.

■ **LOCATION** Durham.

■ **ACCESS** See www.durhamcathedral. co.uk or telephone 0191 386 4266 for opening times and other details.

which it still does today. Remains of the monastic buildings lie behind the church, and the nearby tourist attraction of Bede's World endeavours to recreate the life and times of St Bede through archaeological displays.

■ **LOCATION** 4 miles E of Newcastle upon Tyne; on A184.

■ **ACCESS** St Paul's Church is a working parish church and is open to the public. Bede's World: www.bedesworld.co.uk or telephone 0191 489 2106 for opening times and other details. Admission charge.

REFUGE AND ARCHIVE

⓯ Durham Cathedral

Durham Cathedral, on a peninsula carved by the River Wear, began as a simple church structure in AD998 to house St Cuthbert before being dismantled under the Normans. Construction of a new cathedral on the same site began in 1093 and continued until 1133. Additions such as the Chapter House, Galilee Chapel and Porch and the Chapel

Southern Scotland

This is an area of great beauty that has often been dominated by struggles along the borders. The Roman invasion and subsequent building of the Antonine Wall was an important factor in dividing Britain and beginning to delineate the hill country that would emerge as the kingdom of Scotland. To the north of the region, Iron Age crannogs were an important part of the prehistoric settlement pattern. Early Christian influence is represented by sites such as Whithorn, while in the medieval era towns or 'burghs' evolved, of which Edinburgh is a key example. Fortified houses or 'bastles' from the 17th century are a unique feature of the area. The story of post-medieval Scotland is one of both farming and increasing industrialization.

N

Inverurie ①

ABERDEEN

A96

A93

A90

A9

A93

⭐ **Crannog Centre**

Inchtuthil ⑦

DUNDEE

PERTH

Bonawe ②

A84

A9

Inchmahome ⑥

Poltalloch ③

A82

A811

M90

Antonine Wall ⑧

FALKIRK

DUNFERMLINE

GREENOCK

Edinburgh Castle ⑨

EDINBURGH

A1

Dun Nosebridge ④

M80

GLASGOW

Soutra ⑩

Machrie Moor ⑤

A77

KILMARNOCK

Jedburgh, Melrose and Dryburgh abbeys

Smailholm ⑪

⑫

A83

AYR

Glenochar ⑮

A708

⑬

Roxburgh

Slack's Tower ⑭

A76

A713

A74 (M)

DUMFRIES

Creetown ⑰

Caerlaverock Castle ⑯

A77

Drumtroddan ⑱

⭐ **Whithorn**

Barsalloch ⑲

0   20 m
0   20 k

The Scottish Crannog Centre
Experimental archaeology

600BC to the present

CRANNOGS ARE settlements built in lakes, using stone and timber to create artificial islands and platforms. The term usually refers to Scottish and Irish sites, but lake communities of one sort or another are found all over Britain and Europe. Time Team dug the only known one in Wales at Llangorse (see page 100) in the first series, and the settlements in the Somerset Levels at Meare and Glastonbury (see page 26) were also set

in a wet environment. The most famous lake villages of all are on lake Zürich in Switzerland, where many structures were dramatically discovered on its shores in the 1850s.

Crannogs might seem a rather alien concept to our modern minds, but they were a familiar part of life in Scotland for thousands of years. Iron Age crannogs are most common, but some date as far back as 5,000 years to the Neolithic period, and many were occupied on and off until the 17th century. They provided a defended home or refuge in troubled times, a safe place to keep animals and a rich environment to support a community. Some, like the royal crannog at Llangorse, were status symbols and a large focus for lots of people, but many

▼ An authentic reconstruction of a Bronze Age defensive home: a crannog, perched above the loch on stilts.

were just single homesteads – the one we excavated at Loch Migdale in a recent Time Team series probably housed just one family.

Underwater archaeology

The Scottish Crannog Centre has its origins in a series of pioneering underwater excavations that began in the 1980s. Although hundreds of crannogs have been discovered in Scotland since they were first recognized in the 19th century, not much is known about them because they can be so difficult to dig. So archaeologists from Edinburgh University decided to launch major investigations at Oakbank Crannog, a collection of 18 surviving mounds near Fearnan on Loch Tay. Some of the mounds can still be seen from the bank, covered in trees, but others are totally underwater and required specialist archaeological techniques.

The underwater excavations revealed an enormous amount of information about the crannogs and the lifestyle of their Iron Age builders. The cold, acidic water had preserved the timbers, hurdles and posts used in the construction of the crannog, as well as many artefacts and organic remains, from kitchen utensils to textiles, seeds and pollen, dung, even food like butter and sloes. They showed that the crannog dwellers were Iron Age farmers, keeping livestock and growing cereal crops, as well as making varied and abundant use of local resources, from bracken and moss as building materials to many wild plants and herbs as food.

However, as with a great deal of archaeology, the excavations produced lots of questions: how – and why – were the island and roundhouse built?

To try to answer some of these questions, and take advantage of the unique evidence recovered, Barrie Andrian and her colleagues from the Scottish Trust for Underwater Archaeology decided to build a full-size reconstruction of what they'd found at Oakbank, several miles further along the loch shore. Experimental archaeology is a fascinating process. You learn a huge amount from the inspired combination of guesswork, practice and common sense you have to use to achieve the end result – something that resembles the excavated evidence as closely as possible.

The team recreated the crannog from scratch, felling trees with Iron Age replica axes and experimenting with different ways of driving the sharpened timber piles into the loch bed, until the stone and timber island was recreated, with a wooden platform on stilts supporting a thatched roundhouse on top. It would have been a massive task building a crannog, even a small, single-homestead one like this. Some elements were strenuous, like driving the timber piles into the mud, while others, such as thatching the roundhouse and giving it a secure platform, required specialist skills.

You can still see the reconstructed crannog as it might have looked 2,600 years ago at the centre. Even though the initial building of the crannog is finished, the archaeological team are still learning a great deal from the reconstruction. As it ages and is repaired, it sheds new light on the process of living there. And as Barrie Andrian has commented, when you see it in bad weather it's easy to understand why people chose to build houses on stilts: its flexible construction survives high winds and stormy waters.

■ **GETTING THERE** The Scottish Crannog Centre is ½ mile W of Kenmore, Loch Tay, Perth and Kinross, off the A827. See www.crannog.co.uk or telephone 01887 830583 for opening times and other details. Admission charge.

■ **OUR VIEW** More crannogs are discovered every time the lochs are surveyed, so this is a growing area of archaeology.

Whithorn
Early Christian centre

Founded in the AD400s?

WHITHORN IS ARGUABLY one of the earliest centres of Christianity in Britain and one of the first sites in Scotland to have a bishop and monastery. Along with places like Iona (see page 258), it is one of a group of key sites.

In the 1980s, new excavations were carried out by Peter Hill. Next to the remains of the later cathedral and monastery he also found earlier material, including evidence of trade with the continent. As with many ecclesiastical sites, the problem for archaeologists is that later medieval buildings are often sited as close as possible to the earlier monastic remains. Archaeologists have

therefore to work their way through the later material, which may have damaged evidence of the earlier period. Peter Hill was able to get as close as he could to the central part of the monastery and by a stroke of luck the paddocks to the south and west of the later church turned up evidence of some of the earliest buildings from the 6th and 7th centuries, and also from the 8th, 9th and 10th centuries.

It is rare to find evidence from these periods on ancient ecclesiastical sites and at Whithorn this has enabled an excellent sequence of occupation to be examined. Whithorn is producing material 150 to 200 years earlier than some of the other major sites, such as Jarrow. It is difficult to compare with Iona in detail what has been found here, but it seems possible that Whithorn may have been founded at an earlier date.

▲ *A carved cross from Whithorn, now in the visitor centre. These stones can be key evidence for early occupation of the site.*

▶ *Whithorn Priory is one of the earliest Christian sites in Scotland, and as is the case with many of these monuments, later medieval buildings, seen here, tend to obscure the earlier material.*

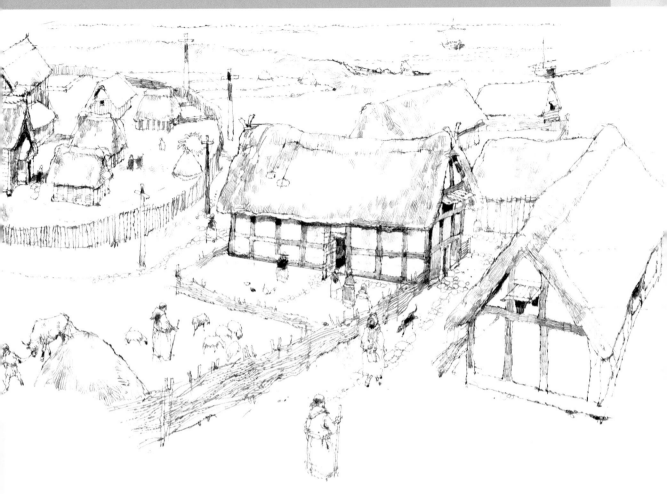

The person principally associated with Whithorn is Ninian. Bede (AD673–735) refers to Ninian's role and the founding of Whithorn, and talks of him converting the southern Picts. Ninian is believed to have come here in the 5th century.

Dating evidence

Early medieval writers wrote a lot about Ninian, but as they were writing 500 years after his death their evidence cannot be seen as conclusive. As more solid dating evidence, Mick points to the stones at nearby Kirk Madrine, which are probably 5th century and mention the presence of priests in the area. One of the stones at Whithorn, the Latinus Stone, might be 5th century.

The business of carving crosses was to become a major feature of medieval life on the site. Whithorn eventually became a pilgrimage centre and attracted many visitors, including royalty, before the dissolution.

▲ Small Christian settlements in Britain started humbly like this. Traces from the period can be difficult for archaeologists to detect.

■ **GETTING THERE** Whithorn is in Dumfries and Galloway, on the A746. See www.historic-scotland.gov.uk or telephone 01988 500508 for opening times and other details. Admission charge.

■ **OUR VIEW** In the main street of Whithorn is the archway of the original entrance to the medieval abbey; you go through this to the visitor centre and museum. The museum contains an excellent range of early Christian stones with inscriptions but it is a good idea to get a general feel for the site first. The site has recently been excavated and the resulting structures laid out so that you can see the plan on the ground.

Other sites to visit

❶ Inverurie

The graveyard at the south end of Inverurie has four stones displaying some fine examples of Pictish art. Around 1,500 years old, the stones depict repetitive geometric designs, usually abstract in nature, although one of the stones features a clear and realistic picture of a horse, showing that the art of the Picts did not always follow the traditional style of complicated patterns. As the Picts adopted Christianity, they incorporated the religion's symbolism into their expressive carving. Some stones, such as the Migvie Cross at St Finan's Church, Migvie, have a complicated woven pattern within a cross shape. The inclusion of more traditional dots, bars and rings within the four quadrants made by the cross show an interesting transition between the ancient artistic style and the new Christian symbolism.

■ **LOCATION** 13 miles NW of Aberdeen; off A96. Migvie: 8 miles NW of Aboyne; off A97.
■ **ACCESS** Public access to churchyards at both Inverurie and Migvie.

❷ Bonawe

The 17th and 18th centuries witnessed a growth in industrial iron-making in Scotland. Abundant timber supplies to fuel the process and a suitable waterway transport network encouraged English iron manufacturers to come to Scotland with their ore and set up furnaces. Built in 1752–3, Bonawe is one such furnace. For 120 years it produced pig iron (ingots of pure cast iron for later reuse) and 40,000 balls of cannon shot.

Built into a slope, the top-loading furnace was fed with charcoal, iron ore and limestone chippings from the sheds above the hearth. Water-powered bellows forced air through the furnace to achieve temperatures in the region of 1,500°C. The molten iron was then regularly tapped and channelled into casts on the casting floor.

The site today is in the care of Historic Scotland. A number of displays and a museum reveal life in the Scottish iron industry. The surrounding village of workers' houses and store sheds, centring on the furnace, stands within the beautiful landscape over Loch Etive.

■ **LOCATION** 13 miles E of Oban, Argyll and Bute; off A85.
■ **ACCESS** See www.historic-scotland. gov.uk or telephone 01866 822432 for opening times and other details. Admission charge.

▼ *18th-century furnaces, such as this one at Bonawe in Argyll, were often built into the slope of a hill so that the raw material could be fed in from above.*

❸ Poltalloch

One of the most intriguing examples of ancient art can be seen at Poltalloch in western Scotland. The precise carvings into a natural outcrop of stone represent the artistic expression of Neolithic and later Bronze Age peoples living in the Argyll area some 5,000 years ago.

The beautiful designs of small cups surrounded by concentric rings appear to be made by the painstaking chipping away of rock using a hammer stone of a harder material. It's not known what the impressions mean, though there are speculations (see also Drumtroddan on page 250). The designs aren't unique to this area. Similar cup-and-ring patterns have been found across the world, though timescales and distances mean it's unlikely they are all connected. Many, such as Poltalloch, are carved into horizontal surfaces, which allow them to hold water when it rains. Whatever their significance, they are fascinating and captivating ancient symbols.

■ **LOCATION** 2 miles SW of Kilmartin, Argyll and Bute; off B8025, 200m SW of ruined Poltalloch House.
■ **ACCESS** See OS Landranger map 55.

❹ Dun Nosebridge

To the south-east of Bridgend on Islay, Dun Nosebridge is a prominent fortification looking out over the Laggan Valley. A substantial defensive site in any location, it appears more so when viewed within the context of the small 20-by-25-mile island.

The stone and earth ramparts are fashioned out of the hillside, creating terraces that surround a central rectangular platform at the top. This unusual style of fortress construction has led many archaeologists to the conclusion that Dun Nosebridge is an adaptation of earlier methods of hillfort building. Though a specific date is not known, it is assumed that

the defences date to the later Iron Age or possibly the Roman period.

■ **LOCATION** 3 miles SE of Bridgend, Isle of Islay; minor road off A846.
■ **ACCESS** See OS Landranger map 60.

❺ Machrie Moor

Machrie Moor on the west side of the Isle of Arran has the most extensive collection of ancient Neolithic and Bronze Age monuments in Scotland. The most

▲ *Machrie Moor 2, one of the amazing collection of monuments on the Isle of Arran. This circle has the tallest stones: over 5m (16ft) high.*

renowned are the Bronze Age stone circles, which date from around 1800 to 1600BC.

Six stone circles lie within a short distance of each other and all vary in diameter and height. At nearly 5m (16ft) high, the tallest stones on Arran are those in the circle known as Machrie Moor 2, but only three remain standing. Machrie Moor 3 is the least impressive circle, as only one tall stone still stands. Machrie Moor 1 originally had a timber circle on the site before being replaced by a ring of alternately arranged granite boulders and sandstone slabs, of which 11 out of 12 remain.

Perhaps the most impressive monument is Machrie Moor 5, which has an inner circle of eight large granite boulders surrounded by an outer ring of 15 smaller stones. It's known as Fingal's Cauldron Seat, in honour of the warrior giant famed in local folklore. Although the stones date from the Bronze Age, there is plenty of archaeological evidence to suggest that the site was in use during the Neolithic period, as it appears that (like Machrie Moor 1) a number of timber circles were created before the stone circles were built. In addition to the stone circles, Machrie Moor is also littered with standing stones, chambered cairns and the remains of hut circles.

■ **LOCATION** 3 miles N of Blackwaterfoot, Isle of Arran; off A841.
■ **ACCESS** See www.historic-scotland. gov.uk for further details. 1 ½ mile walk to site from road.

AUGUSTINIAN MONASTERY

❻ Inchmahome

Inchmahome Priory is a small Augustinian monastery built on one of the little islands in the middle of the Lake of Menteith, the only lake (not loch) in Scotland. It was founded in 1238 by the Earl of Menteith, who also built a castle on another of the islands (Inchtalla). Accessed by boat, the priory ruins are generally in good condition, with the component parts of an Augustinian monastery, such as the church, refectory, chapterhouse and cloisters, all present in varying states. The east gable with its five lancet windows is particularly impressive, and the plan of the site can be seen to make good use of the available

space on the island. It's believed that Mary Queen of Scots stayed at the priory in 1547 when fleeing from the English army after the Battle of Pinkey. The reformation of Inchmahome in 1560 gave allowance for the remaining canons to reside in the monastery buildings, which had been converted to secular use.

■ **LOCATION** On an island in the Lake of Menteith, Stirling. Ferry from Port of Menteith, 8 miles S of Callander; off the A81.
■ **ACCESS** See www.historic-scotland. gov.uk or telephone 01877 385294 for opening times and other details. Admission charge.

ROMAN FORT

❼ Inchtuthil

The legionary fortress at Inchtuthil was built in the 1st century AD by the XX Legion under General Julius Agricola, governor of Britain, during his campaign to defeat the Caledonians. This formidable fortress held around 5,500 men and was one of the northernmost forts of the Roman Empire. In addition to barracks, administration offices and hospital, the fortress had a large workshop where the legion's maintenance and repair work was carried out.

However, Inchtuthil fortress was never fully completed and was only occupied for a brief period. The Roman frontier fell back, the garrison pulled out and it seems that orders were given to destroy everything so that nothing was left for the enemy to make use of. Excavations have revealed that the houses had their timber frames removed and the wattle burnt. A pottery store was discovered where every pot had been smashed to pieces, and the drains and sewers had been filled with gravel.

One of the most significant finds from excavation was a 7-ton hoard of more than 875,000 handmade iron nails. Sizes ranged from 5cm to 40cm (2–16in) and many of the nails

still retained clean-cut heads and edges. It appears that the retreating Romans had hidden the nails in a pit at least 3.5m (12ft) deep and packed almost 2m (6ft) of earth on top to prevent them from being found by the enemy, who might have reused them, or melted them down and made them into weapons.

■ **LOCATION** 6 miles SW of Blairgowrie, Perthshire; off A984.
■ **ACCESS** No public access. Finds, including part of the nail hoard, on display at National Museum of Scotland; see www.nms.ac.uk or telephone 0131 247 4422 for opening times and other details. Admission charge.

ROMAN FRONTIER

❽ Antonine Wall

The Roman invasion of Caledonia (Scotland) was a turbulent affair. Agricola eventually conquered the Picts following the decisive land battle of Mons Graupius in AD84, but the northern territories were difficult to retain and the Romans were soon made to withdraw south. The Picts continued to resist the Roman presence, which prompted the Romans to build Hadrian's Wall (see page 216). Around AD140, some

▲ *The banks and ditches of the Antonine Wall might look less impressive than stretches of Hadrian's Wall, but this was the true northern frontier of the Roman Empire.*

▼ *The volcanic plug that now supports Edinburgh Castle has been an attractive location since prehistoric times.*

20 years later, Emperor Antonius Pius ordered the northern frontier to be extended further into Caledonia. Work commenced on a new wall about 141.

The Antonine Wall became the Roman Empire's most northerly frontier. It was 37 miles long, stretching across the valley from the Forth to the Clyde, and it differed in construction from Hadrian's Wall. The Antonine Wall had a stone foundation covered with a rampart of turf and soil measuring around 3m (10ft) high and 4m (13ft) thick. An intimidating V-shaped ditch, 12m (40ft) wide and more than 3.5m (12ft) deep, protected the northern side of the wall. Running along the wall's south side were at least 17 forts, staggered two miles apart, and 40 fortlets linked by a cobbled road known as the Military Way. Hostility from the north continued unabated regardless of these awesome defences, and it is believed that the wall was completely abandoned between 160 and 180.

Stretches of the wall can still be seen today, particularly at Watling Lodge near Tamfourhill. The impression of the huge ditch is evident here, together with some remains of the turf rampart. Lines of the Antonine ditch can also be seen in Polmonthill, Callendar Park and Seabegs Wood, and excavations at Rough Castle and Kinneil Estate have uncovered remains of Antonine forts.

■ **LOCATION** 2 miles W of Tamfourhill, Stirlingshire; off B816.
■ **ACCESS** See www.historic-scotland. gov.uk or telephone 0131 668 8600 for further details.

MILITARY BASE

❾ Edinburgh Castle

With over one million visitors per year, Edinburgh Castle is second only to the Tower of London as the most visited historic monument in Britain. This magnificent and formidable fortress overlooks the city from its perch of volcanic rock some 25m (80ft) above sea level. The castle has a long and illustrious history, and there is evidence to suggest that, long before the castle, a Bronze Age

settlement existed here around 1000BC. Malcolm III erected a stone fort on this commanding site in the 11th century and it developed into a royal fortress in the twelfth century, during the reign of David I. Over the centuries the Scots and English fought many times for possession of the castle; it even served as headquarters for Cromwell's army. Successive conflicts ensured that the castle was continuously strengthened until the Napoleonic wars in the 1700s, and it remains as a military base today.

Edinburgh Castle is famous for the One O'clock Gun that fires every day (except Sunday), a time check for the people of the city. Moreover, the Scottish crown jewels – the Honours of Scotland, consisting of crown, sceptre and sword – have been on display in the Crown Room since 1818, when they were found by Sir Walter Scott after having been hidden since 1707. Sitting alongside is the inaugural Stone of Destiny, returned to Scotland in 1996 – 700 years after its removal from Scone Abbey to London in 1296.

The oldest building in the castle complex is St Margaret's Chapel, a small Norman structure that has survived numerous conflicts, while a small iron wall-fountain known as Witches' Well marks the site where women accused of witchcraft were burnt at the stake.

■ **LOCATION** Edinburgh.
■ **ACCESS** See www.historic-scotland. gov.uk or telephone 0131 225 9846 for opening times and other details. Admission charge.

ROMAN ROAD

⑩ Soutra Hill

The Roman road of Dere Street was an extensive and direct route constructed in the late 1st century AD to link the legionary fortress at York (Eboracum) with Inchtuthil (see page 244) in Perthshire, in order for essential supplies to reach the troubled northern territories from the south. Dere Street connected with Watling Street, which ran from York to Dover, and its name is thought to come from the Anglo-Saxon kingdom of Deira. Dere Street was originally a road of considerable width, measuring 17m (55ft) from

▼ *Soutra has revealed evidence of a medieval hospital. It's likely that the site, strategically positioned on Dere Street, saw the aftermath of many a bloody battle.*

ditch to ditch on either side, thus allowing two columns of soldiers to pass each other unhindered.

At Soutra Hill, a section of the Dere Street has been preserved. This stretch ran from near Hadrian's Wall at Corbridge to the fort and port at Crammond on the Firth of Forth. Running alongside the road are pits from where the gravel was quarried to be used in its construction. Medieval armies later used the route. Excavations along Dere Street at Soutra have revealed evidence of a large medieval hospital founded by the Augustinian order of canons in the 12th century.

■ **LOCATION** Soutra Aisle, Borders; off A68, on B6368.
■ **ACCESS** See www.historic-scotland. gov.uk or telephone 0131 668 8600 for further details.

BORDER STRONGHOLD

⑪ Smailholm Tower

The property of the Pringle family during the 1400s, the exact date of Smailholm Tower's construction is unknown. The Pringles were squires to the Black Douglases, and the tower, which stands on a craggy hillock near Kelso, is similar in design to Douglas Newark Castle, which would suggest it was built in the early 15th century. Smailholm Tower remained the property of the Pringles until 1513, when David Pringle and four sons were killed at the Battle of Flodden.

The tower's role as a border stronghold saw it attacked by the English in 1543 and 1546, before being sold to the Scotts of Harden in 1645. However, the Scotts moved to nearby Sandyknowe in 1700 and the tower became derelict. As a child in the 18th century, Sir Walter Scott frequently visited Sandyknowe and Smailholm Tower, and the history of the tower influenced his writing. He persuaded the Duke of Buccleuch to restore the tower in the 1800s and it stands today as a fine example of a border tower house.

► *If you live on the Borders, this is the sort of place you need. Smailholm Tower provided defence against the English in the 16th century. In the 18th, it inspired Sir Walter Scott.*

The rectangular tower, with the foundations of kitchen and halls, stands within a small wall that was entered through a stalwart gateway. The arched entrance to the tower was guarded by a heavy outer door and iron grid 'yett' gate; a gun-loop remains directly above. A spiral staircase near the door accesses all floors and leads to the roof where the original watchman's seat remains (next to the chimneystack for warmth), complete with a recess for holding a lantern.

■ **LOCATION** 6 miles W of Kelso, Borders; on A6089.
■ **ACCESS** See www.historic-scotland. gov.uk or telephone 01573 460365 for further details. Admission charge.

DESERTED TOWN

⑫ Roxburgh

Roxburgh is first mentioned in the foundation charter of Selkirk Abbey in 1113. The town grew into a bustling economic centre in the 12th and 13th centuries, becoming a medieval equal to places such as Edinburgh. Records, and archaeological investigation by Time Team show that the Borders town suffered its share of action during the Wars of Independence, and it has changed hands on more than one occasion.

King David I made the Scottish town a royal burgh in the 1100s. It became a successful and thriving community with three churches, a castle and a royal residence, together with civic buildings and a school. The settlement was known to trade with the continent and even hosted visiting bankers from Italy. After a series of battles, Roxburgh was delivered to Edward III in 1334. It then remained in English hands as a vital northern centre of administration until it was taken

back by siege in 1501. By this time the town had practically ceased to function and had fallen into serious decay. Today the old town of Roxburgh lies under pastureland between the Teviot and Tweed rivers.

■ **LOCATION** 3 miles SW of Kelso, Borders; on minor roads off A698.
■ **ACCESS** Nothing to see at Time Team excavation site; private land, no public access.

RULING FAMILIES

⑬ Jedburgh, Melrose and Dryburgh abbeys

During the 12th century, King David I established the feudal system in Scotland, along with 15 religious houses. Among these were Melrose (built by the Cistercian monks of Old Melrose under the king's orders in 1136) and Jedburgh (founded by the king as an Augustinian priory

in 1138). His friend Hugh de Moreville established Dryburgh. This system of building religious houses served two purposes. First, it enabled the founder to guarantee himself a place in heaven, and second it showed the local population, and the English, how powerful the Scottish ruling families were. However, the Borders location of these religious houses was to be their downfall, as the repeated actions between the English and Scots saw them right in the middle of disputed lands.

The wonderful high arches along the nave are a spectacular feature of Jedburgh still to be seen today. The building was severely damaged during the 13th-century Wars of Independence by Edward I and repeatedly rebuilt. Melrose was hugely successful and became one of the most powerful monasteries

▷ *Melrose Abbey. The 12th- and 13th-century builders might, on reflection, have thought of a better location than the main battleground between England and Scotland.*

in Scotland, but, again, the 1296 invasion by Edward I saw it seriously damaged. Later, during the 14th-century attacks by Edward II, Melrose was completely vandalized.

Dryburgh has a more remote setting, possibly at the behest of the austere order of Premonstratensian (Norbertine) canons who helped Hugh de Moreville establish the site in 1150. The ringing of the bells in 1322 is said to have drawn the attention of the withdrawing troops of Edward II, who subsequently set fire to the monastery. This site, like its sister religious houses, suffered repeated attacks but is a remarkable site to visit today, with a wonderful nave, transepts and choir, together with clearly defined cloisters and associated monastic buildings.

■ **LOCATION** Jedburgh, Borders; on A68; Melrose: 6 miles SE of Galashiels, Borders; off A6091. Dryburgh: 1 mile E of Newtown St Boswells, Borders; off A68.
■ **ACCESS** All are in the care of Historic Scotland; see www.historic-scotland.gov.uk for opening times and other details. Admission charge at all three sites.

FORTIFIED FARM
⓮ Slack's Tower, Southdean

The base level of Slack's Tower and the surrounding rubble spills are all that remains of a once thriving defended farm of the Borders, or peel house. Standing several metres high today, the original tower structure dates to the 1500s and in typical defensive style has few openings on the ground floor. Survey work carried out by antiquarians in the 17th century highlighted a variety of enclosures and outbuildings associated with the tower, as well as others that could relate to an earlier agricultural use of the landscape. Much of the stone from the

decayed buildings has been reused to create small enclosures for sheep.

These remains, together with a similar ruin at nearby Mervinslaw, represent typical defended agricultural settlements of their time. The often disputed lands of the Borders must have made for a hard life for the Middle Marches farmers.

■ **LOCATION** 12 miles SE of Hawick, Roxburghshire; off A6088.
■ **ACCESS** 1-mile walk to site, on open hillside NW of Southdean. See OS Landranger map 80.

BASTLE HOUSE
⓯ Glenochar

Glenochar in South Lanarkshire is the site of a fortified settlement known as a 'bastle and fermtoun'. These were built across the turbulent Scottish–English border area in the 16th and 17th centuries to protect the inhabitants and their livestock from border raiders ('reivers'). The bastle house (similar to the French word 'bastille') was a two-storey stone building surrounded by the fermtoun — several timber longhouses, which faced each other across a cobbled roadway.

Glenochar was built around 1603 as part of a series of defensive measures taken by James VI of Scotland when he became James I of England. Cattle and people would

have shared the longhouses, but in the bastle house livestock were stalled on the ground floor while the family lived upstairs. Excavations have revealed the bastle's strong construction and barrel-vaulted roof; as the only stone building in the settlement, it would have been an important refuge if raiders attacked.

Artefacts found in the bastle itself include cups and clay pipes from Staffordshire, which may indicate that imported goods from the New World, such as tea and tobacco, had reached the area quite early on. In the Fermtoun, two silver coins,

German and Dutch, dating from 1606 and 1610, helped to date the site and provide further evidence of long-range contacts. A 'Union Jack' flag carved into a slate appears to indicate that the new union of England and Scotland under James I had already had some impact on the local population.

■ **LOCATION** Glenochar, Lanarkshire; on A702.
■ **ACCESS** On open hillside 600 yds W of main road. OS Landranger map 78. Finds and exhibition at Moat Park Heritage Centre, Biggar, Lanarkshire. Telephone 01899 221050 for opening times and other details. Admission charge.

⑯ Caerlaverock Castle

Between Gretna Green and Dumfries, on the Solway Firth, lies Caerlaverock Castle, a beautiful 13th-century stronghold with a unique design. The three-sided castle presents a formidable challenge to the attacker. Its northern gate has two large drum towers, and the other two corners were protected by further large towers that provided a domineering vantage point over the surrounding landscape. Set within a broad moat, the triangular design belongs to the late-13th-century rebuilding of the Maxwell family base.

So close to the Borders, Caerlaverock naturally became embroiled in the conflicts of the Wars of Independence and came under siege by Edward I in 1300. One of the best-recorded sieges of the period, in the French poem 'Le Siège de Karlavreock', Caerlaverock reputedly withstood 87 knights and 3,000 men before submitting. It then became an English stronghold for the next twelve years. The Maxwell family were under siege once again in 1356 when their loyalty to Scottish royalty was questioned. The 15th and 16th centuries saw phases of rebuilding and some relative peace until the English took the castle briefly once again in 1544.

The castle was for a time converted into a fortified manor house, with the fine Nithsdale Lodgings built within the walls by the first earl of Nithsdale in 1634, but by 1640 the castle was in action again, this time against the Covenanters, who were fighting for a revision of how Scotland was governed by Charles I, and who subsequently took the castle. A large section of the castle's curtain wall

◄ *Caerlaverock Castle from the west. The formidable walls were well able to withstand attacks – a necessity in an area like the Borders.*

was destroyed, and the damage was such that the castle was never lived in again. The site has a display on siege weaponry.

■ **LOCATION** 8 miles SE of Dumfries, Borders; on B725.

■ **ACCESS** See www.historic-scotland. gov.uk or telephone 01387 770244 for opening times and other details. Admission charge.

⓱ Creetown

Lying on a hill 6 miles from Creetown, overlooking Wigtown Bay, are two wonderfully complete Neolithic burial cairns. The Cairnholy chambered tombs date from around 4000BC and are believed to have been places of worship and burial throughout prehistory. The cairns stand approximately 25m (80ft) apart. Cairnholy 1 is around 45m

▲ *Creetown cairn, showing one of the chambered tombs that dates to 4000BC. Finds here have been fascinating, but of limited number because of plunder.*

(150ft) long and 10m (33ft) wide and the best preserved of the two. Its curved forecourt facade is lined with six tall, narrow stones and the chamber is in two sections. Excavations have yielded pottery fragments, a leaf-shaped arrowhead, part of a jadeite stone axe (a green stone believed to have originated in the Alps) and charred human remains.

Standing on a hillock and measuring about 20m by 12m (66ft x 40ft), Cairnholy 2 also has two chambers but no trace of a facade has been found. The entrance is flanked by a portal stone of almost 3m (10ft) in height, and a large capstone lies over the inner chamber. Deposits

found on this site include pieces of Beaker pottery (see page 40), a leaf-shaped arrowhead and a flint knife.

Unfortunately, both sites have been extensively plundered. Although what remains looks relatively complete, a great deal of evidence has been lost from the archaeological record.

■ **LOCATION** 6 miles SE of Creetown, Dumfries and Galloway; off A75.

■ **ACCESS** On open hillside off minor road north of A75. OS Landranger map 83.

⓲ Drumtroddan

Ancient standing stones, cairns and rocks featuring intricate marks carved many centuries ago are abundant in many parts of Scotland. The field south of Drumtroddan Farm has two significant prehistoric sites: the first, two 3m (10ft) standing stones (with a third lying between

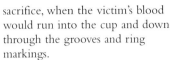

them), and the second, three distinct groups of rocks with well-defined cup-and-ring markings.

Cup-and-ring rock art (petroglyphs) are believed to be typical of the Bronze Age period but the exact reasons for such art are unknown. It has been suggested that the carvings were used as maps of the area, as astrological maps, or that they indicated tribal ownership of land by marking boundaries; others believe they had religious significance.

The markings vary in size, and would have been carved using a hard hammer stone in a 'pecking' technique. Some cup marks are simple hollows, while others have larger 'basins'. Many are accompanied by additional ring markings, some of which are connected to the cup by a groove. The markings with grooves running through them hold water after rainfall and this has led some to suspect that they were used during

▼ *Ancient stone complete with cup and ring markings. These enigmatic carvings, pecked into the surface of the rock, were created in the Bronze Age.*

sacrifice, when the victim's blood would run into the cup and down through the grooves and ring markings.

Cup-and-ring markings are common in Galloway and many have also been found in Ireland, Brittany and in north-west Spain. The preservation of these examples of mysterious art is paramount; the markings of the Drumtroddan groupings have clearly grown fainter from erosion over the past decade.

■ **LOCATION** 3 miles E of Port William, Dumfries and Galloway; off B7085.
■ **ACCESS** See www.historic-scotland. gov.uk or telephone 0131 668 8600 for further details.

IRON AGE FORT

⑲ Barsalloch

The shores around Port William have revealed evidence of human activity and settlements dating back around 6,000 years. Excavations have uncovered a Mesolithic site showing signs of habitation in the south of the region, and flint-working deposits have been found in the north. On the headland of Barsalloch Point, overlooking Luce Bay and the North Sea, lies an Iron Age fort that has also yielded evidence of Mesolithic encampments, making it one of Galloway's earliest dated sites of human settlement.

Situated on top of cliffs some 18m (60ft) above sea level, the promontory fort is enclosed by a large horseshoe-shaped ditch, which would have made it virtually impregnable. Barsalloch Fort's ramparts are surprisingly well preserved and its strategic location suggests that the occupants enjoyed a comfortable subsistence from the good farmland to the rear as well as the resources of the sea below.

■ **LOCATION** ¾ mile W of Monreith, Dumfries and Galloway; on A747.
■ **ACCESS** See www.historic-scotland. gov.uk or telephone 0131 668 8600 for further details.

Scottish Highland and Islands

Some of the most fascinating evidence from Scotland's past is found in this area, and on the Orkney Islands are monuments that are among the most important in Britain and Ireland, and which tell a key part of the story of our past. Early Christian settlement on Iona played a major role in Scotland's history, and it is also along the coastal regions that we see the influence of Scandinavian settlers. The distinctiveness of Scotland's archaeology continues into the Iron Age with the appearance of brochs; excavations have done much to interpret these. The 18th century was a time of turmoil that saw the Battle of Culloden and the end of the rebellion against union with England. Forts from this period indicate the intensity of the conflict.

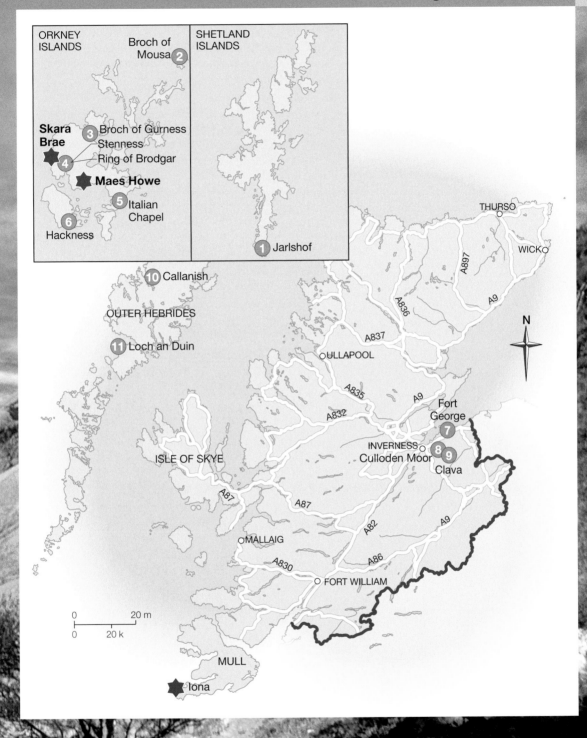

ORKNEY
ISLANDS

Broch of
Mousa ②

SHETLAND
ISLANDS

③ Broch of Gurness
Stenness
Ring of Brodgar

**Skara
Brae**

④

Maes Howe

⑤ Italian
Chapel

⑥

Hackness

① Jarlshof

⑩ Callanish

OUTER HEBRIDES

⑪ Loch an Duin

THURSO

WICK

A897

A836

A9

N

A837

ULLAPOOL

A835

A9

Fort
George

A832

⑦

INVERNESS
Culloden Moor

⑧ ⑨
Clava

ISLE OF SKYE

A87

A87

A82

A9

MALLAIG

A830

A86

FORT WILLIAM

0   20 m
0   20 k

MULL

Iona

Skara Brae
Neolithic homes
3100-2500BC

WHEN MICK AND I first stared down into the Neolithic houses of Skara Brae, it was the nearest I felt we'd come to entering the world of the prehistoric past. We'd seen artefacts before, and monuments, but these were homes.

People were living here when the first phases of Stonehenge were being built. These structures pre-date the Pyramids.

Here in the Orkneys a small community of people lived closely together and created all the home comforts – hearths, beds, shelves, containers for water – out of the local flagstone. There are even what might be called cupboards. This could be the oldest and best-preserved furniture in Europe.

My favourite bit of furniture is the

▶ Skara Brae was occupied over hundreds of years and the people who lived here had the riches of the sea to eat, and reared sheep and cows. You can imagine the pleasure of creeping into one of the wonderful houses and sharing the warmth of the fire.

stone dresser; when this was excavated, a stone pot was found still standing on the surface. You might like to speculate as to the use of the stone-lined boxes, which appeared, when excavated, to have had joints sealed with clay. One suggestion has been that they were temporary containers for seafood – a sort of stone aquarium.

The houses were linked by passages, which you can still see. The passageways had stone doors that could be locked off by bars. Each building was roofed over with turf supported probably on wooden beams, although whalebones were found on the site, and in other houses of a similar date these have been found to have structural uses. The exteriors were huge middens – rubbish pits – and it has been suggested that the temperature inside would possibly have been 1 or 2 degrees warmer because of rotting debris outside. This material was held in place by a drystone wall, which made a sandwich-like structure, ideal for keeping out the draughts.

Continuity of design

A natural disaster paradoxically saved Skara Brae for the future. A violent storm covered the settlement in sand, and when Gordon Childe excavated here in the 1920s he found it extraordinarily well preserved.

After looking at the main complex, if you go to the west you can see a more oval-shaped building that might have been a space for communal ritual. Archaeologists found burnt remains here and some evidence of workshops for creating bone and flint tools. As in other Neolithic sites in Scotland, Skara Brae has its collection of stone balls, whose function is a matter of speculation.

Some aspects of Skara Brae replicate features of the contemporary funeral monuments, such as Maes Howe (see page 256). Side cells or rooms project off central chambers, and there are series of

low passageways in both. Miles Russell in his book on the Neolithic period suggests that more than one area of Skara Brae had a ritual function. It may be that in the Neolithic period, the ritual and the mundane parts of life existed side by side. As you gaze into hut number seven, it is worth remembering that two women died here and their bodies are buried beneath the slabs that are usually referred to as a bed.

Miles Russell also notes the similarity of construction between this kind of structure and the galleries running from the base of shafts in Neolithic flint mines. There is a continuity of design and thought here, which makes the site even more fascinating.

The site was last excavated nearly 75 years ago. Unfortunately the excavations in 1928 removed a lot of material regarded at the time as rubbish. It's likely that the general clearing out of the contents lost some of the evidence.

▲ *Originally the outside walls would have been covered by midden material and thatch and turf roofs.*

■ **GETTING THERE**
Skara Brae is 19 miles NW of Kirkwall, Orkney, on the B9056. See www.historic-scotland.gov.uk or telephone 01856 841815 for opening times and other details. Admission charge.

Skara Brae is part of the Orkney UNESCO World Heritage Site.
■ **OUR VIEW** The visitor centre is excellent; it includes some of the original artefacts and a reconstructed house. Francis Pryor highly recommends this site, and adds: 'The reconstructed house is superbly done and manages to convey a genuinely ancient atmosphere despite the usual visual intrusions imposed by the health and safety people.'

Maes Howe
Neolithic sacred burial site

3100–2500BC

WHEN MICK AND I first made our way down the 15m (50ft) passage into the centre of the Maes Howe monument, it was after a long, wet and arduous Time Team shoot. We were both short of sleep and the Orkney mists had left us unable to catch our return flights. It was late in the year, and we had the place to ourselves. With voices reduced to a whisper, we entered the central tomb and stared at the amazing stonework, and the Norse runes carved by an earlier set of visitors, over 1,000 years before. A few places create an experience you will remember for years afterwards, and Maes

Howe is one of these. Built around 2700BC, a date derived from material found in the surrounding ditch, it was a sacred house of the dead.

When you enter the central chamber, the first thing that strikes you is the quality of the stonework. The local stone naturally splits into slabs and this enabled the builders to create a huge interior space with fine joints. Some of the side slabs along the passageway are over 5.6m (18ft) in length. It would have required a high level of skill and organization to manoeuvre the slabs into place. The top of the current roof is a modern reconstruction, but when it was originally built it would have seemed a huge space – an effect created and enhanced by the tight, low entrance passage.

The monument was excavated in 1861 and sadly no record of what lay on the floors has survived. It is likely that bones, pottery and other artefacts would have been found, which would have proved invaluable in interpreting its function. When Isbister on South Ronaldsay was excavated in the 1970s, two of the side cells contained human bones, including skulls. These were from a range of dates that indicated long-term continuity of use. Pottery and, enigmatically, the remains of sea eagles were among the finds, and it makes you realize just how much may have been lost in the original excavations here.

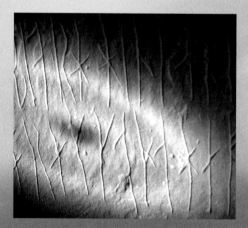

▶ According to the runes left by the Norse raiders, some of them had come here looking for treasure.

▼ Maes Howe is part of a huge ceremonial and ritual landscape. It is important to look at it in its wider context.

It is possible that some of the contents of Maes Howe were removed by the Norse raiders, who left their mark on the stones. Over 30 inscriptions can be seen, including a beautiful engraving of what could be a lion.

'Prehistoric presence'

Francis Pryor regards Maes Howe as one of the best prehistoric sites in north-western Europe. He points to recent archaeological work that suggests the inside may have been painted and that the finely jointed stone surface would have created what he describes as an 'acoustic effect'. He emphasizes the need to see it as part of a landscape full of monuments. Altogether about ten mounds with internal passages are set into a prehistoric ceremonial space that includes the stones of Stenness and the Ring of Brodgar (see page 262), and they represent the final flowering of Neolithic architecture. 'It was not until I visited these famous sites that I became aware that they still possessed some strange, and completely indefinable "prehistoric presence",' says Francis. 'Filming within the great stone chamber after dark was a transcending moment which my more analytical colleagues would regard as an irrelevance, but which has had a lasting effect on me.'

Recent excavations at Maes Howe outside the main tomb have found

evidence of a wall around the mound and another large standing stone at the rear of the tomb. The hill and its entrance are orientated to the south-west and, like Newgrange (see page 284), this produces the effect of light shining down the passage at midwinter sunset. Clearly there were events going on at Maes Howe that were not purely pragmatic; sacred space, shamanic ritual, mind-altering acoustics and light effects are all areas that few archaeologists are willing to discuss, but anyone who visits Maes Howe will experience a space beyond the mundane.

▲ *The passage that takes you into the centre of Maes Howe is a unique experience.*

■ **GETTING THERE**
5 miles NE of Stromness, W of minor road off the A965. See www.historic-scotland. gov.uk or telephone 01856 761606 for opening times and other details. Admission charge.

■ **OUR VIEW** The interior today looks rather well swept and clean, but it's worth imagining the floor and the side cells littered with bones and possibly the decaying bodies of the ancestors of those who built the tomb. Carenza adds, 'The Neolithic construction is awesome – but do make sure you also see the Viking additions. Vandalism, of course ... but it's astonishing how like modern graffiti it is.'

Iona
Early Christian settlement

AD563 to the present

IT IS BELIEVED THAT St Columba founded the first religious settlement on Iona around AD563. He was probably motivated by a desire to spread Christianity to the northern Picts, but legend has it that he was also in need of an act of repentance after his prayers assisted his family's army to kill 3,000 men at the battle of Cooldrevny in AD561. Columba was required, so it is said, to convert the same number of souls that were killed in the battle.

He sought a home away from Ireland as part of his penance. It was said that one of Iona's attractions was that Ireland could be seen from its shores. His was not the first arrival on the island, however. A Bronze Age barrow and a small Iron Age fort are evidence of earlier occupation.

Life of Columba

It is likely that the early settlement was laid out in a pattern of a banked and ditch enclosure surrounding individual monks' cells and a wooden church, but it's important also to remember that Columba had royal connections and a short time after the monastery was established he was able to call on fairly sophisticated imports and good-quality meat supplies, evidence for which has been found by archaeologists.

Before you go, it is worth getting hold of a copy of Adomnán's *Life of Columba*, written by an abbot of Iona in around 679–704, only about 100 years after Columba's death. This contains a mass of information about the saint's life and the details of life on the island. Time Team's expert Richard Reece and other archaeologists say that this mass of written information is a bit daunting for those excavating there. Certain parts of the site, including the small hill called Torr Abb which is said to be the site of

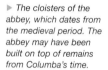
▶ The cloisters of the abbey, which dates from the medieval period. The abbey may have been built on top of remains from Columba's time.

the hut in which Columba used to write, are referred to by Adomnán, and excavations on such features have to take into account Adomnán's descriptions.

From 794, the island suffered from attacks by the Vikings and after increasingly violent raids a decision was made to move the monastery to Kells in Ireland. It is possible that the *Book of Kells* was written on Iona. This magnificent document is a late flowering of a range of artistic skills that developed on the island in the mid-8th century prior to the main Viking attacks. Similar artistic styles exist on some of the oldest crosses on Iona and in the decorative elements in the *Book of Kells*.

Medieval abbey

The buildings you see date from no earlier than the medieval period. The area has been repeatedly built on and little survives from Columba's time other than a vague sense that certain buildings were in approximate locations, and that some of the ditch and bank was contemporary with the saint. The main area is over 80 hectares (200 acres), and it is likely that the original church stood in the same area and on the same orientation as the present abbey, which is medieval. The best places to see the remains of the ditch and bank are to the north-west of the abbey.

The tradition of bringing kings to the island for burial began around the 7th and 8th centuries, although the wonderfully named 'Street of the Dead' is medieval. Some of the crosses are 8th century, but many of the buildings are much later.

The 10th century witnessed renewed settlement on Iona and by the 13th century a Benedictine abbey had been established here. Since Columba's time, Iona has been a focus for Christian belief and legend, as well as the resting place for Scottish kings.

■ **GETTING THERE** The island of Iona is in the Western Isles, reachable by public ferry from Fionnphort, Mull. For the abbey, see www.historic-scotland.gov.uk or telephone 01681 700512 for opening times and other details. Admission charge. There are no cars on Iona.
■ **OUR VIEW** Richard Reece likes the tortuous bus-and-ferry route to Iona, as this emphasizes the original isolation of the site, as well as how different modern ideas of travel are from those of Columba's time, when journeys would have been by boat. Early monks were dependent on sailing and navigating skills, and some writers have written about 'the sea roads of the saints'.

Other sites to visit

❶ Jarlshof

Anyone flying into the main island of Shetland will pass very close to the ancient settlement of Jarlshof. Excavations at the site, near Sumburgh airport, have uncovered occupation dating back over 4,200 years.

The discovery of a Bronze Age smith's house was comprehensive evidence for metalworking. The finds included a selection of moulds used for casting bronze swords and a variety of axes. As the growing farming and fishing community at Jarlshof entered the Iron Age they constructed a broch, or defensive site, hinting at the growing status of their settlement. The unique wheelhouse structures, built using extremely high standards of dry stone coursing, are an interesting aspect of this period, a time when many southern groups were still living in timber roundhouses.

Jarlshof also had an established Viking settlement, which clearly indicates a committed and stable fishing and farming tradition, one that lasted for over 400 years. Artefacts recovered during excavation demonstrate the Norse settlers' crafts and their skills in producing cloth and tools for fishing. Among the finds are some captivating depictions of ships and birds engraved into stone.

The settlement at Jarlshof continued with a medieval farmhouse and hall, indicating that the area was occupied continuously over thousands of years.

■ **LOCATION** Sumburgh, Shetland; off A970.

■ **ACCESS** See www.historic-scotland. gov.uk or telephone 01950 460112 for opening times and other details. Admission charge. Finds and exhibition in Shetland Museum, Lerwick: www.shetland-museum.org.uk or telephone 01595 695057 for opening times and other details.

▼ Continuous occupation from the Bronze Age through the Viking and medieval periods makes Jarlshof an archaeological treasure.

❷ Broch of Mousa

Brochs are fortified towers dating from the Iron Age period in Scotland. They were formidable structures with some evidence of fighting platforms near the roof, reached by stairs running inside a gap between the main outer wall and the inner chambers. The walls of Mousa broch contain three cells, which were probably complemented by rooms leading into galleries that would have been supported by wooden structures inside the broch.

There are over 500 examples of brochs in Scotland and they fall somewhere between a fort and a fortified house. They have features that appear to be defensive, including a single door into a guard chamber and a single door into the floor on each level, which may have reduced the danger from attacks. On the other hand, they appear to have had no slots or windows from which to observe any attacking enemy, and the main door could easily have been breached. A fire started in the ground floor would have quickly

▲ *The magnificent location of the Broch of Mousa gives a good sense of the possible defensive nature of this Iron Age structure.*

destroyed the interior, and some of the brochs do have internal evidence of fire damage.

At best they may have provided a limited refuge. The Broch of Mousa is a massive structure but archaeologists are still in doubt whether its monumental structure was for genuine defence or merely an extension of the 'dun' or small Scottish fortified house that preceded it. See also the Broch of Gurness (right).

■ **LOCATION** Isle of Mousa, Shetland.
■ **ACCESS** Broch is on W side of the island, access by ferry only, from Sandwick, 14 miles S of Lerwick on A970. For ferry details, telephone 01950 431367. See OS Landranger map 4.

❸ Broch of Gurness

The Broch of Gurness is an outstanding example of the Iron Age trend towards impressive structures that were not only defensive but also acted as status symbols for their owners. Orkney has over 100 brochs. They represent a time in Iron Age society when a threat was perceived to exist, either the possibility of raiding groups from elsewhere or direct competition for land from other settlers.

Gurness broch is in very good condition, from the outlying defensive ditch to the stone walls and remains of the tower. Sited on the main island of Orkney, on the Aikerness peninsula, the central site measures some 45m (150ft) across. A single entrance leads to the formidable central tower, which is over 20m (65ft) in diameter.

The inclusion of stone partitions, cupboards, hearths, stairs and an unusual well create a home that is familiar to us today and makes the site relatively easy to interpret, which is astonishing considering its age: before 200BC. A surrounding settlement also survives although in ruins, composed of small stone houses with yards. Though the site appears to have been abandoned well before the Viking history of the islands began, a single Viking burial was discovered at the site when it was excavated in the late 1920s.

■ **LOCATION** Aikerness, 14 miles NW of Kirkwall, Orkney; on A966.
■ **ACCESS** See www.historic-scotland. gov.uk or telephone 01856 751414 for opening times and other details. Admission charge.

❹ Brodgar and Stenness

The Ring of Brodgar is massive and its position at the edge of an island in a region that has never been developed in modern times adds to its impressiveness. The stones are huge, one of them being nearly 4.5m (15ft) high. Brodgar is one of the largest stone circles in Britain. About half the original stones still stand in a circle that is over 100m (330ft) in diameter. It is likely that the Ring of Brodgar and the stones of Stenness were connected as part of the ceremonial ritual landscape that includes Maes Howe (see page 256). Stenness is about a mile away and Maes Howe a mile and a half. The stone just outside the circle is called the Comet Stone.

Stenness may have originally been larger than Brodgar but it suffered badly in the 19th century. Excavations in the 1970s were able to locate the position of some of the stones and features inside the circle. It has been dated to around 3000–2500BC. The stones are an amazing sight because they combine height with relative thinness. Francis Pryor talks about the finding of a hearth at the centre, and about the large amounts of grooved-ware pottery that were found in the excavation. This may indicate that this was a place of the living, as Francis calls it, as opposed to the area around Maes Howe, which focused on the dead.

We are lucky to have these few remaining stones. Other large stones stood nearby, including the magnificent, holed Stone of Odin, which was destroyed in the 19th century. In the centre of Stenness you can see the remains of a cove, a setting of stones that may represent a burial chamber.

■ **LOCATION** Ring of Brodgar: 4 miles NE of Stromness, Orkney; off B9055. Stones of Stenness: 5m NE of Stromness, Orkney; on B9055.
■ **ACCESS** Brodgar: Close to the W side of the road, on E shore of Loch of Stenness; OS Landranger map 6. Stenness: See www.historic-scotland. gov.uk or telephone 01856 841815 for further details.

❺ Italian Chapel

Lamb Holm island has a small chapel with a remarkable story to tell. During the Second World War, a large contingent of Italian prisoners of war, captured during the North African campaign, were sent north to Orkney to help construct 'roads' between the islands. Known as the Churchill Barriers and designed to stop submarines, these concrete obstructions were more than a mile long and 15m (50ft) deep.

Of the thousands of Italians brought to the islands, the prisoners of Camp 60 on Lamb Holm showed an undying dedication to a cause championed by one artistic prisoner, Domenico Chiocchetti. Arriving at the camp in 1942, Chiocchetti was greeted by a grey selection of 13 corrugated-iron Nissen huts as his

▼ *A remarkable testament to one man's artistic vision, and faith: the Italian chapel on Lamb Holm island. A small piece of Italy on a Scottish island.*

Intended to deter Napoleon, these guns were never fired in anger. Hackness has undergone considerable research into its past.

future home. His fellow prisoners started brightening up the camp with flowerbeds, while Chiocchetti used leftover concrete and barbed wire to make a statue of St George slaying the dragon (still to be seen today in the camp's centre). His inspiring work didn't go unnoticed, and when the prisoners asked for a chapel, they were given use of two Nissen huts.

Chiocchetti started work on what was to become an obsession. The two huts were joined and internally clad, and Chiocchetti created a beautiful altar painting of the Madonna and Child, copied from a picture he had in his wallet. The work of painting the interior, building a rood screen, shuttering and moulding the magnificent entrance and finally cladding the entire structure in concrete was all undertaken by the inmates. When the Italians finally left at the end of the war, Chiocchetti remained behind to finish his work. Chiocchetti returned several times after the war, together with his family and other ex-inmates; he died in 1999 and was mourned by the

people of the island, who maintain a special relationship with the people of Chiocchetti's home town of Moena.

- **LOCATION** 8 miles S of Kirkwall, Orkney; on minor road off A961.
- **ACCESS** Public access; see OS Landranger map 6.

BATTERY

❻ Hackness

Hackness battery, on the island of Hoy, is part of a defensive network designed to provide support to British vessels threatened by American and French privateers in Longhope Sound during the early 19th century. The artillery placements were constructed next to a Martello tower (see page 163), one of only three in Scotland. The site has recently opened to the public following a period of conservation by Historic Scotland. Excavations have confirmed the written history of the site's development: from its origins towards the end of the Napoleonic Wars (1803–15) through to several mid-19th-century fracas

with France and service in the First World War, before being converted into a farmhouse in the 1920s.

Initially equipped with eight 24-pound guns, the battery was upgraded with four 68-pounders in 1866. A firing drill held in 1892 was completed with some success when the 68-pounders achieved a range of over a mile into the sea, but the battery never saw action.

- **LOCATION** 2 miles E of Longhope, Isle of Hoy, Orkney; N of minor road off B9047.
- **ACCESS** See www.historic-scotland. gov.uk or telephone 01856 811397 for opening times and other details. Admission charge.

ANTI-ARTILLERY FORT

❼ Fort George

Built almost a hundred years after the similar fortification at Tilbury Fort in Essex (see page 161), Fort George illustrates just how effective

▶ *Fort George was built in the 18th century to the highest known standards of fortification and was virtually impregnable.*

the artillery-proof design was still considered to be by the 18th century. Built between 1748 and 1769 in the age of artillery-led warfare, the geometrically shaped stronghold relies on deep earthen banks behind low stone walls, which themselves are staggered at indirect angles to deflect artillery impacts. Casemates (enclosed gun positions) are constructed within the walls to house artillery pieces and provide 360 degrees of covering fire around the fort.

Fort George was built as a strategic base for the English administration after Culloden, in the heart of the centuries-long disputed lands of the highlanders. The site is self-contained and covers some 16 hectares (40 acres). Its position on a finger of land pushing out into the Moray Firth means it is surrounded on three sides by water. The main entrance from the landward side is via an extended drawbridge from an independent barbican, which itself can be brought under direct fire from the main fort if necessary. Though the site is still an active barracks today, it is open to the public and is an exceptional, untouched example of 18th-century military design.

■ **LOCATION** 6 miles W of Nairn, 11 miles NE of Inverness, Highland; off A96.
■ **ACCESS** See www.historic-scotland. gov.uk or telephone 01667 460232 for opening times and other details. Admission charge.

BATTLE SITE

❽ Culloden Moor

In 1688 King James II of England (and VII of Scotland) was deposed and replaced by William of Orange in a Protestant purge against a perceived Catholic threat. This started a civil war, in which at different times the French and Spanish nations would also become involved. By

1746 William's successor, George II, was still in conflict with King James's grandson, Bonnie Prince Charlie, and events came to a head at the Battle of Culloden.

The year before, Bonnie Prince Charlie had led the Jacobean army as far south as Derby before his commanders, who were convinced they had overstretched themselves, pleaded for a return to Scotland. In an age of poor communications, Bonnie Prince Charlie agreed, while unknown to him Welsh Jacobean forces had risen in his support and the government in London was starting to falter.

The withdrawal placed the initiative in the hands of government troops, who rallied under the son of

George II, the Duke of Cumberland. In 1746 Charles was based in Inverness, while the gathering government forces were based in Aberdeen. Preparing for pitched battle, the Jacobites moved to Culloden Moor on 15 April. On learning that the government forces were celebrating the Duke of Cumberland's birthday at Nairn 12 miles east, they commenced a night march, only to withdraw when they didn't reach the town by daybreak. The Jacobites were exhausted by the time they reached Culloden once again on 16 April.

The government forces duly arrived and devastated the Jacobites with their coordinated artillery and musket fire, bringing the civil war to an end. The widespread English follow-up actions after the Battle of Culloden were brutal and cruel, and devastated much of the Highlands.

■ **LOCATION** 4 miles E of Inverness, Highland; off B9006.

■ **ACCESS** For visitor centre and battle site see www.nts.org.uk or telephone 01463 790607 for details. Admission charge to visitor centre.

PREHISTORIC BURIAL MOUNDS

❾ Clava

▲ *The north-east passage grave at Clava. Careful searching will reveal cup marks on a surrounding kerb stone.*

The cairns at Balnuaran of Clava are around 3,500 years old. There are two types of monument, and they follow mortuary practice seen across Inverness-shire at this period. The first type of monument is known as a passage grave: a stone mound surrounded by large kerb stones, with a central chamber accessed by a passage, typical of an Early Bronze Age tomb. The passage grave to the north-east of the site, measuring 17m (55ft) across, has a particularly good example of clearly defined passage-grave art in one of the kerb stones; other less clear examples can be found elsewhere on the site.

The second type of cairn is a ring cairn, again measuring 17m (55ft) in diameter, with no obvious entrance to the central chamber. This cairn is surrounded by standing stones, some of which are attached to it by low earthen causeways.

■ **LOCATION** 4 miles E of Inverness, Highland; off B851.
■ **ACCESS** See www.historic-scotland. gov.uk or telephone 01667 460232 for further details.

The monument remained in use until the beginning of the 9th century BC, by which time peat expansion might have made the site unusable.

Following peat extraction in the mid-19th century, the site was fully exposed and can be visited today under the guardianship of Historic Scotland.

■ **LOCATION** 12 miles west of Stornoway, Isle of Lewis, Western Isles; off A859.
■ **ACCESS** For visitor centre and site, see www.historic-scotland.gov.uk or telephone 01851 621422. Admission charge to visitor centre.

CRANNOG

⑪ Loch an Duin

The artificial island, or crannog, of Loch an Duin on Taransay, in the Hebrides off far north-western Scotland, is a well-preserved example of this fascinating type of structure. (For more on crannogs, see page 238.) The clear waters are crossed by a rubble causeway about 30m (100ft) long that connects the broch with the foreshore. In antiquity this causeway may well have been submerged, creating the illusion to newcomers that the island was inaccessible without a boat.

The broch itself, approximately 12m (40ft) square, is constructed of rubble and still holds the substantial walls of a roughly square dwelling enclosing around 20 square metres (215 square feet) of space.

The date of the crannog is unknown, but it could have Bronze Age origins, as many crannogs in Scotland do. This popular water-bound means of settlement was equally favoured during the Iron Age, and some crannogs were still being used during the medieval period.

■ **LOCATION** S end of Loch an Duin, Taransay, Western Isles.
■ **ACCESS** The island is privately owned; there are no roads, and the site is very isolated. Access by prior arrangement only: telephone 01859 550260. See OS Landranger map 18.

STANDING STONES

⑩ Callanish

The oldest part of this collection of prehistoric standing stones is some 5,000 years old. This extraordinary ritual landscape in the Western Isles is centred on a large cruciform monument called Callanish I. A large monolith nearly 5m (16ft) high is surrounded by a ring of 13 standing stones. A stone-lined avenue exits the ring and heads in a northerly direction, while the south, east and west points are marked with single lines of standing stones which are thought to be a later (1500BC) addition to the site.

Often overlooked in comparison are Callanish II, a roughly circular monument 18m (60ft) wide marked with its ten stones, and Callanish III, an intriguing small double ring monument with 20 standing stones.

Northern Ireland

The division of Ireland into two is relatively recent, but the northern region has some of its own distinctive features, including Mesolithic settlements in the north-east, and the important Iron Age settlement of Navan. In the prehistoric period the stone outcrops of Tievebulliagh were exploited to produce axes that were traded throughout the British Isles. Early Christianity is represented at Nendrum and, later, White Island and Devenish. The Normans established control in the 12th century. In the 17th century English rulers created settlements – a process called 'plantation'. The 18th century saw a period of small-scale industrialization, particularly of textiles, and the growth of ship-building at Belfast. During the 1840s famine, a period of emigration, particularly to America, was begun.

Map of Northern Ireland showing:
- 1 Derry town walls (O LONDONDERRY)
- 2 Dunluce
- O COLERAINE
- Tievebulliagh 4
- 3 Ballymacaldrack
- O STRABANE
- BALLYMENA O
- LARNE O
- A36
- A6
- A5
- M22
- Carrickfergus 11
- A505
- A29
- COOKSTOWN O
- OMAGH O
- Tullaghogue Fort 10
- BELFAST O
- Ballycopeland 12
- 6 White Island church
- A4
- Tully Castle 5
- Nendrum
- Devenish Island 7
- Clogher 9
- M1
- 8 Enniskillen Castle
- Navan Fort
- ARMAGH O
- Inch 13
- A22
- A1
- A28
- NEWRY O

N

0 ——— 20 m
0 ——— 20 k

Navan Fort
Pre-Christian religious sanctuary

100BC TO AD400

W HEN TIME TEAM DUG near the Navan site in 1996, we used an Irish craftsman to recreate the trumpet mouths of the Bronze Age horns found at Loughnashade. He insisted that our discussions should be carried out, at least from his side, in Irish. This left Phil a little perplexed, but it did perhaps make the point that when we visit ancient sites we forget that the language once spoken there was a lot different from ours.

Here at Navan the spoken word was important. The community lived at a time when oral legend was at the heart of community life. Bards or their Celtic equivalent told stories of heroic deeds, and like the great heroic tales of Homer, these served to celebrate and fix past events in the collective mind. Francis Pryor explains: 'As a prehistorian I sometimes feel cheated that personal touches, on the lines of "King Ethelbert slept here", are denied me. When personalities are attached to sites, they are invariably much later – and very often involve the mythical King Arthur. But at Navan, the legendary capital of the prehistoric kingdom of Ulster, we have a name, *Emain Macha*, which has roots in the Iron Age. Parts of the site were excavated between 1963 and 1971 by Dudley Waterman. These were among the best excavations ever undertaken in Britain or Ireland, and they revealed a series of extraordinary features that recalled a heroic age we know about from the narrative poems of the so-called "Ulster Cycle", which is believed to have its roots in the last two centuries BC.' In the programme Tony Robinson quoted a few lines from the legendary texts. The tales feature great heroes and heroines, and refer to the existence of great palaces at Navan: one for meeting, one for housing the spoils of war and the heads of their enemies, and one for housing swords and shields.

Ceremonial destruction
The earthwork mound of Navan itself is part of a ritual landscape, in which it probably acted as a meeting place. An intriguing feature of the mound is that the rampart bank is on the outside of the ditch, indicating that the 'fort' played a role more ceremonial than defensive. The landscape also includes the King's Stables, Loughnashade where the beautiful trumpets were found – only one now remains and it can be seen in the National Museum of Dublin – and another feature called Haughey's Fort, a hillfort excavated in 1988.

The mound at Navan is the site of a huge destructive sacrificial act in which, around 94BC, a vast ceremonial building was burned to the ground. Dudley Waterman was able to find the postholes that gave the clues to the size of the building and its distinctive shape, which again was apparently more ritualistic than practical. Five successive rings of postholes marked the location of over 270 upright timber posts positioned around a large central wooden pillar, creating a structure over 40m (131ft) across. All the archaeological evidence points to this structure being burned down very soon after it was completed. In his record of Iron Age Britain, Caesar referred to the practice of creating huge wooden structures and ceremonially destroying them; Navan is one such site.

The labour to create these sites would have involved the whole community and it is likely that areas like the King's Stables would have been part of a ceremonial walkway that may have ended with some kind of place of sacrifice. Chris Lynn's excavations in

1976 found Bronze Age sword moulds and the front of a skull.

Aesthetic appreciation

The other point our Irish craftsman was illustrating was the high level of metalworking skills that must have existed on this kind of site, and the effort that was put into objects associated with ritual events and the willingness to destroy them as a kind of sacrifice. One object I would like you to be able to hold is a beautiful fibula brooch decorated in a typical Celtic Iron Age design, known to archaeologists as La Tène (named after an archaeological site in Switzerland). This features a distinctive, sometimes asymmetrical pattern of twirls and spirals, and seems to have taken inspiration from the natural forms of plants.

The area around Navan is called Creevenoe, or 'red branch', and it is thought that this refers to the red yew branches that were sacred to the Celts and formed part of the structure of their houses. *The Cattle Raid of Cooley*

describes a house:
'Thirty feet was the height of each bronze front that was in the house, Carvings of red yew therein – the Compartment of Conchibar was in the forefront of the house, with hoards of silver with pillars of bronze. Their head-pieces glittering with gold and set with carbuncles.'

One of the most extraordinary finds at Navan was the skull of a Barbary ape. This animal or its remains must have undertaken the journey from Africa to Northern Ireland in order to become the high-status gift for a chieftain. It emphasizes that this was a culture where the giving of gifts, the performing of heroic deeds and the telling of tales was essential to the tribe's life. The huge scale of Navan and the structure that was destroyed represents a heroic scale that is rarely uncovered in archaeological evidence from this period.

▲ *The trumpets from Loughnashade announce the approach to* Emain Macha. *Victor's drawing gives a good impression of how the structure might have been before it was ceremonially destroyed.*

■ **GETTING THERE** Navan Fort is 1 mile W of Armagh; off A28. See www.ehsni.gov.uk, go to 'Places to Visit' then 'Historic Monuments' or telephone 028 9054 6552 for details. At the time of going to press, the visitor centre is closed but the site has open access.
■ **OUR VIEW** Francis Pryor says: 'The site itself recalls an earlier age: it is green, leafy and pleasant and a botanist's dream. Some of its ancient magic undoubtedly survives, despite a recent unsuccessful attempt to quarry it away.' If you get the chance, read the early Irish mythological tales before you go.

Nendrum
Early Christian monastery

AD700-800 to 1400s

NENDRUM MONASTERY LIES on an island in Strangford Lough. Originally it could be reached only by crossing a deep ford, but it now has a modern road connecting it to the mainland. The name Strangford is Viking in origin: it means 'strong ford', and reflects the strength of local tides, which can be dangerous. When I first visited Nendrum with Mick, what impressed me most was the air of peace and quiet, and the fact that you could see the cells where monks had prayed in the early days of Christianity. You also get the sense of a self-sufficient community surviving in this beautiful and, at the time, cut-off place. Mick believed there was evidence to suggest early fishponds, near the water's edge, which had been managed to provide food for the monks.

Rare finds

Early Christian sites rarely survive as well as this – its island location in the Strangford Lough probably helped. The site was left untouched until the 19th century when a local historian realized that a ruinous building thought to be a lime kiln was in fact the base of a round tower.

Excavations at Nendrum in the 1920s unearthed beautifully incised tablets with drawings of animals, stones with runic writing and evidence of metalworking. This made Nendrum, in terms of finds, one of the finest archaeological monastic sites in Ireland. However, some restoration work was done at this time which to the modern eye may not have been ideal. Nor was the archaeological work done carefully enough to find traces of the earliest buildings, almost certainly made of wood and dating from when the monastery was founded by St Mochaoi, around AD700–800.

The site includes a round tower and the foundation of the church in which burials, many of them with decorated grave slabs and crosses, were found during excavations in 1954. Three main enclosures, the largest of which is about 360m (400yds) in diameter, divide the site into a central church and graveyard space – outside this is an area of huts, and beyond that, an area that might have been used for farming. The remains of the tower, which was probably built after AD900, allow you to see a feature that was common in Irish monasteries but whose purpose was unclear. Was it a retreat and safe storage place, or a convenient location for

▼ The base of the round tower. This would originally have stood to a height of up to 30m (100ft), and the doorway, situated a few metres off the ground, would have faced the door of the main church.

housing the sacred objects, including a hand bell, that were an important part of monastic life?

During the 9th and 10th centuries, like most Christian sites, Nendrum was attacked by the Vikings. There is a record of the abbot being killed in 976, which may have been in a Viking attack. None the less, Nendrum was a small self-contained monastic community where Christianity survived during a time when it was under threat in much of mainland Europe.

Daily monastic routine

A lot of what the daily life was like here has been learnt from documents, and it makes you wonder what might have been discovered had analysis of environmental and organic remains been possible. Investigations around the fishpond area in 1999 revealed the base of a 7th-century tidal mill, which was possibly used to produce flour for the community.

At Nendrum you can also see a very rare sundial; this and the hand bells were part of the way the monks regulated their day. Many sites in Ireland have produced

hand bells. The cases that contained them were often beautifully decorated. The bell and the crozier were two of the rare objects of value associated with the early Christian monks, and examples of early Christian bells can be seen in the Ulster Museum in Belfast. The first monastic settlement at Nendrum in the later medieval period was Benedictine, built around 1177.

After the 15th century, all evidence of Nendrum was forgotten until it was rediscovered in the 19th century. There are probably other Nendrums waiting to be found, and it is likely that with modern techniques more details of the monks' life can be uncovered.

The buildings and enclosing walls of this monastery generally survive at foundation level only. Each area of the monastic settlement was divided off; here you are looking towards the central church and graveyard area.

■ **GETTING THERE**: Nendrum is just S of Comber, Down, off the A22. See www.ehsni. gov.uk, go to 'Places to Visit' then 'Historic Monuments' or telephone 028 9181 1491 for opening times and other details. The Ulster Museum is at the Botanic Gardens, Belfast. See www. ulstermuseum.org.uk or telephone 028 9038 3000 for details.

■ **OUR VIEW** The visitor centre gives you a good background to the site; it has reproductions of some of the objects found and a model of what the site would have looked like. But what is best about Nendrum is that it can still recreate the atmosphere and sanctity of an early Christian monastery, especially if visited on a quiet day.

Other sites to visit

▶ *The walls of Dunluce Castle on Ireland's north coast, with their many chimney stacks and roof gables, emerge from the natural rock as if part of the geology.*

❶ Derry town walls

The defensive walls of Derry were constructed by the 'City of London' after it had been given the town by James I in 1613. From this point the town, located on the site of an early monastery of St Columba, became known to the English as Londonderry. The walls stand as one of the most complete sets of town walls in Europe. Unbroken, they circle the town centre for just over a mile and in places are over 6m (20ft) thick. Reaching to a height of over 5m (16½ft), the ramparts can be accessed using stone steps at various points.

Though the gateways have been rebuilt and some of the bastions removed, the majority of the walls themselves are original, and witnessed several sieges in the turbulent 17th century, including the famous Jacobite siege of 1688 where combined French and Irish forces found after 105 days of trying that they still couldn't break the walls.

- **LOCATION** Londonderry, Derry.
- **ACCESS** Full public access to town walls.

❷ Dunluce Castle

Dunluce Castle is the most dramatic of a series of clifftop castles along Ireland's north coast. Built about six centuries ago, it occupies a site that was first fortified about one thousand years ago, to judge by the word dún ('fort') in its place-name. A souterrain (underground passage) close to the cliff-edge is all that survives from this period.

The MacQuillan lords of north Antrim built this castle around 1400. Other than the two great circular towers that cling precariously to the rock on the eastern side of the castle, very little architecture survives from this period.

The MacDonnell family, from the Hebrides in western Scotland, captured the Dunluce region from the MacQuillans by military force at the start of the 16th century, and most of what we see at the castle today represents their 'modernization' of it: the Scottish-style gatehouse, the Renaissance loggia or arcaded gallery and the great house in the upper courtyard were all built under their patronage. Also, there is an extensive but long-abandoned garden area – with terraces and raised beds – on the headland immediately west of the castle, and this too was probably laid out by the MacDonnells. Dunluce remained a residence of the MacDonnells and their descendents, the earls of Antrim, until the middle of the 17th century, although it was briefly captured by the English in 1584.

The raging seas have played an important part in Dunluce's history. In 1588 the *Girona*, a vessel of the Spanish Armada, hit the rocks beneath the castle and sank. Almost half a century later parts of the castle's domestic and service quarters collapsed into the sea, carrying a number of servants to their death.

- **LOCATION** 4 miles W of Bushmills, Antrim; off A2.
- **ACCESS** See www.ehsni.gov.uk, go to 'Places to Visit' then 'Historic Monuments' or telephone 028 2073 1938 for opening times and other details. Admission charge.

❸ Ballymacaldrack

The 5,000-year-old tomb at Ballymacaldrack is a fine example of a court tomb, so called because the burial chamber has a small courtyard defined by stones in front of the entrance. The purpose of the 8m by 6m (26ft x 20ft) 'court' is unknown, but is presumably related to the mortuary and ritual practice of the day, which may have involved ancestor worship. Unlike the chambered barrows of England, this court tomb appears to have held cremated remains rather than naturally decayed bones.

Excavations in the 1930s and 1970s indicated that the passage tomb, itself lined with kerb stones, was once timber-roofed. The additional discovery of high concentrations of carbon and bone fragments indicated that part of the 4m-long (13ft) passage, entered via two portal stones, had seen concentrated burning, suggesting cremations had been carried out

inside the tomb. Finds from the site include pottery, flint tools and a stone axe, all of which are at the Ulster Museum in Belfast.

■ **LOCATION** 8 miles SE of Ballymoney, Antrim; off B93.

■ **ACCESS** See www.ehsni.gov.uk, go to 'Places to Visit' then 'Historic Monuments' or telephone 028 9054 6552 for opening times and other details. For Ulster Museum, see www.ulstermuseum.org.uk or telephone 028 9038 3000 for opening times and other details.

❹ Tievebulliagh

The striking outline of Tievebulliagh mountain dominates the Glencorp and Glenaan landscapes. Among the craggy rocks on the south-eastern side, a natural outcrop of particularly beautiful stone was recognized by our Neolithic ancestors and exploited to create stone tools. Porcellanite, an unusual natural combination of laterite and lithomarge rock, has similar properties to flint, making it ideal for working into strong and durable tools. The consistent quality of the stone, together with its beautiful dark colour, resulted in the Tievebulliagh resource developing into an established Stone Age 'factory'.

Hundreds, possibly thousands, of blanks were quarried from Tievebulliagh to be traded, exchanged and then finely crafted by their owners into workable tools. Because the outcrop of porcellanite is so unusual (another source is on the island of Rathlin), the spread of the material throughout Ireland and the British Isles indicates the extensive economic networks that were in place some 5,000 years ago. The community that quarried Tievebulliagh created and supplied an industry that must have supported them for a considerable time. Only the gradual acceptance of an agricultural way of life, which enabled permanent settlement within a landscape, allowed this kind of enterprise to mature. Tievebulliagh represents an early example of people fully exploiting their local resources in an industrial way.

■ **LOCATION** 3 miles W of Cushendall, Antrim; off B15.

■ **ACCESS** See OS Discoverer map D5 for footpaths.

❺ Tully Castle

The province of Ulster was 'planted' with new settlers from Scotland and England in the early 17th century. The settlers invariably built castles to protect their lands, and Tully Castle is one of the finest of those castles to survive.

A Scot, Sir John Hume, settled at Tully in 1610. His castle was built by 1613, and a small village was founded nearby around the same time. The castle itself is a T-shaped house with a walled enclosure (bawn) in front of it. The house was his residence, but there was also living space – presumably for soldiers – in the small towers at the corners of the wall around the bawn. Aspects of the design of the house, such as the use of wicker matting in the making of the vaulted ceiling inside it, suggest to archaeologists that Irish masons built it for Sir John. Excavations inside the bawn revealed cobbled pathways but no buildings, suggesting

that the area was a garden with walkways through it. A garden of 17th-century type has been recreated within it.

Tully Castle was abandoned after 1641 when, it is alleged, the local Gaelic chieftain put its occupants, save the Hume family, to the sword.

■ **LOCATION** 10 miles SE of Belleek, Fermanagh; off A46.
■ **ACCESS** See www.ehsni.gov.uk, go to 'Places to Visit' then 'Historic Monuments' or telephone 028 9054 6552 for opening times and other details.

❻ White Island Church

White Island had a church-site or monastery in the early middle ages, but nothing is known of its history. We do not know the name of its founder, nor do we know of any saint that was venerated here. Our ignorance is all the more remarkable, and frustrating, given the extraordinary archaeological remains on the island.

▲ *Now lined up against a wall of White Island church, these unique and remarkably early Christian carvings were once part of a complex piece of ritual architecture.*

Located inside the denuded ramparts of a large enclosure is a small stone church built in the Romanesque style around 1200. Excavations in 1959 revealed the remains of an earlier wooden church underneath this stone church; we know from historical sources that churches of wood were common in early Ireland, and examples have been found beneath stone churches in a number of excavations.

Built into the wall of the stone church and clearly older than it are eight remarkable and mysterious sculptured pillars, one of them unfinished. Each of the pillars bears a carving of an individual person. In one case the person is obviously an ecclesiastic (he/she carries a bell and staff). Another carries a sword and shield and is evidently a soldier or warrior. Another carries a staff and

a bag, and another again holds two winged birds by their necks.

These unusual works of art are products of Christian culture and they may date from the 9th century or thereabouts, but we do not know where and for what purpose they were originally used. Notches cut in the tops of the four larger sculptured pillars suggest that they supported some timber structure, possibly a pulpit or a shrine.

■ **LOCATION** 10 miles N of Enniskillen in Lower Lough Erne, Fermanagh; off B82.
■ **ACCESS** See www.ehsni.gov.uk, go to 'Places to Visit' then 'Historic Monuments' or telephone 028 9054 6552 for opening times and other details.

MONASTIC SITE

❼ Devenish Island

One of the most interesting ecclesiastical sites in Ireland is on Devenish Island. A monastery was founded on this island by St Molaise in the 6th century, and it had an active life up to the 17th century.

Very little remains from the early phases of the monastery's history, other than some carved stones and part of a cross-slab. There is a large embanked enclosure, as is normal on early monastic sites, but we do not know when it was built. The outstanding building on the island is the later 12th-century round tower. The Devenish tower is one of the finest in Ireland, and has some carved Romanesque stonework just underneath its conical roof. Foundations of a second tower at Devenish were discovered in excavations in the 1950s. In the 12th century the local population burned their king alive inside a round tower, and it is very likely that this tower, of which only the foundations survive, is that very one.

There are two churches beside the round tower: the smaller of the two is known as St Molaise's House, and would have contained his relics if not his actual grave; the larger was a parish church. A short distance away, but outside the old enclosure, is the

▲ *The perfectly preserved round tower dominates the small holy island of Devenish. Visitors can now enter by ladder, where once only the monastic elite could gain entrance.*

ruin of a 15th-century Augustinian monastery.

■ **LOCATION** Just N of Enniskillen in Lower Lough Erne, Fermanagh.
■ **ACCESS** See www.ehsni.gov.uk, go to 'Places to Visit' then 'Historic Monuments' or telephone 028 9054 6552 for opening times and other details.

15TH-CENTURY STRONGHOLD

❽ Enniskillen Castle

This impressive castle was built in the 15th century overlooking the waterway between the lakes of Enniskillen by the influential Maguire chieftains. In this strategic position, the castle witnessed great turbulence, and was often contested by both the O'Neills and the O'Donnells. It was captured by Niall O'Donnell together with the English in 1602, and this led to a phase of development that saw the twin-turreted Watergate built *c.* 1611.

Barrack blocks were built around the old castle keep in the 19th century. Small-scale excavations carried out in the mid-1990s in advance of some cabling works found that much of the material underlying the present surface of the castle was connected to the recent barracks. However, considering that the stronghold had been in continued use for over 600 years, wider exploration might have uncovered more evidence. An earlier auger survey indicated that archaeological deposits could lie as far down as 3m (10ft) in the waterlogged conditions.

The castle keep now holds the Enniskillen Museum, with displays about the castle and the town. The vaults also have reconstructions of castle life from the 15th century onwards. A heritage centre on the site houses collections from the Fermanagh County Museum.

- **LOCATION** Enniskillen, Fermanagh.
- **ACCESS** See www.ehsni.gov.uk, go to 'Places to Visit' then 'Historic Monuments' or telephone 028 9054 6552 for opening times and other details.

IRON AGE HILLFORT
❾ Clogher

Clogher hillfort is in a prominent position overlooking the Clogher valley and appears to have been a focus of activity for thousands of years. Excavations have uncovered evidence stretching back to the Neolithic period, when a hearth, pottery and flint tools were uncovered beneath a later bank.

The discovery of early and late Bronze Age pottery shows that the site continued to be in use during those periods, but the biggest developments on the site came with the transition into the Iron Age, when the first large bank and ditch defensive enclosure was built. Several complicated phases of building continued over the following centuries as the hillfort became a prominent centre for the region. Romano-British pottery and metalwork finds indicate established trade connections with Roman Britain. The fort fell into decline during the medieval period.

- **LOCATION** Just N of Clogher, Tyrone; off A4.
- **ACCESS** See www.ehsni.gov.uk, go to 'Places to Visit' then 'Historic Monuments' or telephone 028 9054 6552 for opening times and other details.

INAUGURAL SEAT
❿ Tullaghogue Fort

A small hill near Cookstown was once the inaugural seat of the powerful O'Neill family, rulers of Tyrone from the early 11th century until the early 17th century. Referred to as a hillfort, the enclosure at Tullaghogue appears to be designed more to designate an important area of land than defend against an attack. The double bank and ditch enclose an area over 30m (100ft) in diameter, while a causeway allows entrance to the interior.

From the 11th century, each head of the O'Neill family was effectively crowned as 'the O'Neill' in a special ceremony that centred round a stone chair reputed to have been blessed by St Patrick. In 1602, Queen Elizabeth's deputy, Mountjoy,

◄ Carrickfergus Castle is one of Ireland's finest Norman fortresses. It is dominated by its great keep, built in the decades around the year 1200 but similar to earlier English keeps.

destroyed the stone chair, and the following year the leading O'Neill of the time (Hugh) was able to be subdued. Nothing remains of the inauguration chair, but the earthworks are still impressive today.

■ **LOCATION** 2½ miles SE of Cookstown, Tyrone; off B162.
■ **ACCESS** See www.ehsni.gov.uk, go to 'Places to Visit' then 'Historic Monuments' or telephone 028 9054 6552 for opening times and other details.

NORMAN CASTLE

⑪ Carrickfergus

Carrickfergus near Belfast has one of the best-preserved medieval castles in

Ireland. The Norman baron John de Courcy, who ruled over Ulster for some 27 years following his campaign of 1177, started work on the castle around 1178. A large keep over 17m (55ft) square together with a hall were built at this time. De Courcy was ousted from power by Hugh de Lacy, and he in turn was expelled by King John in 1210. This marked the beginning of Carrickfergus as an English stronghold, which it remained for hundreds of years.

The early 13th century saw de Lacy reinstated and the continued development of the castle, with an upward extension to the keep, making it over 27m (90ft) high, and the addition of the curtain wall. By the middle of the 1200s, the imposing gatehouse and portcullis were complete. The 17th century saw the castle taken from James II's forces by the Duke of Schomberg for William III, and the castle saw action again in 1760 when a French attack captured and ransacked the town and its castle.

The castle's more recent history includes its use as a weapons store in the First World War and as an air-raid shelter in the Second World War.

■ **LOCATION** Carrickfergus, Antrim; on A2.
■ **ACCESS** See www.ehsni.gov.uk, go to 'Places to Visit' then 'Historic Monuments' or telephone 028 9054 6552 for opening times and other details.

18TH-CENTURY WINDMILL

⑫ Ballycopeland

Dating from the late 1700s, Ballycopeland is a fine example of a grain mill, kiln and miller's house. There were once over a hundred of these small industrial concerns in Co. Down, and Ballycopeland is the only remaining one in full working order.

Originally used for flour and animal feed, the mill was in full time

work until 1914. A programme of conservation by the Department of the Environment has seen the site restored to its former glory. It now houses an informative museum, featuring displays on this once prominent industry.

The mill itself is contained within a large stone tower and driven by four sails attached via a windshaft to gearing in the rotating timber cap. This is a type of mill that was first engineered in France during the 14th century.

■ **LOCATION** 1 mile W of Millisle, Down; on B172.
■ **ACCESS** See www.ehsni.gov.uk, go to 'Places to Visit' then 'Historic Monuments' or telephone 028 9054 6552 for opening times and other details.

CISTERCIAN ABBEY

⑬ Inch

Built on raised ground in the Quoile Marshes, the Cistercian abbey of Inch was founded in 1187 by John de Courcy as a daughter house of Furness in Lancashire (see page 224). The 12th-century remains visible today sit on top of an earlier monastic building, known to have been in use by the late 8th century, which was subsequently wrecked by raiding Vikings, and later the Irish.

The abbey was constructed in a typical Cistercian location, away from the general population, to enable the monks to follow their strict lifestyle of manual labour combined with worship and study. Built in the gothic style, only the east gable and its attached north and south walls now stand to any great height. Its three lancet windows crowned by a larger opening in the gable ridge are flanked by further lancets in the side walls. The northern transept end also stands with a vaulted chapel.

■ **LOCATION** ¾ mile N of Downpatrick, Down; off A7.
■ **ACCESS** See www.ehsni.gov.uk, go to 'Places to Visit' then 'Historic Monuments' or telephone 028 9054 6552 for opening times and other details.

Republic of Ireland

The first settlers in Ireland were Mesolithic hunter-gatherers who arrived around 7000BC. Farmers appeared around 4000BC, ushering in a period that saw the building of megalithic tombs. The emergence of metal, first copper, then bronze, from about 2000BC changed the nature of society. Ireland's rich gold deposits began to be exploited at this time. The Iron Age developed around 500BC, and Ireland came into contact with Celtic influences. Christianity flourished from the 5th century onwards and the Irish Church became famous across medieval Europe for its art and learning. The Vikings raided and then settled in the country between the 9th and 10th centuries. The Anglo-Normans arrived in the 12th century, while the 16th century saw the 'plantation' of Ireland. In the 18th century English landlords were in control. The 1847 famine caused the depopulation of many areas, particularly in the west.

N

Newmills ①

DONEGAL

N56

② SLIGO
Carrowmore

③ Carrowkeel

BANGOR ERRIS

N59

④ Boyle Abbey

CAVAN

WESTPORT

N5

TULSK

N55

N3

Fore ⑦

Newgrange
Bective
Abbey ⑧
Trim

⑨ Monasterboice
⑩ Drogheda
⑪ Fourknocks
Tomb

Tara

Roscommon Castle ⑤

⑥ Corlea

CLIFDEN

N59

Athenry

N4

Maynooth
Castle ⑫

Dublin

N5

GALWAY

⑮

⑯ Dún Aonghasa

Turoe

Clonmacnoise

N1

Clonfert

Portumna

PORTLAOISE

N7

⑬ Glendalough

⑭ Baltinglass Abbey

⑱ Quin Friary

⑲ Bunratty Castle

LIMERICK

N8

N9

N11

Adare ⑳

Rock of Cashel ㉒

Kilree ㉓ ㉔

Jerpoint Abbey

㉕ Vinegar Hill Mill

CAHIR

N17 Dingle Peninsula

N21

N20

Glanworth Castle ㉑

WATERFORD

ROSSLARE

KILLARNEY

KENMARE

N22

CORK

N25

N71

0   50 m

0   50 k

Newgrange, Knowth and Dowth
World Heritage Site

3300–3000BC

THE AREA KNOWN as the Bend of the Boyne is about 4 miles long and contained within a great curve of the river Boyne. During the Neolithic period this landscape was chosen for a cemetery of megalithic graves, known as passage graves or tombs. There are three principal tombs – Newgrange, Knowth and Dowth – on high ground overlooking the river, and they date from between 3300 and 3000BC.

Newgrange

Newgrange is the best-known tomb. It consists of a large mound of layered natural material 11m (36ft) high and 91m (300ft) in diameter, which is ringed by a kerb of large stones, a number of them decorated with abstract carved art. The most impressive of these stones is that which marks the entrance to the tomb. A 19m-long (62ft) passage of orthostats (large upright stones), many of them with carvings, gives access to the cruciform burial chamber. Here, the actual burials – cremations, accompanied by bone pins, small stone pendants and handmade round-bottomed pottery – were placed on stone basins within small recesses, the walls of which were decorated. The open space at the centre of the chamber was

▶ The great tumulus of Newgrange sits on a low rise overlooking the river Boyne. The quartz wall on the left is a controversial reconstruction of how the mound might have appeared 5,000 years ago.

presumably used for ritual. The chamber's roof is corbelled, with the supporting stones tipped in such a way that water percolating through the mound would be deflected away from the roof. The result is that the chamber remains dry 5,000 years after it was built.

On the winter solstice – the shortest day of the year, 21 December – the sun shines through a small opening above the entrance to the passage and spectacularly illuminates the back wall of the burial chamber. Such astronomical alignments are quite commonly found among megalithic tombs.

The exterior of the tomb has a wall of quartz with interspersed small round granite stones. This wall is a suggested – and very controversial – reconstruction

◄ *You can still walk the full length of the passage of Newgrange, even though some of the orthostats (upright stones) have been pushed over a little by the weight of the mound material.*

▶ *Victor's illustration captures the magic of the moment when light enters the Newgrange tomb. Knowing that our ancestors could predict these events and created rituals around them is an important addition to our understanding of their lives.*

of how the front of the tomb may originally have appeared, based on the discovery during excavation of large amounts of tumbled quartz in front of the tomb's entrance. The ring of tall standing stones outside the mound was erected after about 2500BC. A number of smaller passage tombs are positioned beside this great mound, though their remains are rather slight. Two of them pre-date the great tomb.

▼ *The decorated kerbstone at the back of the great tumulus has a selection of classic motifs of the Neolithic artists, including spirals and diamonds.*

Knowth and Dowth

The other two tombs are at Knowth, located to the west, and Dowth, to the east. Dowth is somewhat neglected, but Knowth has seen extensive excavations over the past 40 years, and these have revealed its complex history and yielded spectacular material. The mound is again

massive, 12m (40ft)
high and 67m (220ft) in
diameter. Like Newgrange, the mound
has a kerb of large stones, but unlike
Newgrange it has two burial chambers
inside it, both reached by passages that
run towards the centre of the mound
from opposite sides without actually
meeting. There are 17 small tombs
clustered around the big mound at
Knowth, some of them pre-dating it.

This extensive great cemetery of
more than 30 megalithic tombs, with
three massive examples among them,
was well known in early historic times.
The Celtic Gof Dagda allegedly lived
here, Roman visitors of the pre-Christian
era paid homage to the gods by
depositing coins and gold ornaments
in front of Newgrange, and it is
recorded that the last pre-Christian
kings of Tara (see page 286) were buried
here. The Battle of the Boyne of 1690,

at which William of Orange defeated
James II, securing a Protestant succession
on the throne of England, took place to
the east of Dowth.

■ **GETTING THERE**
Newgrange is 1½
miles west of Donore,
County Meath, on the
L21, signposted from
Drogheda (off N1),
and from Slane (off
N2). See www.
heritageireland.ie or
telephone 041 98
80300 for opening
times and other
details. Admission
charge.
■ **OUR VIEW** For
Francis Pryor, these
sites are 'perhaps

best seen as funerary
theatre rather than as
permanent tombs.
Experiments have
shown they were
constructed to
enhance certain
acoustic and lighting
effects. The great
passage graves at
Knowth and
Newgrange have
been excavated and
"restored" in order to
enhance their appeal
to visitors – but not
entirely successfully.'

Tara
Centre of burial, ritual and protest

3000BC-AD1843

TARA IS ONE OF THE most famous of all Irish archaeological sites, and arguably the single most important place in ancient and medieval Irish history. Tara was known in early Irish society as the home of Celtic gods (such as Lug) and goddesses (such as Medb), and the kingship of Tara was the most sought-after political prize in early medieval Ireland.

Tara is not so much one site as many dozens of sites, or rather monuments, concentrated on a low hilltop – the Hill of Tara itself – but also spread around the local countryside. It is a concentration of monuments of unrivalled density in the Irish archaeological record. The visitor to Tara might be disappointed at first, as it presents itself as a landscape of grassy humps and bumps with no building other than an early-19th-century church, but closer inspection reveals its great richness, and tempts the visitor to imagine what might lie under the ground.

▶ This phallus-shaped standing stone (from the Iron Age) is popularly identified as the Lia Fáil, the Stone of Destiny, and legend has it that it roared its approval when worthy kings of Tara were inaugurated.

Stone Age beginnings

About 30 monuments are visible on the hill, some of them so denuded that very good light is needed for them to be seen. About another 30 sites are known through geophysical and geochemical survey. You will see that many of the visible monuments on the hilltop have names. These names were recorded in an account of about AD1000, but the monuments to which they referred originally are not known. Nineteenth-century antiquarians made the identifications we know today.

The earliest monument on the hill, revealed in excavation, seems to be a buried palisaded enclosure of Neolithic date (3000–2200BC). The so-called Mound of the Hostages, a megalithic tomb (of the passage-tomb type), was built between 3000 and 2500BC, and is the oldest prominent monument that can be seen on the hilltop. Its burial chamber contained the cremated remains of a large number of people, accompanied by pottery vessels and other artefacts. Around the same time the long earthbanked avenue (or cursus monument) known as the Banqueting Hall was built. It was aligned on the passage tomb, suggesting ritual processions along it to the place of burial.

Bronze and Iron Age additions

In the Bronze Age there was a flurry of activity on the hilltop and in its immediate landscape, with new burials stuck into the Mound of the Hostages, and a great henge – known as Rath Maeve – constructed a mile to the south. That burial-related activity continued into the Iron Age with the apparent construction during this period of many, if not most, of Tara's dozens of barrows and ring ditches. The great enclosure around the top of the hill – Ráith na Ríg, the Fort of the Kings – dates from

this period; its name suggests it was a fortification, but in fact it was originally a great ceremonial enclosure. Dating from the end of the pre-Christian period is the Rath of the Synods, a complex earthwork in which Roman material was found. There is relatively little archaeology from the Christian period, reinforcing our impression of this place as a great prehistoric cemetery and ritual centre.

Tara's importance in the history of Ireland and of Irish identity is indicated by the fact that it featured prominently in political revolts in 1641, 1798 and 1843. Perhaps the most curious episode in its modern history is when a group known as the British-Israelites 'excavated' the Rath of the Synods from 1899 to 1903 in the firm belief that the biblical Ark of the Covenant was buried in it.

▲ This view of Tara from the air shows the great royal enclosure and some of the monuments inside it, including the small Mound of the Hostages. At the top of the picture is the 'Banqueting Hall', a Neolithic cursus.

■ **GETTING THERE**: The Hill of Tara is 9 miles south of Navan, County Meath, off the N3. See www.heritageireland.ie or telephone 046 90 25903 for opening times and other details.

Admission charge.
■ **OUR VIEW** There were important excavations on the hilltop in the 1950s, the results of which are only now being published, and there were

extensive topographical, geophysical and geochemical surveys in the 1990s. The site has been in the news recently, with a proposal to construct a motorway through it.

Clonmacnoise
Medieval monastic site

AD500s-1169

CLONMACNOISE IS ONE of the greatest of all Irish monastic sites of early medieval date. It was a centre of learning, of architectural endeavour and of artistic production, and it had an important role in regional and national politics up to the time of the Anglo-Norman invasion of 1169.

The monastery was founded by St Ciarán in the middle of the 6th century. He died within months of its foundation, but this did not prevent its rise as the pre-eminent monastery of the Irish midlands. Its golden age was between the 9th and 12th centuries, when royal money supported workshops producing architecture, sculpture, metalwork and manuscripts. Its decline starts with the arrival of the Anglo-Normans, whose shattered castle can still be seen on the

large earthen mound beside the car park. Since the 17th century it has been venerated as an ancient holy place.

Standing stone remains

Nothing survives from the first couple of centuries of Clonmacnoise's history, although an ogham stone (see page 306), possibly 6th-century though probably earlier, was discovered in excavations in 1990. The original monastic buildings were probably of timber or post-and-wattle and would have been contained within an enclosing bank. Of the stone buildings on the site, the 12th-century round tower is the most eye-catching. This was a bell-tower but it would have served other functions as well, including the storage of relics.

The cathedral is the largest (and one of the more complete) of the eight stone churches on the site. Probably built at the start of the 10th century, this church was altered in many ways over the centuries but it retains much of its original, and rather simple, character.

▼ The graves of many dead generations surround the small ruined churches of the former monastic settlement of Clonmacnoise. The small canopied structure at the edge of the site was erected in 1979 for the visit of Pope John Paul II.

◀ *The 12th-century church of Temple Finghin, built on the boundary of the monastic enclosure and overlooking the mighty river Shannon, is famous for its round tower.*

One curious feature of it are the antae at both ends; these are shallow projections of the side walls past the end walls, and while they are quite common in early Irish churches their purpose is still debated. Another interesting church is called Temple Ciarán. This is traditionally the burial place of the saint himself, and a relic – his hand! – was stored here in the 17th century. Temple Finghin, the church with the attached round tower at the edge of the old graveyard, was built in the 12th century. Temple Melaghlin (or Temple Rí as it is sometimes called) is behind the cathedral and dates from around 1200.

A short distance to the east of the monastery along a pilgrim road is the Nuns' Church, a small Romanesque church with beautiful detail. It dates from the eve of the Anglo-Norman invasion.

The High Crosses of Clonmacnoise are justly celebrated. The Cross of the Scriptures – decorated with scenes from the scriptures – is the best and was carved in the early 900s. There is a much-defaced inscription at the bottom of one of its sides. The crosses are displayed in the visitor centre, as well as a selection of the 600 complete or fragmentary early medieval grave slabs from the site, the largest collection in Britain or Ireland.

■ **GETTING THERE** 8 miles NE of Shannonbridge, Offaly, off the R444. See www.heritage ireland.ie or telephone 090 96 74195 for opening times and other details.

There is an admission charge.
■ **OUR VIEW** Three of the High Crosses of Clonmacnoise are on display in the visitor centre, with excellent replicas on the site itself.

Dublin
One of Europe's oldest capitals

AD841 to the present

ALTHOUGH SMALL AND intimate, Dublin is one of Europe's great capital cities. A city of culture that was once home to many of the greatest literary figures of the 20th century, it enjoys a reputation today as the lively and welcoming metropolitan centre of Ireland's 'Celtic Tiger' economy. Dublin is an essential port of call for any explorer of Ireland's heritage.

Viking origins

The city is one of Europe's oldest capitals. Though there was a Christian settlement in its vicinity back in the early middle ages, its origins as a city must be traced to the Vikings. These pirates from Scandinavia were regular visitors to Ireland's shores in the late 700s and early 800s. In 841 they set up a permanent camp or fort near the mouth of the Liffey, Dublin's river. The local population expelled them in 902. Fifteen years later they returned, and they created the town that then developed over many centuries into the modern city. That Viking town was downriver from the present city centre, in the vicinity of Christ Church Cathedral and Dublin Castle. Nothing survives above ground from this period, but very extensive archaeological excavations of the past half-century have revealed Viking

▼ *Dublin's most famous bridge, the cast-iron Ha'penny Bridge, was built in around 1820 at a cost of £3,000. It takes its name from the toll that had to be paid to cross it.*

Dublin's prosperous and sophisticated culture, as well as its international connections.

The civic offices that overlook the Liffey at Wood Quay stand on the site of the most famous excavation ever conducted in Ireland. Archaeologists showed this site – one of the richest urban archaeological sites in Europe – to be at the heart of Viking Dublin. The site was earmarked for development by Dublin Corporation. A campaign in the late 1970s to preserve it for posterity included public demonstrations on the streets of Dublin and even a pro-preservation resolution from the Council of Europe. Alas, Dublin Corporation

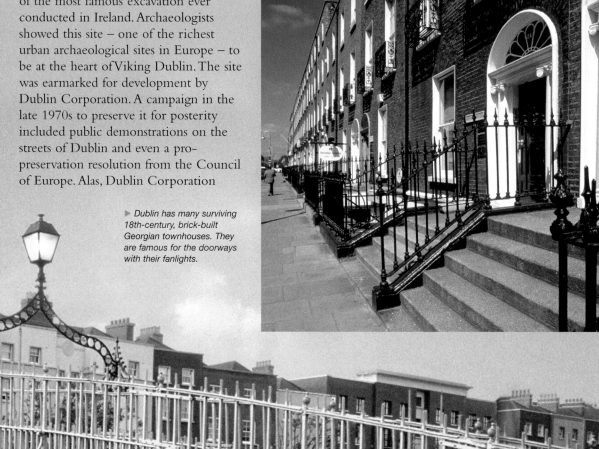

▶ Dublin has many surviving 18th-century, brick-built Georgian townhouses. They are famous for the doorways with their fanlights.

resisted the pressure and erected the civic offices in the early 1980s. Some silver lining: the Wood Quay saga did raise public consciousness of heritage, and today Ireland has stricter heritage laws than most other countries anywhere in the world.

Development of the city

The cathedral and castle mentioned already date from the period when the Normans came to Ireland and established Dublin as their capital. Christ Church Cathedral is one of two Norman cathedrals in Dublin; the other, St Patrick's, was built near by as a rival cathedral to serve the same diocese. Both churches are impressive examples of 13th-century Gothic architecture. Their architects were almost certainly trained in western parts of England. The castle, which was built by the crown, was the centre of English administration in Ireland from the 13th century to the early 20th century. Little of the original castle survives, but walls exposed in excavations in the 1980s are displayed.

Dublin was a city of extraordinary wealth in the 18th century. The city expanded eastwards towards the present city centre from its medieval core, and great public buildings were constructed. Dublin's Georgian houses (with their famous fanlight doorways) were built at this time, usually in terraces along streets or facing onto squares. After the Act of Union in 1801 Dublin lost its status as a capital city and the owners of these houses de-camped to England, specifically to London. The great houses were thereafter occupied by multiple families, often living in squalor. They naturally fell into decay. Regarded as symbols of English power after Ireland achieved independence, they were allowed to decay further in the 20th century, and many were demolished as recently as the 1970s. Today, they are regarded as some of Dublin's greatest cultural assets.

The National Museum

The National Museum of Ireland on Kildare Street has one of the greatest museum collections in Europe. It houses more than two million objects dating from earliest prehistory to the 20th century. Of the prehistoric material on display, the goldwork from the Bronze Age (2000–500BC) is probably most impressive: there are hundreds of gold artefacts, most of them personal

▼ *Completed in 1922, the government building on Merrion Street is among Dublin's finest Edwardian buildings.*

A bronze open-work object of Iron Age date from Cornalaragh, Co. Monaghan, in the National Museum of Ireland. It was designed with the aid of a compass, and chiselled by hand.

ornaments such as neck-rings and bracelets. Ireland was one of the most important places for the production of gold objects in prehistory.

The museum's collection of early medieval objects includes a number of the most famous treasures from early medieval Europe, such as the unique 8th-century liturgical chalices from Ardagh and Derrynaflan, and the Tara Brooch. The 12th-century treasures include various shrines, such as that made to contain St Patrick's bell, and the Cross of Cong, an exquisite processional cross made to carry a fragment of the True Cross. Artefacts from the time of the foundation of the state – the 1916 Proclamation of Independence, for example – are also exhibited in the museum. Ireland's famous Christian manuscripts, such as the *Book of Durrow* and the *Book of Kells* (see also page 259), can be visited in Trinity College in the city centre.

■ **GETTING THERE**: The National Museum of Ireland (Archaeology and History) is on Kildare Street, Dublin 2.

See www.museum.ie or telephone 01 67 77444 for opening times and other details.

■ **OUR VIEW** The museum is unmissable, and the Georgian streetscapes of Dublin are well worth a visit.

Turoe Stone, Clonfert and Portumna
The Celts to the Renaissance

Multi-period site

THE CELTS, OR *Keltoí*, were a people of central Europe in the immediate pre-Christian period. Ireland identifies itself as a Celtic country, but the nature and extent of the Celts' involvement with Ireland is a matter of great dispute. Some scholars have suggested, for example, that Celtic warriors invaded Ireland, while others have suggested that there was a peaceful migration to Ireland of Celtic people. Whatever the case, Ireland has a small but impressive body of Celtic material, much of which is housed in the National Museum in Dublin (see page 292).

The Turoe Stone

The most impressive and intriguing Celtic object to be seen in the landscape is the Turoe Stone. It is the finest one of the five monoliths (large stones) in Ireland that are decorated with the curled, organic style of Celtic art that is described as La Tène (see also page 271). It is a phallic-shaped granite monolith more than 1.5m (5ft) high, with a complex curvilinear design at the top and a band of fretwork about halfway down. It was probably carved in the 1st century BC, possibly in imitation of the often square decorated monoliths of Celtic Europe. Some commentators have argued that this stone, which obviously served a ritual-religious function, is an omphalos stone, rather like that which stood at Delphi in Greece.

The Turoe Stone is not in its original position. It used to be located beside a small earthen fortification at a place called Feerwore, several miles away.

Clonfert Cathedral

St Brendan the Navigator, who allegedly discovered America long before the Vikings or Christopher Columbus, founded an important monastery on the banks of the river Shannon at Clonfert around 560. The monastery is well documented but the only feature that survives to any degree is the great church built in the 10th century. This church was designated a cathedral in the 12th century when a new diocese of Clonfert was created.

The church was originally a long, one-cell, rectangular church with antae

▼ The Turoe Stone, a carved granite boulder with complex, abstract ornament, dating from the Celtic Iron Age.

(see page 289). These buttress-like features are still visible today. Alterations were made to this church in the late 12th century – it was enlarged, and it was given a new Romanesque doorway – and then again in the 15th century, when it was further enlarged and a west tower was built.

The Romanesque doorway at Clonfert is justly famous. It is a masterpiece of medieval Irish stone-carving. Dating from around the year 1180, it features a dazzling array of ornamental motifs both on its arches and on the triangular gable or pediment above it. Some of the motifs come from within the native Irish carving tradition, others from the Viking art tradition, and others again from the Romanesque tradition of western France. Particularly striking but puzzling are the stone heads, both human and animal, that decorate virtually every part of the doorway.

Portumna Castle

Portumna Castle is one of Ireland's finest Renaissance houses, dating from the start of the 17th century. It was built by Richard Burke, earl of Clanricarde and governor of Galway, at a cost of £10,000. In 1826 it fell victim to an accidental fire and was abandoned. Restoration and conservation began in 1968 and still continues.

The house itself has a very wide facade as you approach it along a long avenue, but it is actually a very narrow building, with two parallel sets of rooms, one at the front and one at the back. Internal partitions, now gone, separated various public, private and semi-private rooms, most of them well lit and with fireplaces.

There was some slight provision for the protection of the household by firearms, but this was on the whole an unfortified house.

A small circular porch was added on one side in 1797 and this bears an unusual inscription that immortalizes a family dog.

▲ The late-12th-century west doorway of Clonfert Cathedral, with its mysterious iconography, is one of Ireland's finest works of Romanesque art.

■ **GETTING THERE** These sites are in County Galway. Turoe Stone is 4 miles N of Loughrea, off the R350 at Turoe Pet Farm. Clonfert Abbey is 6 miles N of Banagher, on minor roads off the R356. For Turoe, telephone 091 841580 for further details. For Clonfert and Portumna details, go to www.irelandwest.ie or telephone 091 537700.
■ **OUR VIEW** The Turoe Stone is a beautiful and remarkable monument and deserves your full attention. Ideally it should be seen with side lighting from the sun to enhance its design.

Trim
Medieval town

12th–14th centuries

THE SMALL MARKET TOWN of Trim is one of the jewels in Ireland's heritage crown. It is dominated by the largest and finest Norman castle in Ireland, but it also contains other important medieval buildings. The town itself was founded in the middle ages, but there was a great monastery here in the pre-Norman period; indeed, it was that monastery, as well as the river Boyne, that attracted the Normans to settle here.

Trim Castle

The castle was built by Hugh de Lacy, one of the most powerful of the Norman aristocrats to settle in Ireland in the aftermath of the successful invasion of 1169. De Lacy's first castle on the site was of earth and timber. It was burned down by an Irish army in 1173, when Hugh was in France in the service of Henry II. Traces of this early fortification have been discovered in archaeological excavations.

The rebuilding of Trim Castle in stone started around 1175. The great keep or donjon was built in the first campaign; most of the other structures, such as the ruined great hall overlooking the river and the barbican gate, which originally allowed one to enter the castle across a now dried-up moat, were built in the 13th century.

The design of the keep is unusual: it is basically square in shape with larger square turrets projecting from the middle of each face. Its interior is labyrinthine, with chambers and halls and connecting

▼ Trim Castle is one of the most complete Norman fortresses in Ireland. The great keep (seen here in the background) was built in the late 12th century and is of international importance as a work of architecture. The curtain wall was built in the 13th century.

stairs and passages. Water was collected in a cistern at the top of the building and supplied to rooms by lead pipes. Originally the keep was a much lower building than the one we see today. Its height was raised over a period of 25 years, and building work had finished by the time King John and his entourage stayed here in 1210. We have this detailed knowledge of the architectural history of the keep thanks to the fortuitous survival inside in its wall of stumps of timber hoarding and scaffolding, securely dated by dendrochronology.

Yellow Steeple

Across the river from the castle is another of Trim's treasures, the Yellow Steeple. The massive west tower of a largely destroyed Augustinian monastic church, this was built in the 14th century and blown up in 1649. A statue of the Blessed Virgin, known as the Idol of Trim, was venerated here in the middle ages, but was destroyed during the Reformation. The site that the Yellow Steeple occupies is presumably the site on which the original pre-Norman church stood.

There are other medieval buildings in the town, such as St Patrick's Protestant Cathedral, as well as parts of the old town wall, but visitors to Trim should not miss the ruins of Newtown Trim Cathedral, about a mile downstream from the town. This cathedral was founded by the local Norman bishop in 1206 and its church was probably the largest in Ireland in the middle ages. It was served by Augustinian canons and their domestic quarters survive on the site.

Close to the cathedral but on the other side of the bridge you can see what remains of a medieval friary and hospital.

■ **GETTING THERE**
Trim is in County Meath. For the castle, go to www.heritageireland.ie or telephone 046 94 38619 for opening times and other details. Admission charge.
■ **OUR VIEW** A visit to Trim is a real pleasure and you should give yourself enough time to enjoy both the town and the impressive historic remains.

Other sites to visit

❶ Newmills

The corn and flax mills of Newmills, on the south banks of the Swilly river, are a beautifully preserved example of this thriving 17th-century industry. Originally built in 1683, the mills were later run by the Gallagher family for 90 years until they closed business in 1982. The state purchased the mills four years later and embarked on a programme of restoration and preservation. The lower corn mill also ground barley and oats, and was driven by a cast-iron waterwheel measuring over 7.5m (25ft) in diameter. The upper flax mill was used in the manufacture of cloth and was powered by a smaller waterwheel nearly 4m (13ft) across.

The water to power the wheels was channelled down a millrace that tapped the Swilly some quarter of a mile upstream. The channel, which

▼ *Newmills represents a rare chance to see still-operating industrial machinery in the rural County Donegal landscape.*

▶ *Many of the tombs in the Carrowmore cemetery have been stripped of their earthen mounds, leaving skeletal stone chambers and outer kerbs.*

was piped in some sections, fed both wheels in turn. Visitors can see the large corn-mill wheel turning today as it drives the old machinery, a rare example of preserved industrial archaeology.

■ **LOCATION** 3 miles W of Letterkenny, County Donegal; off R250.
■ **ACCESS** See www.heritageireland.ie or telephone 074 91 25115 for opening times and other details. Admission charge.

❷ Carrowmore

With its collection of stone burial monuments, Carrowmore is the largest prehistoric cemetery in Ireland and undoubtedly an area of great significance to Neolithic and Bronze Age predecessors. More than a hundred individual burial tombs are distributed over 1.5 square miles of landscape. Though many tombs were destroyed by enthusiastic antiquarians in the 1800s, and later gravel extraction claimed even more, over 60 still remain to be seen.

The tombs are a selection of passage tombs, portal dolmens and

barrows lined with kerb stones. Some of the circles of stones that can be seen are actually kerbs from barrows that have been excavated. The majority of the monuments are gathered around an area to the south by the Seafield road, distributed in a roughly oval pattern that is about a quarter of a mile wide and half a mile north to south. However, additional standing stones and tombs are also present further north, including an interesting stone with a hole near the Rathcarrick–Sligo road.

The date range for the tombs stretches from the Neolithic period around 6,500 years ago to the Early Iron Age, some tombs having been reused or converted into ritual enclosures around the 5th century BC.

■ **LOCATION** 3 miles W of Sligo; off N17.
■ **ACCESS** See www.heritageireland.ie or telephone 071 91 61201 for opening times and other details. Admission charge.

❸ Carrowkeel

An impressive cemetery of megalithic tombs of Neolithic date crowns a number of summits in the Bricklieve mountains. The tombs, which were probably built between 3000 and 2000BC, are mainly passage graves. Their cross-shaped burial chambers are accessed by passages – hence their name – and are contained within circular cairns. Carrowkeel is one of four great cemeteries of tombs of this type, the others being in the Bend of the Boyne (see page 282), Loughcrew and Carrowmore (see left).

There has been no modern excavation in this cemetery, but earlier excavations of tombs yielded bone pins, stone pendants and beads, as well as a very characteristic type of handmade, round-bottomed pottery (now called Carrowkeel ware) which is decorated with incised patterns.

Settlements associated with cemeteries such as Carrowkeel are rarely identified, but a low plateau to the east of the cemetery has the extensive remains of small stone-built huts which may be Neolithic. It is a rare and valuable survival.

- **LOCATION** S of Castlebaldwin, County Sligo; on minor road off N4.
- **ACCESS** Open site with full public access. OS Discovery map D25.

❹ Boyle Abbey

The large Cistercian abbey at Boyle was founded in the later 12th century, and populated by monks from Mellifont in Louth. Apart from being raided by Richard de Burgo in 1235, and then later used as a military barracks after Cromwell's troops vandalized it in 1659, the abbey appears to have largely escaped continuing troubles and enjoyed a successful time for the majority of its use.

The well-preserved ruins of the cruciform design have two aisles to the nave and chapels in each transept. The arches of the north wall of the nave have pointed tops, while their opposing arches on the south wall are rounded. Though possibly built

▼ The nave of the church of Boyle Abbey with its rows of Romanesque columns and piers was built in the early 13th century.

in different stages, both sets would have been complete in the early 13th century when the church was consecrated. The pillars supporting the arches are also different, with rounded examples on the south and square on the north. Both have interesting carved stone capitals, many with figures pulling surprised faces.

Though much of the monastic complex, including the cloister, is no longer intact, it is possible to see traces of its existence, such as blocked-up doorways, in the fabric of the walls. There is a visitor centre at the site, built in the restored gatehouse.

- **LOCATION** Boyle, County Roscommon; off N4.
- **ACCESS** See www.heritageireland.ie or telephone 071 96 62604 for opening times and other details. Admission charge.

❺ Roscommon Castle

Roscommon Castle is one of the great castles built by Edward I in the late 13th century. Although less spectacular and certainly less famous than the castles of north Wales such as Conwy (see page 102) and Harlech, it is nevertheless one of that group.

In the late 1260s Roscommon was identified as a suitable place for a castle to protect English interests in western Ireland from the Irish. A castle was built here around 1270 but the Irish burned it soon after. A new castle – built at considerably greater expense, and the one we see today – was begun in 1275 and largely finished a decade later. Today the castle is a shell – the buildings which lined the interior of the castle have all been destroyed – but its large D-shaped corner towers and two-towered gatebuilding are still impressive.

The castle changed hands many times in its history. One of its owners was Sir Nicholas Malby, the English governor of Connacht, who obtained it in 1578. He modernized the old castle by constructing new buildings inside it and by replacing some of the narrow arrow-slits with the large windows we still see today.

The castle overlooks on one side a now-dried lake. This would have been a part of its defences, but it is likely also that it provided an aesthetically pleasing watery landscape of the type that is increasingly identified at castles of the same date in Britain.

■ **LOCATION** The castle is on a hillside just outside the town of Roscommon, County Roscommon.
■ **ACCESS** See www.visitroscommon.com for more information. National monument; open access.

IRON AGE TRACKWAY

❻ Corlea

The discovery of ancient preserved timbers at Corlea near Kenagh in 1984 led to the uncovering of a remarkable wooden trackway. Further excavation in 1985 revealed another four tracks leading out into the bog, while peat extraction has uncovered traces of even more. A large section of the main trackway is now preserved in a specially sealed environment within the visitor centre, and a parallel conservation project has ensured that the

▲ Oak trackways of prehistoric date criss-cross the bogs of the Irish midlands. The Corlea trackway is among the most impressive ever discovered.

remaining timbers left in the bog are protected by a maintained environment.

The purpose of the main trackway and its associated similar structures has been a subject of debate among archaeologists. Here's Francis Pryor's view: 'I like mysteries, and this one is a cracker. The remarkable prehistoric road known as Corlea One was constructed of massive split oak planks in the year 148BC. The huge planks, each one of which was over 3m (10ft) long and would have taken two or more men to carry, were laid on two parallel rails, or bearers, rather like un upside-down railway track. It is known to have run for a mile and a half across soft boggy ground. There is also possible evidence for rituals, not like Flag Fen (see page 146), but odd nonetheless – for example, parts of an Iron Age cart were found directly below the timbers. But the strangest, most mysterious, aspect of Corlea concerns its use, or non-use. Some sections appear to have remained incomplete. There is also good

scientific evidence to suggest that it was so heavy that it sank into the bog very shortly after its construction. Now there are over 100 *toghers* (trackways) known in the bogs around Corlea, and it is inconceivable that the prehistoric engineers who built it did not realize it would sink. So why did they build it? My personal theory is that it was built *to* sink – as some kind of massive offering. But that's just a guess. In all honesty, I don't think anyone really knows.'

■ **LOCATION** 6 miles NW of Ballymahon, County Longford; on R392.
■ **ACCESS** For the visitor centre go to www.heritageireland.ie or telephone 043 22386 for opening times and other details. Admission charge.

EARLY MONASTIC SITE

❼ Fore

The remains of a small church at Fore are the only surviving parts of an early 7th-century monastery founded by St Feichin. At one time the monastery was reputed to have housed more than 250 monks, and records show that it was raided and burned down on many occasions from the 8th century through to the 12th century.

▲ The ruined Norman Benedictine priory at Fore is the most impressive of a series of important archaeological sites in this historic, secluded valley in the Irish midlands.

The church got a chancel early in the 13th century. Also at the beginning of the 13th century, the influential de Lacy family built a priory near by, one of only a small number held in Ireland by the Benedictine order. The remains of the priory, some of which have been reconstructed, can be seen, including 15th-century additions. Stone gateways, once part of the medieval town, can also be found on the outskirts of the village.

■ **LOCATION** 3 miles E of Castlepollard, County Westmeath.
■ **ACCESS** See www.eastcoastmidlands ireland.com (go to 'Visitor Attractions' then 'Visitor Attractions in Westmeath', then 'Fore Abbey') or telephone 044 40861 for opening times and other details.

CISTERCIAN MONASTERY

❽ Bective Abbey

The substantial ruins of Bective Abbey lie between the dominant historic landscapes of Tara (see page 286) and Trim (see page 296).

Founded by Murdach O'Melaghlin, the king of Meath, in 1147 as a daughter house of Mellifont in Louth, this Cistercian abbey is one of the earliest of the order in Ireland.

In 1186 the community was involved in a dispute over the remains of the influential and extremely wealthy character Hugh de Lacy. He was a supporter of the abbey, but also a benefactor of the Augustinian abbey of St Thomas's in Dublin. The ensuing wrangling, which also included disputes about the inheritance of his lands, resulted in Bective Abbey handing over de Lacy's remains in 1205 (St Thomas's already had his head).

In the 13th century Bective was further developed and partly defended so that it provided a safe place for visitors. By the 15th century the abbey appears to have fallen into decline and some parts of the monastic complex were decommissioned. The abbey was finally dissolved in 1536. Records show that the abbey roof was taken down in 1540 for reuse during the repair of a mill.

■ **LOCATION** 5 miles NE of Trim, County Meath; on minor road off R161.
■ **ACCESS** Open site with full public access.

MEDIEVAL MONASTERY

❾ Monasterboice

This monastery was founded around AD500 by a little-known saint called Buite. It was an important centre of art and learning up to the 12th century, but the arrival of the Cistercians nearby in 1142, and the invasion of the Anglo-Normans 30 years later, accelerated its decline.

The round tower dominates the site from afar. It was built in the 10th century, and burned out in the 1090s in circumstances that are not recorded. The monastery's treasures were lost with it. The two churches that survive in the monastery are fairly nondescript later medieval buildings, which presumably replace older churches.

Monasterboice's chief claim to fame is its high crosses. Two of these – Muiredach's Cross (which is near the entrance to the site) and the West Cross (which stands in front of the round tower) – are among the most celebrated works of medieval art to survive in Ireland. Both were carved in the early 10th century. Their iconography features scenes from the scriptures, many of them easily identifiable. One of the most striking images, to be found on

Muiredach's Cross, is of people whose souls are damned being prodded towards hell by a trident-waving devil.

- **LOCATION** 6 miles N of Drogheda, County Louth; off N1.
- **ACCESS** Open site, full public access.

MEDIEVAL DEVELOPMENT

⑩ Drogheda

Drogheda was one of the biggest towns in Ireland during the 14th and 15th centuries, controlling a prominent port on the river Boyne that managed significant imports and exports for the country. The first indications of settlement belong to the Vikings, who established themselves here in the early 10th century, but a thorough programme of archaeological assessment has found that most of the evidence under the present streets belongs to the medieval occupation of the town.

The middle ages saw the town heavily fortified by the Normans, including the substantial St Lawrence's Gateway, and the founding of the St Mary Magdalene church under the Dominicans in 1224. The town was devastated by Oliver Cromwell's forces in 1649 when a massacre took place, and never recovered its status after surrendering to King William after the Battle of the Boyne in 1690.

- **LOCATION** Drogheda, County Louth; on N1.
- **ACCESS** See www.eastcoastmidlands ireland.com or telephone 042 93 35484 for further details. For Drogheda Museum: www.millmount.net or telephone 041 98 33097 for opening times and other details. Admission charge.

PREHISTORIC BURIAL

⑪ Fourknocks Tomb

Ten miles south-east of the extraordinary Newgrange site (see page 282) lies Fourknocks, a collection of three burial mounds. The largest is a Neolithic chambered tomb, which was excavated in the

1950s and remains open to the public. Though the top of the mound is a modern reconstruction, it does allow the visitor to experience the interior of a passage tomb as it would have been. Of particular interest is the rock art within the tomb, found on the left as you enter. The face stone, made up of carved diamond shapes for an eye and nose together with a double-lined smile, is the earliest known representation of a face in Ireland.

The large main chamber of the tomb has three niches, which were found to contain the remains of more than 60 individuals. Additional burials were discovered in the mound itself, indicating the continued importance of the site as burial practice developed.

The other two mounds have not been excavated and are on private land.

- **LOCATION** 11 miles S of Drogheda, County Meath.
- **ACCESS** See www.knowth.com then 'Fourknocks'. Only the main mound here is open to the public.

13TH-CENTURY CASTLE

⑫ Maynooth Castle

Gerald Fitzgerald, the influential first Baron of Offaly, had Maynooth Castle built at the beginning of the 13th century as a stronghold to defend his extending lands and holdings. The Fitzgerald family became one of the most powerful in Ireland, and Maynooth gained renown as one of their greatest houses.

Developed in several phases, the castle keep was surrounded by a curtain wall. At one time it also had a great hall, evidence for which can be seen by the arches in the fabric of the east wall. The base has two stone vaults, which are thought to be a later addition, possibly built when the 6th earl strengthened the defences in the 15th century.

Maynooth held a prominent position in the administrative and

political culture of the 15th and 16th centuries as successive earls of Kildare took the seat as representatives of the King of England. Abandoned in the 17th century, the castle is now in the care of the state.

- **LOCATION** In County Kildare, on R148; 7 miles W of Dublin.
- **ACCESS** See www.eastcoastmidlands ireland.com or telephone 01 62 86744 for opening times and other details. Admission charge.

ECCLESIASTICAL CENTRE

⑬ Glendalough

The ruined monastery in Glendalough – 'the valley of the two lakes' – is associated with St Kevin, a 6th-century holy man. He was drawn to this place because of its isolation, an isolation it has retained despite its many visitors today. The monastery is well known in history, and we have the names of many of its abbots and bishops, as well as information on the number of times local kings gave it patronage or enemy armies burned its churches. It fell into decline after the Anglo-Normans united the diocese of Glendalough with that of Dublin.

The principal cluster of monastic buildings is dominated by the round tower, one of the finest and most complete in Ireland. The large church nearby is the cathedral, possibly built in the 10th century. It was modified in the 12th century, not least with the addition of a chancel. Close by is a small church that is popularly called St Kevin's Kitchen on account of having a small chimney-like round tower projecting from its stone roof!

There are other churches in the vicinity, including the 11th-century Reefert Church, deeper into the valley to the west of the main cluster,

▶ *The monastery in Glendalough is spread out along the two lakes that give it its name, but at its centre is the group of buildings shown here: the round tower (top), cathedral (right) and St Kevin's church (bottom).*

▲ *Glendalough remains tranquil, despite the many visitors to the site.*

and the lovely little St Saviour's priory church, a Romanesque church built in the 12th century, in the valley to the east.

- **LOCATION** 1 mile W of Laragh, County Wicklow; off R756.
- **ACCESS** See www.heritageireland.ie or telephone 0404 45325/45352 for opening times and other details. Admission charge to visitor centre.

CISTERCIAN MONASTERY

⑭ Baltinglass Abbey

To the north of Baltinglass town, by the river Slaney, lies Baltinglass Abbey, a Cistercian monastery founded by Dermot MacMurrough in 1148. The monks came from the mother house at Mellifont, and Baltinglass itself would later send out monks to establish other monasteries, such as the daughter house at Jerpoint (see page 311).

The aisles to the nave have alternating square and round piers, which are decorated on both their capitals and bases in a transitional style between Irish and Cistercian architecture. The ruins of the church and associated cloister are well kept. Their carved stone details can be attributed to the 12th century. The fine tower is a 19th-century addition. The abbey was dissolved in 1541 and passed into private hands. Records show that before suppression, Baltinglass was one of the richest abbeys in Ireland.

An interesting feature of the site is a large pyramid-shaped granite mausoleum from the 19th century. It was built by the Stratford family, who held influence and owned estates in the area during the 1800s.

- **LOCATION** In County Wicklow on N81; 35 miles SW of Dublin.
- **ACCESS** See www.wicklow.ie (go to Navigation Menu and 'Tourism', then 'Attractions', then 'Heritage') or telephone 0404 20100 for further details.

CASTLE AND FRIARY

⑮ Athenry

The settlement of Athenry became established as a town after Meiler de Bermingham gained a charter to build a castle here in 1235. His large three-storey tower was enclosed with a heavy curtain wall incorporating drum towers. The early 14th century saw the fortification of the town with bastion-supported walls and a large moated area. In 1316 the O'Connors fought de Bermingham outside the town. The 15th century saw the building of gables and a new roof to the extended tower. In the 16th century the town was contested by the O'Donnells and almost destroyed by fire. The castle is well preserved and has a good visitor centre.

Meiler de Bermingham also founded a friary at Athenry in 1241 for the Dominicans. Records show that the different parts of the friary were built by different prominent members of the Athenry community, rather than the friary having been completely built by de Bermingham. Only the ruins of the church remain from the original complex, displaying evidence within the fabric of the walls of successive periods of development. The friary avoided dissolution in the 16th century only to be confiscated later by Queen Elizabeth and burnt out in 1574.

▲ Not a place for the nervous! The Atlantic Ocean crashes against the cliffs beneath this lfort, Dún Aonghasa, on the Aran Islands at the edge of Europe.

However, by 1644, the new prior, Dominick de Burgo, had restored the buildings and established the friary as a university. This was not to last. Oliver Cromwell's troops seized the site in 1652 and banished the friars.

■ **LOCATION** Athenry, County Galway.
■ **ACCESS** For the castle, see www.heritageireland.ie or telephone 091 844797 for opening times and other details. Admission charge. For the priory, telephone Athenry Arts & Heritage Centre, 091 844661.

STONE FORT

⑯ Dún Aonghasa

This stone fort or *cashel* in the Aran Islands stands at the edge of a vertical cliff nearly 90m (300ft) high and has views for almost 100 miles along the Atlantic seaboard. It is one of the most spectacular – and frightening! – archaeological sites in Europe. It is a great semi-circular enclosure of about 5.5 hectares (14 acres) in area defined by three concentric enclosing walls of dry-stone construction, as well as by a 'chevaux de frise' (a band of jagged pillars of rock through which attackers could not move quickly; see also Castell Henllys, page 98).

There is relatively little in the folklore of the Aran Islands about this extraordinary monument; even its name seems to be relatively modern. Archaeological survey and excavation in the early 1990s cast light on its antiquity. Much of what we see today was constructed around 2,000 years ago and remodelled about 1,000 years ago, but digs revealed that the site was first occupied around 1500BC and that it was first enclosed around 1100BC. Indeed, its inhabitants at that time lived in timber huts on stone footings, had a mixed diet that included shellfish and meat, used moulds to cast objects of bronze, made their own pots, and possessed amber, an exotic material imported from the Baltic.

■ **LOCATION** The Aran Islands are in Galway Bay. Dún Aonghasa is on Inishmore.
■ **ACCESS** By ferry and air: www.visitaran islands.com or telephone 091 563081 for further details. There's a visitor centre on Inishmore.

🄱 Dingle Peninsula

This beautiful peninsula is exceptionally rich in archaeological remains, especially of the period between the 6th and 12th centuries. At the west end of the peninsula are three important early church sites, Reask, Gallarus and Kilmalkedar.

Reask was excavated in the 1970s. It is a stone-built enclosure within which are the remains of a small stone church, some circular huts and an exceptionally beautiful cross-inscribed pillar. Imported pottery from the Mediterranean was found here, reminding us of the distant origins of early monasticism in Ireland.

Like Reask, little is known historically about the site of Gallarus. The site is best known today for its small, fully roofed church, built without mortar. Churches of this type are often described as 'boat-shaped' because they resemble upturned boats. They are largely confined to the west coast of Ireland. Their dates of construction are not known; some scholars have suggested that they may have been built as late as the 12th century, but the likelihood is that they date from around the 9th century. Gallarus is the most complete example.

The small monastic site of Kilmalkedar was allegedly founded by a St Maolcethair, who died in 636. The principal feature is a fine Romanesque church built around 1140, complete with interesting carved details. There are some early crosses at the site, and an early Christian sundial to remind us of the importance of time-keeping in monastic communities. The oldest archaeological feature on the site is the ogham stone, one of about 360 known in Ireland. Ogham was a script that used short lines or strokes to represent letters. It was used by Christian communities in Ireland from at least the early 5th century,

◀ *The small huts, walled cemeteries and gardens of this early monastic site on remote Skellig Michael have survived almost intact.*

fragmentary remains of a small oratory even higher up on the rock. One wonders how many monks of Skellig in centuries past misjudged their steps and fell to their deaths.

■ **LOCATION** Gallarus Oratory and Kilmalkedar are on the Dingle Peninsula, 4 and 5 miles NW of Dingle, County Kerry; off R559. Once you're there on the peninsula, you'll find Reask is signposted.
■ **ACCESS** See www.corkkerry.ie, go to 'Visitor Attractions' then 'Visitor Attractions in South Kerry' or telephone 066 91 55333 for opening times and other details of the oratory. Admission charge. Kilmalkedar is an open site with full public access. Access to Skellig Michael is difficult and weather-dependent. Boats depart from Portmagee. Telephone 021 42 55100 for further details.

FRANCISCAN FRIARY

⑱ Quin Friary

The tiny village of Quin possesses one of the most interesting and unusual of Ireland's many medieval monuments: a superbly constructed Franciscan friary of the 15th century which sits within the shell of an abandoned 13th-century Norman castle.

The castle – originally a square courtyard with large circular corner towers and, presumably, various buildings against the inside of the enclosing wall – was built by one Thomas de Clare, the Norman ruler of Thomond (north Munster), around 1280, but was attacked and burned out by the Irish. In 1433 the local Irish chieftain, one of the Macnamara family, founded a monastery for Franciscan friars within the ruins. The symbolism would not have escaped contemporary visitors.

The new friary buildings were carefully measured in order to fit fairly precisely within the shape of the old building. The result is very

compact architecture. The friary is dominated by its slender tower above the church, which is a typical feature of Irish Franciscan monasteries. Beside the church are the domestic and other buildings of the monastery, arranged around a central court or cloister. The covered walkway around the cloister is one of the finest of its type in Ireland.

■ **LOCATION** 6 miles SE of Ennis, County Clare; on R469.
■ **ACCESS** See www.shannonregion tourism.ie (go to 'Visitor Attractions' then 'Monuments, Castles and Historic Houses') for details.

RESTORED CASTLE KEEP

⑲ Bunratty Castle

Bunratty Castle has been the scene of fighting for hundreds of years. With Viking origins as a trading settlement, which may later have been fortified, the first castle was begun on the site in the mid-13th century by Thomas de Clare under order of Edward I to create an English strongpoint. Two hundred years of battles and fires followed as the castle became a highly contended strategic site on the river Shannon, heavily plundered by the Irish. Most of the castle seen today belongs to 15th-century developments under the Macconmara family, and later the O'Briens.

The castle was restored in 1954, complete with reconstructed chambers and a large banqueting hall, which are open to the public. The site also has a folk park, which has reconstructions of different types of houses found in Clare together with their furnishings. This living museum regularly re-enacts the past, with both medieval and Victorian events.

■ **LOCATION** Off N18 between Limerick and Ennis, County Clare.
■ **ACCESS** See www.shannonregion tourism.ie, go to 'Visitor Attractions' then 'Monuments, Castles and Historic Houses' or telephone 061 360788 for opening times and other details. Admission charge.

often to commemorate the dead on pillar-stones. The Kilmalkedar pillar carries the inscription ANM MAILE-INBIR MACI BROCANN, which means 'The name of Mael Inbir, son of Brocan'.

Some of the small islands off the Dingle Peninsula have monasteries on them, though access is difficult. The most famous island monastery of all is further south, off the next peninsula. Skellig Michael is a craggy, uninhabitable rock that juts out of the Atlantic. Hundreds of stone steps lead from sea level to a cluster of churches and six beehive huts that sit precariously on terraces high above the waves. There are very

⑳ Adare

Adare is a beautiful, picture-postcard
village. It owes this to the
benevolence of its local landlord in
the early 19th century. There was an
older, medieval settlement here –
probably not on the exact site of the
present village, but close by – and a
remarkable assortment of
monuments survives.

Adare was one of the centres of
Norman political power in north
Munster in the early 13th century.
A castle was built here around 1200,
and permission was given for the
holding of a fair in 1226. A small
town developed here, and provision
was made for building a town wall

▼ The Norman and later cathedral dominates
the summit of the Rock of Cashel, but two
buildings survive intact from the early 12th
century: the slender round tower (right) and
Cormac's Chapel (partly hidden on the left).

▲ The river Maigue laps
against the walls of Adare
Castle, a multi-period fortress
of exceptional interest. The
much ruined keep overlooks
the castle at the back.

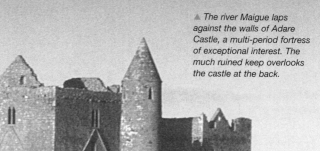

round it (although we don't know if any such wall was ever built).

The castle, which overlooks the river, was built by the local Norman lord Geoffrey de Marisco. It has an inner and outer courtyard, both originally protected by moats drawing water from the river. There is a ruined keep in the inner courtyard and two fine halls, one of them built around 1200, in the outer courtyard. Close to the castle is the ruined parish church (dedicated to St Nicholas of Myra) and a Franciscan friary, founded in 1464 and built over many years, which enjoyed patronage from various local families; John Wesley preached in the friary.

There are two other monastic houses in Adare. The Augustinian friary, which is at the edge of the village, was founded in the early 14th century. Its church is still in use. In the village itself is Ireland's only example of a monastery of – wait for it – the Trinitarian Canons of the Order of the Redemption of Captives. It was founded in the 13th century and its church is still in use.

■ **LOCATION** Adare is 10 miles SW of Limerick; on N21.
■ **ACCESS** See www.shannonregion tourism.ie, go to 'Visitor Attractions' then 'Visitor Attractions in Limerick' or telephone 061 396666 for further details. Admission charges to castle and Heritage Centre exhibition.

CASTLE AND PRIORY

㉑ Glanworth Castle

Glanworth Castle is in a prominent position on rocky high ground guarding the river Funshion. It dates from the mid-13th century and was built by the Roche family. At its core is the ruin of a large square keep, three storeys high, and its walls are an impressive 1.5m (5ft) thick at the base. The original stairway must have been made of wood – there are no traces of internal stone stairs within the keep.

A curtain wall follows an eccentric path around the site to the top of the rocky cliff over the old Glanworth mill below. The wall has intermittent turrets to provide additional protection at vulnerable points. At some point in the 15th century an additional phase of construction was undertaken, where quarters were added together with a tall tower that transcends the keep. The castle was abandoned after the 16th century.

The ruins of Glanworth Priory can also be seen near by, complete with a tall square tower. The priory was founded by the Roche family around 1475 for the Dominican order.

■ **LOCATION** 4 miles NW of Fermoy, Cork; on R512.
■ **ACCESS** Open site, full public access.

RELIGION AND MYTH

㉒ Rock of Cashel

Standing sentinel where the boggy lowlands of central Ireland give way to the fertile grasslands and high mountain ranges of Munster is the Rock of Cashel. Nestling on the summit of this dramatic landmark, which is also known as St Patrick's Rock because the saint is alleged to have been here, is one of Ireland's most important clusters of medieval ecclesiastical buildings. For much of the middle ages, Cashel was second only to Armagh in importance in Irish Christianity.

The Rock itself is, of course, a product of geological history, but two origin tales have attached to it. One is that the devil was passing over Ireland, felt hungry, took a bite out of a mountain to the north, disliked the taste, and spat out what we now know as the Rock. In the other tale the Rock did not exist until it was revealed in a vision to an ancestor of one of the royal dynasties of medieval Munster.

The Rock was a secular fortress – the name Cashel comes from the Latin *castrum*, 'castle' – in early historic times, but in 1101, at a synod of the Irish Church held on it or beside it, the then-king granted it in perpetuity to the Church.

You enter the complex today through the Hall of the Vicars' Choral, the restored 15th-century residence of the clergy who worked in the cathedral. That cathedral is the dominant building on the Rock. Built in several phases during the 13th century, it replaced an older cathedral. It has been roofless and ruined since the 18th century, but there are periodic proposals to re-roof it. A number of important sculptured tombs of the 15th and 16th centuries are preserved inside it.

The oldest building still standing on the Rock is the round tower. It is one of the best preserved of the 70 or so that still survive in Ireland. This was originally a freestanding building. Probably built under royal patronage

around the time of the synod, it was ostensibly a bell-house associated with a long-disappeared church, with wooden ladders ascending to the top floor where (hand) bells were rung to signal the timing of rituals. The tower may have had other functions as well, such as the storage of relics and other treasures. It has recently been suggested that the top floors of towers like this were actually chapels that were accessible to a select few.

The most famous building on the Rock is Cormac's Chapel, a small and perfect Romanesque church – Ireland's finest, in fact – dating from around 1130. Masons from England helped to construct it. The two towers that rise on either side of it are Germanic in appearance, and may

reflect Cashel's long-standing political connections with Bavaria. There are good traces of wall paintings inside it. Particularly impressive is the 12th-century sarcophagus (grave-chest) inside the main entrance, with Viking-style slender, intertwined animals carved on it.

Visitors to the Rock of Cashel should also pay a visit to the town, which is an old Norman market town, and to Hore Abbey, a rather gaunt Cistercian abbey that stands in the shadow of the Rock.

■ **LOCATION** In Cashel on N8, County Tipperary.
■ **ACCESS** See www.heritageireland.ie under 'Rock of Cashel', or telephone 062 61437 for opening times and other details. Admission charge.

ROUND TOWER

23 Kilree

The round tower at Kilree gives us clues to an earlier monastic settlement here. Standing nearly 30m (100ft) tall, the tower is in fine condition apart from its damaged top which no longer carries a roof. Originally constructed as a stronghold for use by the monks in times of trouble, the doorway can be seen set off the ground to hinder access once a ladder had been withdrawn. The Kilree doorway is relatively low compared to other examples in Ireland, such as Turlough in Mayo.

Close to the tower is a high cross thought to be 9th century in origin. The geometric designs are rather worn, yet still include prominent rounded nodes at the points of the cross in high relief. From the top of the cross projects a tenon, so at some point it must have had a capstone.

■ **LOCATION** 3 miles S of Kells, Kilkenny; on minor road off R697 or N10.
■ **ACCESS** Open site, full public access.

◀ *Kilree is one of the best preserved round towers in County Kilkenny. It was probably built in the 11th century. The battlements at the top are probably 15th century.*

▲ *Jerpoint is possibly Ireland's finest Cistercian abbey. It dates from the end of the 12th century and has a large 15th-century crossing tower. The arcaded walkway round the cloister has attractive sculptural details.*

CISTERCIAN ABBEY

㉔ Jerpoint Abbey

The impressive ruins at Jerpoint are the remains of a highly successful monastic community. Founded for the Benedictine order by King Donal of Ossory in the mid-12th century, the monastery was repopulated with Cistercian monks by 1180. The house rapidly grew into a thriving enterprise, which by the dissolution owned thousands of acres of land, watermills, fisheries and many domestic houses. Jerpoint also became the mother house to abbeys in Killenny, Kilcooly and Tipperary, and was strongly associated with the formidable Cistercian abbey at Fountains in Yorkshire (see page 207).

The large plan of the monastery was suitably designed for the isolated lifestyle of the Cistercians. The self-contained complex included gardens, an infirmary, kitchens, refectory and associated outbuildings, all situated round a large cloister. Most of the buildings can still be determined on the site today. The site also features some interesting stonework, including grotesque heads and the tombs of two knights dating to the 13th century.

■ **LOCATION** 1½ miles SW of Thomastown, County Kilkenny; on N9.
■ **ACCESS** See www.heritageireland.ie or telephone 056 77 24623 for opening times and other details. Admission charge.

SCENE OF UPRISING

㉕ Vinegar Hill Mill

The ruins of a windmill at Vinegar Hill mark the site not only of an industrial-age corn mill, but also of a vicious battle during the Irish uprising of 1798. In 1791 the Society of United Irishmen worked together with Catholics and Protestants in an effort to gain independence from England. In 1798, with the uprising spreading across the country, a rebel army of between 10,000 and 15,000 troops assembled on Vinegar Hill. On 21 June General Gerard Lake surrounded the hill with 20,000 soldiers. In a massed artillery attack the rebel forces were devastated and the rebellion in the south-east was subdued. However, rebel leaders continued to stage reprisals, which attracted retribution from the English.

The rebellion of 1798 ultimately backfired, resulting in the 1801 Act of Union which brought with it further restrictions. Today the stout base of the windmill occupies a wonderful position with fantastic views over Enniscorthy and the landscape beyond, a peaceful spot that marks a dark hour between two nations.

■ **LOCATION** Just outside the town of Enniscorthy, County Wexford; off N11.
■ **ACCESS** For further details of the 1798 battle visitor centre in Enniscorthy, telephone 054 37596/7. Admission charge.

Top Ten sites

WE ASKED MEMBERS of the team to select their 'must-see' sites, the places that if they *had* to choose would be top of their list. This produced, as you might expect, some interesting and eclectic choices, but there was also a degree of unanimity with regard to the key sites.

As you would expect, Carenza was very keen on some of the major sites like Bath, and found the Viking graffiti at Maes Howe an intriguing addition that pushed it to somewhere near the top of her list. For personal reasons – it was the first site she dug – she had fond memories of Vindolanda, together with Hadrian's Wall, but just topping this was Avebury. Avebury was the top site for Phil Harding and Henry Chapman, and Newgrange and Tara were high in many people's lists.

Phil was keen to include Grimes Graves, Creswell Crags and the Langdale axe factory. His choices were, not surprisingly, prehistoric, although he has a soft spot for HMS *Victory*, which features fairly high on Guy de la Bédoyère's list. Guy lists Lullingstone as his favourite Roman site.

A surprise choice was Conwy Castle, which featured on several lists, including Helen Geake's where it appeared alongside Sutton Hoo and other sites nearer to her particular area of expertise on Time Team. Stuart Ainsworth's selection was highly individualistic, including some larger landscape sites like Dunstanburgh Castle in Northumberland and Wharram Percy.

The Geophysics Team clearly have a keenness for the Irish and Orkney sites – both John and Chris put the Stones of Stenness and Ring of Brodgar at the top, and all of John's top ten were in Orkney. The Graphics Team came up with an eclectic mix featuring, as might be expected, some substantial structures – Raysan choosing the Temple of Mithras, Bath and Fountains Abbey, and Neill putting Glastonbury and Hampton Court Palace in his top ten.

Mick, as you can imagine, put some of the great medieval ecclesiastical sites at the top of his list, including Gallarus, Jarrow, Hexham and Ripon, but Chysauster came high in his list, as did Ironbridge.

Time Team's Top Ten

Having forced them all to make their choices, we then came up with the definitive Time Team Top Ten sites, and here they are, in age order:

- **Grimes Graves**, Norfolk (page 144)
- **Avebury**, Wiltshire (page 38)
- **Newgrange**, County Meath (page 282)
- **Maes Howe**, Orkney (page 256)
- **Flag Fen**, Peterborough (page 146)
- **Maiden Castle**, Dorset (page 12)
- **Bath**, Somerset (page 18)
- **Sutton Hoo**, Suffolk (page 150)
- **Conwy Castle**, Gwynedd (page 102)
- **Ironbridge**, Shropshire (page 124)

We then asked Francis Pryor to expand on the five sites that came top in order of popularity. His knowledge is encyclopedic, and he brings to this what we feel is a crystallizing of Time Team's approach. So these are Time Team's five favourite archaeological sites, in Francis's words.

Flag Fen

This has to be top of my list for all sorts of personal reasons, but having said that I still understand that it is the only place anywhere in the world (although there are rumours of another such site in Japan) where you can see prehistoric timbers actually in situ. Hundreds of bronze and other objects were placed in the water alongside a later Bronze Age timber trackway, built between 1300 and 900BC. Flag Fen is one of the few prehistoric sites in Britain where finds can be seen on site. Too often finds have to be viewed in distant museums, which is fine, except that they have been wrenched out of context. The ancient timbers are in a special building that is part of a large archaeological park, which includes reconstructed buildings and ancient

▲ For anyone who has not made the journey to the Orkney Islands, sites such as Maes Howe and the wonderful interior chamber are a good reason to make the effort.

breeds of livestock. Flag Fen is largely staffed by volunteers and it has very much become a part of the local community. What it may lack in corporate slickness is made up for in warmth and enthusiasm.

Maes Howe

I'd include here the other sites round about, such as the Stones of Stenness, the Ring of Brodgar and Skara Brae. It took me a long time eventually to find my way so far north, although I did steam past Orkney in a trawler from Grimsby when I was 16 (back in the Bronze Age). Later, I was making a mini-series, *Britain BC*, for Channel 4 and felt I ought to include these famous sites and it was not until I visited them that I became aware that they still possessed some strange, and completely indefinable, 'prehistoric presence'. Filming within

the great stone chamber at Maes Howe after dark was quite literally a transcending moment, which my more analytical colleagues would regard as an irrelevance, but which has had a lasting effect on me. Alternatively, if you want to stay clear of prehistorians having New Age moments, I strongly recommend a visit to Skara Brae, the well-known settlement contemporary with the nearby later Neolithic ritual sites (sometime between 3100 and 2500BC). The reconstructed house is superbly done and manages to combine a genuinely ancient atmosphere, despite the usual visual intrusions imposed by the health and safety people.

Avebury

This landscape is very different in feel from that around Stonehenge. I prefer it, and not just because there is a very crowded and touristy pub in the middle of the great Avebury stone circle. I suppose it's the variety of sites in this landscape that appeals: the famous West Kennet long barrow, Silbury Hill (which one is supposed not to climb), the West Kennet Avenue, the Sanctuary and so on. One can spend a good two days in and around Avebury. I prefer to go there in winter, simply because there are fewer people around the place; cold, wet stones are less pleasant to hug. A couple of times I have been given a nasty shock when I happened to stumble across stone-huggers, deep in meditation. One cannot be too careful.

Maiden Castle

This is, I think, the most spectacular prehistoric site in Britain, which is doubtless what its Iron Age builders intended. I like the site for its vast ramparts and awe-inspiring remains, but I also like the effect it has on the imagination. The great archaeologist Sir Mortimer Wheeler excavated here and I will never forget a BBC *Chronicle* film which featured the great man standing bolt-upright in a Land Rover as he was driven through the imposing main entranceway. Similarly, who can forget Julie Christie and Terence Stamp frolicking on the ramparts in *Far from the Madding Crowd*? Doubtless Sir Mortimer would have approved. The site is also important as a fine example of natural downland. If you have a bent for botany, it's worth taking a good wild flower book with you too. Spring with its clear air is a good time to appreciate the superb views.

Newgrange

Undoubtedly the most famous 'ritual landscape' in Ireland consists of about 40 barrows and other monuments enclosed on three sides by a great bend of the River Boyne (the Brugh na Bóinne). Many of the barrows cluster around three massive so-called passage graves beneath large round mounds at Knowth, Newgrange and Dowth. (Maes Howe in Orkney is also such a site.) They consist of a chamber buried deep within the mound which is entered by a long, low passage intended, among other things, to distance the chamber from the world outside. Often the passages were aligned on the midwinter sunrise and the great stones are decorated with the circles and spirals of so-called 'megalithic art' that flourished in Ireland in the later 4th millennium BC. These sites are perhaps best seen as funerary theatre than as permanent tombs as we would understand the term today. Experiments have also shown that they were constructed to enhance certain acoustic and lighting effects. Today two of the three great passage graves at Knowth and Newgrange have been excavated and 'restored' in order to enhance their appeal to visitors. I have to say I find the 'restoration' at Newgrange stark, unconvincing and plain ugly. The only surviving large passage grave, that at Dowth, was quite extensively 'excavated' in the early 19th century. So much for joined-up thinking.

... and Francis's 11th site?

Would be the one you experience for yourself. Nothing can ever beat the feeling every archaeologist, professional or otherwise, gets when he or she takes part in actual research. This doesn't necessarily require excavation, but it often takes place out-of-doors, maybe on a field-walking or survey project. Sometimes it may involve searching through documents in an archive. But in my experience doing archaeology gives you ownership of the past, which then becomes a special part of your own, personal history.

What happened when?

ARCHAEOLOGISTS HAVE A number of ways of dividing up the past. These can at times give the misleading impression that distinct transitions have taken place from one technology to another, whereas in reality these transitions are blurred. In practice, however, most of the archaeologists we work with on Time Team use these descriptions as a form of general shorthand and it allows an approximate separation of periods, within which a more detailed analysis can take place. Mick suggests this as the broad range that is most useful.

- **Palaeolithic** *(Old Stone Age; divided into Lower and Upper Palaeolithic)*
  before 8000 BC
- **Mesolithic** *(Middle Stone Age)*
  8000–4000 BC
- **Neolithic** *(New Stone Age)*
  4000–2500 BC
- **Bronze Age**
  2500–700 BC

- **Iron Age**
  700 BC–AD 43
- **Roman**
  AD 43–410 (the late Roman period is increasingly called Late Antique)
- **Early Medieval** *(also Anglo-Saxon, formerly the Dark Ages)*
  Late Saxon *c.* AD 900; Viking period AD 800–1100
- **Late Medieval** *(sometimes called High Medieval)*
  from 1066 to 1530s; Late Medieval is sometimes also used for post-1350 (the Black Death)
- **Post Medieval** *(increasingly called Historical Archaeology)*
  the 1530s onwards
- **Early Modern**
  from 1850 onwards

▼ *Every time a new dig is undertaken, there is always a feeling of excitement – of not knowing if the next layer of the soil beneath our feet will reveal its secrets of the way that we used to live and help to fix a date on bygone lives.*

Index

abbeys *see* monasteries
Adare, Co. Limerick 308–9
Addingham, West Yorkshire 209–10
air-raid shelter 201
airfield 90
Albert Docks, Liverpool 186–7
Alexander Keiller Museum 38
amphitheatres 63, 114
Ancaster 62
animal relics 24, 80, 101, 109, 171, 212
antler picks 144–5
Antonine Wall 218–19, 244–5
aqueducts 32, 109–11
Arbor Low, Derbyshire 168–9
Arras culture 212
Arromanches 56
arrowheads, flint 147
art works 166–7, 242, 243
Arthurian legends 20–1, 22, 148
Arts and Crafts movement 66–7
Athelney, Somerset 25–6
Athenry, Co. Galway 304–5
Atlantic Wall 55
Atrebates tribe 87
Aubrey Holes 43
Augustinians 244, 297
Avebury, Wiltshire 28–9, 38–41, 168, 312, 313–14
Aveline's Hole, Somerset 27–8
Avoncroft Museum, Worcestershire 138
axes 145, 147–8, 227

Back to Backs Museum, Birmingham 137
Ballycopeland, Co. Down 279
Ballymacaldrack, Co. Antrim 274–5
Baltinglass Abbey, Co. Wicklow 304
Baptist Mills, Bristol 31
barn, timber-framed 162
barrows 41, 42, 52, 91, 168–9, 172–4, 212
Barsalloch, Dumfries and Galloway 251
bastle house 248–9
Bath 18–19, 46, 312
baths, Roman 18–19, 120–1, 177, 227
battery 263
Battle, East Sussex 93
battle sites 92, 178, 211–12, 264–5, 285
Beaker relics 147
Beamish 233
Beaumaris Castle 102
Bective Abbey, Co. Meath 301
Beeston, Cheshire 191–3
Belfast, HMS 75
Benedictines 207–8, 222, 259, 311
Berkeley Castle, Gloucestershire 50
Bewl Valley Gun Casting, East Sussex 91–2
Billingsgate Bathhouse, London 63
Billown, Isle of Man 194
Birmingham Canals 128–31
Birmingham Metal Company 31
Black Death 203, 205
Blackstone Edge, Lancashire 210
Blaenavon, Gwent 106–7
Bluestones 43
boats, Bronze Age 94–5, 175–7, 213

Bodiam Castle, East Sussex 93–4
Boleigh, Cornwall 17
Bolsover Castle, Derbyshire 174–5
Bonawe 242
Book of Durrow 293
Book of Kells 259, 293
Boulton and Watt Factory, Birmingham 137
Boxgrove, Sussex 80–1
Boyle Abbey, Co. Roscommon 299
Bradford-on-Avon, Wiltshire, chapel of
    St Laurence 51
Bradwell-on-Sea 47, 162–3
Bridestones, Cheshire 193
bridges 126–7, 159
Brigantes tribe 198
Bristol 29–31
British Museum, London 71
Brixworth, Northamptonshire 178–9
Broch of Gurness, Orkney 261
Broch of Mousa, Shetland 260–1
brochs 16, 247, 260–1
Brodgar, Ring of, Orkney 257, 262, 312, 313
brooch, Roman 217
Brunel, Isambard Kingdom 29
Brycheiniog 100
buckle, gold, Sutton Hoo 153
Bunratty Castle, Co. Clare 307
burhs 34–5, 52
burial sites 13, 14, 27–8, 73, 113, 140, 150–3,
    168, 172, 175, 193, 211–12, 246, 250,
    256–7, 282–5, 298–9, 302

Cadiz, blockade of 56
Caerlaverock Castle, Borders 249–50
Caerleon, Gwent 114
Caernarvon castle 102
Caerwent, Monmouthshire 115
cairns 226–7, 250
caissons 55–6
Callanish, Western Isles 247
camps, Mesolithic 212
    POW 233
canals 128–31
Canterbury, Kent 94
Carlisle 230–1
Carn Euny 17
Carreg Coetan, Pembrokeshire 112
Carrickfergus, Co. Antrim 279
Carrowkeel, Co. Sligo 299
Carrowmore, Co. Sligo 298
Carthusians 206–7
carvings, early Christian 276–7
Castell Henllys, Pembrokeshire 98–9
Castle Acre Priory, Norfolk 157–8
Castle Ring, Staffordshire 137
Castlerigg, Cumbria 228
castles 92–4, 102–5, 140–1, 158–9, 172, 174–5,
    193, 200, 210–11, 226, 230–1, 245–6,
    249–50, 274, 276, 277–8, 279, 295, 296–7,
    299–300, 302, 307, 309
    motte-and-bailey 54–5, 122–3, 133, 139, 158,
    177, 200, 210–11
cathedrals 111–12, 171, 200–1, 235, 292, 294–5,
    297, 302
cavalry training depot, Roman 139
caves 24, 27, 109, 112-13, 166–7
cemeteries *see* burial sites
chariot burials 212
Cheddar Man 27

Cheddar, Somerset 27, 167
Chedworth, Gloucestershire 50
Chester 190–1
Christianity 61–2, 85, 171, 188–9, 193, 222–3,
    258–9
churches 160–3, 171, 172, 175, 178–9, 300–1,
    303–4, 306–7
Chysauster, Cornwall 16–17, 312
Cirencester, Gloucestershire 50–1
Cistercians 202–3, 208, 224–5, 279, 299, 301,
    304, 311
cities, Roman 170–1
Civil War 24–5
Clacton-on-Sea, Essex 163
Clausentum 55
Clava, Highland 246
Clifton Suspension Bridge 29
Clogher, Co. Tyrone 278
Clonfert Cathedral, Co. Galway 294–5
Clonmacnoise 288–9
Coalbrookdale, Shropshire 31, 124–7
Colchester, Essex 163
Conwy Castle, Gwynedd 102–5, 312
Corfe Castle, Dorset 33–4
Corgis 101
Corieltauvi tribe 170
Corlea, Co. Longford 300
Cornovii tribe 136
country park 109
Coventry, City of 138–9
crannogs 100–1, 238–9, 247
Creetown, Dumfries and Galloway 250
Cressing, Essex 162
Creswell Crags, Nottinghamshire 166–7
Crew's Hole Copper Works 31
crosses 193, 258, 289, 301–2
Crown Jewels 73
Cuerdale Hoard 184–5
Culloden Moor 264–5
cup-and-ring designs 243, 246, 250–1
cursus monuments 31–2, 212–13
Cutty Sark, Greenwich 76

Dartmoor 23–4
Derry, town walls 274
Devenish Island, Co. Fermanagh 277
Dingle Peninsula, Co. Kerry 306–7
docks 186–7
Dominicans 304, 309
Dorchester 32–3
Dorset County Museum 32
Dorset Cursus, Cranborne Chase, Dorset 31–2
Dover, Kent 94–5
Drogheda, Co. Louth 302
Drumtrodden 250–1
Dublin 290–3
Dumnonia 22
Dun Aonghusa, Aran Islands 305
Dun Nosebridge 243
Dunluce, Co. Antrim 274
Dunstanburgh Castle, Northumberland 226,
    312
Durham Cathedral 235
Durotiges tribe 13
Durrington Walls 44

Eddisbury, Cheshire 191
Edinburgh Castle 245–6
Elgin Marbles 71

Elizabeth I, Queen, visit to Kenilworth 123
Enniskillen Castle, Co. Fermanagh 277–8
Exeter, Devon 25

factories 136–7, 174, 209–10, 227
farming settlement, prehistoric 156
Fengate, Cambridgeshire 156
fens 146–9
Fishbourne, West Sussex 86–7
Flag Fen, Peterborough 146–9, 312–13
flagon, Roman 60–1
Flint castle 102
flints, flint tools 25, 115
floorstone 145
fogous 17
footprints, Mesolithic 115
Fore, Co. Westmeath 301
forest, submerged 25
Fort George, Highland 263–4
forts, ancient 305
  anti-artillery 264
  blockhouse 160–1
  Iron Age 251, 270–1
  Roman 162–3, 182–3, 211, 216–21, 244, 245
Forts of the Saxon Shore 46–7
Fountains Abbey, North Yorkshire 88, 207–8,
  312
Fourknocks Tomb, Co. Meath 302
Franciscans 307
furnace, iron 242
Furness Abbey 224–5

Gallarus, Co. Kerry 306, 312
Gas Street Basin, Birmingham 131
George Inn, Southwark, London 76
Gib Hill, Derbyshire 168–9
Glanworth Castle, Co. Cork 309
Glastonbury, Somerset 20–1, 312
  Abbey 20–1
  lake village 26, 238
  Tor 21
Glendalough, Co. Wicklow 302–4
Glenochar, Lanarkshire 248–9
Globe theatre, London 64–5
Gloucester, Cathedral 48–50
Goldcliff, Gwent 114–15
Goodrich, Herefordshire 140–2
granaries 218
grave goods see burial sites
Great Fire of London 72
Great Northern Railway 76
Great Orme, Conwy 109
Great Western Railway 29–31
greenstone 147–8
Greenwich Park, London 76
Grimes Graves, Norfolk 144–5, 312
Guildhall Art Gallery, London 63
Guildhall, Leicester 177
gunpowder mills 160–1

Hadrian's Wall 46, 216–19, 312
Halliggye, Cornwall 17
Hampton Court Palace, Surrey 68–9, 312
Hamwic 55
Harland & Wolff shipyard, Belfast 75
Harlech castle 102
Harperley, Co. Durham 233
Hawkcombe Head, Somerset 25
Hayes Barton manor house 25

helmets, Roman cavalryman's 183
  Sutton Hoo 150–3
henges 32, 38–45, 168–9, 207, 228, 286–7
Hexham, Northumberland 233, 312
hillforts 12–15, 52, 98–9, 132, 134–6, 137, 179,
  191–3, 226, 243, 278
hoards, Viking 184–5
Holy Jesus Hospital, Newcastle 233
hominid bones 80–1, 109
Homo heidelbergiensis 81
Hospital of St Leonard, York 200–1
Hound Tor 24
houses, Georgian 292
  stone 16, 254–5
Humber Estuary, East Yorkshire 213
hunter-gatherers 90–1, 108–9, 212
hypocausts 83, 87

Inch, Co. Down 279
Inchmahome, Stirling 244
Industrial Revolution 29–31, 124–7, 137,
  209–10
Inverurie 242
Iona, Western Isles 240, 258–9
Ironbridge Gorge and Coalbrookdale,
  Shropshire 124–7, 312
ironworks 106–7
Isleham Priory Church, Cambridgeshire 158–9
Italian Chapel, Orkney 262–3

Jarlshof, Shetland 260
Jarrow 234–5, 240, 312
Jedburgh, Melrose and Dryburgh abbeys 247–8
Jerpoint Abbey, Co. Kilkenny 311
Jewel Tower, Westminster, London 69–70
Jewry Wall, Leicester 177
Jorvik Viking Centre, York 198–200

Kenilworth, Warwickshire 122–3
Kents Cavern, Devon 24–5, 167
Kilmalkedar, Co. Kerry 306–7
Kilree, Co. Kilkenny 312
Kirk Madrine, Dumfries and Galloway 241
Kits Coty House, Kent 91
Knights Hospitaller 68, 162
Knights Templar 162
Knowlton Rings, Dorset 32

lake villages 26, 238
landscape, prehistoric 194, 226–7
Lanercost Priory, Cumbria 231–3
Langdale Axe Factory, Cumbria 227
leatherwork, Roman 211
Leicester 18, 177
letters, Roman 220–1
Lia Fáil (Stone of Destiny) 286
Liberty's, Regent Street, London 67
Lincoln 18, 170–1
Lindisfarne 163, 222–3, 233
Lindow Man 188–9
Little Kits Coty House, Kent 91
Little Moreton Hall, Cheshire 193–4
Littledean House of Correction,
  Gloucestershire 48
Liverpool, docks and railway 186–7
Liverpool to Manchester railway 187
Llangorse, Powys 100–1, 238
Llyn Cerrig Beach, Anglesey 108
Llys Rhosyr, Anglesey 108

Loch an Duin, Western Isles 247
Loch Migdale 239
London, Roman 60–3
London Wall 63
Long Meg and her Daughters 229–30
Longstones 41
Lullingstone, Kent 82–5
Lunt Roman Fort, West Midlands 139
Lydney, Gloucestershire 48

Machrie Moor, Isle of Arran 243–4
Maes Howe, Orkney 255, 256–7, 262, 312, 313
Maiden Castle 12–15, 99, 312, 314
Manchester, city 188
manor houses 133–4, 183–5
marble monument, Roman 95
Mary Rose, Portsmouth Harbour 57
mass grave 175
Masson Mills, Derbyshire 174
Maumbury Rings, Dorset 32
mausoleum 85
Mayburgh, Cumbria 228
Maynooth Castle, Co. Kildare 302
Meare 26, 238
Meols, Merseyside 190
Merton Abbey Mills, London 66–7
Merton Priory, London 66
milecastles 217
military supplies 188
military testing station 163
mills, corn and flax 298, 311
  textile 174, 209–10
mines, copper 109
  flint 144–5
Mines Royal Act 31
Mint Wall, Lincoln 170
Mithras, temple of, London 61–2, 313
Monasterboice, Co. Louth 301–2
monasteries 20–1, 48, 52, 66, 70, 88, 116–17,
  123, 138, 157–8, 160–1, 178–9, 188, 191,
  202–3, 206–8, 222–5, 231–3, 240–1, 244,
  244–5, 247–8, 259, 272–3, 277, 279, 288–9,
  296, 299, 300–11
monoliths, Celtic 294
mosaics 82–5, 86
Moulton, Suffolk 159
Mount Grace Priory, Northallerton 206–7
Mucking, Essex 155
Mulberry Harbours 55–6
Museum of London 73
museums 73, 88–90, 137, 138, 177, 182–3, 233,
  292–3

Naseby, Northamptonshire 178
National Maritime Museum, London 76
Navan Fort 270–1
Neanderthal objects 24, 109
Nendrum, Co. Down 272–3
Newgrange, Knowth and Dowth, Co. Meath
  257, 282–5, 302, 312, 313
Newmills, Co. Donegal 298
Newport Arch, Lincoln 170
Newport Ship, Gwent 114
Newtown Trim Cathedral 297
Nine Ladies, Derbyshire 172–4
Nonsuch Palace, Cheam, Surrey 66, 88
Nornour, Isles of Scilly 22
North Ferriby, East Yorkshire 213
Norton Priory, Cheshire 191

Norwich Castle 158
nymphaeum 50

Oakbank Crannog, Perth and Kinross 239
Offa's Dyke 132–3
Old Berwick Moor, Northumberland 226–7
Old Royal Observatory, Greenwich 76
Old Sarum 54–5
Orford Ness, Suffolk 163
Oswestry, Shropshire 132
Oxford, city 52–4

palaces, Romano-British 86–7
    Tudor 88
    Welsh 108
passage tombs 282–5, 286, 298, 314
Paviland Cave, West Glamorgan 112–13
Pevensey, East Sussex 47, 92–3
Peveril Castle, Derbyshire 172
Picts 242, 244
Poltalloch 243
Pontcysyllte Aqueduct 109–11
Pontnewydd Cave, Denbighshire 109
Porlock Beach, Somerset 25
port, ancient 190
portal-dolmen monument 112
Portchester, Hampshire 46–7, 87
Portumna Castle, Co. Galway 295
pottery 136
Prime Meridian Clock, Greenwich 76
prison, WWII 263–4

Quin Friary, Co. Clare 307

railways 186–7
Rath of the Synods 287
Raunds, Northamptonshire 179
Ravenglass, Cumbria 227
Reask, Co. Kerry 306
reaves 23
Reculver 47
'Red Lady of Paviland' 113
Repton, Derbyshire 175
Rhuddlan castle 102
Ribchester, Lancashire 182–3
Richard's Castle, Shropshire 133
Richborough, Kent 95
Rievaulx Abbey, North Yorkshire 88, 202–3,
    225
Ripon, North Yorkshire 207, 233, 312
ritual sites 28–9, 108, 212–13, 270–1
roads, Roman 210, 246
Robin Hood's Cave 167
Rock of Cashel 309–10
Rockingham Castle, Northamptonshire 177–8
Roscommon Castle 299–300
Rose theatre, London 64–5
Rosetta Stone 71
roundhouses 99
Royal Naval College, Greenwich 76
Rudston, East Yorkshire 212–13

St Albans, Hertfordshire 160
St Cuthbert's Isle 223
St Davids 111–12
St Laurent 56
St Leonard's Tower, Kent 91
St Paul-in-the-Bail, Lincoln 171
St Paul's Cathedral, London 71

St Peter's Church, Barton-upon-Humber,
    Lincolnshire 172
St Stephen Walbrook, London 72
Samian Ware 14, 216
Sandal Castle, West Yorkshire 210–11
Sandbach Crosses, Cheshire 193
sarsens 43
Savigny order 224
Scilly, Isles of 22
Scottish Crannog Centre 238–9
Serapis, head of 61
Shardlow, Derbyshire 175–7
shield, Battersea, London 69
shipbuilding 57, 114
shore fort 92
shrine 50
Silbury Hill, Wiltshire 41, 314
Silures 115
Skara Brae, Orkney 254–5, 313–14
Skellig Michael 307
Slack's Tower, Southdean, Roxburghshire 248
slave trade 29, 31, 186
slingshot stones 12, 99
Smailholm, Borders 246–7
Snettisham, Norfolk 156
Somerset Levels 21, 26, 238
Southampton 55
Soutra, Borders 246
spear, Clacton 163
Spitalfields, London 73
springs, hot 18–19
standing stones 286, 288
Stanton Drew, Somerset 28–9, 169
Stanton Moor, Derbyshire 172-4
Stanwick, Northamptonshire 179
Star Carr, North Yorkshire 212
Stenness, Orkney 257, 262, 312, 313
Stockton and Darlington Railway 186–7
Stokesay, Shropshire 133–4
Stone Point Lepe, Solent, Hampshire 55–6
stone circles 38–45, 228–30, 243–4, 262
stone tools 80–1, 90–1, 275
Stonehenge, Wiltshire 29, 38, 40, 42–5, 168
stones, standing 247
stonework, Roman 120–1
storage pot, Iron Age 14
Sutton Hoo, Suffolk 150–3, 312
Swanscombe, Kent 90–1

Tangmere Airfield, West Sussex 90
Tara, Co. Meath 286–7, 301, 312
temples, Roman 48, 163
Thames, river, front 69
Thornborough Circles, North Yorkshire 207
Tievebulliagh, Co. Antrim 275
Tilbury Fort, Essex 161–2
timber, pre-Roman 149
timber-framed buildings 193–5
tin 16, 149
Tintagel, Cornwall 22
Tintern Abbey, Monmouthshire 88, 116–17
tomb, court 274–5
tombs, megalithic 282–5
Tower Hill, London 63
Tower of London 73–5
towers 73–5, 91, 233, 246–7, 248, 310
    Martello 163, 263
towns, medieval 247
    Roman 115, 163

Towton, North Yorkshire 211–12
trackway, Iron Age 300
Trafalgar, Battle of 56
treasure, Iron Age 156
Trilithons 43, 44
Trim, Co. Meath 296–7, 301
Trinovantes tribe 163
Tullaghogue Fort, Co. Tyrone 278–9
Tully Castle, Co. Fermanagh 276
Turoe Stone, Co. Galway 294
Tyneham Village, Dorset 33

Uffington White Horse, Oxfordshire 52

Vauxhall, London 69
viaduct 106–7
Victory, HMS, Portsmouth Harbour 56, 312
Vikings 25, 33, 55, 114, 175, 184–5, 189, 193,
    198–201, 206, 223, 260, 261, 273, 290, 302
villages, Anglo-Saxon 154–5
    medieval 204–5
villas, Roman 50, 82–5
Vindolanda 63, 219, 220–1, 312
Vinegar Hill Mill, Co. Wexford 311
votive objects 19, 22

walls, town 274
Walmgate, York 199
Waltham Abbey Gunpowder Mills,
    Hertfordshire 160–1
Walton-le-Dale, Lancashire 188–9
war industry 91
Wareham, Dorset 34–5
Wars of Independence 249
Warwick Castle 139
Wasperton, Warwickshire 140
Waverley Abbey, Surrey 88
Wayland's Smithy, Oxfordshire 52
Weald and Downland Museum, West Sussex
    89–90
Wedgwood Factory, Staffordshire 136
Wells, Somerset, Bishop's Palace 26
West Heslerton, Yorkshire 155
West Kennet, Wiltshire 41, 314
West Stow, Suffolk 154–5
Westminster Abbey, London 70
Wetwang, East Yorkshire 212
Whalley Abbey 188
Wharram Percy, North Yorkshire 204–5, 312
Whitby Abbey, North Yorkshire 206
White Island church, Co. Fermanagh 276–7
Whitehall Palace, London 70–1
Whitford Dyke 132–3
Whithorn, Dumfries & Galloway 240–1
Winchester 55
Windmill Hill, Wiltshire 41
windmills 279, 311
Woodhenge 44
Wrekin, Shropshire 134–6
Wroxeter, Shropshire 120–1, 136

Yellow Steeple, Co. Meath 297
York 198–201
    Minster 200–1
York House, London 70

Acknowledgements

This book would not have been possible without the help and support of the members of Time Team and the many experts who provided their advice and guidance on a regular basis. Their willingness to be interviewed at length, answer endless questions and check facts has been a critical contribution to producing the book.

I would particularly like to thank my senior editorial assistant Matt Reynolds for his dedication to the project, and our other editorial assistants Dr Nick Corcos, Dr Jenni Butterworth, Steve Bumford, Marcus Dahl, Dr Nadia Durrani and Victoria Batten for their work on the secondary sites. These were ably assisted by Jackie Stinchcombe, who was, thankfully, able to decipher my writing, and, along with Jo Pye in the Bristol office, keep us organized.

Mick and I would like especially to thank Tadhg O'Keeffe for his work on Irish sites and Francis Pryor for his general help and encouragement, and our general editor Mari Roberts who managed to pull the whole enterprise together.

Picture Credits

Key: L=left; R=right; A=above; B=below

2–3 Alamy: Homer Sykes; 6 and 8 Channel 4: Chris Bennett; 10–11 Alamy: Peter Adams Photography; 12 Alamy: Apex News and Pictures Agency/Marc Hill; 14 Corbis: Werner Forman; 15 lastrefuge.co.uk: Adrian Warren/Dae Sasitorn; 17 English Heritage Photographic Library: Skyscan Balloon Photography; 18 Alamy: Arcaid/John Edward Linden; 19 Stephen Arnold; 20 Alamy: Robert Harding Picture Library/Christopher Nicholson; 21 Alamy: Robert Harding Picture Library/R Cowins; 22–23A English Heritage Photographic Library: Skyscan Balloon Photography; 22–23B Alamy: Peter Adams Photography; 24 Alamy: Andrew Palmer; 26 Alamy: Stuart Crump; 27 Cheddar Caves & Gorge; 28 Cheddar Caves & Gorge; 29 Corbis: Macduff Everton; 30 Corbis: London Aerial Photo Library; 32–33 Alamy: Peter Titmuss; 34–35 Alamy: National Trust Photographic Library/Matthew Antrobus; 36–37 Alamy: Jon Arnold Images; 38–39A Corbis: Adam Woolfitt; 39B National Trust Photographic Library: David Noton; 40 English Heritage Photographic Library: Sky Eye Aerial Photography; 43 English Heritage Photographic Library; 45 Alamy: Patrick Eden; 46 Corbis: Jason Hawkes; 49 Alamy: Bildarchiv Monheim GmbH/Horian Monheim; 50 National Trust Photographic Library: Ian Shaw; 51 Corbis: John Heseltine; 52 Alamy: Steve Jant; 53 Corbis: Yann Arthus-Bertrand; 54 English Heritage Photographic Library; 56 Louise Thomas; 57 Alamy: Travel-Shots; 58–59 Alamy: John Prior Images; 60 Corbis: Hulton-Deutsch Collection; 62 © Museum of London; 63 Louise Thomas; 64 Corbis: Eye Ubiquitous/David Cumming; 65 Shakespeare's Globe: John Tramper; 68 Alamy: Howard Sayer; 69 © Copyright The Trustees of The British Museum; 70 English Heritage Photographic Library: Paul Highnam; 71 Alamy: Ace Stock Limited; 72A Corbis: John Heseltine; 72–73B John Hamill; 74–75 Corbis: Joel W Rogers; 76 National Trust Photographic Library: Mike Caldwell; 77 Corbis: London Aerial Photo Library; 78–79 Alamy: Pat Behnke; 82 Corbis: Hulton-Deutsch Collection; 83 and 84 English Heritage Photographic Library: Jonathan Bailey; 85 Stephen Arnold; 86 Alamy: Rolf Richardson; 87 Stephen Arnold; 88 Alamy: Brian Seed; 89 Corbis: Cordaiy Photo Library/Monika Smith; 90 © Museum of London; 91 Corbis: Robert Estall; 92–93 National Trust Photographic Library: Oliver Benn; 94–95 lastrefuge.co.uk: Adrian Warren/Dae Sasitorn; 96–97 Alamy: Robert Harding Picture Library/R Rainford; 98 Courtesy of Pembrokeshire Coast National Park; 100–101B Cadw Crown Copyright; 101A Brecknock Museum and Art Gallery Collection; 103 Corbis: Jason Hawkes; 106 and 107 Cadw Crown Copyright; 108 National Museums & Galleries of Wales (Item Reference: 44.32/75); 109 Great Orme Mines Limited; 110–111 Alamy: Travel Ink/Dorothy Burrows; 112 Cadw Crown Copyright; 113BL National Museums & Galleries of Wales (Item Reference: L_034T); 113R Alamy: Wild Places Photography/Chris Howes; 114–115A and 115B Cadw Crown Copright; 116–117 Cadw Crown Copyright; 118–119 Alamy: Arcaid/Martine Hamilton Knight; 121 English Heritage Photographic Library: Paul Highnam; 122 Corbis: London Aerial Photo Library; 125 Courtesy of Ironbridge Gorge Museum Trust; 126 Alamy: Rob Rayworth; 127 Alamy: John James; 128–129 Alamy: GP Bowater; 130–131 Alamy: Andrew Fox; 132 Oswestry Borderland Tourism Ltd:Van Rhijn Aerial Photography; 133 Corbis: Homer Sykes; 135 Alamy: Peter Barritt; 136 By courtesy of The Wedgwood Museum Trust, Barlaston, Staffordshire; 137 National Trust Photographic Library: Dennis Gilbert; 138 Alamy: Pat Behnke; 139 Courtesy of Warwick Castle; 140–141 Alamy: Peter Barritt; 142–143 Alamy: David Moore; 144 English Heritage Photographic Library: Skyscan Balloon Photography; 145 English Heritage Photographic

Library: Alun Bull; 147 English Heritage Photographic Library: John Critchley; 148A and 148B John Byford; 149 Courtesy of Flag Fen; 150–151 National Trust Photographic Library: Joe Cornish; 152 and 153 © Copyright The Trustees of The British Museum; 154 St Edmundsbury Borough Council/West Stow Anglo-Saxon Village Trust; 155 Alamy: GeoPhotos; 156 © Copyright The Trustees of The British Museum; 157 Alamy: Arcaid/Mark Fiennes; 159A English Heritage Photographic Library: Jonathan Bailey; 158–159B English Heritage Photographic Library: Steve Cole; 160–161 English Heritage Photographic Library; 162 Alamy: Justin Kase; 164–165 Alamy: Rob Edwards; 166 and 167 Courtesy of The Creswell Heritage Trust; 168 Alamy: Geoffry Morgan; 170 Courtesy of Lincoln County Council; 171 Corbis: Michael S Yamashita; 172 English Heritage Photographic Library: Jonathan Bailey; 173 Alamy; 174–175 Sir Richard Arkwright's Masson Mills; 178 Alamy: Elmtree Images; 178A Alamy: Popperfoto; 178–179B John Hamill; 180–181 Alamy: The National Trust Photographic Library; 182 Courtesy of Ribchester Museum; 183 © Copyright The Trustees of The British Museum; 184 © Copyright The Trustees of The British Museum; 187A Corbis: Hulton-Deutsch Collection; 186–187B Alamy: Tropix; 189 © Copyright The Trustrees of The British Museum; 190–191 Courtesy of Chester City Council; 192 English Heritage Photographic Library: Paul Highnam; 193 English Heritage Photographic Library: Chris Belcher; 194 © Copyright Manx National Heritage; 195 National Trust Photographic Library: Roy Twigge; 196-197 Alamy: Frantisek Staud; 198 and 199 York Archaeological Trust; 200–201 Corbis: Jason Hawkes; 202 English Heritage Photographic Library: Paul Highnam; 206 Alamy: Mike Kipling; 207 lastrefuge.co.uk: Adrian Warren/Dae Sasitorn; 208–209 Alamy: The National Trust Photographic Library/Oliver Benn; 210 Alamy: Photofusion Picture Library/John Morrison; 211 English Heritage Photographic Library: John Critchley; 213 Alamy: Angra Mainyu; 214–215 Alamy: The National Trust Photographic Library/David Norton; 216 Alamy: Leslie Garland Picture Library; 218 National Trust Photographic Library: Paul Wakefield; 220 English Heritage Photographic Library: Skyscan Balloon Photography; 221 © Copyright The Trustees of The British Museum; 222 Alamy: John Potter; 223 Corbis: Bettmann; 224 and 225 English Heritage Photographic Library: Johnathan Bailey; 226–227 National Trust Photographic Library: Joe Cornish ; 229A English Heritage Photographic Library: Keith Wood; 228–229 National Trust Photographic Library; 230 Alamy: David Crausby; 232 Corbis: Wild Country/David Paterson; 234 Alamy: Leslie Garland Picture Libary; 235 English Heritage Photographic Library: Graeme Peacock;

236–237 Alamy: Cliff Whittem; 238 Courtesy of Undiscovered Scotland www.undiscoveredscotland.co.uk; 240A and 240B Courtesy of Undiscovered Scotland www.undiscoveredscotland.co.uk; 242 Courtesy of Undiscovered Scotland www.undiscoveredscotland.co.uk; 243 Alamy: Worldwide Picture Library/Iain Sarjeant; 244–245A and 245B Courtesy of Undiscovered Scotland www.undiscoveredscotland.co.uk; 246 Courtesy of Undiscovered Scotland www.undiscoveredscotland.co.uk; 247 Alamy: Doug Houghton; 248 and 248–249B Courtesy of Undiscovered Scotland www.undiscovered scotland.co.uk; 250 Alamy: Worldwide Picture Library/David Williams; 251 Ancient Sites Directory: Chris Tweed (www.henge.org.uk); 252–253 Alamy: Fergus Mackay; 255 Corbis: Adam Woolfitt; 256A and 257A Courtesy of Undiscovered Scotland www.undiscoveredscotland.co.uk; 256–257B Corbis: Adam Woolfitt; 258 Courtesy of Undiscovered Scotland www.undiscoveredscotland.co.uk; 259 Corbis: Homer Sykes; 260 and 261 Courtesy of Shetland Islands Tourism; 262 and 263 Courtesy of Undiscovered Scotland www.undiscoveredscotland.co.uk; 264–265Courtesy of Undiscovered Scotland www.undiscoveredscotland.co.uk: Image courtesy of Historic Scotland; 266–267 Courtesy of Undiscovered Scotland www.undiscoveredscotland. co.uk; 268–269 Alamy: Peter Adams Photography; 272 Alamy: David Nixon; 273 Harrisons Photos.com: Marie-Therese Hurson; 275 Corbis: Michael St Maur Sheil; 276 Corbis: Richard T Nowitz; 277 Corbis: Michael S Yamashita; 278–279 Corbis: Michael St Maur Sheil; 280–281 Alamy: David Noton Photography; 282–283B Corbis: Geray Sweeney; 283A Corbis: Gianni Dagli Orti; 284 Corbis: Adam Woolfitt; 286 and 287 Photo © Department of the Environment, Heritage and Local Government; 288 Corbis: Bob Krist; 289 Alamy: Art Kowalsky; 290–291B Alamy: Art Kowalsky; 291A Alamy: Jon Arnold Images; 292 Alamy: Andre Jenny; 293 Corbis: Werner Forman; 294 Alamy: David Lyons; 295 Corbis: Kevin Schafer; 296–297 Alamy: chromepix.com; 298B, 299B and 298–299A Photo © Department of the Environment, Heritage and Local Government; 300 Photo © Department of the Environment, Heritage and Local Government; 301 Corbis: Zuma/Barry Cronin; 303 Corbis: Felix Zaska; 304 Corbis: Museart/Bertrand Rieger; 305 Alamy: David Lyons; 306 Corbis: Michael St Maur Sheil; 308A Alamy: Leslie Garland Picture Library; 308–309B Alamy: David Noton Photography; 310 Corbis: Edifice/Heini Schneebell; 311 Photo © Department of the Environment, Heritage and Local Government; 313 Courtesy of Undiscovered Scotland www.undiscovered scotland.co.uk.; 315 Channel 4: Chris Bennett.